Lecture Notes in Computer Scien

T0238289

Commenced Publication in 1973
Founding and Former Series Editors:
Gerhard Goos, Juris Hartmanis, and Jan van Leeuwen

Vijay Atluri (Ed.)

Data and Applications Security XXII

22nd Annual IFIP WG 11.3 Working Conference
on Data and Applications Security
London, UK, July 13-16, 2008
Proceedings

 Springer

Volume Editor

Vijay Atluri
MSIS Department and CIMIC
Rutgers University
Newark, NJ, USA
E-mail: atluri@rutgers.edu

Library of Congress Control Number: 2008930129

CR Subject Classification (1998): E.3, D.4.6, C.2, F.2.1, J.1, K.6.5

LNCS Sublibrary: SL 3 – Information Systems and Application, incl. Internet/Web and HCI

ISSN   0302-9743

ISBN   978-3-540-70566-6 Springer Berlin Heidelberg New York

Springer is a part of Springer Science+Business Media

springer.com

© IFIP International Federation for Information Processing 2008

Typesetting: Camera-ready by author, data conversion by Scientific Publishing Services, Chennai, India
Printed on acid-free paper   SPIN: 12438716   06/3180   5 4 3 2 1 0

Preface

This volume contains the papers presented at the 22nd Annual IFIP WG 11.3 Working Conference on Data and Applications Security (DBSEC) held in London, UK, July 13–16, 2008. This year's working conference continued its tradition of being a forum for disseminating original research results and practical experiences in data and applications security.

This year we had an excellent program that consists of 9 research paper sessions with 22 high-quality research papers, which were selected from a total of 56 submissions after a rigorous reviewing process by the Program Committee members and external reviewers. These sessions included such topics as access control, privacy, auditing, systems security and data security in advanced application domains. In addition, the program included a keynote address, an invited talk and a panel session.

The success of this conference was a result of the efforts of many people. I would like to extend my appreciation to the Program Committee members and external reviewers for their hard work. I would like to thank the General Chair, Steve Barker, for taking care of the organization aspects of the conference and for arranging the keynote address and the panel session. I would also like to thank Claudio Ardagna for serving as the Publicity Chair and for promptly updating the conference Web page, and Don Lokuadassuriyage for serving as the Local Arrangements Chair. Special thanks go to Alfred Hofmann, Editorial Director at Springer, for agreeing to include these conference proceedings in the *Lecture Notes in Computer Science* series.

Last but not least, my thanks go to all of the authors who submitted papers and to all of the attendees. I hope you find the program stimulating and beneficial for your research.

July 2008   Vijay Atluri

Organization

Executive Committee

General Chair	Steve Barker, King's College, London University, UK
Program Chair	Vijay Atluri, Rutgers University, USA
Publicity Chair	Claudio Ardagna, Universita di Milano, Italy
Local Arrangements Chair	Paul Douglas, University of Westminster, UK
IFIP WG 11.3 Chair	Vijay Atluri, Rutgers University

Program Committee

Gail-Joon Ahn	University of North Carolina, USA
Vijay Atluri	Rutgers University, USA
Steve Barker	King's College London University, UK
Sabrina De Capitani di Vimercati	Universita di Milano, Italy
Soon Ae Chun	City University of New York, USA
Jason Crampton	Royal Holloway, London University, UK
Steve Demurjian	University of Connecticut, USA
Csilla Farkas	University of South Carolina, USA
Eduardo Fernandez-Medina	Univ. of Castilla-La Mancha, Spain
Qijun Gu	Texas State University, USA
Ehud Gudes	Ben-Gurion University, Israel
Tsau Young Lin	San Jose State University, USA
Peng Liu	Pennsylvania State University, USA
Patrick McDaniel	Pennsylvania State University, USA
Sharad Mehrotra	University of California, Irvine, USA
Ravi Mukkamala	Old Dominion University, USA
Peng Ning	North Carolina State University, USA
Sylvia Osborn	University of Western Ontario, Canada
Brajendra Panda	University of Arkansas, USA
Joon Park	Syracuse University, USA
Indrakshi Ray	Colorado State University, USA
Indrajit Ray	Colorado State University, USA
Pierangela Samarati	Universita di Milano, Italy
Ravi Sandhu	University of Texas, San Antonio, USA
Andreas Schaad	SAP Research, Germany
Dongwan Shin	New Mexico Tech, USA
Basit Shafiq	Rutgers University, USA
Anoop Singhal	NIST, USA

Table of Contents

Access Control

Dynamic Meta-level Access Control in SQL 1
   Steve Barker

On the Formal Analysis of a Spatio-temporal Role-Based Access
Control Model 17
   Manachai Toahchoodee and Indrakshi Ray

Audit and Logging

A Unified Audit Expression Model for Auditing SQL Queries 33
   Vikram Goyal, S.K. Gupta, and Anand Gupta

A New Approach to Secure Logging 48
   Di Ma and Gene Tsudik

Keynote

Security, Functionality and Scale?: (Invited Talk) 64
   Ross Anderson

Privacy I

P4A: A New Privacy Model for XML 65
   Angela C. Duta and Ken Barker

Privacy-Aware Collaborative Access Control in Web-Based Social
Networks 81
   Barbara Carminati and Elena Ferrari

A Privacy-Preserving Ticketing System 97
   Kristof Verslype, Bart De Decker, Vincent Naessens, Girma Nigusse,
   Jorn Lapon, and Pieter Verhaeghe

Systems Security

The Analysis of Windows Vista Disk Encryption Algorithm 113
   Mohamed Abo El-Fotouh and Klaus Diepold

Shared and Searchable Encrypted Data for Untrusted Servers 127
   Changyu Dong, Giovanni Russello, and Naranker Dulay

Secure Construction of Contingency Tables from Distributed Data 144
  Haibing Lu, Xiaoyun He, Jaideep Vaidya, and Nabil Adam

Invited Talk

Web Services Security: Techniques and Challenges
(Extended Abstract) 158
  Anoop Singhal

Certificate Management

Empirical Analysis of Certificate Revocation Lists 159
  Daryl Walleck, Yingjiu Li, and Shouhuai Xu

Using New Tools for Certificate Repositories Generation in MANETs ... 175
  Candelaria Hernández-Goya, Pino Caballero-Gil,
  Oscar Delgado-Mohatar, Jezabel Molina-Gil, and
  Cándido Caballero-Gil

Privacy II

Exclusive Strategy for Generalization Algorithms in Micro-data
Disclosure 190
  Lei Zhang, Lingyu Wang, Sushil Jajodia, and Alexander Brodsky

Protecting the Publishing Identity in Multiple Tuples 205
  Youdong Tao, Yunhai Tong, Shaohua Tan, Shiwei Tang, and
  Dongqing Yang

Panel

Panel Session: What Are the Key Challenges in Distributed
Security? 219
  Steve Barker, David Chadwick, Jason Crampton, Emil Lupu, and
  Bhavani Thuraisingham

Trusted Computing Platforms

On the Applicability of Trusted Computing in Distributed
Authorization Using Web Services 222
  Aarthi Nagarajan, Vijay Varadharajan, Michael Hitchens, and
  Saurabh Arora

Sharing but Protecting Content Against Internal Leakage for
Organisations 238
  Muntaha Alawneh and Imad M. Abbadi

Security Policies and Metrics

Regulating Exceptions in Healthcare Using Policy Spaces 254
  Claudio Agostino Ardagna, Sabrina De Capitani di Vimercati,
  Tyrone Grandison, Sushil Jajodia, and Pierangela Samarati

Towards Automation of Testing High-Level Security Properties 268
  Aiman Hanna, Hai Zhou Ling, Jason Furlong, and Mourad Debbabi

An Attack Graph-Based Probabilistic Security Metric 283
  Lingyu Wang, Tania Islam, Tao Long, Anoop Singhal, and
  Sushil Jajodia

Web and Pervasive Systems

An Opinion Model for Evaluating Malicious Activities in Pervasive
Computing Systems 297
  Indrajit Ray, Nayot Poolsappasit, and Rinku Dewri

DIWeDa - Detecting Intrusions in Web Databases 313
  Alex Roichman and Ehud Gudes

Securing Workflows with XACML, RDF and BPEL 330
  Vijayant Dhankhar, Saket Kaushik, and Duminda Wijesekera

Author Index 347

Dynamic Meta-level Access Control in SQL

Steve Barker

Dept Computer Science
King's College London
Strand, WC2R 2LS, UK
steve.barker@dcs.kcl.ac.uk

Abstract. Standard SQL is insufficiently expressive for representing many access control policies that are needed in practice. Nevertheless, we show how rich
forms of access control policies can be defined within SQL when small amounts
of contextual information are available to query evaluators. Rather than the standard, relational structure perspective that has been adopted for fine-grained access
control, we consider instead the representation of dynamic fine-grained access
control (DFMAC) policy requirements at the access policy level. We also show
how DFMAC policies may be represented in SQL and we give some performance
results for an implementation of our approach.

1 Introduction

SQL only permits limited forms of DAC (GRANT-REVOKE) and RBAC policies to
be represented and only at coarse levels of granularity. A consequence of this limited
expressive power is that many access control policy requirements, that need to be employed in practice, cannot be adequately represented in SQL. Of course, views can
sometimes be used, in conjunction with SQL's sublanguages for DAC and RBAC representation, to express access control requirements. However, this combined approach
does not provide a complete solution to the problem of SQL's limited support for access policy specification and it can introduce additional problems (e.g., the problem of a
mass proliferation of view definitions if a user-based view of access control is adopted).

The problem of SQL's limited provision of language features for expressing access
control policies (henceforth referred to as the AC representation problem) has been
recognized ever since the first SQL standard was published. To address this problem,
the language constructs that have been included in SQL, for representing access control requirements, have been progressively extended. However, the AC representation
problem has, in a sense, become more acute because the gap between SQL's sublan-
guage for access control specification and what database practitioners need has grown
wider. Moreover, we believe that the AC representation problem is a multi-faceted and
wide-ranging problem that will not be adequately solved by small extensions to SQL's
sublanguages for access control. Different aspects of the problem have emerged over
time as it has become better understood and as applications of databases have changed.
For instance, interest in the AC representation problem has been recently rekindled as
a consequence of researchers investigating issues in database privacy; for that, various

V. Atluri (Ed.): DAS 2008, LNCS 5094, pp. 1–16, 2008.
© IFIP International Federation for Information Processing 2008

approaches for representing *fine-grained access control (FGAC)* policies have been proposed (see, for example, [13], [17] and [19]). However, these approaches simply deal with a particular manifestation of the AC representation problem under standard assumptions (e.g., that access control policy information is relatively static).

Aspects of the AC representation problem have also been recognized and addressed by RDBMS vendors and relational database programmers. For example, Oracle's *Virtual Private Database (VPD)* [15] allows programmers to define functions, which may be written using PL/SQL, C or JAVA, to express access control requirements that are not expressible in standard SQL. More generally, for all forms of RDBMSs, database programmers will often write application programs to enhance SQL's provision and to thus enable richer forms of access control policies to be represented. However, neither of these approaches is especially attractive. As many researchers have observed, access control requirements must be expressed in high-level, declarative languages that have well-defined semantics, that permit properties of policies to be proven for assurance purposes, and that enable users to express access control requirements succinctly and in a way that makes it possible for them to understand the consequences of making changes to a policy. Conversely, it is inappropriate to use low-level languages that do not have well-defined semantics, that embed *ad hoc* and often hard-coded representations of policies in applications, that compromise attempts at formal verification of requirements, that make it difficult for security administrators to understand the consequences of policy change, and that thus makes policy maintenance a difficult task. Moreover, the programming-based approach requires that two languages (with very different semantics) be used and often results in complex forms of SQL query being executed inefficiently.

The work that we describe in this paper addresses an aspect of the AC representation problem that has not previously been considered in the context of SQL databases. Specifically, we address the issue of providing support for representing, in SQL, formally well-defined, dynamic fine-grained meta-level access control (DFMAC) policies for category-based access control models. By meta-level policy representations we mean representations of closed access control policies, open access control policies, and various forms of hybrid policies. As we allow for open policies, it follows that we admit negative authorizations (for expressing denials of access) as well as positive authorizations in our representation. In our approach, the meta-policies that are applicable to users can change dynamically and autonomously as a consequence of modifications to a database. To accommodate changing policies, we make use of contextual information; specifically, user identifiers and system clock time. By enabling DFMAC policies to be represented and implemented in SQL, we preserve the semantics of SQL and we are able to utilize existing RDBMS technology to implement DFMAC policies. Although FGAC policies have previously been discussed in the access control literature, to the best of our knowledge, no previous work has been described that is based on representing multiple forms of DFMAC policies directly in SQL. For our implementation, we use *query rewriting* [18]. Query rewriting for FGAC has recently been investigated by several researchers (see, for example, [17], [13], and [19]); the novelty of our rewriter stems from the focus we adopt on the exploitation of DFMAC information rather than FGAC information.

The rest of the paper is organized in the following way. In Section 2, a number of preliminary notions are described. In Section 3, we describe the general features of category-based access control models to which our approach may be applied. In Section 4, we describe policy representation in SQL. In Section 5, we explain how our query modifier is used to rewrite SQL queries to enforce DFMAC policies. In Section 6, we use a detailed example to explain more fully what is involved in our proposal. In Section 7, we discuss a candidate implementation for our approach and we give performance measures for this implementation. In Section 8, we discuss the related literature. Finally, in Section 9, conclusions are drawn, and further work is suggested.

2 Preliminaries

In this section, we briefly describe some key technical issues, to make the paper self-contained, to highlight the language that we propose for specification, and to explain the theoretical foundations of our approach. We assume that the reader is familiar with basic relational (SQL) terminology, like relation (table), attribute (column) and tuple (row). Otherwise, we refer the reader to [10].

In our approach, *tuple relational calculus (TRC)* [10] is used for specifying DFMAC policy requirements. For that, a many-sorted first order language is used over an alphabet Σ that includes:

- Countable sets of (uninterpreted) constants, variables, and n-ary relation symbols (some of which have a fixed interpretation);
- A functionally complete set of connectives;
- The singleton set of quantifiers: $\{\exists\}$;
- The comparison operators: $\{=, <, \leq, \neq, >, \geq\}$;
- The set of parenthetic symbols $\{(,), [,]\}$ and the punctuation symbols ',' and '.'.

Rather than restricting attention to a minimal set of connectives that are functionally complete, we assume that policy specifiers will choose some subset of the 2^{2^n} n-ary connectives in 2-valued logic for representing DFMAC policies of interest.

The following sorts are of interest:

- A countable set $\mathcal{U}$ of user identifiers.
- A countable set $\mathcal{C}$ of category identifiers.
- A countable set $\mathcal{A}$ of named *actions* e.g., $SELECT, INSERT, UPDATE$, and $DELETE$.
- A countable set $\mathcal{T}$ of *table identifiers*.
- A countable set Θ of *time points*.

By tables, we mean base tables and views. On times, we assume a one-dimensional, linear, discrete view of time, with a beginning and no end point. That is, the model of time that we choose is a total ordering of time points that is isomorphic to the natural numbers. Clock times are an important form of contextual information. The function $current\_time$ is used to generate the current system clock time, a structured term from which more specific temporal information may be produced. For example,

$current\_time.year$, $current\_time.month$ and $current\_time.day$ can be used to, respectively, extract the current year, month and day from $current\_time$. Our focus is on user queries and hence the $SELECT$ action. The extension of what we propose to the case of update operations is straightforward.

A TRC query, expressed in terms of Σ, is of the following general form

$$\{\tau_1.A_1, \tau_2.A_2, \ldots, \tau_n.A_n : \mathcal{F}(\tau_1, \tau_2, \ldots, \tau_n, \overrightarrow{\tau_{n+1}}, \overrightarrow{\tau_{n+2}}, \ldots, \overrightarrow{\tau_m})\}$$

where $\tau_1, \tau_2, \ldots, \tau_n$ are tuple variables (not necessarily distinct), $A_1, A_2, \ldots, A_n$ are attributes, and

$$\mathcal{F}(\tau_1, \tau_2, \ldots, \tau_n, \overrightarrow{\tau_{n+1}}, \ldots, \overrightarrow{\tau_m})$$

is a subformula of TRC, expressed in terms of Σ, with $\tau_1, \tau_2 \ldots \tau_n$ as free variables in $\mathcal{F}$ and with bound variables $\overrightarrow{\tau_{n+1}}, \overrightarrow{\tau_{n+2}}, \ldots, \overrightarrow{\tau_m}$.

In our approach, rewritten queries are formulated with respect to a pair (Q, Π) where Q is an SQL query submitted for evaluation by a user u and Π is the DFMAC policy information that is applicable to u at the time at which u submits its query. For query evaluation, Q and Π are combined to generate a rewritten query Q'.

The model of a DFMAC policy Π, which we assume to be expressed in a language as expressive as hierarchical programs [14], includes a set of *authorizations*. An authorization, in turn, is expressed in terms of *permissions* or *denials*, which may be expressed conditionally in terms of contextual information. A permission is expressed in terms of a 2-place predicate $per(a, o)$ where a is an access privilege and o is a database object (a table); the meaning of $per(a, o)$ is that the a access privilege may be exercised on o. A denial is expressed in terms of a 2-place predicate $den(a, o)$ where a is an access privilege, o is a database object (a table), and $den(a, o)$ denotes that the a access privilege cannot be exercised on o. An authorization is a triple $auth(u, a, o)$ with the semantics that user u may exercise the access privilege a on o.

A Herbrand semantics [1] is applicable to the databases that we consider. In this context, the intended model of a relational database Δ is the set of ground instances of atoms from the Herbrand Base of Δ, $HB(\Delta)$, that are true in the unique least Herbrand model of Δ. In our approach, the set of ground atomic consequences that a user u may retrieve (i.e., *select*) from a database Δ to which the DFMAC policy Π applies is expressed thus:

$$\{A : A \in HB(\Delta) \wedge \Delta \models A \wedge authorized(u, select, A)\}.$$

3   Category-Based Access Control

In this section, we briefly discuss the essential features of a range of category-based access control models to which our approach can be applied. We also briefly describe goal-oriented access control for which DFMAC policies are applicable.

In contrast to DAC/GRANT-REVOKE models, a number of access control models are based on the idea of categorizing users on some general criterion. In this context, user-category assignment is adopted as a basis for access control. That is, users are assigned to categories and permissions are assigned to categories of users too. A user acquires the permissions assigned to a category when the user is assigned to the category. Assigning users and permissions to categories raises the level of abstraction (relative to lower-level policies, like DAC policies) and reduces the number of permission and denial assignments that need to be specified. The downside of the approach is that it is often necessary to express that, for example, exceptions apply to certain users within a general category. Hence, negative authorizations need to be specified as well as positive authorizations. However, the need for conflict resolution strategies then arises.

Category-based access control models include groups (with discretionary assignment of users to a group), sets of users categorized according to their security clearance (as in MAC models [6]), sets of users that are categorized according to the job function that they perform in an organization (as in RBAC models [11]), sets of users catagorized according to a discretely defined trust level, and sets of users that are categorized according to the combination of an ascribed and action status (as in ASAC [4]).

Category-based access control models have a fairly common definition of an authorization (u, a, o) and meta-policies are defined in terms of this general interpretation of authorizations. In the case of closed meta-policies for category-based access control models: permissions (each of which is a pair (a, o) where a is an access privilege and o is a database object) are assigned to a category c; a user u is assigned to a category c; when the user is assigned to a category c the user may exercise a privilege a on object o iff the permission (a, o) is assigned to c. For an open meta-policy the authorization (u, a, o) holds iff u is assigned to category c and there is no denial of the permission (a, o) to c. A variety of additional meta-policies may be defined in terms of the open and closed meta-policies. For example, a "denials override" policy may be used to express that the authorization (u, a, o) holds iff u is assigned to category c, the permission (a, o) is assigned to c and there is no denial of the permission (a, o) to c category users.

DFMAC polices are required to provide fine-grained access control where "fine-grained" information is interpreted as fine-grained at the meta-policy level rather than at the level of data. That is, DFMAC policies are applicable when security administrators want to be able to specify that a particular meta-policy (a closed policy, an open policy, a hybrid policy, etc) is to apply to different categories of users in different contexts. The different contexts may be temporally-based (e.g., an open policy is to apply on weekdays but not weekends) or they may be location-based or the policy that applies may depend on the contents of the database.

DFMAC policies are especially important when goal-oriented access control requirements need to be represented. In goal-oriented access control, organizational and individual goals may change as a consequence of the occurrence of events and this, in turn, may cause access control policy requirements to change. For example, an organization may wish to restrict access to information on "special offers" to the category of *preferred* customers, but may need to change dynamically and autonomously this policy constraint to allow access to all customers if sales figures are "poor".

4   Access Policy Representation

For the representation of our approach, we use four base tables; each of the tables has a fixed purpose. We use a table named *category* to record which users of a DBMS are assigned to which categories and we use a table named *policy* to store meta-level access control information that our query rewrite procedure uses at runtime to evaluate a user's access request. We also use a table named *pca* (shorthand for permission category assignment) and a table name *dca* (shorthand for denial category assignment) to, respectively, store tuples that represent the permissions and denials that apply to categories of users that may request to perform some action on some database object. The *category*, *policy*, *pca* and *dca* tables may include conditions that must be satisfied in order for a category, policy, permission or denial to apply. The query rewrite procedure also uses this information at runtime in the evaluation of a user's access request.

The four tables and brief details of their intended semantics may be described thus:

- $category(userID, catID, CC_u)$: $\langle u, c, cc_u \rangle \in category$ iff $u \in \mathcal{U}$, $c \in \mathcal{C}$ and u satisfies the cc_u condition for assignment to the category c.
- $policy(catID, action, objectID, PC_t)$: $\langle c, a, t, p \rangle \in policy$ iff $c \in \mathcal{C}$, $a \in \mathcal{A}$, $t \in \mathcal{T}$, and p is a boolean condition defined in terms of *pca*, *dca*, or other tables in the database.
- $pca(catID, action, objectID, pca\_condition)$: $\langle c, a, t, q_{pca} \rangle \in pca$ iff $c \in \mathcal{C}$, $a \in \mathcal{A}$, $t \in \mathcal{T}$, q_{pca} is a boolean condition, and the permission (a, t) applies to c users if q_{pca} is true.
- $dca(catID, action, objectID, dca\_condition)$: $\langle c, a, t, q_{dca} \rangle \in dca$ iff $c \in \mathcal{C}$, $a \in \mathcal{A}$, $t \in \mathcal{T}$, q_{dca} is a boolean condition, and the denial (a, t) applies to c users if q_{dca} is true.

The set of authorizations $\mathcal{AUTH}$ that is defined by a DFMAC policy is expressed in terms of the core set of tables that are described above. For example, we have for a closed DFMAC policy (expressed using TRC and ignoring PC_t conditions):

$$\mathcal{AUTH} = \{\langle t_1.userid, t_2.action, t_3.objectid \rangle : category(t_1)$$
$$\wedge\ t_1.cc_u\ \wedge\ [policy(t_2)\ \wedge\ t_1.catid = t_2.catid$$
$$\wedge\ \exists t_3[pca(t_3)\ \wedge\ t_3.catid = t_1.catid$$
$$\wedge\ t_3.catid = t_2.catid\ \wedge\ t_3.pca\_condition]]\}.$$

A number of points should be noted. We envisage access policy information being represented in TRC before being transferred into SQL for implementation. Any number of meta-level policies can be expressed in the same way as the closed policy information that is represented above. When a category c of users can access information about all of the attributes in a table t then the subset of the rows in the table that a c category user can access is expressed as a value of PC_t. When only a subset of the attributes of a base table is accessible to a category of users then access to this data is via a view v. However, the subset of tuples accessible to the category of users via v is also defined as a value of PC_t. We make the simplifying assumption that $(catID, objectID)$ is the primary key for *policy*. In practice, an extra attribute (e.g., *policyID*) would be used to allow for multiple DFMAC policies to apply to different categories of users, for different actions on different objects when different forms of contextual information apply. Access control information in the form of certificates can also be naturally accommodated in our approach. Notice too that we represent DFMAC policy information at the meta-level level *and* at the level of permissions and denials. That is, conditions on the meta-level policy that applies at any instance of time may be specified in *category* and *policy* and conditions that define when permissions and denials are applicable are expressed in *pca* and *dca*, respectively. The values that are admitted for CC_u, PC_t, *pca* and *dca* are boolean expressions that are formulated using SQL and are automatically appended to a user's SQL query in the process of query modification.

5   Query Modification

Recall that an SQL query is of the following basic form:

$$SELECT\ A_1, \ldots, A_m$$
$$FROM\ t_1, \ldots, t_n$$
$$WHERE\ Q;$$

Here, $A_1, \ldots, A_m$ are attributes that define the structure of the required result relation and $t_1, \ldots, t_n$ are the tables on which the condition Q is evaluated. Of course, an SQL $SELECT$ statement can be expressed in terms of other constructs (e.g., aggregate functions) but these elements are not important in the discussion that follows.

In our approach, the query modifier automatically appends references to the *category* and *policy* tables to a user's query when the user submits the query to an RDBMS for evaluation. The user has a unique $userID$, which is accessible to the query modifier as soon as a user has been authenticated (a range of different authentication methods may be used). In order for the user's query to be performed, the user must be authorized, according to the information stored in *category* and *policy*, to access each of the $t_1 \ldots t_n$ tables (or views) that are referred to in Q; otherwise, the user's query will automatically fail. The reason for this should be clear: the join of $t_i, \ldots, t_n, t_i \bowtie \ldots \bowtie t_n$, cannot be performed for user u if access to some t_i $(1 \leq i \leq n)$ is not authorized for u.[1] For a user that submits a query Q, the CC_u condition (if any) is appended to Q. For a user that is permitted to access each t_i $(1 \leq i \leq n)$ table that is referred to in Q, the condition on accessing t_i is appended to the query as a conjunct PC_{t_i} $(1 \leq i \leq n)$ where PC_{t_i} denotes the condition from *policy* that holds on u's access to t_i as a consequence of u's assignment to a category c. Hence, the rewritten query is of the following general form (where $t_i (1 \leq i \leq n)$ is the table name for t_i):

$$SELECT\ A_1, \ldots, A_m$$
$$FROM\ t_1, \ldots, t_n, category, policy$$
$$WHERE\ Q$$
$$AND\ category.userID = \$userID$$
$$AND\ category.categoryID = policy.categoryID$$
$$AND\ category.CC_u$$
$$AND\ (policy.objectID = t_1\ AND\ PC_{t_1}$$
$$\ldots$$
$$AND\ policy.objectID = t_n\ AND\ PC_{t_n};$$

---

[1] cf. the null-based semantics used in [13].

A query Q is rewritten with respect to a DFMAC policy Π to generate a query Q' for evaluation. If the tables $t_1, \ldots, t_n$ are interpreted as sets of tuples then for Q' to succeed for user u we require that $t_1 \cup \ldots \cup t_n \models Q$ and $(u, select, t_i) \in \mathcal{AUTH}$, $\forall t_i$ such that $t_i \in \{t_1 \ldots t_n\}$. It should also be noted that $Q' \sqsubseteq Q$ holds where $\sqsubseteq$ is a query containment operator [1].

When an SQL query is expressed as a collection of n ($n \in \mathbb{N}$) nested subqueries $Q_1, \ldots, Q_n$ in the form

$$Q_1(Q_2(Q_3(Q_4 \ldots (Q_n))))$$

then the rewritten query (ignoring the CC_u condition) is of the form

$$Q_1 \ AND \ C_1(Q_2 \ AND \ C_2(Q_3 \ AND \ C_3(Q_4 \ AND \ C_4 \ldots (Q_n \ AND \ C_n))))$$

where C_i ($1 \leq i \leq n$) is the conjunction of PC_{t_i} conditions that apply to Q_i.

When an SQL query is expressed in terms of the union of two subqueries ($Q_1 \cup Q_2$), or difference ($Q_1 - Q_2$) or interersection ($Q_1 \cap Q_2$) then, respectively, the rewritten queries are of the form $Q_1 \ AND \ C_1 \cup Q_2 \ AND \ C_2$, $Q_1 \ AND \ C_1 - Q_2 \ AND \ C_2$ and $Q_1 \ AND \ C_1 \cap Q_2 \ AND \ C_2$ where C_i ($i \in \{1, 2\}$) is the conjunction of PC_{t_i} conditions that apply to Q_i.

Next, we consider various forms of meta-level specification that may be represented in SQL and that are useful for representing DFMAC policy requirements. Recall that these different meta-policies are stored in the $policy$ table as values of the attribute PC_t and are defined in terms of pca and dca.

The condition for a closed policy on table t_i may represented, as a value for PC_{t_i}, in a fragment α of SQL, thus:

$EXISTS(SELECT * FROM pca$
$WHERE \ policy.catID = pca.catID \ AND \ pca.action = \text{``}select\text{''}$
$AND \ pca.object = policy.objectID \ AND \ pca\_condition).$

If the conjunction of conditions for a closed policy to apply are true then a user u assigned to category c will be authorized to select the requested tuples from a table t (where t is the $objectID$) iff c category users are recorded in pca as being permitted to exercise the select privilege on t and the condition $pca\_condition$ on the permission applicable to c category users of t evaluates to true at the time of the access request.

The policy condition for an open policy on table t_i may be represented as a fragment β of SQL and as a value for PC_{t_i}, thus:

$NOT \ EXISTS(SELECT * FROM dca$
$WHERE \ policy.catID = dca.catID \ AND \ dca.action = \text{``}select\text{''}$
$AND \ dca.object = policy.objectID \ AND \ dca\_condition).$

In the case of an open policy, a user u assigned to category c will be authorized to select the requested tuples from a table t iff c category users are not currently recorded in dca as being prohibited from exercising the select privilege on t. Here, t is the $objectID$ and the $dca\_condition$ must evaluate to true in order for the prohibition on t to apply to c category users at the time of an access request.

Recall that one of our aims is to define complex policies in terms of more primitive forms. For example, a "denials override" policy can be defined as the conjunction $\alpha \; AND \; \beta$. However, multiple forms of meta-policies can be similarly constructed using the specification language that we admit. On that, policy authors will make use of a subset of the 2^{2^n} n-ary operators in 2-valued logic for specifying DFMAC policies. For instance, a conditioned disjunction operator $[c, \alpha, \beta]$ (where $[c, \alpha, \beta] \equiv c \wedge \neg \phi_1 \vee \neg c \wedge \phi_2$) may be used with c denoting $sales > 1000$ to specify that a closed policy applies when $sales$ are greater than 1000 and an open policy otherwise. Similarly, $(c \rightarrow \phi_1) \wedge (\neg c \rightarrow \phi_2) \equiv (\neg c \vee \phi_1) \wedge (c \vee \phi_2)$ can be used to express an IF-ELSE condition. Notice too that by combining subconditions, conditions of arbitrary complexity may be generated to enable expressive forms of policy algebras to be defined.

In addition to meta-level representation via the *policy* table, policy information that applies to the permissions and denials of access, expressed via *pca* and *dca*, respectively, are expressed as values of *pca_condition* and *dca_condition*. As in the case of the conditions that apply to meta-level information included in *policy*, the values of *pca_condition* and *dca_condition* are boolean conditions expressed in SQL.

To conclude this section, we outline the 4-step procedure for the query rewrite method that we use for DFMAC policy enforcement (see also Section 7):

Step 1: Rewrite a user's query Q to give the following modified query Q_1:

$$SELECT \; A_1, \ldots, A_m$$
$$FROM \; t_1, \ldots, t_n, category, policy$$
$$WHERE \; Q$$
$$AND \; category.userID = \$userID$$
$$AND \; category.categoryID = policy.categoryID$$
$$AND \; category.CC_u$$
$$AND \; policy.objectID = t_1 \; AND \; PC_{t_1}$$
$$\ldots$$
$$AND \; policy.objectID = t_n \; AND \; PC_{t_n};$$

Step 2: Expand Q_1 by PC_{t_i} ($\forall i \in \{1 \ldots n\}$) to give Q_2.
Step 3: Expand Q_2 by *pca_condition* or *dca_condition* to give Q'.
Step 4: Evaluate Q'.

It should be clear from the rewrite method and previous discussion that a query expansion approach is used by us. That is, if $\rightsquigarrow_i$ is read as "expands to using i" (where i is some source of DFMAC information) then the rewrite sequence is

$$[Q \rightsquigarrow_c Q_1, Q_1 \rightsquigarrow_t Q_2, Q_2 \rightsquigarrow_m Q']$$

where c denotes the category condition, t denotes the table access conditions and m denotes the meta-policy information. Moreover, $Q \wedge c \wedge t \wedge m \rightsquigarrow Q'$.

6   DFMAC Policy Examples

Before we consider the implementation of the 4-step query modification procedure, we provide a (quite general) example to illustrate our approach. Our example is based on a variant of Date's *supplier-part-project* database [10] and includes the following relational schemes:

$$supplier(s\#, sname, status, scity),$$
$$part(p\#, pname, color, unitcost, stock),$$
$$project(j\#, jname, jcity),$$
$$spj(s\#, p\#, j\#, qty).$$

Consider next the following DFMAC policy requirements on *part*:

During the month of March (in any year), a closed access control policy on the retrieval of part information is to apply to users that are categorized as preferred but only if the stock is greater than 1000 units and the user has not been suspended. At all other times, an open policy on retrieving information from part applies to preferred users, but only if the stock level of an item is less than 450 units and unit cost is greater than 0.9.

In TRC, the full expression of the policy information is:

$$\{\langle t_1.p\#, t_1.pname, t_1.color, t_1.unitcost, t_1.stock \rangle :$$
$$part(t_1) \wedge \exists t_2[category(t_2) \wedge t_2.userid = \$userid$$
$$\exists t_3[policy(t_3) \wedge t_2.policyid = t_3.policyid \wedge$$
$$[\$currenttime.month = ``march'' \wedge t_1.stock > 1000 \wedge$$
$$\exists t_4[pca(t_4) \wedge t_3.catid = t_4.catid \wedge$$
$$t_4.action = ``select'' \wedge t_3.objectid = t_4.objectid \wedge$$
$$\neg\exists t_5[suspended(t_5) \wedge t_5.userid = t_2.userid]]] \vee$$
$$[\$currenttime.month \neq ``march'' \wedge$$
$$t_1.stock < 450 \wedge t_1.unitcost > 0.9 \wedge$$
$$\neg\exists t_6[dca(t_6) \wedge t_3.catid = t_6.catid$$
$$t_6.action = ``select'' \wedge t_3.objectid = t_6.objectid]]]]\}.$$

Notice that two exclusive disjuncts are required to express the DFMAC policy requirements. For the closed policy, which applies in March, the TRC translates into the following fragment γ of SQL code:

```
$current_time.month = "march" AND stock > 1000
AND EXISTS(SELECT *
FROM pca
WHERE policy.catID = pca.catID AND pca.action = "select"
AND pca.object = policy.objectID AND pca_condition)
```

where the *pca_condition* is represented by the following fragment δ of SQL code:

```
NOT EXISTS(SELECT *
FROM suspended
WHERE suspended.userID = category.userID).
```

That is, a *preferred* user is authorized in March to access tuples in *part* where the *stock* value is greater than 1000 if there is a permission to allow u access on *part* and u is not a suspended user. For the open policy, the required fragment ϵ of SQL code is as follows:[2]

> *NOT $current_time.month = "march"*
> *AND stock < 450 AND unitcost > 0.9*
> *AND NOT EXISTS(SELECT * FROM dca*
> *WHERE policy.catID = dca.catID AND dca.action = "select"*
> *AND dca.object = policy.objectID).*

The PC_{part} value that is stored in *policy* is the disjunction of the fragments $\gamma \wedge \delta$ and ϵ; the SQL fragment δ is stored in *pca*.

Next, consider the following query Q for user κ with *preferred* status:

> *SELECT p#*
> *FROM part*
> *WHERE unitcost > 0.25*

but where *preferred* users are only permitted to see a subset (view) of *part* such that *unitcost* ≥ 0.5 (thus making the *unitcost* > 0.25 condition redundant) and only if these users are located in Europe (as recorded in a table named *region*).

It follows, from the discussion above, that the query rewriter that we use will generate the following modified form of Q for κ:

> *SELECT p#*
> *FROM part, category, policy*
> *WHERE unitcost > 0.25*
> *AND category.userID = $userID*
> *AND category.categoryID = policy.categoryID*
> *AND policy.objectID = "part" AND unitcost $\geq$ 0.5*
> *AND EXISTS(SELECT * FROM region*
> * WHERE $userID = region.ID AND region.name = "europe")*
> *AND $current_time.month = "march" AND stock > 1000*
> *AND EXISTS(SELECT * FROM pca*
> * WHERE policy.catID = pca.catID*
> * AND pca.action = "select" AND pca.object = policy.objectID*
> * AND NOT EXISTS (SELECT **
> *   FROM suspended*
> *   WHERE suspended.userid = category.userid))*
> *OR NOT $current_time.month = "march"*
> *AND stock < 450 AND unitcost > 0.9*
> * AND NOT EXISTS(SELECT * FROM dca*
> * WHERE policy.catID = dca.catID*
> * AND dca.action = "select" AND dca.object = policy.objectID);*

---

[2] Notice that there is no *dca_condition* value that is applicable.

Thus:

> If κ submits its query on March 1st (at which point κ has preferred status and
> is located in Europe) then κ is authorized to access part numbers for all tuples
> in part where $unitcost \geq 0.5$ but only if stock values are greater than 1000
> units and a permission holds for κ that is not overridden as a consequence of κ
> being a suspended user at the time of κ's access request. In contrast, if, on the
> 1st April (say), κ submits its query then it can access all part numbers where
> $unitcost > 0.9$ provided that stock level is less than 450 units and κ is not
> explicitly prohibited from accessing this information.

For the example DFMAC policy requirements described above, the SQL query that is
generated is quite complex and requires that a number of subqueries be used. However,
for many practical queries the rewritten form will be much simpler. For all approaches
that are used for access control there is an overhead involved in checking access constraints, and there will always be a trade-off between complex policy representation and
query efficiency. In the next section, we provide arguments to suggest that many queries,
that require the representation of some quite complex DFMAC policy requirements, can
be evaluated without significant enforcement overheads.

7   Practical Considerations

In this section, we describe the testing of an implementation of our approach and we
give some performance measures.

For the testing, we use large-scale versions of the tables that we previously described.
Specifically, we use the *supplier-part-projects* database with (of the order of) 100000 tuples in each of the *part*, *supplier* and *project* tables and with (of the order of) 500000
tuples in the *spj* table.

For implementation, we use PostgreSQL 8.3 [16]. We use rewrite rules to transform
a query tree for a user query Q into a modified form Q' that incorporates access control
information that may be stored in *category*, *policy*, *pca* or *dca*. Our testing is performed using a 1.9GHz AMD Athlon X2 Dual-Core machine (with a 128KB Level 1
data cache, a 512KB level 2 cache, and 1GB of memory) running Red Hat Linux 7.3.
The results are generated by using the PostgreSQL *timing* function.

The principal purpose of our testing is to determine the extent to which the DFMAC
policy information, which is added to Q to generate Q', affects performance. No effort was made to tune the implemented system (to avoid the results becoming set-up
specific). We perform our tests using data and queries for "expensive case" evaluation.
Hence, we also test the scalability of the approach.

An example of the type of query that we use is: *retrieve all suppliers names for
suppliers that supply red parts to no project in London*, to wit:

$$\{\langle t_1.sname \rangle : supplier(t_1) \wedge \exists t_2[part(t_2) \wedge t_2.color = \text{``red''} \wedge$$
$$\neg \exists t_3[project(t_3) \wedge t_3.jcity = \text{``london''} \wedge \exists t_4[spj(t_4) \wedge t_1.s\# = t_4.s\# \wedge$$
$$t_2.p\# = t_4.p\# \wedge t_3.j\# = t_4.j\#]]]\}$$

Various policy combinations were tested with various queries for a single user that
is assigned to a single category to which $SELECT$ access is defined in *policy* on

the tables in the *supplier-parts-projects* database. We also performed some queries that generate large numbers of tuples in intermediate tables in the process of query evaluation. For example, we perform a query that involves computing the cartesian product of three subsets of the tuples in *part* (each subset having a cardinality of 100). The meta-policy information, based on the example from Section 6, is stored in *policy* and the *pca* conditions and *dca* conditions that are defined in terms of *suspended* are, respectively, stored in *pca* and *dca*.

The key measure for our implementation is the overheads that are incurred as a consequence of adding the DFMAC policy information in the process of query evaluation. On that, we have observed typical extra overheads of the order of 10-15% (for the majority of our test queries). For example, for the query above, the query evaluation time (averaged over 10 runs) is 1.9s. In contrast, when the DFMAC policy information, described in Section 6, is compiled into the query, the average time is 2.2s. (The overheads involved in rewriting are negligible.) Similar results were generated for a range of queries on the *supplier-part-project* database. Nevertheless, a test of a hybrid policy with an expensive subquery evaluation that involves accessing an instance of *suspended* with 15000 tuples did push the DFMAC overhead up to 26% over the non-DFMAC case. For the processing of this query (with $|$ *suspended* $|$ $=$ 15000) the computational overheads are pushed towards a bound of unacceptability. However, if this type of query were performed frequently, in practice, on a table of similar cardinality then the possibility of optimizing access to *suspended* would be considered by a DBA. Clearly, it is always possible to find worst case scenarios that incur high costs in terms of processing DFMAC information. In all cases, a DBA must consider the trade-off between automatic DFMAC policy enforcement and the computational overheads that are incurred as a consequence of evaluating queries that are rewritten to incorporate DFMAC policy information.

8 Related Work

In this section, we describe the literature that relates to our approach. We first describe work from the access control community that is concerned with the specification of flexible forms of access control information for protecting databases. Thereafter, we consider how our approach relates to work that has been focused on the specific issue of query rewriting on SQL databases for implementing FGAC policy requirements.

The importance of developing access control models, in terms of which flexible forms of access control policies may be defined, has long been recognized. The work by Bertino, Jajodia and Samarati [9] is especially significant in this respect. In [9], a well-defined authorization model that permits a range of discretionary access policies to be defined on relational databases is described. However, the emphasis in [9] is principally on discretionary policies rather than the range of DFMAC policies for category-based access control models that we have considered. The importance of using contextual information in access control for helping to protect databases is also well-known. For example, the idea of utilizing temporal restrictions on access to information in databases has been discussed by Bertino et al. [7], and an event-based approach for flexible access to databases that is based on triggers has been presented in [8]. An extension of the approach, which allows for the dynamic enabling and disabling of roles, has been described in [12]. However, these approaches are not concerned with the direct representation of DFMAC policies in SQL, they do not consider the range of category-based models that we do, and they are not concerned with query modification. We also note that an approach for the representation of flexible forms of access control policies for deductive databases has been described [2,3] as well as flexible specifications of access control meta-policies when contextual factors like system clock times may be taken into account [5]. However, the approaches that are described in [3],[2], and [5] are theoretical and cannot be naturally used with SQL databases (not least because query evaluation with respect to policy specification is tied to the operational semantics that are used in deductive databases and constraint databases).

On the issue of using query rewriting for access control, we discuss three recent contributions to the literature: the work by Rizvi et al. [17], Wang et al. [19], and LeFevre et al. [13]. The work by Rizvi et al. [17] has certain similarities with ours in that context is taken into account when evaluating access requests. However, the key contribution of Rizvi et al.'s work is to define validity rules that control access to data via parameterized views. A user's access request can be performed if and only if the access is consistent with the validity rules that apply to the access; otherwise, the user's query is rejected. Rizvi et al.'s work is concerned with FGAC policies at the level of data whereas our approach is focused on fine-grained access control from a policy-level perspective. It should also be noted that Rizvi et al.'s concern is with developing what the authors call a "non-Truman" approach to database access control. The issue of distinguishing queries that users can execute from those that they cannot execute, to ensure that non-Truman databases can be supported, is a different aspect of the AC representation problem than we have addressed. Rizvi et al.'s motivation for non-Truman databases is what they suggest to be possible misinterpretations of query answers that arise as a consequence of security restrictions. However, it is not clear that such confusions are exhibited by users. Moreover, Rizvi et al.'s work aims to resolve "inconsistencies" between what a user "expects" and what a system returns (in terms of answers to a query). These terms are not well defined by Rizvi et al. and it is not clear that rejecting queries as "inconsistent" is what users would "expect". A number of more specific problems apply to Rizvi et al.'s approach. For example, legitimate forms of queries can be rejected and the query validation problem is undecidable, in general, for the inference rules that are proposed for identifying acceptable queries.

The work by Wang et al. [19], is also concerned with FGAC for relational databases. More specifically, Wang et al. consider the problem of defining and demonstrating the correctness of FGAC enforcement. In contrast, our approach is concerned with DF-MAC policies. Moreover, our approach is correct in the sense that the set of atomic consequences that are accessible by a user of an SQL database are those that SQL computes to satisfy the definition of correctness that we specified in Section 2. That is, the set of ground atomic consequences that a user u may retrieve (i.e., *select*) from a database Δ to which the DFMAC policy Π applies is:

$$\{A : A \in HB(\Delta) \wedge \Delta \models A \wedge authorized(u, select, A)\}.$$

We have not considered the richer interpretation of correctness that Wang et al. consider, but that has not been the focus in this paper.

The work that we have described is perhaps closest is spirit to Lefevere et al.'s work [13]. Like LeFevre et al., we make use of a high-level specification language for representing policy requirements and we translate this specification into SQL for implementation. However, the specification language that we use is tuple relational calculus (rather than P3P) and our concern is with access control policies for SQL database in general (rather than privacy policies for Hippocratic databases). What is more, our concern is with the representation and processing of very different types of meta-level information because we do not interpret fine-grained access control at the data level as LeFevre et al. do. Instead, our concern has been to represent DFMAC policies. As such, we address a different aspect of the AC representation problem (as we explained in Section 1). The work in [13] is based on a nullification-based semantics (i.e., a null value is substituted for a data value that should remain private); this semantics may be appropriate in the privacy context, but is less obviously so in the DFMAC case.

In more general terms, it should be noted that our approach is focused on DF-MAC policies for category-based access control models, specifically. By focusing on category-based models, the potential problem of view proliferation is much more manageable than it is when a user-based view is adopted (as in, for example, [17]). Neither [17] nor [13] identify well defined access control models to which their approaches apply. Moreover, negative authorizations are not considered and so neither [17] nor [13] discusses issues like policy overriding. It is also worth noting that, unlike [13], [17] and [19], our concern is with dynamic and autonomous *changing* of access control policy requirements.

9 Conclusions and Further Work

The contributions that we have described in this paper can be summarized in the following way: we introduced an approach for dynamic, fine-grained access control policy representation (in tuple relational calculus and SQL) that differs from related work in terms of its focus; we demonstrated how DFMAC policy information may be used by a query modifier for enforcing access control policy requirements; and we discussed an implementation and performance results for a real application of the approach. The approach that we have described can be applied to various category-based access control models and, as such, is quite general. As far as we are aware the particular aspect of the AC representation problem that we have considered (the representation and implementation of DFMAC policy requirements) has not been previously addressed in the literature on representations of access control policy requirements in SQL.

In future work, we intend to investigate yet finer grained DFMAC policy representations where, for example, DFMAC policies may be expressed on individual columns within a table. We also want to consider extending our approach to accommodate additional information of relevance to extended forms of DFMAC policies (e.g., DFMAC policies that include specifications of obligations on users and constraints on policy specifications). The efficient implementation of these forms of extended DFMAC policies in SQL is also a matter for further work as is an investigation of the feasibility of combining DFMAC and FGAC policies proposed by other authors.

References

1. Abiteboul, S., Hull, R., Vianu, V.: Foundations of Databases. Addison-Wesley, Reading (1995)
2. Barker, S.: Access Control for Deductive Databases by Logic Programming. In: Stuckey, P.J. (ed.) ICLP 2002. LNCS, vol. 2401, pp. 54–69. Springer, Heidelberg (2002)
3. Barker, S.: Protecting deductive databases from unauthorized retrieval and update requests. Journal of Data and Knowledge Engineering 23(3), 231–285 (2002)
4. Barker, S.: Action-status access control. In: SACMAT, pp. 195–204 (2007)
5. Barker, S., Stuckey, P.: Flexible access control policy specification with constraint logic programming. ACM Trans. on Information and System Security 6(4), 501–546 (2003)
6. Bell, D.E., LaPadula, L.J.: Secure computer system: Unified exposition and multics interpretation. MITRE-2997 (1976)
7. Bertino, E., Bettini, C., Ferrari, E., Samarati, P.: An access control model supporting periodicity constraints and temporal reasoning. ACM TODS 23(3), 231–285 (1998)
8. Bertino, E., Bonatti, P., Ferrari, E.: TRBAC: A temporal role-based access control model. In: Proc. 5th ACM Workshop on Role-Based Access Control, pp. 21–30 (2000)
9. Bertino, E., Jajodia, S., Samarati, P.: A flexible authorization mechanism for relational data management systems. ACM Trans. Inf. Syst. 17(2), 101–140 (1999)
10. Date, C.: An Introduction to Database Systems. Addison-Wesley, Reading (2003)
11. Ferraiolo, D.F., Sandhu, R.S., Gavrila, S.I., Kuhn, D.R., Chandramouli, R.: Proposed nist standard for role-based access control. ACM Trans. Inf. Syst. Secur. 4(3), 224–274 (2001)
12. Joshi, J., Bertino, E., Latif, U., Ghafoor, A.: A generalized temporal role-based access control model. IEEE Trans. Knowl. Data Eng. 17(1), 4–23 (2005)
13. LeFevre, K., Agrawal, R., Ercegovac, V., Ramakrishnan, R., Xu, Y., DeWitt, D.J.: Limiting disclosure in hippocratic databases. In: VLDB, pp. 108–119 (2004)
14. Lloyd, J.: Foundations of Logic Programming. Springer, Heidelberg (1987)
15. Oracle. Oracle 11g, http://www.oracle.com
16. PostgreSQL 8.3: User Manual, http://www.postgresql.org/docs/
17. Rizvi, S., Mendelzon, A.O., Sudarshan, S., Roy, P.: Extending query rewriting techniques for fine-grained access control. In: SIGMOD Conference, pp. 551–562 (2004)
18. Stonebraker, M., Wong, E.: Access control in a relational data base management system by query modification. In: Proc. 1974 Annual Conf (ACM/CSC-ER), pp. 180–186 (1974)
19. Wang, Q., Yu, T., Li, N., Lobo, J., Bertino, E., Irwin, K., Byun, J.-W.: On the correctness criteria of fine-grained access control in relational databases. In: VLDB, pp. 555–566 (2007)

On the Formal Analysis of a Spatio-temporal Role-Based Access Control Model*

Manachai Toahchoodee and Indrakshi Ray

Department of Computer Science
Colorado State University
{toahchoo,iray}@cs.colostate.edu

Abstract. With the growing use of wireless networks and mobile devices, we are moving towards an era where spatial and temporal information will be necessary for access control. The use of such information can be used for enhancing the security of an application, and it can also be exploited to launch attacks. For critical applications, a model for spatio-temporal-based access control is needed that increases the security of the application and ensures that the location information cannot be exploited to cause harm. Consequently, researchers have proposed various spatio-temporal access control models that are useful in pervasive computing applications. Such models typically have numerous different features to support the various application requirements. The different features of a spatio-temporal access control model may interact in subtle ways resulting in conflicts. We illustrate how the access control model can be formally analyzed to detect the presence of conflicts. We use Alloy, a formal language based on first-order logic, for the purpose of our analysis. Alloy is supported by a software infrastructure that allows automated analysis of models and has been used to verify industrial applications. The results obtained by analyzing the spatio-temporal access control model will enable the users of the model to make informed decisions.

1 Introduction

With the increase in the growth of wireless networks and sensor and mobile devices, we are moving towards an era of pervasive computing. The growth of this technology will spawn applications such as, the Aware Home [8] and CMU's Aura [11], that will make life easier for people. Pervasive computing applications introduce new security issues that cannot be addressed by existing access control models and mechanisms. For instance, access to a computer should be automatically disabled when a user walks out of the room. Traditional models, such as Discretionary Access Control (DAC) or Role-Based Access Control (RBAC) do not take into account such environmental factors in determining whether access should be allowed or not. Consequently, access control models and mechanisms that use environmental factors, such as, time and location, while determining access are needed.

Researchers have proposed various access control models that use contextual information, such as, location and time, for performing access control [1, 4, 5, 6, 8, 11,

---

* This work was supported in part by AFOSR under contract number FA9550-07-1-0042.

V. Atluri (Ed.): DAS 2008, LNCS 5094, pp. 17–32, 2008.

13, 14, 15, 16, 17, 20] Many of these were developed for commercial applications and are based on RBAC. Examples include TRBAC [4], Geo-RBAC [5], and STRBAC [15]. These models are more expressive than their traditional counterparts, and have various features which the users can selectively use based on the application requirements. The different features of these models interact in subtle ways resulting in inconsistencies and conflicts. Consequently, it is important to analyze and understand these models before they are widely deployed.

Manual analysis is tedious and error-prone. Analyzers based on theorem proving are hard to use, require expertise, and need manual intervention. Model checkers are automated but are limited by the size of the system they can verify. In this paper, we advocate the use of Alloy [12], which supports automated analysis, for checking access control models. Alloy is a modeling language capable of expressing complex structural constraints and behavior. Moreover, it has been successfully used in the modeling and analysis of real-world systems [10,24].

In this paper, we illustrate how to specify and analyze properties of a spatio-temporal role-based access control model. Alloy is supported by an automated constraint solver called Alloy Analyzer that searches instances of the model to check for satisfaction of system properties. The model is automatically translated into a Boolean expression, which is analyzed by SAT solvers embedded within the Alloy Analyzer. A user-specified scope on the model elements bounds the domain, making it possible to create finite Boolean formulas that can be evaluated by the SAT-solver. When a property does not hold, a counter example is produced that demonstrates how it has been violated.

The rest of the paper is organized as follows. Section 2 describes the related work. Section 3 shows the relationship of each component of Core RBAC with location and time. Sections 4, 5 and 6 propose different types of hierarchies and separation of duty constraints that we can have in our model. Section 7 discusses how the model can be analyzed using Alloy. Section 8 concludes the paper with some pointers to future directions.

2   Related Work

Ardagna et al. [1] discuss how location information of the requester can be ascertained and how such information can be used to evaluate and enforce location-based predicates used in access control. Location-based access control has been addressed in other works as well [11,14,16].

Role-based access control model [9] is used for addressing the access control needs of commercial organizations. Several works exist that improve RBAC functionality, some of which focus on how RBAC can be extended to make it context aware. Sampemane et al. [19] present a new access control model for active spaces. Active space denotes the computing environment integrating physical spaces and embedded computing software and hardware entities. Environmental aspects are adopted into the access control model for active spaces, and the space roles are introduced into the implementation of the access control model based on RBAC. Covington et al. [8] introduce environment roles in a generalized RBAC model (GRBAC) to help control access control to private information and resources in ubiquitous computing applications. The environments roles differ from the subject roles in RBAC but do have similar properties including role activation, role hierarchy and separation of duty. However, the environment roles are activated according to the changing conditions specified in environmental conditions, thus environmental properties like time and location are introduced to the access control framework. In a subsequent work [7], Covington et al. describes the Context-Aware Security Architecture (CASA) which is an implementation of the GRBAC model.

Other extensions to RBAC include the Temporal Role-Based Access Control Model (TRBAC) proposed by Bertino et al. [4]. The authors in this paper introduce the concept of role enabling and disabling. Temporal constraints determine when the roles can be enabled or disabled. A role can be activated only if it has been enabled. Joshi et al.[13] extend this work by proposing the Generalized Temporal Role Based Access Control Model (GTRBAC). In this work the authors introduce the concept of time-based role hierarchy and time-based separation of duty. These works do not discuss the impact of spatial information.

Researchers have also extended RBAC to incorporate spatial information. The most important work in this regard is the GEO-RBAC [5]. In this model, role activation is based on the location of the user. For instance, a user can acquire the role of teacher only when he is in the school. Outside the school, he can acquire the role of citizen. The model supports role hierarchies but does not deal with separation of duties. Another work incorporating spatial information is by Ray et al. [17]. Here again, the authors propose how each component of RBAC is influenced by location. The authors define their formal model using the Z specification language. Role hierarchy and separation of duties is not addressed in this paper. None of these work discuss the impact of time on location.

The paper proposed by Chandran et al. [6] combines the main features of GTRBAC and GEO-RBAC. Here again, role is enabled by time constraints. The user can activate the role if the role is enabled and the user satisfies the location constraints associated with role activation. Another work which falls into this category is GST-RBAC by Samuel et al. [20]. In this work, the authors develop a framework to incorporate topological spatial constraints to the existing GTRBAC model. The authors do this by augmenting GTRBAC operations, namely, role enabling, user-role assignment, role-permission assignment, and role-activation with spatial constraints. The operations are allowed only if the spatial and temporal constraints are satisfied. The model also introduces the notion of Spatial Role Hierarchy and Spatial Separation of Duty (spSoD) constraints. Our early work [15] extends RBAC with spatial and temporal constraints. Although the goal of this work is similar to those proposed by Chandran et al. and Samuel et al., our model can express some real-world constraints that are not possible in the other ones. Atluri et al proposed Geotemporal RBAC model in [2,3] for protecting the information in Geospatial databases. In this model, user can acquire a role based on his spatial-temporal information. For instance, a user can assume the role of a professor in a classroom during the day time. This allows the user to access some resource only when he satisfies spatial and temporal constraints. The Geotemporal RBAC model, however, does not discuss the impact of spatial and temporal constraints on role hierarchy and separation of duties.

A lot of work appears in the area of analysis of security policies. Some have used the Z modeling language for specifying RBAC [25] and LRBAC [17]. Although Z language can represent RBAC and its constraints in the formal manner, the language itself lacks the tool to support the automatic analysis of the formalized model. Others have used an extension of the Unified Modeling Language (UML) [18] called parameterized UML to visualize the properties of RBAC constraints. However, it still lacks the ability to perform automated model analysis.

Researchers have advocated the use of Alloy for modeling and analyzing RBAC specifications. Schaad et al. model user-role assignment, role-permission assignment, role hierarchy, and static separation of duties features of RBAC extension using Alloy in [22]. The authors do not model role activation hierarchy or the dynamic separation of duties. The authors briefly describe how to analyze conflicts in the context of the model. Samuel et al. [20] also illustrate how GST-RBAC can be specified in Alloy. They describe how the various GST-RBAC functionalities, that is, user-role assignment, role-permission assignment, and user-role activation, can be specified by Alloy. However, this work does not focus on how to identify interactions between features that result in conflicts. Our work fills this gap.

3   Relationship of Core-RBAC Entities with Time and Location

In this section, we describe how the entities in RBAC are associated with location and time[1]. We discuss how the different entities of RBAC, namely, *Users*, *Roles*, *Sessions*, *Permissions*, *Objects* and *Operations*, are associated with location and time.

Users
We assume that each valid user, interested in doing some location-sensitive operation, carries a locating device which is able to track his location. The location of a user changes with time. The relation $UserLocation(u,t)$ gives the location of the user at any given time instant t. Since a user can be associated with only one location at any given point of time, the following constraint must be true. Note that in this and all the subsequent formulae, we omit the quantification symbols.

$$UserLocation(u,t) = l_i \wedge UserLocation(u,t) = l_j \Leftrightarrow (l_i \subseteq l_j) \vee (l_j \subseteq l_i)$$

We define a similar function $UserLocations(u,d)$ that gives the location of the user during the time interval d. Note that, a single location can be associated with multiple users at any given point of time.

Objects
Objects can be physical or logical. Example of a physical object is a computer. Files are examples of logical objects. Physical objects have devices that transmit their location information with the timestamp. Logical objects are stored in physical objects. The location and timestamp of a logical object corresponds to the location and time of

---

[1] For lack of space, we do not give details on location and time representation. Please refer to our earlier paper [15] for more details.

the physical object containing the logical object. We assume that each object is associated with one location at any given instant of time. Each location can be associated with many objects. The function *ObjLocation(o,t)* takes as input an object *o* and a time instance *t* and returns the location associated with the object at time *t*. Similarly, the function *ObjLocations(o,d)* takes as input an object *o* and time interval *d* and returns the location associated with the object.

Roles

We have three types of relations with roles. These are user-role assignment, user-role activation, and permission-role assignment.

We begin by focusing on user-role assignment. Often times, the assignment of user to roles is location and time dependent. For instance, a person can be assigned the role of U.S. citizen only in certain designated locations and at certain times only. To get the role of conference attendee, a person must register at the conference location during specific time intervals. Thus, for a user to be assigned a role, he must be in designated locations during specific time intervals. In our model, a user must satisfy spatial and temporal constraints before roles can be assigned. We capture this with the concept of *role allocation*. A role is said to be *allocated* when it satisfies the temporal and spatial constraints needed for role assignment. A role can be assigned once it has been allocated. *RoleAllocLoc(r)* gives the set of locations where the role can be allocated. *RoleAllocDur(r)* gives the time interval where the role can be allocated. Some role *s* can be allocated anywhere, in such cases *RoleAllocLoc(s) = universe*. Similarly, if role *p* can be assigned at any time, we specify *RoleAllocDur(p) = always*.

Some roles can be activated only if the user is in some specific locations. For instance, the role of audience of a theater can be activated only if the user is in the theater when the show is on. The role of conference attendee can be activated only if the user is in the conference site while the conference is in session. In short, the user must satisfy temporal and location constraints before a role can be activated. We borrow the concept of *role-enabling* [4,13] to describe this. A role is said to be *enabled* if it satisfies the temporal and location constraints needed to activate it. A role can be activated only if it has been enabled. *RoleEnableLoc(r)* gives the location where role *r* can be activated and *RoleEnableDur(r)* gives the time interval when the role can be activated.

The predicate *UserRoleAssign(u,r,d,l)* states that the user *u* is assigned to role *r* during the time interval *d* and location *l*. For this predicate to hold, the location of the user when the role was assigned must be in one of the locations where the role allocation can take place. Moreover, the time of role assignment must be in the interval when role allocation can take place.

$$UserRoleAssign(u,r,d,l) \Rightarrow (UserLocation(u,d) = l) \wedge$$
$$(l \subseteq RoleAllocLoc(r)) \wedge (d \subseteq RoleAllocDur(r))$$

The predicate *UserRoleActivate(u,r,d,l)* is true if the user *u* activated role *r* for the interval *d* at location *l*. This predicate implies that the location of the user during the role activation must be a subset of the allowable locations for the activated role and all times instances when the role remains activated must belong to the duration when the role can be activated and the role can be activated only if it is assigned.

$UserRoleActivate(u,r,d,l) \Rightarrow$
$\quad (l \subseteq RoleEnableLoc(r)) \wedge (d \subseteq RoleEnableDur(r)) \wedge UserRoleAssign(u,r,d,l)$

The additional constraints imposed upon the model necessitates changing the preconditions of the functions *AssignRole* and *ActivateRole*. The permission role assignment is discussed later.

Sessions

In mobile computing or pervasive computing environments, we have different types of sessions that can be initiated by the user. Some of these sessions can be location-dependent, others not. Thus, sessions are classified into different types. Each instance of a session is associated with some type of a session. The type of session instance s is given by the function $Type(s)$. The type of the session determines the allowable location. The allowable location for a session type st is given by the function $SessionLoc(st)$.

When a user u wants to create a session si, the location of the user for the entire duration of the session must be contained within the location associated with the session. The predicate $SessionUser(u,s,d)$ indicates that a user u has initiated a session s for duration d.

$SessionUser(u,s,d) \Rightarrow (UserLocation(u,d) \subseteq SessionLoc(Type(s)))$

Since sessions are associated with locations, not all roles can be activated within some session. The predicate $SessionRoles(u,r,s,d,l)$ states that user u initiates a session s and activates a role for duration d and at location l.

$SessionRole(u,r,s,d) \Rightarrow UserRoleActivate(u,r,d,l) \wedge l \subseteq SessionLoc(Type(s)))$

Permissions

The goal of our model is to provide more security than their traditional counterparts. This happens because the time and location of a user and an object are taken into account before making the access decisions. Our model also allows us to model real-world requirements where access decision is contingent upon the time and location associated with the user and the object. For example, a teller may access the bank confidential file if and only if he is in the bank and the file location is the bank secure room and the access is granted only during the working hours. Our model should be capable of expressing such requirements.

Permissions are associated with roles, objects, and operations. We associate three additional entities with permission to deal with spatial and temporal constraints: user location, object location, and time. We define three functions to retrieve the values of these entities. $PermRoleLoc(p,r)$ specifies the allowable locations that a user playing the role r must be in for him to get permission p. $PermObjLoc(p,o)$ specifies the allowable locations that the object o must be in so that the user has permission to operate on the object o. $PermDur(p)$ specifies the allowable time when the permission can be invoked.

We define another predicate which we term $PermRoleAcquire(p,r,d,l)$. This predicate is true if role r has permission p for duration d at location l. Note that, for this predicate to be true, the time interval d must be contained in the duration where the permission can be invoked and the role can be enabled. Similarly, the location l must be contained in the places where the permission can be invoked and role can be enabled.

$PermRoleAcquire(p,r,d,l) \Rightarrow (l \subseteq (PermRoleLoc(p,r) \cap RoleEnableLoc(r)))$
$\wedge (d \subseteq (PermDur(p) \cap RoleEnableDur(p)))$

The predicate $PermUserAcquire(u,o,p,d,l)$ means that user u can acquire the permission p on object o for duration d at location l. This is possible only when the permission p is assigned some role r which can be activated during d and at location l, the user location and object location match those specified in the permission, the duration d matches that specified in the permission.

$PermRoleAcquire(p,r,d,l) \wedge UserRoleActivate(u,r,d,l)$
$\wedge (ObjectLocation(o,d) \subseteq PermObjectLoc(p,o)) \Rightarrow PermUserAcquire(u,o,p,d,l)$

4   Impact of Time and Location on Role-Hierarchy

The structure of an organization in terms of lines of authority can be modeled as an hierarchy. This organization structure is reflected in RBAC in the form of a role hierarchy [21]. Role hierarchy is a relation among roles. This relation is transitive, and anti-symmetric. Roles higher up in the hierarchy are referred to as senior roles and those lower down are junior roles. The major motivation for adding role hierarchy to RBAC was to simplify role management. Senior roles can inherit the permissions of junior roles, or a senior role can activate a junior role, or do both depending on the nature of the hierarchy. This obviates the need for separately assigning the same permissions to all members belonging to a hierarchy.

Joshi et al. [13] identify two basic types of hierarchy. The first is the permission inheritance hierarchy where a senior role x inherits the permission of a junior role y. The second is the role activation hierarchy where a user assigned to a senior role can activate a junior role. Each of these hierarchies may be constrained by location and temporal constraints. Consequently, we have a number of different hierarchical relationships in our model.

[**Unrestricted Permission Inheritance Hierarchy**]. Let x and y be roles such that $x \geq y$, that is, senior role x has an unrestricted permission-inheritance relation over junior role y. In such a case, x inherits y's permissions but not the locations and time associated with it. In other words, the permission can be applied wherever the senior role is at that time. This is formalized as follows:

$(x \geq y) \wedge PermRoleAcquire(p,y,d,l) \Rightarrow PermRoleAcquire(p,x,d',l')$

In the above hierarchy, a senior role inherits the junior roles permissions. However, unlike the junior role, these permissions are not restricted to time and location. Account auditor role inherits the permissions from the accountant role. He can use the permissions at any time and at any place.

[**Unrestricted Activation Hierarchy**]. Let x and y be roles such that $x \succcurlyeq y$, that is, senior role x has a role-activation relation over junior role y. Then, a user assigned to role x can activate role y at any time and at any place. This is formalized as follows:

$(x \succcurlyeq y) \wedge UserRoleActivate(u,x,d,l) \Rightarrow UserRoleActivate(u,y,d',l')$

Here again a user who can activate a senior role can also activate a junior role. This junior role can be activated at any time and place. A project manager can activate the code developer role at any time and at any place.

[Time Restricted Permission Inheritance Hierarchy]. Let x and y be roles such that $x \geq_t y$, that is, senior role x has a time restricted permission-inheritance relation over junior role y. In such a case, x inherits y's permissions together with the temporal constraints associated with the permission. This is formalized as follows:

$$(x \geq_t y) \wedge PermRoleAcquire(p,y,d,l) \Rightarrow PermRoleAcquire(p,x,d,l')$$

In the above hierarchy, a senior role inherits the junior roles permissions. However, the duration when the permissions are valid are those that are associated with the junior roles. A contact author can inherit the permissions of the author until the paper is submitted.

[Time Restricted Activation Hierarchy]. Let x and y be roles such that $x \succeq_t y$, that is, senior role x has a role-activation relation over junior role y. Then, a user assigned to role x can activate role y only at the time when role y can be enabled. This is formalized as follows:

$$(x \succeq_t y) \wedge UserRoleActivate(u,x,d,l) \wedge d \subseteq RoleEnableDur(y) \Rightarrow$$
$$UserRoleActivate(u,y,d,l')$$

Here again a user who can activate a senior role can also activate a junior role. However, this activation is limited to the time when the junior role can be activated. A program chair can activate a reviewer role only during the review period.

[Location Restricted Permission Inheritance Hierarchy]. Let x and y be roles such that $x \geq_l y$, that is, senior role x has a location restricted permission-inheritance relation over junior role y. In such a case, x inherit's y's permissions together with the location constraints associated with the permission. This is formalized as follows:

$$(x \geq_l y) \wedge PermRoleAcquire(p,y,d,l) \Rightarrow PermRoleAcquire(p,x,d',l)$$

In the above hierarchy, a senior role inherits the junior roles permissions. These permissions are restricted to the locations imposed on the junior roles. A top secret scientist inherits the permission of top secret citizen only when he is in top secret locations.

[Location Restricted Activation Hierarchy]. Let x and y be roles such that $x \succeq_l y$, that is, senior role x has a role-activation relation over junior role y. Then, a user assigned to role x can activate role y only at the places when role y can be enabled. This is formalized as follows:

$$(x \succeq_l y) \wedge UserRoleActivate(u,x,d,l) \wedge l \subseteq RoleEnableLoc(y) \Rightarrow$$
$$UserRoleActivate(u,y,d',l)$$

Here again a user who can activate a senior role can also activate a junior role. However, this activation is limited to the place where the junior role can be activated. A Department Chair can activate a Staff role only when he is in the Department.

[Time Location Restricted Permission Inheritance Hierarchy]. Let x and y be roles such that $x \geq_{tl} y$, that is, senior role x has a time-location restricted permission-inheritance relation over junior role y. In such a case, x inherits y's permissions together with the temporal and location constraints associated with the permission. This is formalized as follows:

$$(x \geq_{tl} y) \wedge PermRoleAcquire(p,y,d,l) \Rightarrow PermRoleAcquire(p,x,d,l)$$

In the above hierarchy, a senior role inherits the junior roles permissions. These permissions are restricted to time and locations imposed on the junior roles. Daytime doctor role inherits permission of daytime nurse role only when he is in the hospital during the daytime.

[Time Location Restricted Activation Hierarchy]. Let x and y be roles such that $x \succcurlyeq_{tl} y$, that is, senior role x has a role-activation relation over junior role y. Then, a user assigned to role x can activate role y only at the places and during the time when role y can be enabled. This is formalized as follows:

$$(x \succcurlyeq_{tl} y) \wedge UserRoleActivate(u,x,d,l) \wedge d \subseteq RoleEnableDur(y)$$
$$\wedge l \subseteq RoleEnableLoc(y) \Rightarrow UserRoleActivate(u,y,d,l)$$

Here again a user who can activate a senior role can also activate a junior role. However, this activation is limited to the time and place where the junior role can be activated. User who has a role of mobile user can activate the weekend mobile user role only if he/she is in the US during the weekend.

It is also possible for a senior role and a junior role to be related with both permission inheritance and activation hierarchies. In such a case, the application will choose the type of inheritance hierarchy and activation hierarchy needed.

5   Impact of Time and Location on Static Separation of Duties

Separation of duties (SoD) enables the protection of the fraud that might be caused by the user [23]. SoD can be either static or dynamic. Static Separation of Duty (SSoD) comes in two varieties. First one is with respect to user role assignment. The second one is with respect to permission role assignment. In this case, the SoD is specified as a relation between roles. The idea is that the same user cannot be assigned to the same role. Due to the presence of temporal and spatial constraints, we can have different flavors of separation of duties – some that are constrained by temporal and spatial constraints and others that are not. In the following we describe the different separation of duty constraints.

[Weak Form of SSoD - User Role Assignment]. Let x and y be two roles such that $x \neq y$. $x,y \in SSOD_w(ROLES)$ if the following condition holds:

$$UserRoleAssign(u,x,d,l) \Rightarrow \neg UserRoleAssign(u,y,d,l)$$

The above definition says that a user u assigned to role x during time d and location l cannot be assigned to role y at the same time and location if x and y are related by $SSOD_w$. An example where this form is useful is that a user should not be assigned the audience role and mobile user role at the same time and location.

[Strong Temporal Form of SSoD - User Role Assignment]. Let x and y be two roles such that $x \neq y$. $(x,y) \in SSOD_t(ROLES)$ if the following condition holds:

$$UserRoleAssign(u,x,d,l) \Rightarrow \neg\ (\exists d' \subseteq always \bullet UserRoleAssign(u,y,d',l))$$

The above definition says that a user u assigned to role x during time d and location l cannot be assigned to role y at any time in the same location if x and y are related by $SSOD_t$. The consultant for oil company A will never be assigned the role of consultant for oil company B in the same country.

[Strong Spatial Form of SSoD - User Role Assignment]. Let x and y be two roles such that $x \neq y$. $(x,y) \in SSOD_l(ROLES)$ if the following condition holds:

$$UserRoleAssign(u,x,d,l) \Rightarrow \neg\ (\exists l' \subseteq universe \bullet UserRoleAssign(u,y,d,l'))$$

The above definition says that a user u assigned to role x during time d and location l, he cannot be assigned to role y at the same time at any location if x and y are related by $SSOD_l$. A person cannot be assigned the roles of realtor and instructor at the same time.

[Strong Form of SSoD - User Role Assignment]. Let x and y be two roles such that $x \neq y$. $(x,y) \in SSOD_s(ROLES)$ if the following condition holds:

$$UserRoleAssign(u,x,d,l) \Rightarrow \neg\ (\exists l' \subset universe, \exists d' \subseteq always \bullet UserRoleAssign(u,y,d',l'))$$

The above definition says that a user u assigned to role x during time d and location l, he cannot be assigned to role y at any time or at any location if x and y are related by $SSOD_s$. The same employee cannot be assigned the roles of male and female employee at any given corporation.

We next consider the second form of static separation of duty that deals with permission role assignment. The idea is that the same role should not acquire conflicting permissions. The same manager should not make a request for funding as well as approve it.

[Weak Form of SSoD - Permission Role Assignment]. Let p and q be two permissions such that $p \neq q$. $(p,q) \in SSOD\_PRA_w$ if the following condition holds:

$$PermRoleAcquire(p,x,d,l) \Rightarrow \neg\ PermRoleAcquire(q,x,d,l)$$

The above definition says that if permissions p and q are related through weak SSoD Permission Role Assignment and x has permission p at time d and location l, then x should not be given permission q at the same time and location.

[Strong Temporal Form of SSoD - Permission Role Assignment]. Let p and q be two permissions such that $p \neq q$. $(p,q) \in SSOD\_PRA_t$ if the following condition holds:

$$PermRoleAcquire(p,x,d,l) \Rightarrow \neg\ (\exists d' \subseteq always \bullet PermRoleAcquire(q,x,d',l))$$

The above definition says that if permissions p and q are related through strong temporal SSoD Permission Role Assignment and x has permission p at time d and location l, then x should not get permission q at any time in location l.

[Strong Spatial Form of SSoD - Permission Role Assignment]. Let p and q be two permissions such that $p \neq q$. $(p,q) \in SSOD\_PRA_l$ if the following condition holds:

$$PermRoleAcquire(p,x,d,l) \Rightarrow \neg\ (\exists l' \subset universe \bullet PermRoleAcquire(q,x,d,l'))$$

The above definition says that if permissions p and q are related through strong spatial SSoD Permission Role Assignment and x has permission p at time d and location l, then x should not be given permission q at the same time.

[Strong Form of SSoD - Permission Role Assignment]. Let p and q be two permissions such that $p \neq q$. $(p,q) \in SSOD\_PRA_s$ if the following condition holds:

$$PermRoleAcquire(p,x,d,l) \Rightarrow \neg\ (\exists l' \subset universe, \exists d' \subseteq always \bullet PermRoleAcquire(q,x,d',l'))$$

The above definition says that if permissions p and q are related through strong SSoD Permission Role Assignment, then the same role should never be given the two conflicting permissions.

6   Impact of Time and Location on Dynamic Separation of Duties

Static separation of duty ensures that a user does not get assigned conflicting roles or a role is not assigned conflicting permissions. Dynamic separation of duty addresses the problem that a user is not able to activate conflicting roles during the same session.

[Weak Form of DSoD]. Let x and y be two roles such that $x \neq y$. $(x,y) \in DSOD_w$ if the following condition holds:

$$SessionRole(u,x,s,d,l) \Rightarrow \neg\ SessionRole(u,y,s,d,l))$$

The above definition says that if roles x and y are related through weak DSoD and if user u has activated role x in some session s for duration d and location l, then u cannot activate role y during the same time and in the same location in session s. In the same session, a user can activate a sales assistant role and a customer role. However, both these roles should not be activated at the same time in the same location.

[Strong Temporal Form of DSoD]. Let x and y be two roles such that $x \neq y$. $(x,y) \in DSOD_t$ if the following condition holds:

$$SessionRole(u,x,s,d,l) \Rightarrow \neg\ (\exists d' \subset always, \bullet SessionRole(u,y,s,d',l))$$

The above definition says that if roles x and y are related through strong temporal DSoD and if user u has activated role x in some session s, then u can never activate role y any time at the same location in the same session. In a teaching session in a classroom, a user cannot activate the the grader role once he has activated the student role.

[Strong Spatial Form of DSoD]. Let x and y be two roles such that $x \neq y$. $(x,y) \in DSOD_l$ if the following condition holds:

$$SessionRole(u,x,s,d,l) \Rightarrow \neg\ (\exists l' \subseteq universe \bullet SessionRole(u,y,s,d,l'))$$

The above definition says that if roles x and y are related through strong DSoD and if user u has activated role x in some session s, then u can never activate role y in session s during the same time in any location. If a user has activated the Graduate Teaching Assistant role in his office, he cannot activate the Lab Operator role at the same time.

[Strong Form of DSoD]. Let x and y be two roles such that $x \neq y$. $(x,y) \in DSOD_s$ if the following condition holds:

$SessionRole(u, x, s, d, l) \Rightarrow \neg (\exists l' \subset universe, \exists d' \subseteq always \bullet SessionRole(u, y, s, d', l'))$

The above definition says that if roles x and y are related through strong DSoD and if user u has activated role x in some session s, then u can never activate role y in the same session. An user cannot be a code developer and a code tester in the same session.

7 Model Analysis

An Alloy model consists of *signature* declarations, *fields*, *facts* and *predicates*. Each signature consists of a set of *atoms* which are the basic entities in Alloy. Atoms are *indivisible* (they cannot be divided into smaller parts), *immutable* (their properties do not change) and *uninterpreted* (they do not have any inherent properties). Each field belongs to a signature and represents a relation between two or more signatures. A relation denotes a set of tuples of atoms. Facts are statements that define constraints on the elements of the model. Predicates are parameterized constraints that can be invoked from within facts or other predicates.

The basic types in the access control model, such as, *User, Time, Location, Role, Permission* and *Object* are represented as signatures. For instance, the declarations shown below define a set named *User* and a set named *Role* that represents the set of all users and the set of all roles in the system. Inside the *Role* signature body, we have four relations, namely, *RoleAllocLoc, RoleAllocDur, RoleEnableLoc,* and *RoleEnableDur* which relates *Role* to other signatures.

```
sig User{}
sig Role{
 RoleAllocLoc: Location,
 RoleAllocDur: Time,
 RoleEnableLoc: Location,
 RoleEnableDur: Time}
```

The different relationships between the STRBAC components are also expressed as signatures. For instance, *RoleEnable* has a field called *member* that maps to a cartesian product of *Role, Time* and *Location*. Similarly, *RoleHierarchy* has a field *RHmember* that represents a relationship between *Role* and *Role*. Different types of role hierarchy are modeled as the subsignatures of RoleHierarchy.

```
sig RoleEnable { member: Role -> Time -> Location}
sig RoleHierarchy { RHmember: Role -> Role}
sig UPIH, TPIH, LPIH, TLPIH, UAH, TAH, LAH, TLAH extends
    RoleHierarchy{}
```

The various invariants in the STRBAC model are represented as facts in Alloy. For instance, the fact *URActivate* states that for user u to activate role r during the time interval d and location l, this user has to be assigned to role r in location l during time d. Moreover, the location of the user must be a subset of the locations where the role is enabled, and the time must be in the time interval when role r can be enabled. This is specified in Alloy as shown below. Other invariants are modeled in a similar manner.

```
fact URActivate{
all u: User, r: Role, d: Time, l: Location, uras: UserRoleAssignment,
urac: UserRoleActivate |
((u->r->d->l) in urac.member) => (((u->r->d->l) in uras.member) &&
(l in r.RoleEnableLoc) && (d in r.RoleEnableDur))
}
```

To represent the effects of STRBAC hierarchical structure, we use Alloy's *fact* feature. The fact *UPIHFact* represents the Unrestricted Permission Inheritance Hierarchy's property. The fact states that senior role sr can acquire all permission assigned to itself together with all permissions assigned to junior role jr.

```
//Unrestricted Permission Inheritance Hierarchy
fact UPIHFact{
     all sr, jr: Role, p: Permission, d: Time, l: Location, upih: UPIH,
         rpa: RolePermissionAssignment, pra: PermRoleAcquire |
         ((sr->jr in upih.member) && (jr->p->d->l in pra.member) &&
         (sr->p !in (rpa.member).Location.Time)) =>
              (sr->p->sr.RoleEnableDur->sr.RoleEnableLoc) in pra.member}
```

The separation of duty constraints are modeled as predicates. Consider the Weak form of Static Separation of Duties User Role Assignment. This constraint says that a user *u* assigned to role *r*1 during time *d* and location *l* cannot be assigned to its conflicts role *r*2 at the same time and location. The other forms are modeled in a separate manner.

```
//Weak Form of SSoD-User Role Assignment
pred W_SSoD_URA(u: User, disj r1, r2: Role,
ura: UserRoleAssignment.member, d: Time, l: Location){
((u->r1->d->l) in ura) => ((u->r2->d->l) not in ura)
}
```

Finally, we need to verify whether any conflicts occur between the features of the model. We rely on the powerful analysis capability of the ALLOY analyzer for this purpose. We create an *assertion* that specifies the properties we want to check. After we create the assertion, we will let ALLOY analyzer validate the assertion by using *check* command. If our assertion is wrong in the specified scope, ALLOY analyzer will show the counterexample.

For instance, to check the interaction of the Weak form of SSOD User Role Assignment and the Unrestricted Permission Inheritance Hierarchy, we make the assertion shown below. The assertion does not hold as illustrated by the counterexample shown in Figure 1.

```
// WSSoD_URA violation in the present of UPIH Hierarchy
check TestWSSoD_URA
assert TestConflict1_1{
no u: User, disj x, y: Role, upih: UPIH,
     d: Time, l: Location, ura: UserRoleAssignment |
((x->y in ^(upih.member)) &&
```

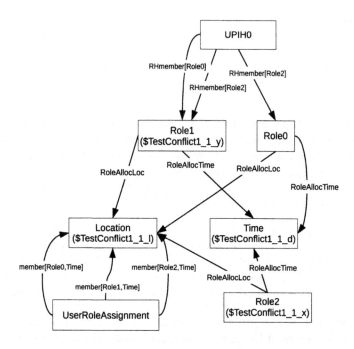

Fig. 1. Counterexample for assertion TestConflict1_1

```
          (u->x->d->l in ura.member)) =>
W_SSoD_URA[u, x, y, u->(x+y)->d->l, d, l]
}
check TestConflict1_1
```

The counterexample shows one possible scenario. In this case, it uses the following instances to show the violation.

1. $Role = \{Role0, Role1, Role2\}$
2. $UPIH0 = \{Role0 \rightarrow Role1, Role2 \rightarrow Role0, Role2 \rightarrow Role1\}$
3. $Time = d, Location = l$
4. $UserRoleAssignment = \{User \rightarrow Role0 \rightarrow Time \rightarrow Location, User \rightarrow Role1 \rightarrow Time \rightarrow Location, User \rightarrow Role2 \rightarrow Time \rightarrow Location\}$

Substituting x and y in W_SSoD_URA predicate with $Role2$ and $Role1$ respectively, we get the violation. We checked the assertion on a HP-xw4400-Core2Duo-SATA with two Core2Duo 1.86Ghz CPU and 2 Gb memory running Linux 64. We used Version 4.1.2 Alloy Analyzer. The time taken to check this assertion was 25,916 ms.

Similar types of analysis reveals that the various forms of SSoD permission role inheritance conflict with the different forms of permission inheritance hierarchy. Conflicts were also detected with the various forms of SSoD user role assignment with different forms of permission inheritance hierarchy. Also, the various forms of DSoD constraints conflict with the different forms of role activation hierarchy. Another source of conflict occurs between role activation and permission when the corresponding location constraints or the temporal constraints do not overlap. Checking all these conflicts took 914,558 ms in our setup.

8 Conclusion and Future Work

Traditional access control models do not take into account environmental factors before making access decisions. Such models may not be suitable for pervasive computing applications. Towards this end, we proposed a spatio-temporal role based access control model. We identified the entities and relations in RBAC and investigated their dependence on location and time. This dependency necessitates changes in the invariants and the operations of RBAC. The behavior of the model is formalized using constraints. We investigated how the different constraints interact with each other and their relationships.

A lot of work remains to be done. We also plan to implement our model. We need to investigate how to store location and temporal information in an optimal manner. We also need to investigate how to use triggers for automatically detecting role allocation and role enabling. Once we have an implementation, we plan to validate our model using some example real-world applications. We also plan to adapt our analysis techniques for verifying other types of access control models.

References

1. Ardagna, C.A., Cremonini, M., Damiani, E., di Vimercati, S.D.C., Samarati, P.: Supporting location-based conditions in access control policies. In: Proceedings of the ACM Symposium on Information, Computer and Communications Security, Taipei, Taiwan, March 2006, pp. 212–222 (2006)
2. Atluri, V., Chun, S.A.: An authorization model for geospatial data. IEEE Transactions on Dependable and Secure Computing 1(4), 238–254 (2004)
3. Atluri, V., Chun, S.A.: A geotemporal role-based authorisation system. International Journal of Information and Computer Security 1(1/2), 143–168 (2007)
4. Bertino, E., Bonatti, P.A., Ferrari, E.: TRBAC: a temporal role-based access control model. In: Proceedings of the 5th ACM Workshop on Role-Based Access Control, Berlin, Germany, pp. 21–30 (July 2000)
5. Bertino, E., Catania, B., Damiani, M.L., Perlasca, P.: GEO-RBAC: a spatially aware RBAC. In: Proceedings of the 10th ACM Symposium on Access Control Models and Technologies, Stockholm, Sweden, pp. 29–37 (June 2005)
6. Chandran, S.M., Joshi, J.B.D.: LoT-RBAC: A Location and Time-Based RBAC Model. In: Proceedings of the 6th International Conference on Web Information Systems Engineering, New York, NY, USA, pp. 361–375 (November 2005)
7. Covington, M.J., Fogla, P., Zhan, Z., Ahamad, M.: A Context-Aware Security Architecture for Emerging Applications. In: Proceedings of the Annual Computer Security Applications Conference , Las Vegas, NV, USA, pp. 249–260 (December 2002)
8. Covington, M.J., Long, W., Srinivasan, S., Dey, A., Ahamad, M., Abowd, G.: Securing Context-Aware Applications Using Environment Roles. In: Proceedings of the 6th ACM Symposium on Access Control Models and Technologies, Chantilly, VA, USA, pp. 10–20 (May 2001)

9. Ferraiolo, D.F., Sandhu, R., Gavrila, S., Kuhn, D.R., Chandramouli, R.: Proposed NIST Standard for Role-Based Access Control. ACM Transactions on Information and Systems Security 4(3), 224–274 (2001)

10. Georg, G., Bieman, J., France, R.B.: Using Alloy and UML/OCL to Specify Run-Time Configurati on Management: A Case Study. In: Evans, A., France, R., Moreira, A., Rumpe, B. (eds.) Practical UML-Based Rigorous Development Methods - Countering or Integrating the eXtremists. LNI, vol. P-7, pp. 128–141. German Informatics Society (2001)

11. Hengartner, U., Steenkiste, P.: Implementing Access Control to People Location Information. In: Proceedings of the 9th ACM Symposium on Access Control Models and Technologies, Yorktown Heights, NY, USA, pp. 11–20 (June 2004)

12. Jackson, D.: Alloy 3.0 reference manual (2004), http://alloy.mit.edu/reference-manual.pdf

13. Joshi, J.B.D., Bertino, E., Latif, U., Ghafoor, A.: A Generalized Temporal Role-Based Access Control Model. IEEE Transactions on Knowledge and Data Engineering 17(1), 4–23 (2005)

14. Leonhardt, U., Magee, J.: Security Consideration for a Distributed Location Service. Imperial College of Science, Technology and Medicine, London, UK (1997)

15. Ray, I., Toahchoodee, M.: A Spatio-temporal Role-Based Access Control Model. In: Proceedings of the 21st Annual IFIP WG 11.3 Working Conference on Data and Applications Security, Redondo Beach, CA, pp. 211–226 (July 2007)

16. Ray, I., Kumar, M.: Towards a Location-Based Mandatory Access Control Model. Computers & Security 25(1) (February 2006)

17. Ray, I., Kumar, M., Yu, L.: LRBAC: A Location-Aware Role-Based Access Control Model. In: Proceedings of the 2nd International Conference on Information Systems Security, Kolkata, India, pp. 147–161 (December 2006)

18. Ray, I., Li, N., France, R., Kim, D.-K.: Using UML to Visualize Role-Based Access Control Constraints. In: Proceedings of the 9th ACM symposium on Access Control Models and Technologies, Yorktown Heights, NY, USA, pp. 115–124 (June 2004)

19. Sampemane, G., Naldurg, P., Campbell, R.H.: Access Control for Active Spaces. In: Proceedings of the Annual Computer Security Applications Conference , Las Vegas, NV, USA, pp. 343–352 (December 2002)

20. Samuel, A., Ghafoor, A., Bertino, E.: A Framework for Specification and Verification of Generalized Spatio-Temporal Role Based Access Control Model. Technical report, Purdue University (February 2007), CERIAS TR 2007-08

21. Sandhu, R.S., Coyne, E.J., Feinstein, H.L., Youman, C.E.: Role-based access control models. IEEE Computer 29(2), 38–47 (1996)

22. Schaad, A., Moffett, J.D.: A Lightweight Approach to Specification and Analysis of Role-Based Access Control Extensions. In: Proceedings of the 7th ACM Symposium on Access Control Models and Technologies, Monterey, CA, USA, pp. 13–22 (June 2002)

23. Simon, R., Zurko, M.E.: Separation of Duty in Role-based Environments. In: Proceedings of the 10th Computer Security Foundations Workshop, Rockport, MA, USA, pp. 183–194 (June 1997)

24. Taghdiri, M., Jackson, D.: A lightweight formal analysis of a multicast key management scheme. In: König, H., Heiner, M., Wolisz, A. (eds.) FORTE 2003. LNCS, vol. 2767, pp. 240–256. Springer, Heidelberg (2003)

25. Yuan, C., He, Y., He, J., Zhou, Z.: A Verifiable Formal Specification for RBAC Model with Constraints of Separation of Duty. In: Proceedings of the 2nd SKLOIS Conference on Information Security and Cryptology, Beijing, China, pp. 196–210 (November 2006)

A Unified Audit Expression Model for Auditing SQL Queries

Vikram Goyal[1], S.K. Gupta[1], and Anand Gupta[2]

[1] Department of Computer Science and Engineering, IIT Delhi,
Hauz Khas, New Delhi-16
{vkgoyal,skg}@cse.iitd.ernet.in
[2] Dept. of Comp. Sci. and Engg. N.S.I.T. Delhi, Sector-3, Dwarka,
New Delhi
anand@coe.nsit.ac.in

Abstract. A privacy auditing framework for Hippocratic databases accepts an administrator formulated audit expression and returns all suspicious user queries that satisfy the given constraints in that audit expression. Such an expression should be expressive, precise, unambiguous and flexible to describe various characteristics of a privacy violation such as target data (sensitive data subject to disclosure review), suspicion notion, authorized privacy policy parameters through which the violation is possible, and time duration of the privacy violation. Earlier proposed audit expression models for the auditing are not flexible and do not specify suspicion notion with in the audit expression for the auditing of past user accesses. We propose a unified model for an audit expression which can specify earlier proposed audit expressions along with different suspicion notions. The model includes (i) a suspicion notion model which unifies earlier proposed suspicion notions, and (ii) mechanisms to specify data versions.

1 Introduction

Privacy concerns have become very prominent in e-commerce, e-governance and a host of services delivered through the Internet. Governments have enacted regulatory laws balancing various needs to provide robust and acceptable privacy. Academic and commercial organizations have also carried out research to achieve the holy grail of complete privacy. However, despite considerable efforts [1,2,3,4], privacy intrusions [5,6,7,8,9] continue to rise and raise serious concerns. Providing robust privacy infrastructure remains an elusive and perhaps an Utopian goal.

Faced with the problem of privacy violations, the next step in providing confidence to the involved parties is to detect privacy violation accesses [10,11,12]. In case of privacy violation notification, it is required to determine the source of the privacy violation, i.e., to ask the questions like who? when? and how? etc. This process of privacy violation access determination is termed as *auditing*. Auditing may lead to: (a) putting some individuals under suspicion, (b) acting against those involved in that violation, if confirmed, and (c) locating and fixing the specification or implementation loopholes in the privacy or access control policies. These findings and their maintenance increase the trust of involved parties in the organization and the information system.

V. Atluri (Ed.): DAS 2008, LNCS 5094, pp. 33–47, 2008.

In a post event scenario, the auditing process generally starts from the available information related to privacy violation. Therefore, the need for some specification mechanism for this information in an expression is evident. The information which may be available are: (a) target data view which has caused a privacy violation, (b) notion of suspicion, (c) time interval of attack, and (d) privacy policy specific parameters.

Prior work in the area of SQL query auditing does not facilitate specifying different suspicion notions for the administrator but instead assumes a default suspicious notion. A suspicion notion defines the criterion by which suspicion of a batch of queries is determined. Earlier work includes Agrawal et al. [12] where a simple specification syntax and a notion of suspicion was introduced for single SQL queries in isolation, Motwani et al. [13] where the authors have used a similar syntax and have proposed new suspicion notions for a batch of queries, i.e., semantic suspiciousness, strong syntactic suspiciousness, and weak syntactic suspiciousness. Other work in auditing is Böttcher et al. [14] where the authors have used audit expression for XML databases and used the similar notion of suspicion as proposed by Agrawal et al. in [12]. Consider the following example of an audit expression:

```
AUDIT disease FROM Patients WHERE zipcode='118701'
```

The audit expression asks for auditing of disease information for all the patients living in area 118701. It assumes the default suspicion notion of *indispensable tuple* (formally explained later) for determining suspiciousness of a query, i.e., it marks a query suspicious if it has accessed disease information of at least one patient from the patients which get identified by the audit expression. On the other hand, there may be many other suspicion notions here, e.g., (i) access to disease and area information of at least one patient from the above identified patients, (ii) access to disease information of more than N patients from the above identified patients, and many more. Therefore, the earlier proposed specification syntax is simple but is not expressive enough to specify different suspicion notions. It makes the administrator's task of specifying audit expressions difficult as different privacy violations may require different suspicion notions. Hence, we propose a suspicion model which is capable of expressing different interesting suspicion notions.

Further, auditing generally occurs on past user accesses for a given time interval. In case of database applications, where the database state changes frequently due to various *update* and *insert* operations, two identical queries issued at different times might have accessed different information. As an audit expression specifies the target data, e.g., the disease information of the patient living in area *118701* in the given example, there may be many versions of the data for a given time interval. Existence of such different instances of database emphasizes the need to incorporate version specific information in the audit expression and hence is incorporated in our model. The administrator also specifies the privacy policy specific information in an audit expression to limit the search for intended user accesses [10,12,15], which is also supported in our model.

The motivation for proposing such an audit expression model arises from the need of representing different information in an audit expression by the auditor while auditing, as it is usually done in the context of information search over the Internet. A user usually gets some feedback from the result of first query and tries to embed that information obtained from the result in the next query to get the relevant results. Similarly, the proposed model helps to retrieve relevant suspicious queries as the auditor can express the required information in the proposed audit expression model which was not possible in the earlier cases. In this paper, we contribute the following:

1. Identify components for an audit expression that need to be specified for auditing.
2. A model for suspicion notion which can encompass the earlier defined notions of suspicion as well as other relevant suspicion notions.
3. Incorporates proposed components in an audit expression,
   - giving the flexibility of specifying suspicion notions,
   - specifying precisely target data view in presence of more than one data versions, and
   - specifying precisely limiting information parameters such as privacy policy parameters.

The rest of the paper is organized as follows. In Section 2, related work is presented. Section 3 presents the audit expression model. In Section 3.1, we describe target data view specification in presence of multiple data versions. We present the suspicion model in Section 3.2, limiting parameters for auditing in Section 3.3, and audit expression in Section 3.4. Finally in Section 4, we conclude with suggestions for future work.

2   Related Work

In this section, we describe earlier audit related work done by different authors.

2.1   Data Dependent Auditing of SQL Queries

In [12] Agrawal et al. explore the auditing problem of determining whether any single SQL query in the query log accessed a specific information specified by an audit expression. Their syntax for audit expressions (Figure 1) closely resembles SQL queries.

```
OTHERTHAN PURPOSE    purpose list
DURING               timestamp 1 to timestamp 2
AUDIT                attribute list FROM table names WHERE conditional expression
```

Fig. 1. Audit Expression Syntax as proposed by Agrawal et al. [12]

During normal operation, the text of every query processed by the database system is logged along with annotations such as the execution time, the user-id of a user who submits the query, and the purpose (defined in [4]) for which the query is made by the user. The system uses database triggers to capture and record all updates to base tables in backlog tables. The state of the database at any past point in time is obtained through these backlog tables.

For the audit, the auditor formulates an audit expression that declaratively specifies the data of interest. The audit expression is processed by the audit query generator. It first performs a static analysis over the logged queries to select a subset of logged queries that could potentially disclose the specified information for the given audit expression. The query generator then analyzes the selected queries by running them against the backlog database and yields the precise set of logged queries that accessed the designated data.

An audit expression essentially identifies the tuples of interest via predicates in the *WHERE* clause from the cross-product of tables in the *FROM* clause. Any query which has accessed all the attributes in the audit list and the *WHERE* clause of which gets satisfied by any of the identified tuples is tagged as a suspicious query. We illustrate this with examples from [12]. Consider the audit expression:

```
AUDIT disease FROM Patients WHERE zipcode='120016'
```

This expression tags all queries that returned disease information about any patient living in area *120016*. Now consider the SQL query:

```
SELECT zipcode FROM Patients WHERE disease='cancer'
```

This SQL query will be considered suspicious with respect to the above audit expression if any patient who has *cancer* lives in area *120016*. It would not, however, be suspicious with respect to the following expression if no patient having both *cancer* and *diabetes* exists.

```
AUDIT zipcode FROM Patients WHERE disease='diabetes'
```

This is due to the fact that this audit expression checks only whether the zipcode of any patient with diabetes was disclosed.

Looking at the version related issue, it may be noted that the above expression identifies tuples in the current database instance only, whereas the authors in [12] interpret it as all the versions of zip codes of each *diabetes* patient present in the backlog database table (we use *b-relationname* to specify the backlog table of table *relationname*, e.g., b-Patients for table Patients), whereas the authors in [13] interpret this as zipcode of each diabetes patient in the Patients table of the current database instance, i.e., Patients table. Both interpretations would give different results if there had been updates of zipcode and disease value of a patient. We handle these version related issues in our proposed audit expression model.

It may be noted that all the above examples assumes a suspicion notion of *indispensable tuple* [12] (explained later). Similarly, many other suspicion notions have been proposed in the past for auditing. To explain these notions, we use following formalizations. The SPJ (Select Project Join) queries and audit expressions are considered of the form $Q = \pi_{C_{OQ}}(\sigma_{P_Q}(\mathcal{T} \times \mathcal{R}))$ and $A = \pi_{C_A}(\sigma_{P_A}(\mathcal{T} \times S))$ respectively. Here $\mathcal{T}$ is the cross-product of tables common to both the audit expression and the query. $\mathcal{R}$ and S are the cross-products of the other tables in the *FROM* clause. C_{OQ} is the set of columns projected out in query Q and C_A is the set of columns to be audited in A. P_Q and P_A are the predicates in Q and A respectively specified in *WHERE* clause. We use C_Q to denote all the column names appearing in C_{OQ} and P_Q.

Definition 1. *(Candidate Query) A query Q is a candidate query with respect to an audit expression A, if Q can not be marked syntactically non suspicious with respect to an audit expression A for a given suspicion notion. By syntactically we mean that query and audit expression are not executed over any database instance.*

Definition 2. *(Indispensable Tuple) A tuple $t \in \mathcal{T}$ is indispensable to a query Q if the presence or absence of tuple t creates a difference to the result of the query Q, i.e. $\sigma_{P_Q}(t \times \mathcal{R}) \neq \phi$.*

Definition 3. *(Notion of Semantic Suspicion defined in [12] for a single query) A candidate query Q is suspicious with respect to an audit expression A if both share an indispensable tuple. A candidate query is the query which accesses all the columns listed in the audit expression, i.e., $C_Q \supseteq C_A$.*

Definition 4. *(Notion of Semantic Suspicion defined in [13] for a batch of queries) A batch of queries Q is said to be semantically suspicious with respect to an audit expression A if there is some subset of queries $Q' \subseteq Q$ such that (1) there is a tuple $t \in \mathcal{T}$ for every query $q \in Q'$ that is indispensable to both q and A, and (2) the queries in Q' together access all the columns of the audit list in A. Here $\mathcal{T}$ is the cross product of all tables common to A and the particular $q \in Q'$ in question.*

2.2 Data Independent Auditing of SQL Queries

This type of auditing is done independent of a database instance, i.e., a database instance is not accessed. Due to being independent from a database instance this would be very fast as compared to database dependent auditing as accessing a database is a costly operation. But, unfortunately, it is computationally intractable to determine suspicion for many query types for a given audit expression and a notion of suspicion [13,16,17].

The authors in [16,17] have considered the problem of "perfect privacy" which determines whether a database system discloses *any information* at all about a secret view through various views revealed by it. Here secret view corresponds to the audit expression and the views that were revealed to answered queries. Determining whether "any information" has been disclosed is determined through a notion of suspicion which uses the *critical tuple* concept.

Definition 5. *(Critical Tuple [17]) A tuple $t \in D$, where D is the database, is critical for a query q if there exists a possible database instance I of D for which $q(I - t) \neq q(I)$, i.e., t is critical for q if there exists some instance for which dropping t makes a difference to the result of q.*

Definition 6. *(Perfect Privacy Suspicion Notion [17]) An SQL query q is suspicious with respect to a secret view A, if and only if both q and A share a critical tuple.*

Definition 7. *(Notion of Weak Syntactic Suspicion given in [13]) A batch of SPJ queries Q is weakly syntactically suspicious with respect to an audit expression A, if there exists* *some subset of the queries $Q' \subseteq Q$ and some database instance I such that (1) for every query $q \in Q'$, a tuple $t \in \mathcal{T}$ is indispensable to both q and A in the context of I and (2) the queries Q' together access at least one of the columns of the audit list in A. Here $\mathcal{T}$ is the cross product of all the tables in I common to both A and the query $q \in Q'$ under consideration.*

The difference between perfect privacy suspicion notion and weak syntactic suspicion notion is that the later notion requires accessing of at least one column of audit query by a user query to be tagged as suspicious.

2.3 Auditing Aggregate Queries

The problem of auditing aggregate queries has been extensively studied in the context of statistical databases [18]. Users of statistical databases can retrieve only aggregate results. In this paper, we consider only SPJ queries for relational databases and our work is orthogonal to the body of work done for statistical databases.

3   Audit Expression Model

It may be noted from the previous section that in the auditing research paradigm, several suspicion notions have been proposed by different authors with different objectives but no one has worked for the incorporation of the suspicion notion with in an audit expression. In this section, we present a suspicion model and show that our proposed suspicion model can specify all the above suspicion notions (defined in Section 2) in addition to other relevant suspicion notions. We incorporate the proposed suspicion model in the audit expression which increases the expressiveness of the proposed audit expression. Further, we introduce the notion of data versions specification in the audit expression which helps the auditor to specify precise and unambiguous audit expression.

The model consists of (i) a target data view, (ii) suspicion notion, and (iii) filtering parameters. The target data view describes the sensitive data which is under disclosure review. The suspicion notion identifies the portions of the target data view which, if accessed by a batch of queries make it suspicious. Filtering parameters are the constraints specifying context information such as the time interval of user accesses. Now we shall explain each of these constituents in the following subsections. The following relations (Tables 1, 2, 3) and audit expressions (Figures 2, 3) are used for describing our proposed model.

Table 1. P-Personal

t-id	pid	name	age	sex	zipcode	address
t11	p1	Jane	25	M	177893	A1
t12	p2	Reku	35	M	145568	A2
t13	p13	Robert	29	M	188888	A3
t14	p28	Lucy	20	F	145568	A4

Table 2. P-Health

t-id	pid	ward	doctor	disease	pres-drugs
t21	p1	W23	Hassan	thyroid	drug2
t22	p2	W12	Nicholas	diabetic	drug1
t23	p13	W14	Ramesh	Malaria	drug3
t24	p28	W14	King U	diabetic	drug1

Table 3. P-Employ

tid	pid	employer	salary
t31	p1	E1	12000
t32	p2	E2	20000
t33	p13	E3	9000
t34	p28	E4	19000

```
Audit name,age,address FROM P-Personal WHERE age < 30
```

Fig. 2. Audit Expression-1

```
Audit name, disease, address FROM P-Personal, P-Health, P-Employ
WHERE P-Personal.pid=P-Health.pid and
    P-Health.pid=P-Employ.pid and
    P-Personal.zipcode=145568 and
    P-Employ.salary > 10000 and
    P-Health.disease='diabetic'
```

Fig. 3. Audit Expression-2

3.1 Target Data View

The target data view defines the sensitive data which is in the audit scope. We denote this sensitive data as a set of data facts U and is obtained via predicates in the *WHERE* clause from the cross-product of tables in the *FROM* clause of the audit expression. We define the scheme of data facts U as the union of all attributes in the AUDIT and WHERE clause, and the tuple id attribute for each table present in the *FROM* clause of the audit expression. We denote the tuple-id attribute for a table T by tid_T. For example, target data facts U for the audit expressions given in Figures: 2, 3 and the relations shown in Tables: 1, 2, 3 would be as given in tables 4 and 5.

An auditing process involves analysis of user queries on the actual data contents accessed by them. On the other hand, a database state is updated many times due to insert, update and delete operations. Due to this change in database states, two similar queries q_{t_1} and q_{t_2} executed at different times may have different result set. Hence, due to possibility of many data versions existing for a given time interval, it becomes necessary to have mechanisms for data version specification to specify the intended

Table 4. Target Data Facts U for Audit Expression 2

tid_{PP}	name	age	address
t11	Jane	25	A1
t13	Robert	29	A3
t14	Lucy	20	A4

Table 5. Target Data Facts U for Audit Expression 3

tid_{PP}	pid	name	zipcode	address	tid_{PH}	disease	tid_{PE}	salary
t12	p2	Reku	145568	A2	t22	diabetic	t32	20000
t14	p28	Lucy	145568	A4	t24	diabetic	t34	19000

target data view for auditing. We have identified requirements related to data versions for a precise target view definition through an audit expression. The auditor may need to specify:

1. a set of data versions in a given time interval,
2. the current version of the data, and
3. a specific version of the data other than current data version.

We propose to use a *DATA-INTERVAL* clause in an audit expression. This clause would determine the set of target data versions. It may be noted that semantics of this clause are different from the clause *DURING* (explained later) discussed in [12]. The latter specifies the time interval for user queries which are to be audited. A *DATA-INTERVAL* clause has a pair of starting and ending time stamps (t_s, t_e). We use the keyword *now()* to denote the current time of the system.

As an example, the following expression

```
DATA-INTERVAL   1/5/2004:13-00-00 to now()
Audit           name, age, address From b-P-Personal Where  age < 30
```

would define a target data view with all the data versions from *1/5/2004:13-00-00* to *current system time*. In absence of this clause, we define the default interval as the current day interval, i.e., *current date:00-00-00* **to** *current system time stamp*. A specific data version is specified by giving the same time-stamp as the starting as well as ending time stamp. For example, the current database instance or version can be specified by using *now()* as t_s and t_e.

3.2 Suspicion Model

In query based auditing of privacy violations, the auditor specifies the data which is under disclosure review along with a notion of suspicion. While the earlier proposed audit expression models assumed a default single suspicion notion, we provide the facility to the administrator for specifying suspicion notion in the audit query. This increases the expressiveness of the audit expression model. The notion of suspicion defines *granules* of data such that access to any granule from the set by a batch of queries would label the batch as suspicious. The notion of suspicion is subjective in the real world. However, an auditor needs to specify it precisely in an audit expression. In our case, a suspicion notion defines a set of suspicion granules G defined through the target data view U of the audit expression such that if a batch of queries Q accesses any granule $o \in G$, Q is marked suspicious. We present a model for defining suspicion notion. The model comprises (i) a notion to specify the scheme for granules, (ii) the number of data facts in a granule, and (iii) a notion of accessibility of a granule.

The clauses which define a granule set G are:

1. *AUDIT* and *INDISPENSABLE* clauses: to specify the schemes of granules in G.
2. *THRESHOLD* clause: to define the number of tuples in each granule $o \in G$. For a given threshold value k, a scheme of a granule, and number of tuples n in U, there would be ^nC_k granules with that scheme.

The *AUDIT* and the *INDISPENSABLE* clauses together define the scheme for the granules whereas the *THRESHOLD* clause defines the number of tuples to be selected from U for each granule o. *INDISPENSABLE* clause defines whether tuple ids should be included or excluded in the granules scheme. Determining tuple ids that are to be included for each granule would depend upon the *partial scheme* in case of *INDISPENSABLE* value as *true*. By *partial scheme* of a granule we mean the scheme of granule defined by using only AUDIT clause.

The auditing attributes specified in an audit expression are usually (i) attributes which specify the subject notion whose information has been misused, e.g., an individual identifier or a user category and (ii) the sensitive attributes specifying the sensitive information associated with identifiers. In our opinion, following combinations of these attribute categories, identifiers and sensitive attributes, would be interesting to an administrator for auditing. The administrator would like to:

1. Specify a set of attributes as *optional* attributes such that a batch of queries would be marked suspicious if the batch has accessed *at least one* of the attributes. This requirement is clearly valid in the case of a set of sensitive attributes such that each attribute derives all other attributes in the set. For an example, in case of a set with *Bonus*, and *Salary* attributes and *Bonus* can be determined from *Salary* or vice-versa the case is true. By *optional* we mean 'one or more attributes'.
2. Specify a set of attributes as a combination of *mandatory* and *optional* attributes such that a batch of queries would be marked suspicious if the batch has accessed all the mandatory attributes and at least one attribute from the set of *optional* attributes. This requirement is valid in the case of a set of identifier attributes and a set of sensitive attributes such that each sensitive attribute derives all other sensitive attributes.
3. Specify a set of attributes as *mandatory* attributes such that a batch of queries would be marked suspicious if the batch accesses all the mandatory attributes. It is valid in the case of one sensitive attribute and all other as identifying attributes.

To specify all the above requirements, we use brackets [] to specify a set of *optional* attributes, and parenthesis () to specify mandatory attributes in the audit clause of an audit expression. For example, if an audit list has four attributes a,b,c,d and all attributes are sensitive such that access to any attribute would make a query batch suspicious, then this case can be specified as $[a,b,c,d]$. In order to specify attributes a,b as mandatory with attributes c,d as *optional*, the specification would be $(a,b),[c,d]$ and would mark a batch of queries suspicious accessing attributes a,b,c or a,b,d. The specification (a,b,c,d) would make all four attributes mandatory and hence a query batch accessing all attributes would be marked as suspicious. We define a set of structural rules which describe the equivalence notions for different audit clause specifications in Table 6. Here in the rules specification, a capital letter denotes a set of attributes and a lower case letter denotes a single attribute.

Table 6. Audit Attributes Structural Rules

No.	Rule	Description
1	$[a] = (a)$	An *optional* set containing a single element is equal to a mandatory set having the same element.
2	$(A)(B) = (A,B)$	A sequence of two mandatory sets yields a single mandatory set.
3	$(A,B) = (B,A)$ $[A,B] = [B,A]$	Set commutativity
4	$[a][b] = (a,b)$	Using rule-1 and rule-2
5	$[A][B] = [B][A]$ $(A)(B) = (B)(A)$ $(A)[B] = [B](A)$	Sequence commutativity
6	$[(A,B)] = (A,B)$ $([A,B]) = [A,B]$	Nesting
7	$(A,B)[c] =$ (A,B,c)	Composition

The number of data facts in each granule of set G, as discussed earlier, is decided by the *THRESHOLD* clause. We define the default value for THRESHOLD clause as 1 in case the administrator does not specify it. A special value *ALL* is also defined, which will include as many tuples in each granule as there are in the target data view U of an audit expression.

The notion of accessibility for each granule is decided from the presence or absence of special attribute tuple id, tid. If these attributes are present in granules, then a granule is treated as accessed by a query batch if all the tuples in the granules are *indispensable* for the query batch and the batch has accessed all these tuples. The indispensability notion is defined earlier (Definition 2). On the other hand, if tuple ids are not present in granules, i.e., *INDISPENSABLE = FALSE*, then the entire data in a granule would be treated as accessed by a batch of queries if the batch has accessed an information which contains tuples similar to the ones present in the granule. The presence of tuple id values in granules makes it necessary that the *WHERE* clause predicates of a query in the batch are consistent with the predicates in the *WHERE* clause of the audit expression to mark the batch as suspicious for that audit expression.

It can be seen that for a table U having k columns (assuming one column for tuple id attribute) and n records, $2^k.2^n - 1$ suspicion notions can be defined. We now show the expressability of our presented suspicion model by specifying the earlier discussed suspicion notions [12,13,17].

Notion of Perfect Privacy [17]. This notion of suspiciousness can be classified as the strongest notion of privacy proposed till now as it marks a query batch Q as suspicious if the batch Q has accessed data of any one of the cell in U. The granules set G for this notion would have each cell of U with tuple id attribute as its granules. For example, for the the audit expression in figure 4 the granules set G would be:

Granules Set:
$G=\{(t12,p2),(t22,p2),(t32,p2),(t12,145568),(t12,M),(t12,A2),(t12,Reku),(t22,W12),$
$(t22,Nicholas),(t22,diabetic),(t22,drug1),(t32,E2),(t32,20000)\}$

```
INDISPENSABLE = true
AUDIT [*] FROM P-Personal, P-Health, P-Employ
WHERE P-Personal.pid=P-Health.pid and
    P-Health.pid=P-Employ.pid and
    P-Personal.zipcode=''145568" and
    P-Employ.salary > 10000 and
    P-Health.disease=''diabetic" and
    p-Personal.name='Reku';
```

Fig. 4. Audit Expression for Perfect Privacy

The perfect privacy always considers all the columns of tables specified in the 'from' clause of audit query in the suspicion granules.

Notion of Weak Syntactic Suspicion [13]. This suspicion notion marks a batch of queries Q suspicious if Q accesses any column specified in audit expression and constraints of batch Q are not in conflict with constraints of the audit expression, i.e., there is some indispensable tuple between the batch Q and audit expression A. Therefore, the granules in this case would be each pair of values of the column value of one of the columns specified in the audit list and the tuple id *tid* of the respective row in the table. For example, if we use the audit expression given in figure 5 then the granules set G would be:

Granules Set:
$G=\{(t12,p2),(t12,145568),(t12,Reku),(t12,A2),(t14,p28),(t14,145568),(t14,Lucy),$
$(t14,A4),(t22,diabetic),(t24,diabetic),(t32),(t32,20000),(t34,19000),(t22,p2),(t32,p2),$
$(t24,p28),(t34,p28)\}$

```
INDISPENSABLE = true
AUDIT [name,disease,address,P-Personal.pid,
P-Health.pid, P-Employ.pid, zipcode, salary]
FROM P-Personal, P-Health, P-Employ
WHERE P-Personal.pid=P-Health.pid and
    P-Health.pid=P-Employ.pid and
    P-Personal.zipcode=145568" and
    P-Employ.salary > 10000 and
    P-Health.disease=diabetic"
```

Fig. 5. Audit Expression for Weak Syntactic Suspicion Notion

Notion of Indispensable Tuple [12] or Strong Semantic Suspicion [13]. This suspicion notion is stronger than the earlier explained notions. It marks a batch of queries Q as suspicious if the query batch has accessed all the columns specified in the audit list and the tuple is indispensable. Therefore, for the audit expression from figure 6, the granules set G would be:

Granules Set:
$G=\{(t12,t22,Reku,diabetic,A2),(t14,t24,Lucy,diabetic,A4)\}$

```
INDISPENSABLE = true
AUDIT (name,disease,address)
FROM P-Personal, P-Health, P-Employ
WHERE P-Personal.pid=P-Health.pid and
    P-Health.pid=P-Employ.pid and
    P-Personal.zipcode=''145568" and
    P-Employ.salary > 10000 and
    P-Health.disease=''diabetic"
```

Fig. 6. Audit Expression for Semantic Suspiciousness

3.3 Limiting Parameters

In a privacy enforced information system, any user access to information is filtered through the privacy policy. Therefore, the authorization parameters given in the privacy policy which allow access to the *target data view* can be specified in an audit expression. These parameters are usually *User-id, Purpose-id, Role-id* and can be specified in a negative way; user accesses with these parameters will not be considered for the auditing, or in positive way; user accesses with these parameters are considered for the auditing. In case of a conflict between the authorization parameters in both clauses, i.e., the positive clause allows it and the negative clause denies it, we give precedence to negative clause and the accesses will not be audited. There is no specific reason to give precedence to negative clause here except to resolve the conflict. We would use the following clauses for specification of privacy policy specific parameters.

1. **Neg-Role-Purpose** $\{(r,pr)|(r,-)|(-,pr)\}^*$
2. **Pos-Role-Purpose** $\{(r,pr)|(r,-)|(-,pr)\}^*$
3. **Neg-User-Identity** $\{u-id\}^*$
4. **Pos-User-Identity** $\{u-id\}^*$

Neg-Role-Purpose is a list of ordered pairs of role and purpose, the semantics of which is to not consider the user accesses with these parameters for auditing. The (r, pr) ordered pair in this clause indicates to remove all user accesses having r as a role and pr as a purpose annotation in the User Accesses Log from consideration. The $(r, -)$ ordered pair removes all the accesses having r as their role (- denotes any purpose). Similarly, $(-, pr)$ removes all accesses having pr as the access purpose. If the administrator has the information of role and purpose through which a violation has occurred (i.e., positive aspect) then that can be specified in *Pos-Role-Purpose* clause. If information about user identities is known, it is specified similarly in the *Pos-User-Identity* and *Neg-User-Identity* clauses.

Other limiting information is the time interval for user accesses. We use the *DURING* clause proposed in [12]. The user accesses made to database in the 'DURING' interval are to be audited.

3.4   Final Audit Expression

We now define all the clauses used to specify an audit expression (Figure 7). The clauses having default values are optional and need not to be specified. The limiting parameters filter user accesses from auditing.

The proposed audit expression model facilitate to specify the intended target data view even in presence of data versions. Hence, the model helps to specify precise information and prevents ambiguity. The model is more expressive as it allows to specify suspicion notion along with the version related information. It is flexible as it does not require to specify all the clauses, i.e., some clauses are optional.

```
Neg-Role-Purpose    {(r,pr)|(r,-)|(-,pr)}*
!------(default is to consider all user accesses)
Pos-Role-Purpose    {(r,pr)|(r,-)|(-,pr)}*
!------(default is to consider all user accesses)
Neg-User-Identity  {u-id}*
!------(default is to consider all user accesses)
Pos-User-Identity  {u-id}*
!------(default is to consider all user accesses)
DURING              timestamp 1 to timestamp 2
!------(default is current day)
DATA-INTERVAL       timestamp1 to timestamp2
!------(default is current day)
THRESHOLD       N
!------(default is 1)
INDISPENSABLE       true | false
!------(default is true)
AUDIT               attribute list
FROM                table names
WHERE               conditional expression
```

Fig. 7. Proposed Audit Expression Syntax

DURING clause filters the accesses which are not in the specified interval, whereas *DATA-INTERVAL* helps in determining the target data view. All the satisfying tuples are collected from each specified database state using *DATA-INTERVAL*. The methodology to get database instance as proposed in [12] can be used for this purpose.

It could be seen that the proposed expression syntax and semantics of audit expression is capable of expressing all the identified aspects in the expression. Thus the presented audit expression model is more expressible and fulfills the need of an auditor for the task of determining relevant suspicious queries.

4   Conclusion and Future Work

In query based auditing, the administrator enters an audit expression to identify the suspicious accesses for a given privacy violation. We have presented audit expression model for these expressions. The model unifies earlier proposed audit expressions and consists of target data view, suspicion notions, and limiting parameters. We have given mechanism to define the target data view even in presence of database updates. It is also shown how the earlier notions can be specified using our presented suspicion model. The limiting parameters, one of the constituents of the audit expression model, identifies the context information which can be specified in an auditing expression for privacy violation detection. We use privacy policy parameters and a time duration for this purpose. The proposed audit expression would help the auditor to specify an audit expression to retrieve relevant and intended suspicious queries.

As a future work, it would be interesting to see for what suspicion notions static determination of a query batch suspiciousness for an audit expression is decidable. Further, future work includes designing efficient algorithms to map an audit expression to a set of suspicious batch of queries for a given database instance. In case of on line auditing, there is a need to determine the suspicion rank, closeness value, of a queries batch for a given set of audit expressions. Therefore, an interesting task would be to use the presented audit expression model for computing the degree of suspiciousness for user queries on line.

Acknowledgments

The authors acknowledge with thanks support from the projects "Design and development of Malafide intention based Privacy Violation Detection System" sponsored by Department of Information Technology, and "Advanced Information Systems Security Laboratory".

References

1. OASIS, eXtensible Access Control Markup Language (XACML) TC,
   http://www.oasis-open.org/committees/tc_home.php?wg_abbrev=xacml
2. Ashley, P., Hada, S., Karjoth, G., Powers, C., Schunter, M.: Enterprise Privacy Authorization Language (EPAL 1.1), IBM Research Report (2003),
   http://www.zurich.ibm.com/security/enterprise-privacy/epal

3. Bhattacharya, J., Gupta, S.K.: Privacy Broker for Enforcing Privacy Policies in Databases. In: Proceedings of Fifth international conference on knowledge based computer systems, Hyderabad, India (2004)
4. Agrawal, R., Kiernan, J., Srikant, R., Xu, Y.: Hippocratic Databases. In: Proceedings of the 28th International Conference on VLDB, Hong Kong, China, pp. 143–154 (2002)
5. Rosencrance, L.: Toysrus.com faces online privacy inquiry, http://archives.cnn.com/2000/TECH/computing/12/14/toysrus.privacy.inquiry.idg/toysrus.privacy.inquiry.html
6. Associated Press: Fliers File Suit Against Jetblue (September 23, 2003), http://www.wired.com/politics/security/news/2003/09/60551
7. Barse, E.L.: Logging For Intrusion And Fraud Detection. PhD Thesis, ISBN 91-7291-484-X Technical Report no.28D ISSN 1651-4971, School of Computer Science and Engineering, Chalmers University of Technology (2004)
8. Bruno, J.B.: Security Breach Could Expose 40M to Fraud (June 18, 2005), http://www.freerepublic.com/focus/f-news/1425334/posts
9. Teasley, B.: Does Your Privacy Policy Mean Anything (January 11, 2005), http://www.clickz.com/experts/crm/analyze_data/article.php
10. Goyal, V., Gupta, S.K., Saxena, S., Chawala, S., Gupta, A.: Query Rewriting for Detection of Privacy Violation through Inferencing. In: International Conference on Privacy, Security and Trust (PST06), supported by ACM SIGSAC, Markham, Ontario, Canada, October 30 - November 1, pp. 233–243 (2006)
11. Gupta, S.K., Goyal, V., Patra, B., Dubey, S., Gupta, A.: Design and Development of Malafide Intension Based Privacy Violation Detection System (An Ongoing Research Report). In: Bagchi, A., Atluri, V. (eds.) ICISS 2006. LNCS, vol. 4332, pp. 369–372. Springer, Heidelberg (2006)
12. Agrawal, R., Bayardo, R., Faloutsos, C., Kiernan, J., Rantzau, R., Srikant, R.: Auditing compliance with a Hippocratic database. In: Proceedings of the Thirtieth international conference on Very large data bases, pp. 516–527. VLDB Endowment (2004)
13. Motwani, R., Nabar, S., Thomas, D.: Auditing a Batch of SQL Queries. In: IEEE 23rd International Conference on Data Engineering Workshop, pp. 186–191 (2007)
14. Böttcher, S., Steinmetz, R.: Detecting Privacy Violations in Sensitive XML Databases. In: Jonker, W., Petković, M. (eds.) SDM 2005. LNCS, vol. 3674, pp. 143–154. Springer, Heidelberg (2005)
15. Gupta, S.K., Goyal, V., Gupta, A.: Malafide Intension Based Detection of Violation in Privacy. In: Bagchi, A., Atluri, V. (eds.) ICISS 2006. LNCS, vol. 4332, pp. 365–368. Springer, Heidelberg (2006)
16. Machanavajjhala, A., Gehrke, J.: On the Efficiency of Checking Perfect Privacy. In: PODS 2006: Proceedings of the twenty-fifth ACM SIGMOD-SIGACT-SIGART symposium on Principles of database systems, pp. 163–172. ACM Press, New York (2006)
17. Miklau, G., Suciu, D.: A Formal Analysis of Information Disclosure in Data Exchange. J. Comput. Syst. Sci. 73(3), 507–534 (2007)
18. Reiss, S.P.: Security in databases: A combinatorial study. J. ACM 26(1), 45–57 (1979)

A New Approach to Secure Logging

Di Ma and Gene Tsudik

Computer Science Department
University of California,
Irvine
{dma1,gts}@ics.uci.edu

Abstract. The need for secure logging is well-understood by the security researchers and practitioners. The ability to efficiently verify all (or some) log entries is important to any application employing secure logging techniques. In this
paper, we begin by examining the state-of-the-art in secure logging and identify
some problems inherent to systems based on trusted third-party servers. We then
propose a different approach based upon recently developed Forward-Secure Sequential Aggregate (FssAgg) authentication techniques. Our approach offers both
space-efficiency and provable security. We illustrate two concrete schemes – one
private-verifiable and one public-verifiable – that offer practical secure logging
without any reliance on on-line trusted third parties or secure hardware. We evaluate proposed schemes and report on our experience with implementing them
within a secure logging system.

Keywords: secure logging, forward secure stream integrity, MACs, signatures,
truncation attack.

1 Introduction

System logs are an important part of any secure IT system. They record noteworthy
events, such as user activity, program execution status, system resource usage and data
changes. Logs provide a valuable view of past and current states of almost any type
of a complex system. In conjunction with appropriate tools and procedures, audit logs
can be used to enforce individual accountability, reconstruct events, detect intrusions
and identify problems. Keeping system audit trails and reviewing them in a consistent
manner is recommended by NIST as one of the good principles and practices for securing computer systems [1]. Many types of (especially distributed) software include some
sort of a logging mechanism.

Because of their forensic value, system logs represent an obvious attack target. An
attacker who gains access to a system naturally wishes to remove traces of its presence
in order to hide attack details or to frame innocent users. In fact, the first target of an
experienced attacker is often the logging system [2,3]. To make the audit log secure, we
must prevent the attacker from modifying log data. Secure versions of audit logs should
be designed to defend against such tampering. Providing *integrity* checks, the primary
security requirement for any secure logging system, is informally stated in the Orange
Book [4] as:

V. Atluri (Ed.): DAS 2008, LNCS 5094, pp. 48–63, 2008.
© IFIP International Federation for Information Processing 2008

Audit data must be protected from modification and unauthorized destruction to permit detection and after-the-fact investigation of security violations.

In addition to the traditional meaning of *data integrity* which stipulates no insertion of fake data and no modification or deletion of existing data, integrity of a log file also requires no re-ordering of log entries. We call this property *log stream integrity*.

In many real-world applications, a log file is generated and stored on an untrusted logging machine which is not sufficently physically secure to guarantee impossibility of compromise [5]. Compromise of a logging machine can happen as long as the Trusted Computing Base (TCB) – the system component responsible for logging – is not totally bug-free, which is unfortunately always the case. In systems using *remote logging* (which send audit data to a remote trusted server), if the server is not available, the log is buffered and stored temporarily at the local machine. Once an attacker obtains the secret key of the compromised logging machine, it can modify *post-compromise* data at will. In this case, one important issue is *forward integrity*: how to ensure that *pre-compromise* data can not be manipulated? That is, even if the attacker obtains the current secret key, she must be unable to modify audit data generated before compromise.

No security measure can protect log entries created after an attacker gains control of a logging machine, unless the logging machine's keys are periodically updated with the help of a remote trusted server or a local trusted hardware component (e.g., using key-insulated and intrusion-resilient authentication schemes [6, 7, 8]). We focus on the security of log entries pre-dating the compromise of a logging machine. Consequently, we require *forward-secure stream integrity*, i.e., resistance against post-compromise insertion, alteration, deletion and re-ordering of pre-compromise log entries.

Traditional log integrity techniques include using special write-only hard disks or remote logging where copies of log entries are sent to several geographically distributed machines. Recently, a number of cryptographic approaches have been proposed to address security for audit logs which are generated and stored on local logging servers [2, 3, 5, 9]. Bellare and Yee were the first to define the *forward-secure stream integrity* property required in an audit log system and proposed to use forward-secure MACs and index log entries [2,3]. Schneier and Kelsey proposed a similar system based on forward-secure MACs and one-way hash chain [5]. Holt extended Schneier and Yee's system to the public key setting [9]. Unfortunately, none of these schemes defends against *truncation attack* - a special kind of deletion attack whereby the attacker deletes a contiguous subset of tail-end log entries. Furthermore, private key-based schemes – such as Schneier-Kelsey and Bellare-Yee – also suffer from *delayed detection attack* [1] since they need a trusted server to aid users in verifying log integrity; modifications can not be detected until the entire log data is uploaded to the trusted server. Moreover, all prior schemes are inefficient in storage and communication which makes them impractical for platforms with meager resources, such as implantable medical devices [10]. We overview prior work in more detail in Section 2.

---

[1] For a precise definition, see Section 2.

To mitigate aforementioned shortcomings of prior schemes, we propose a new approach which provides *forward-secure stream integrity* for audit logs generated and stored on untrusted machines. Our scheme is based on a new cryptographic technique called *forward-secure sequential aggregate* (FssAgg) authentication recently proposed in [11, 12]. In an FssAgg authentication scheme, forward-secure signatures (or MACs) generated by the same signer are sequentially combined into a single aggregate signature. Successful verification of an aggregate signature is equivalent to that of each component signature. Whereas, as discussed later, failed verification of an aggregate signature implies that at least one component signature is invalid. An FssAgg signature scheme is thus a good match for secure logging applications: it resists truncation attacks due to its all-or-nothing (aggregate and forward-secure) signature verification. In our scheme, users can verify the log without relying on any trusted server; this obviates delayed detection attacks. Our scheme offers storage and bandwidth efficiency inherited from the underlying FssAgg scheme. Also, depending on the specific FssAgg scheme used, our scheme can be either private- or public-verifiable.

In an FssAgg scheme, individual signatures are erased once they are folded into the aggregate signature. Subsequent validity of individual log entries is implied by the validity of the aggregated signature computed over all log entries. This indirect verification process is costly if the verifier is only interested in the validity of one specific log entry. The need to provide finer-grained verification in certain applications motivates us to keep individual log entry signatures in the log file. However since the aggregation function is public, revealing individual signatures enables anyone to truncate log entries and create new aggregate signature based on existing ones. To prevent this truncation attack (even when individual component signatures are revealed), we need the property refferred to as "immutability" of aggregate authentication. Informally, immutability is the computational infeasibility of computing new valid aggregated signatures from existing signatures. To achieve immutability, we extended existing FssAgg MAC/signature schemes. However, due to space limitation, we refer to [13] for details on immutability extensions.

1.1 Contributions

Our contributions are as follows:

1. We identify some fundamental security issues and architectural limitations in prior secure logging schemes.
2. We propose new secure logging schemes which provide *forward-secure stream integrity* for audit logs generated and stored on untrusted logging machines and avoid the undesirable features of prior schemes. Our schemes inherit the effiency and provable security of the underlying FssAgg schemes.
3. We evaluate proposed schemes by comparing them with prior work in terms of security as well as communication and computation efficiency. Our evaluation shows that new schemes offer better security and incur less computation and communication overhead.
4. We implement existing FssAgg signature schemes and assess their performance in the context of a real secure logging system.

Organization. We begin with the overview of the state-of-the-art in Section 2, followed by introduction of forward-secure aggregate authentication in Section 3. We then show how to use FssAgg schemes in logging applications: we propose a private-verifiable scheme in Section 4 and a public-verifiable scheme in Section 5. We evaluate our schemes in Section 6 and report on some experience with prototype implementations in Section 7. Section 8 overviews related work and Section 9 concludes the paper.

2   Current Approach Analysis

In this section, we examine the state-of-the-art represented by Schneier-Kelsey scheme [5]. It has been used as a foundation by many subsequently proposed secure logging systems. Readers interested in further details of the Schneier-Kelsey scheme are referred to [5].

2.1   Overview of Schneier-Kelsey Scheme

In the Schneier-Kelsey scheme, a logging machine $\mathcal{U}$ opening a new audit log first establishes a shared secret key A_0 with a trusted remote server $\mathcal{T}$. After each audit entry is generated, the current secret key A_i is evolved into A_{i+1} through a one-way function. Log entries are linked using a hash chain. Each log entry L_i is composed of three parts:

1. Log entry data M_i.[2]
2. Element Y_i in the hash chain, where

$$Y_i = H(M_i \| Y_{i-1}) \textbf{ and } Y_0 = H(M_0)$$

3. Forward-secure MAC denoted Z_i, computed as: $Z_i = MAC_{A_i}(Y_i)$.

$\mathcal{U}$ closes the log file by creating a special final-record entry, M_f and erasing A_f as well as other secrets, if any.

There is no constant high-bandwidth channel between $\mathcal{U}$ and $\mathcal{T}$. It is assumed that $\mathcal{U}$ communicates log entries to T infrequently. At times, a moderately-trusted entity, called $\mathcal{V}$, may need to verify or read the audit log, while it is still on $\mathcal{U}$. $\mathcal{V}$ receives from $\mathcal{U}$ a copy of the audit log, $[L_0, L_1, \cdots, L_f]$, where f is the index value of the last record, from $\mathcal{U}$. $\mathcal{V}$ goes through the hash chain in the log entries (the Y_i values), verifying that each entry in the hash chain is correct. $\mathcal{V}$ then sends Y_f and Z_f to $\mathcal{T}$. $\mathcal{T}$ knows A_0 so it can compute A_f; this allows it to verify that $Z_f = MAC_{A_f}(Y_f)$. $\mathcal{T}$ informs $\mathcal{V}$ about the verification result and $\mathcal{V}$ discovers whether the received copy of the log has any problems.

---

[2] [5] provides access control to audit log. Each log entry L_i contains a log entry type W_i and $C_i = E_{K_i}(D_i)$: the actual log data D_i is encrypted with an access control key K_i. Since we focus on log integrity in this paper, to make our discussion clearer, we refer to the combination of W_i and C_i as M_i.

2.2 Analysis

We claim that the Schneier-Kelsey scheme has two security-related drawbacks:

Truncation Attack. A kind of deletion attack whereby the attacker erases a contiguous subset of tail-end log messages. This attack is realistic, since, after breaking in, it is natural for an attacker to want to modify the audit log by deleting the most recent log entries generated right before break-in.

The Schneier-Kelsey scheme uses a hash chain to link log entries such that undetectable log (link) deletion is impossible. This pertains to log entries already off-loaded to T. However, log entries still residing on U are vulnerable to the truncation attack since there is no single authentication tag protecting the integrity of the entire log file. A hash chain element Y_i only protects data records generated before time i. Thus, truncating log entries generated after time i is not detected by T, unless there is synchronization between U and T and the latter knows the current value of f. Without a continuous communication channel, synchronization between U and T would require U to generate log entries at a fixed rate. However, most logging systems are event-driven and events are unevenly spaced. Logging events at a fixed rate hinders the logging machine's ability to fully utilize its computation and storage resources.

Delayed Detection. Recall that, V is unable to verify a log file by itself and needs to ask for help from T. If this occurs before T receives a copy of the most up-to-date log from U, and before U has closed the log file, an attacker can modify pre-compromise records without being detected. Albeit, such modification will be eventually detected, after T receives the updated version of a log file.

We illustrate the delayed detection attack in Figure 1. Suppose that, at time a (≥ 0), U has transmitted log entries $[L_0, \cdots, L_a]$ to T. At time b ($> a$), an attacker breaks into U and obtains the current secret key A_b. Even though the attacker can not recover secret keys used in time intervals $[a+1, b-1]$, she can modify the values of M_i and corresponding Y_i in this interval without touching Z_i. At time f ($\geq b$), V receives a copy of log entries $L_0, \cdots, L_f$. V and sends Y_f and Z_f to T. Since the attacker knows A_b at break-in, she can generate valid MACs from time b. Thus, verification of Y_f with Z_f at T will succeed. The modified log file will translate false information to V and activities conducted within interval $[a+1, f]$ will elude V's detection. In Figure 1, values in the shaded area (M and Y values in time interval $[a+1, b-1]$, all Z values within $[b, f]$) can be manipulated by an attacker. Since there is no continuous high-bandwidth $U \leftrightarrow T$ communication channel and U only communicates with T infrequently, the time interval $[a+1, f]$ can be long.

Since the attacker is unable to fake any values Z_i (for $i \in [a+1, b-1]$), any manipulation in this period can be detected whenever the corresponding log entries are uploaded to T and T scan-verifies all individual MACs.[3]

The two drawbacks of the Schneier-Kelsey scheme seem to be quite fundamental. However, it is rather surprising that they have not been addressed in any later work. In

---

[3] Actually, the authors do not mention any scan-verification (verification of individual MACs) in the paper. They only claim that verification of Z_f equals to verification of all the individual MACs.

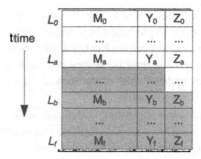

Fig. 1. Delayed detection attack. Data in shaded area is controlled by the attacker. a: time when log entries are uploaded to $\mathcal{T}$; b: time of break-in; f: index of last log entry as well as time when $\mathcal{V}$ receives a copy of log file from $\mathcal{U}$.

addition to the security issues discussed above, the Schneier-Kelsey scheme has some architectural limitations:

Online Server. As mentioned earlier, the scheme employs an assisted verification process and a trusted server $\mathcal{T}$ must be present whenever $\mathcal{V}$ wants to pose an integrity query. In other words, the scheme requires a continuous channel (not necessarily high-bandwidth in this case) between $\mathcal{V}$ and $\mathcal{T}$. As any centralized solution, the scheme has the problem with $\mathcal{T}$ being the single point of failure. Furthermore, the overall security of the scheme scheme relies on the frequency of communication between $\mathcal{U}$ and $\mathcal{T}$. The need for $\mathcal{T}$ can be avoided by adopting a public key approach, as in [9].

Storage Inefficiency. Each log entry contains a hash Y_i and a MAC Z_i. To provide reasonable long-term security guarantees, a minimum security overhead of 512 bits per log entry is needed to accommodate a 256-bit hash and a 256-bit MAC. This per-log-entry overhead makes the Schneier-Kelsey scheme impractical for resource-poor platforms, such as sensors or implantable medical devices. (The latter, especially, need a light-weight secure logging system [10].)

The same set of vulnerabilities/limitations is equally applicable to the Bellare-Yee private key-based scheme [2, 3]. The Holt scheme [9] involves a public key-based approach. Therefore, it avoids the need for an online server and gains security against delayed detection attacks. However it is still vulnerable to truncation attacks and suffers from storage inefficiency.

3 Forward Secure Sequential Aggregate Authentication

In this section, we briefly introduce FssAgg scheme components. We refer to [11, 12] for a more formal and complete definition of an FssAgg scheme.

An FssAgg scheme includes the following components:

[*FssAgg.Kg*] – key generation algorithm used to generate public/private key-pairs. It also takes as input T – the maximum number of time periods (key evolvements).
[*FssAgg.Asig*] – sign-and-aggregate algorithm which takes as input: a private key, a message to be signed and a signature-so-far (an aggregated signature computed

up to this point). It computes a new signature on the input message and combines it with the signature-so-far to produce a new aggregate signature. The final step in *FssAgg.Asig* is a key update procedure *FssAgg.Upd* which takes as input the signing key for the current period and returns the new signing key for the next period (not exceeding T). The key update is part of the sign-and-aggregate algorithm in order to obtain stronger security guarantees.

[*FssAgg.Aver*] – verification algorithm, which, on input of: a putative aggregate signature, a set of presumably signed distinct messages and a public key, outputs a binary value indicating whether the signature is valid.

A secure FssAgg scheme must satisfy the following properties:

1. *Correctness.* Any aggregated signature produced with *FssAgg.Asig* must be accepted by *FssAgg.Aver*.
2. *Forward secure aggregate unforgeability.* No one, even knowing the current signing key, can make a valid FssAgg forgery.

The forward-secure aggregate unforgeability implies two things.

First, a secure FssAgg scheme is append-only - no one can change any message generated before the compromise. Therefore a FssAgg signature can provide integrity protection for the whole message body. An attacker who compromises a signer has two choices: (1) either it includes the intact aggregate-so-far signature in future aggregated signatures, or (2) it ignores the aggregate-so-far signature completely and starts a brand new aggregated signature. What it can not do is selectively delete components of an already-generated aggregate signature.[4] Second, it is computationally hard to remove a component signature without knowing it. Thus, a secure FssAgg scheme is resistant to deletion (including truncation) attacks. These two properties are very useful and we exploit them in our design below.

We claim that FssAgg authentication implies forward-secure stream integrity, i.e.:

Forward Security. In an FssAgg scheme, the secret signing key is updated via a one-way function. An attacker is thus unable to recover previous keys from the current (compromised) key and therefore can not forge signatures from prior intervals.[5]

Stream Security. The sequential aggregation process in an FssAgg scheme preserves the message order and provides stream security; thus, re-ordering of messages is impossible.

Integrity. Any insertion of new messages as well as modification and deletion of existing messages renders the final aggregate unverifiable.

Based on the above, we can now construct a secure logging system from any secure FssAgg authentication scheme.

---

[4] This append-only property resembles the property of a special write-only disk used in traditional log systems.

[5] Assuming, of course, that the plain signature scheme – upon which the FssAgg scheme is built – is CPA-secure.

4 Private-Verifiable Scheme

We first describe a private-verifiable scheme that provides *forward-secure stream integrity*. In a private-verifiable scheme, verifiers are drawn from a small "private" group. Our scheme is based, in turn, on the FssAgg MAC scheme proposed in [11]. *Forward-secure stream integrity* is inherited from the FssAgg MAC scheme. To avoid an online server, two FssAgg MACs are computed over the log file with different initial signing keys. A semi-trusted verifier can only verify one of them. The other MAC is used by the trusted server to finally validate the log file. No one – including the semi-trusted verifier – can alter the contents of the log file without being detected.

We next present the trust model and system assumptions, followed by the description of system operation. Then, we show how to add operations to start/open and close a log file such that total deletion and abnormal stop attacks can be detected. We then evaluate the proposed scheme.

4.1 Security and System Model

There are three types of players in our scheme:

1. $\mathcal{U}$ is an *untrusted* log generator. By "untrusted", we mean that it is not physically secure, bug-free, or sufficiently tamper-resistant to guarantee that it can not be taken over by an attacker. $\mathcal{U}$ does not behave maliciously, unless controlled by the attacker. It generates log entries and replies to $\mathcal{V}$'s query. It only interacts with $\mathcal{T}$ to start a log file or after a log file is closed.
2. $\mathcal{V}$ is a *semi-trusted* verifier that reads and verifies the log file on $\mathcal{U}$. Usually, audit logs can only be accessed by a small group of people, such as system administrators, security personnel and auditors. Therefore, $\mathcal{V}$ is drawn from a small group of authorized entities; it can obtain and verify a copy of the audit log from $\mathcal{U}$. However, $\mathcal{V}$ is not trusted as far as the integrity of the log file.
3. $\mathcal{T}$ is a *trusted* machine in a secure location. It has secure storage sufficient to store audit logs from $\mathcal{U}$. It can authorize a legitimate verifier $\mathcal{V}$ to access the audit log and gives $\mathcal{V}$ the verification key. It also finally validates the log file. $\mathcal{T}$ does not interfere the verification process.

As in [5], we assume that there is no constantly available reliable high-bandwidth channel between $\mathcal{U}$ and trusted storage on $\mathcal{T}$. Consequently, $\mathcal{U}$ and $\mathcal{T}$ communicate infrequently.

The attacker's goal is to tamper with the log file by deleting, modifying, inserting or re-ordering log entries. Clearly, the attacker who compromises $\mathcal{U}$ obtains the signing key used at the time of compromise. We consider two types of attackers: outsiders and insiders. An outsider is an attacker that knows none of $\mathcal{U}$'s secrets before compromising $\mathcal{U}$. A malicious $\mathcal{V}$ is considered to be an insider attacker as it knows some of $\mathcal{U}$'s secrets. An insider is obviously more powerful as far as its ability to tamper with the integrity of the log file. Our scheme is designed to detect both insider and outsider attacks.

4.2 Scheme Description

We use the following notation from here on:

- L_i: i-th message, i.e., the i-th log entry. (We assume that log entries are time-stamped and generally have a well-defined format).
- $\mathcal{F}$: k-bit full-domain hash function with strong collision resistance $\mathcal{F} : \{0,1\}^k \rightarrow \{0,1\}^k$.
- $\mathcal{H}$: one-way hash function with strong collision resistance and arbitrarily long input: $\mathcal{H} : \{0,1\}^* \rightarrow \{0,1\}^k$.
- mac: secure MAC function $mac : \{0,1\}^k \times \{0,1\}^* \rightarrow \{0,1\}^t$ that, on input of a k-bit key x and an arbitrary message m, outputs a t-bit $mac_x(m)$.
- UPD: key update frequency (see below).

At any given time, an authenticated log file consists of two parts: (1) log entries: $[L_1, \cdots, L_i]$ and (2) two authentication tags (forward-secure aggregate MACs): $\mu_{T,i}$ and $\mu_{V,i}$ that are defined below.

Log File Initialization. Before the logging system starts, we require $\mathcal{T}$ to be accessible to $\mathcal{U}$ and assume that $\mathcal{U}$ is not compromised (yet). $\mathcal{U}$ generates two random symmetric keys, A_1 and B_1. Then, it commits these keys to $\mathcal{T}$ along with the other information about the specific log file and the key update interval UPD. We are not concerned with the details of the commitment process. Suffice it to say that, after the commitment process, $\mathcal{T}$ can go off-line and $\mathcal{U}$ can be deployed in an adversarial and unattended environment.[6]

Meanwhile, $\mathcal{U}$ creates the initial "dummy" log entry L_1 which commits to a fixed message (e.g., set to "START") and computes two MACs on L_1 with keys A_1 and B_1, respectively: $\mu_{T,1} = mac_{A_1}(L_1)$ and $\mu_{V,1} = mac_{B_1}(L_1)$. Next, $\mathcal{U}$ evolves its keys through a one-way function $\mathcal{F}$: $A_2 = \mathcal{F}(A_1)$, and $B_2 = \mathcal{F}(B_1)$.

Through the initial interaction, $\mathcal{T}$ knows that $\mathcal{U}$ has started a log file at time t with initial secrets A_1 and B_1. $\mathcal{T}$ stores these values in its database and thereafter knows that a valid log must exist on $\mathcal{U}$ and that that log must contain at least one log entry L_1. The purpose of this initial commitment step is to prevent a total deletion attack, i.e., an attacker breaking into $\mathcal{U}$ at a later time shold not be able to delete the whole log and simply claim that no such log has been started.

Update Frequency. We make no assumptions about key update frequency, except that it must be fixed at log initialization time by $\mathcal{T}$ or $\mathcal{U}$ (or both). Moreover, it must be encoded in the first message from $\mathcal{U}$ to $\mathcal{T}$. UPD can be based on time (e.g., every hour), volume of activity (e.g., every 10 log entries) or some combination thereof. However, to simplify our discussion below, we assume that keys are updated for each log entry.

Generating Log Entries. Before the i-th entry is generated, the log file contains $L_1, \cdots, L_{i-1}$ and two FssAgg MACs $\mu_{T,i-1}, \mu_{V,i-1}$. Current keys of $\mathcal{U}$ are: A_i and B_i.

---

[6] We also assume that the initial commitment as well as each subsequent log entry contains a time-stamp.

Now, a new i-th event occurs and $\mathcal{U}$ creates a corresponding log entry L_i. $\mathcal{U}$ updates[7] authentication tags as follows:

1. $\mathcal{U}$ first generates a MAC for $\mathcal{V}$ as: $mac_{A_i}(L_i)$. It then computes $\mu_{V,i}$ as: $\mu_{V,i} = \mathcal{H}(\mu_{V,i-1}||mac_{A_i}(L_i))$. Here, $\mathcal{H}$ acts as the aggregation function. Note that $\mu_{V,i}$ can be represented (un-rolled) as:

$$\mu_{V,i} = \mathcal{H}(\mathcal{H}(\cdots \mathcal{H}(\mu_{V,1}||mac_{A_1}(L_1))\cdots)||mac_{A_i}(L_i)) \qquad (1)$$

2. $\mathcal{U}$ updates the second FssAgg MAC (for $\mathcal{T}$) in the same manner:
$\mu_{T,i} = \mathcal{H}(\mu_{T,i-1}||mac_{B_i}(L_i))$
3. Finally, $\mathcal{U}$ evolves both keys: $A_{i+1} = \mathcal{F}(A_i)$, and $B_{i+1} = \mathcal{F}(B_i)$. Prior keys A_i and B_i and MACs $mac_{A_i}(L_i)$ and $mac_{B_i}(L_i)$ are immediately and securely erased (e.g., from disk and RAM).

Log File Closure. $\mathcal{U}$ officially closes the log file by creating a special closing message as the final log entry (L_f), updating the two authentication tags ($\mu_{V,f}$ and $\mu_{T,f}$) and securely erasing the remaining keys (A_f and B_f).

This special step is necessary in order to inform users that the log file is closed properly and no longer accepts any new data. Consider that an attacker might prevent the logging system from functioning after gaining control of the logging machine. Without the explicit closing step, we can not determine whether the log file has been closed normally or the logging process has been impeded by an attacker. Once the log file is properly closed, an attacker who breaks into $\mathcal{U}$ cannot modify anything since no keys are available.

Log File Validation. An authorized verifier $\mathcal{V}$ starts the validation process by obtaining A_1 – one of the two initial signing keys – from $\mathcal{T}$. Next, $\mathcal{V}$ queries $\mathcal{U}$ and obtains a copy of log entries $L_1, \cdots, L_f$ as well as $\mu_{V,f}$. $\mathcal{V}$ computes $A_2, \cdots, A_f$ through the key update function, computes $\mu'_{V,f}$ and checks that it matches $\mu_{V,f}$. Verifier's computation costs amount to f invocations of $\mathcal{F}, \mathcal{H}$ and mac.

When $\mathcal{T}$ receives the complete and already-closed log file, it can independently validate it using B_1 and $\mu_{T,f}$. The validation mimics that performed by $\mathcal{V}$. Note that, a malicious verifier $\mathcal{V}$, knowing A_1, has full control and can modify any log entries by generating its own version of $\mu_{V,f}$. However, it can not forge $\mu_{T,f}$.

4.3 Discussion

The private-verifiable scheme is simple and very computation-efficient, since it only involves fast hashing and symmetric key operations. $\mathcal{V}$ can verify a log file without consulting $\mathcal{T}$; thus, no on-line trusted party is needed. Furthermore, it is very storage-efficient: compared with previous schemes which require either f or $2 * f$ units to store authentication-related values, our scheme only needs two storage units for two FssAgg MACs. Considering that log files tend to be very large and can contain millions of log entries, the benefits of storage-efficiency are quite apparent.

---

[7] We use the term "updates", since, at all times, there are only two authentication tags in the secure log.

Our scheme provides *forward-secure stream integrity* through the use of a single FssAgg MAC that covers all log entries. An attacker can not forge this MAC without knowing any pre-compromise MAC keys. Deletion and truncation attacks are readily detectable by any verifier. Furthermore, our scheme detects a total deletion attack, since we use an explicit commitment process when starting a log file. Also, by explicitly closing the log file, our scheme can detect certain DoS attacks that aim to incapacitate the logging system.

However, we concede that a malicious verifier V can tamper with the log without being detected by other verifiers. This tampering can only be detected with the help of T. It is thus possible for a malicious insider to mount a delayed detection attack. This is a definite drawback which leads us to construct an alternative scheme based on public key techniques.

5   A Public-Verifiable Scheme

We now describe a public-verifiable scheme. It can be based on any FssAgg signature scheme proposed in [11] and [12]. A public-verifiable scheme allows auditors outside the system to make sure no tampering takes place within the system. Therefore, it can be used for systems which require public auditing, such as financial records and voting systems. A public-verifiable scheme also avoids the shortcoming of a private-verifiable schemes which, as pointed out above, suffers from delayed detection attacks.

As in the previous section, we begin with the trust model and system assumptions. Next, we describe and evaluate the new scheme. To avoid unnecessary repetiton, we focus on the difference between private- and public-verifiable schemes.

5.1   Trust Model

In this scheme we no longer require a trusted server T. Instead, we need a Certification Authority (CA) that can certify/register U's public key. The scope of V moves from a small private group of semi-trusted entities to the public domain, i.e., anyone who has a copy of the log file can verify it. We no longer need to differentiate between inside and outside attackers. An attacker is thus anyone who behaves maliciously and does not know the system's initial secrets.

5.2   Scheme Description

An authenticated log file in the present scheme consists of two parts: log entries $[L_1, \cdots, L_f]$ and a single FssAgg signature $\sigma_{1,f}$.

Log File Initialization. To initiate a log file, U uses $FssAgg.Kg$ to generate the initial secret key sk_1 and the public key pk. Then it registers pk with a public CA. U's certificate for log file contains (at least) essential information, such as: the log creator, the log ID, starting time and the public key. For example, CA's signature in U's certificate for log file ID_{log} might be as follows:

$$CERT(ID_{log}) = SIGN_{CA}(U, ID_{log}, t, T, pk, \text{timestamp}, \cdots)$$

$\mathcal{U}$ keeps sk_1. Next, it creates the initial log entry L_1 which is set to $CERT(ID_{log})$. Then, $\mathcal{U}$ generates a signature $\sigma_{1,1}$ on L_1 with $FssAgg.Asig$ using the initial private key sk_1. Finally, $\mathcal{U}$ updates its key from sk_1 to sk_2 and securely erases all copies of sk_1.

Generating Log Entries. Before the i-th entry occurs, the log file contains $[L_1, \cdots, L_{i-1}]$ and the FssAgg signature $\sigma_{1,i-1}$. $\mathcal{U}$'s current secret key is sk_i. Now, a new event occurs and triggers $\mathcal{U}$ to creates a new log entry L_i. $\mathcal{U}$ updates its FssAgg signature by invoking $FssAgg.Asig$ with input: L_i, $\sigma_{1,i-1}$ and sk_i. Finally, $\mathcal{U}$ evolves its sk_i into sk_{i+1} via $FssAgg.Upd$ and securely erases sk_i. ($FssAgg.Upd$ is invoked immediately after the aggregate signature is generated.)

Since the maximum number of key update periods T is fixed *a priori*, as the log file grows, the number of updates might eventually to exceed T. To address this issue we can dynamically extend the scheme to support additional key update periods without sacrificing security. One straightforward way is to generate a public key for the next T number of time periods and to use the last (initially certified) secret key sk_T to, in turn, certify a new set of public keys to be used thereafter. In fact, the certification of the next batch of public keys should be treated as a special log entry L_T.

Log File Closure. As in the private-verifiable scheme, $\mathcal{U}$ closes the log file by creating a special closing message as the final log entry L_f, updating the FssAgg signature accordingly, and securely erasing its secret key.

Validating Log File. After receiving a copy of the log file, $\mathcal{V}$ extracts public keys from $CERT(ID_{log})$ contained in the initial log entry L_1 and $\mathcal{V}$ verifies CA's signature on $CERT(ID_{log})$. Then, $\mathcal{V}$ validates the actual log file using $FssAgg.Aver$.

5.3 Discussion

Compared with its private-verifiable counterpart, the present scheme offers better security because of its resistance to delayed detection attacks. It allows anyone – not just a group of semi-trusted verifiers – to validate a log file. It is thus suitable for applications where scalability is important and, more generally, where public verification is required. Except for the log initialization time, no trusted entity is needed for any system operations.

6 Evaluation

We evaluate the proposed schemes by comparing them with prior schemes. We compare our private verifiable scheme with two existing private-key-based schemes: Schneier-Kelsey [5] and Bellare-Yee [3]. We also compare our public-verifiable scheme with Holt's scheme [9]. Our comparison is based on four factors: 1) resilience to truncation attacks; 2) resilience to delayed detection attacks; 3) on-line server requirements; 4) storage efficiency. Comparison results are summarized in Table 6.

Compared with Schneier-Kelsey and Bellare-Yee, our private scheme is resilient to truncation attacks, more storage-efficient and requires no on-line server. However, it is vulnerable to delayed detection attacks. Compared with Holt's scheme, our public scheme is resilient to truncation attacks and more storage-efficient.

Table 1. Comparisons of Various Schemes

	Private Key Based Schemes			Public Key Based Schemes	
	SK [5]	BY [3]	Ours	Holt [9]	Ours
Resilience to truncation attack?	No	No	Yes	No	Yes
Resilience to delayed detection attack?	No	No	No	Yes	Yes
No on-line server?	No	No	Yes	Yes	Yes
Storage efficient?	No	No	Yes	No	Yes

7 Implementation

We investigated the viability of the proposed schemes on an Intel dual-core 1.73GHz Laptop with 1GB RAM running Linux. We used the NTL [14] and the PBC [15] libraries as for necessary cryptographic and number-theoretic primitives.

We prototyped the BLS-$FssAgg$ signature scheme in [11] and the AR-$FssAgg$ and BM-$FssAgg$ signature schemes in [12]. For BM-$FssAgg$ and AR-$FssAgg$ schemes, we selected security parameters $k = 1024$ and $l = 160$. For the BLS-$FssAgg$ scheme, we used a singular curve $Y^2 = X^3 + X$ defined on a field F_q for $|q| = 512$ and the group order $|p| = 160$, where p is a Solinas prime. Such groups have the fastest pairing operations [15]. We measured signer's computation costs by signature generation and key update on a per-log-entry basis. We measured verifier's computation costs over an aggregate signature $\sigma_{1,t}$ when $t = 100, 1,000$ and $10,000$ which corresponds to a small, medium, and large log file, respectively. Experimental results shown in Table 2 show that the BM-$FssAgg$ scheme is the most efficient in terms of computation for both signer and verifier. Its signature generation is approximately twice faster than that of AR-$FssAgg$ and 5.5 times faster than that of the BLS-$FssAgg$. Its signature verification is 4 times faster than that of the AR-$FssAgg$ and 16 times faster than that of the BLS-$FssAgg$. However, it incurs the most storage overhead.

We also investigated storage overhead incurred by each scheme. Let I_a denote the amount of storage needed to to store the secret key and the aggregate signature - the overhead incurred by authentication. Let $|S|$ denote the size of a signature or a key. Let I denote the number of log entries and $|L|$ denote the average size of a log entry. We

Table 2. Comparisons of FssAgg Signature Schemes. (Operation Timing in *msecs.*)

		BLS-$FssAgg$	BM-$FssAgg$	AR-$FssAgg$
Signer Computation Cost	$Asig$	30	2.09	4.39
(per log entry)	Upd	0.002	3.46	7.27
	total	30.00	5.55	11.66
	$t = 100$	2%	162%	3%
Signer Storage Cost	$t = 1000$	0.2%	16.2%	0.3%
	$t = 10000$	0.02%	1.62%	0.03%
	$t = 100$	3.30×10^3	211.97	810.88
Verifier Cost	$t = 1000$	29.3×10^3	2.13×10^3	8.16×10^3
	$t = 10000$	330.72×10^3	21.35×10^3	80.84×10^3

measure storage efficiency by $\frac{I_a*|S|}{I*|L|}$. BLS-$FssAgg$ needs 1 unit of space each for both secret key and signature. BM-$FssAgg$ needs 162 units of storage for secret key and 1 unit for the aggregate signature. BM-$FssAgg$ needs 2 units for secret key and 1 for the aggregate signature. To simply measurements, we assumed log entry size comparable to the size of a signature or a secret key, e.g. $|S| \approx |L|$. The comparison results are also shown in Table 2. BLS-$FssAgg$ is the best in term of storage efficiency, As the number of log entries grows, storage overhead in BLS-$FssAgg$ becomes negligible.

8 Related Work

A number of cryptographic approaches to address secure logging have been proposed to-date. Most prior work focused on three areas: (1) data integrity/authentication, (2) data confidentiality and access control, and (3) searchable encryption. Since we are primarily interested in integrity, only the first area directly relates to this paper.

Bellare and Yee were the first to define the *forward-secure stream integrity* property required in an audit log system and proposed to use forward-secure MACs [2, 3]. They focused on formal definition and construction of forward-secure MAC schemes and applied them to secure audit log applications. In their secure log scheme, multiple log entries are indexed and tagged independently within one time period. At the end of each time period, a special log entry containing the number of log entries in the current time period is created to indicate the end of the current time period. This scheme has the same security as well as the architectural limits as the Schneier and Kelsey scheme analyzed in Section 2.

Schneier and Kelsey proposed a similar system (the SK scheme we analyzed in Section 2) based on forward-secure MAC and one-way hash chains [5, 16, 17]. Unlike Bellare and Yee's scheme, in the SK scheme, rekeying is performed after each log entry is made. Therefore they no longer use per-stage sequence numbers in tagging logs. Instead, each log entry now contains a link in a hash chain and a forward-secure MAC computed over this link to authenticate the values of all pervious entries. Moreover, they presented a precise protocol design for its implementation in a distributed system, describing how messages are sent to external trusted machines upon log creation and closing.

Chong, et. al. discussed the feasibility of using of tamper-resistant hardware in conjunction with a system like Schneier and Yee's in [18]. Holt extended Schneier and Yee's system to the public key setting [9].

Waters, et. al. designed encrypted and searchable audit log [19]. This showed how identity-based encryption (IBE) can be used to make audit logs efficiently searchable. Keywords which relate to each log entry are used to form public keys in an IBE system. Administrators allow searching and retrieval of entries matching a given set of keywords by issuing clients the corresponding IBE private keys. They recommended the use of the Schneier and Yee's technique as their authentication scheme. The two security attacks, truncation attack and delayed detection attack, which we outlined in Section 2, seem to be very fundamental to all the secure audit log schemes as far as we know. It is surprising that they have not been addressed by any later work so far.

9 Conclusion

In this paper, we identified some issues in current secure logging techniques. We then proposed two concrete schemes to provide *forward-secure stream integrity* for logs generated on untrusted machines. Our approach supports forward security and compact aggregation of authentication tags (MACs or signatures). Both of our proposed schemes offer practical secure logging without reliance on trusted third parties or secure hardware. Our schemes are based on the recent proposed FssAgg authentication schemes where a unique authentication tag is used to protect the integrity of underlying message body. We evaluated the performance of our schemes and reported on our experience with the prototype implementation of a secure logging system. In the full version of this paper [13], we also considered the immutability extensions to our schemes.

Although the security of proposed schemes rests entirely on previously proposed techniques (i.e., [11, 12], we still need to construct separate security proofs for each scheme. Furthermore, we pland to conduct more extensive experiments, and perhaps even trace-driven simulations, to better understand the performance of our schemes.

References

1. Swanson, M., Guttman, B.: Generally accepted principles and practices for securing information technology systems. In: NIST, pp. 800–814 (1996)
2. Bellare, M., Yee, B.: Forward integrity for secure audit logs. Technical Report, Computer Science and Engineering Department, University of San Diego (November 1997)
3. Bellare, M., Yee, B.: Forward-Security in Private-Key Cryptography. In: Joye, M. (ed.) CT-RSA 2003. LNCS, vol. 2612. Springer, Heidelberg (2003)
4. U.S. Department of Defense, C.S.C.: Trusted computer system evaluation criteria (December 1985)
5. Schneier, B., Kelsey, J.: Cryptographic support for secure logs on untrusted machines. In: Proceedings of the 7th USENIX Security Symposium (January 1998)
6. Bellare, M., Palacio, A.: Protecting against key exposure: strongly key-insulated encryption with optimal threshold. In Cryptology ePrint Archive, Report 2002/64 (2002)
7. Dodis, Y., Katz, J., Xu, S., Yung, M.: Key-Insulated Public Key Cryptosystems. In: Knudsen, L.R. (ed.) EUROCRYPT 2002. LNCS, vol. 2332, pp. 65–82. Springer, Heidelberg (2002)
8. Dodis, Y., Katz, J., Xu, S., Yung, M.: Strong key-insulated public key cryptosystems. In: Desmedt, Y.G. (ed.) PKC 2003. LNCS, vol. 2567, pp. 130–144. Springer, Heidelberg (2002)
9. Holt, J.E.: Logcrypt: forward security and public verification for secure audit logs. In: ACSW Frontiers 2006: Proceedings of the 2006 Australasian workshops on Grid computing and e-research, Darlinghurst, Australia, pp. 203–211. Australian Computer Society (2006)
10. Halperin, D., Kohno, T., Heydt-Benjamin, T., Fu, K., Maisel, W.: Security and privacy for implantable medical devices, vol. 7(1) (January 2008)
11. Ma, D., Tsudik, G.: Forward-secure sequential aggregate authentication. In: Proceedings of IEEE Symposium on Security and Privacy 2007 (May 2007)
12. Ma, D.: Practical forward secure sequential aggregate signatures. In: ACM Symposium on Information, Computer and Communications Security (ASIACCS 2008) (March 2008)
13. Ma, D., Tsudik, G.: A new approach to secure logging. Cryptology ePrint Archive, Report 2008/185 (2008), http://eprint.iacr.org/
14. Shoup, V.: Ntl: a library for doing number theory, http://www.shoup.net/ntl/
15. Pbc library benchmarks, http://crypto.stanford.edu/pbc/times.html

16. Schneier, B., Kelsey, J.: Secure audit logs to support computer forensics. ACM Transactions on Information and System Security, 159–176 (1999)
17. Kelsey, J., Schneier, B.: Minimizing bandwidth for remote access to cryptographically protected audit logs. In: Recent Advances in Intrusion Detection (RAID 1999) (September 1999)
18. Chong, C., Peng, Z., Hartel, P.: Secure audit logging with tamper resistant hardware. Technical report TR-CTIT-02-29, Centre for Telematics and Information Technology, Univ. Twente, The Netherlands (August 2002)
19. Waters, B., Balfanz, D., Durfee, G., Smeters, D.K.: Building an encrypted and searchable audit log. In: ACM Annual Symposium on Network and Distributed System Security (NDSS 2004) (2004)

Security, Functionality and Scale?
(Invited Talk)

Ross Anderson

University of Cambridge Computer Laboratory
JJ Thomson Avenue
Cambridge CB3 0FD, UK
ross.anderson@cl.cam.ac.uk

Abstract. Since 2002 the UK has been attempting to build a system of federated databases containing all the nation's medical records. This project has encountered numerous problems and some feel that it is becoming the world's largest ever software disaster. One aspect of the problem is security. This means different things to different stakeholders: the government and its contractors boast about their ability to keep out 'hackers', while medics and patients' groups worry that making records available to large numbers of authorised insiders will lead to abuses that will fatally undermine privacy. A security policy that I developed for the BMA and that I discussed at DBSEC in 2002 was not used; instead the developers went for a combination of role-based access control plus a 'legitimate relationship'. This has been found insufficient and 'sealed envelopes' are planned as well. Medical databases are the first application involving very sensitive personal data being kept in large-scale systems which their operators hope will develop rich functionality over time. This combination of a stringent security requirement, complex functionality and great scale poses the most serious problems yet known to the security architect. I will discuss the options and ask whether it is in fact the case that you can have any two of these attributes - security, functionality and scale - but not all three.

V. Atluri (Ed.): DAS 2008, LNCS 5094, p. 64, 2008.

P4A: A New Privacy Model for XML

Angela C. Duta and Ken Barker

University of Calgary
2500 University Drive
Calgary, Alberta, Canada

Abstract. We propose a new privacy model for XML data called Privacy for All (P4A) to capture collectors privacy practice and data providers privacy preferences. Through P4A data collectors specify the purpose of data collection along with recipients, retention time and users. Data providers can agree to the collectors' practice or impose their own privacy preferences. P4A offers more flexibility to both data collectors and providers in specifying privacy statements and preferences, including but not limited to full permission, denial, and conditional access to information.

A privacy practice defines purposes, recipients, retention period, and uses of data collection. Data providers share their private information with data collectors under restrictions specified by privacy preferences. P4A offers individuals multiple options for restrictions such as conditional access, return results as range intervals for each data item and purpose.

Keywords: privacy preference, privacy statement, flexible privacy policy, privacy map.

1 Introduction

Several representations for privacy policies have been proposed in the literature to address the growing concern of private information protection. Current research in the database community considers privacy [3] [4] [9] [11] in databases where data providers[1] agree to a set of predefined policies. This is a restrictive solution as data providers have limited options. If they do not agree with any of company's policy they are left with no real option [10] except to sign an unsatisfying privacy agreement or to refuse the company's services. Neither option is considered acceptable.

We propose a solution to preserve data privacy where providers set their own conditions. Data collection has two major players: the data collector and the data provider. Both have different viewpoints regarding privacy. The collector's view is expressed as the privacy practice and the provider's view is captured in privacy preferences. A privacy policy considers two major elements: data and the purpose of its use. Each provider decides which personal information is private and all possible purposes for which it can be used.

---

[1] **Data provider** or **provider:** people that share their private information with collectors possibly in the exchange for a product or service, i.e. patients, customers, *etc.*

V. Atluri (Ed.): DAS 2008, LNCS 5094, pp. 65–80, 2008.

1.1   Motivation

Agrawal *et al.* identified the ten principles of privacy in databases. Two of them, the principles of limited collection and limited use require that only data necessary to fulfill specified purposes is collected and used. However, a company could have several "minor" purposes in addition to its main one, as it has several additional business activities in addition to its main one. Thus, the principle of limited use allows for a broad variation depending on company goals. Instead of leaving this decision to the collector, we suggest that data providers determine what data is reasonable to be used for each purpose. Obviously, providers options generates considerable overhead that must be resolved. Categorizing privacy policies in hierarchies is not a viable option as offering predefined privacy contracts is not flexible enough and a multitude of options can be expressed by providers (thus, no hierarchy). Current approaches to privacy do not offer the flexibility people desire because they do not treat each privacy contract individually. This is the challenge we address in this paper: each data provider expresses individual options for privacy with a minimum of overhead for the database system.

1.2   Contributions

This paper proposes a new XML data model that considers privacy protection called Privacy for All (P4A). In P4A privacy policies offer maximum flexibility to each provider of personal information in choosing the desired protection. Collector's privacy practice is included in the metadata and forms the general guidelines for data query. In P4A providers actively decide upon the use of their data by allowing, denying access to it, or setting additional conditions that must be meet before access to their data is allowed. Privacy preferences are stored in a privacy map. P4A has several advantages: (1) sensitive data is used according to providers preferences; (2) data providers can request conditional access to their private data; (3) information leakage is avoided as unaccessible nodes are not reached.

1.3   Paper Organization

The balance of this paper is organized as follows. Section 2 summarizes related current approaches in privacy and security. Section 3 defines the problem and introduces a working example that is used next in the privacy model description (Section 4). Some conclusions regarding this new privacy model for XML are drawn in Section 5.

2   Related Work

Work in the privacy area must look at its sociological aspect. Privacy is characterized differently by philosophers, sociologists, economists, computer scientists, *etc.* [16]. Our research incorporates the current trend to create more complex privacy rules such as "no-release-by-legal-right" [16] to protect individuals. A simple solution to privacy protection is to perturb sensitive values [3]. Creating range values to hide sensitive values if it is in concordance with the purpose of a data query is reasonable but not sufficient. Research in the privacy area is developed in two main directions: (1) regulate the use of data stored in databases and (2) regulate data collection during Web surfing. In the first area, work on Hippocratic databases [4] [11] [14] translate the Hippocratic Oath into modern privacy policy tables. Regulation of data collection for Web users is first considered by W3C through the privacy specification standard called the Platform for Privacy Preferences (P3P1.0) [5]. Subsequent research criticizes P3P because it does not guarantee Web sites have the means to implement and respect their privacy policies ([2], [6], [8]). Social Contract Core (SCC) [10] extends P3P by allowing users to choose privacy preferences that suit them. Users "vote" for the policy that is closest to their preferences so they are able to visit the site. Both the collection of private data through the Internet and its use are considered in some approaches. The Platform for Enterprise Privacy Practices (E-P3P) [9] defines a methodology to enforce P3P by using an *Obligations Engine* to fulfill contractual obligations (i.e. delete records older than 3 years) and a *Policy Evaluation Engine* to control user access to personally identifiable information. The Paranoid Platform for Privacy Preferences (P4P) [2] envisions a world where personal agents help individuals to control the destination, type, scope and duration of use of released personal information. Our work considers XML data collections where each query has a purpose assigned as in Hippocratic databases [4]. We extend the Social Contract Core [10] by allowing providers to decide on the accessibility of each data item not just offering them several policy options. From this perspective we support and incorporate in P4A the use of authorization table for each customer that accommodates individual privacy preferences as in the approach of Massacci *et al.* [14].

In the security area, a standard XML access control XACML [12] that deals with specification of complex policies is created as a component of distributed systems. The advantage brought by XACML is related to its ability to integrate in heterogenous systems and act as a successful intermediary language due to the XML extensible and expressive format.

3   P4A Privacy Model

3.1   Problem Definition

As pointed out by Walters [16] the term *privacy* has several definitions, some more detailed, not only among categories of scientists, but the general public as well. We start defining privacy by looking at some definitions.

First the definition provided by *The Canadian Oxford Dictionary* [1] states that: Privacy is *the state of being private and undisturbed; a persons right to this; freedom from intrusion or public attention; avoidance of publicity.*

This definition probably captures our view of privacy in our day-to-day activities relating it to *anonymity*. The *Canadian Privacy Act*[2] refers to the legal aspects of privacy and provides a more complete definition. In this act, the term used is *personal information*, as the key element of privacy.

"Personal information" means information about an identifiable individual that is recorded in any form including, without restricting the generality of the foregoing.[3]

The definition provided by the Canadian Privacy Act sets the grounds for privacy in databases. The *Organization for Economic Cooperation and Development* sets the guidelines for collections of private data in the 1980s, later used by governments in legislative privacy standards. The OECD defines eight principles[4] for data collection and usage with respect to privacy: (1) Collection Limitation Principle, (2) Data Quality Principle, (3) Purpose Specification Principle, (4) Use Limitation Principle, (5) Security Safeguards Principle, (6) Openness Principle, (7) Individual Participation Principle, and (8) Accountability Principle.

Whatever the definition for privacy or personal information we use, just by looking at the definition of database systems it is clear that they are not yet ready to handle it. A database is defined as *"a collection of related data"* [7], and a database management system is *"a collection of programs that enables users to create and maintain a database"*. Nothing about privacy is specified in these definitions. Database administrators are usually concerned in current database systems by user authorizations referred to as discretionary access control. Even more, one reason for collecting data is to apply data mining or knowledge discovery to search data for patterns and "discover" new information.

Thus, a different approach must be developed in creating database systems, one that incorporates privacy. A simplified view of a database management system (DBMS) environment is composed by: application, access control, query management, concurrency control, and metadata with stored data. Privacy must be considered and implemented at each of these components. Implementation at the application level generates no changes to the database model and is the most flexible. However, it is the least reliable because the responsibility lies with programmers. Frequent changes to an application may leave open holes in privacy protection. If data is utilized also by a different application, then the process of implementing data privacy starts again. Access control may solve some of the privacy issues by accepting only authorized users to access data. However, a user once authorized, has access to data no matter what privacy concerns are specified. Query management and concurrency control rely on the data model. Any additions, such as privacy, to the query management should be reflected in the underlined data model. Last, but not least, is the data model. This includes data descriptions, that is, the domains. All the other components of a DBMS are based on the data model. By adding privacy to the data model, the database becomes fully equipped to handle privacy more reliably regardless

---

[2] http://lois.justice.gc.ca/en/P-21/text.html

[3] http://lois.justice.gc.ca/en/P-21/text.html

[4] http://www.cdt.org/privacy/guide/basic/oecdguidelines.html

of the application, access control, query management, and concurrency control mechanisms implemented. However, as components of security policies are implemented at all levels of a DBMS for increased reliability, efficiency, and protection, so should privacy policies.

This work is aimed at constructing a data model for XML data to incorporate privacy being the milestone of a privacy concerned database. The following is the definition of a privacy concerned database we refer to in the rest of the paper.

Definition 1. *[Privacy Concerned Database] A* privacy concerned database *is a database where private data is stored, retrieved, and used according to purposes to which their owners have agreed as specified by associated privacy policies (privacy practice and providers' preferences).* ∎

An example of privacy concerned database is presented next.

3.2   A Working Example

BrightStar is a financial institution offering credit card services to individuals from which it collects private data as depicted in Figure 1. BrightStar requires personal information such as name, address, phone number, SIN, employer, income, credit card information, and transactions on it. To fulfill its business goal, BrightStar performs credit evaluations, studies clients purchase habits, and exchanges credit information with other financial institutions regarding common customers. It also performs data mining on collected data to determine new trends in customers' behavior likely to influence their credit score, to suggest new financial products (credit cards or loans), or to detect suspicious transactions. Affiliated banks, such as TotalBank and NorthBank, query the BrightStar's database regarding credit information to perform their credit evaluations. BrightStar has agreements with several merchants, such as SellStar LTD and SellAll LTD, to sell sell non-financial products to BrightStar's customers. BrightStar is a modern institution that wants to respect its customers privacy concerns. It decides to allow its clients to choose how private data is used for different purposes implied by its business activities by implementing P4A.

3.3   Privacy Metadata

Privacy policies permit data owners to actively determine the purpose for the data collection but do not provide the means to verify their correct implementation. A privacy policy evaluates the legitimacy of a query with respect to its purpose and requested data before the query is executed. Unanswerable queries are rejected with no additional waste of computational time. Further, information leakage is avoided as unaccessible nodes are never reached.

A complete definition of a privacy policy must include a combination of privacy constraints $<$ *Purpose, Object, Recipient, Retention* $>$ and access constraints $<$ *Purpose, Object, User* $>$ as suggested in Hippocratic Databases [4], where *Recipient* and *User* refer to who has access to data. We argue that

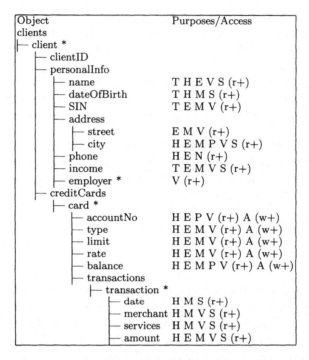

Fig. 1. Purpose-constraints

the Hippocratic Database [4] introduces unnecessary redundancy in its privacy tables by specifying purposes for each object in connection with recipients (in privacy constraints) and users (in access constraints) as detailed above. In Hippocratic Databases [4] privacy policies are defined in addition to security policies < *User, Access right* > that specify authorizations for users. It is more important that the *access right* be correlated to the query purpose rather than to the subject. Thus, we suggest the following privacy model, P4A, formed by Purpose-constraints < *Object, Purpose, Access right* > (Figure 1), Recipient-constraints < *Recipient, Purpose, Retention time* > (Table 1), and User-constraints< *User, Recipient* > (Table 2). Purpose-constraints (Figure 1) structure captures the purposes for which each data is collected. For example, the name of a client is used for "income tax purpose" (T) to refer to its declared income, for "purchase habits purpose" (H) to call the client in case a suspicious transaction is executed in its account, for "credit inquiries purpose" (E) when other banks or financial institutions want to verify his credit history, for "credit evaluations purpose" (V) conducted by BrightStar, and for "sell products purpose" (S) by BrightStar's partners that sell non-financial products. The type of access required for these purposes is specified between parenthesis following purpose specification (i.e. for read is r+). Recipient-constraints (Table 1) describes connections between recipients and purposes, by identifying which recipients are entitled to query for which purposes. The retention time is included in this table as it specifies the duration data is stored and used for a

Table 1. Recipient-constraints

Recipient	Purpose	Retention
Canada Revenue	(T) income tax	5 years
BrightStar	(H) purchase habits	2 years
TotalBank	(E) credit enquiries	1 month
BrightStar	(M) data mining	2 years
BrightStar	(P) payment	while ∃ card
BrightStar	(V) credit evaluation	6 months
SellStar LTD	(S) sell products	1 months
BrightStar	(A) approve credit card	3 month

Table 2. User-constraints

User	Recipient
Alice	BrightStar
Susan	BrightStar
Bob	TotalBank
Oliver	SellSTar

particular purpose. This time can vary for each recipient and purpose. When a data element is not required by any purpose of any recipient then it must be deleted from the database according to the Minimum Retention Time Principle enunciated by Agrawal *et al.* [4]. The third component of our proposed model, the user-constraints structure extends security policies by specifying all users associated with each recipient.

P4A defines attributes' accessibility for each purpose in the Purpose-constraints table (Figure 1) and recipients rights to query for specific purposes in the Recipient-constraints table (Table 1). In P4A, access rights are associated with query purposes as the concern in privacy policies is focused on the purpose rather than on the user as in security policies. P4A has the benefit of less redundancy compared with Hippocratic Databases [4] as relationship purposes - objects are specified once. Further, the retention period is correlated with query purposes instead of objects. A purpose requires instances of several objects to be available. Instead of multiple retention periods for combinations purpose-object [4] only one tuple per purpose is specified. An object is queried with multiple purposes, so instances of an object are stored for as long as one purpose needs this data. Thus, the retention period is included in Recipient-constraints table and it allows multiple specifications for one purpose depending on the recipient. In P4A, different recipients query private data with the same purposes but have different data visibility. The retention time for a collector is the maximum period allowed to store data. The retention time for a recipient is the maximum allowed time to query data as specified by the purpose. Table 2 specifies users[5] that are allowed to query data on behalf of each recipient.

P4A implements conditional access in addition to traditional permission and denial. The following sections describe the access codes and conditions that apply to private data.

3.4   Complex Conditions

A major contribution of our approach is to offer more flexibility to data providers in expressing a variety of conditions that must be respected to have access to

---

[5] An individual or group that accesses data stored in a database on behalf of the recipient or collector (not the one "on whose behalf a service is accessed and for which personal data exists" [5] as in W3C terminology).

data. In previous approaches the only options providers had were permission or denial. Additional restrictions are included in P4A such as: interval values, perturbed values, and conditions that refer to the knowledge of more "private" information. For example, a condition is "my name can be accessed only if the user provides my correct client ID". This condition denies execution of queries such as "who are BrightStar's clients?" or "is X a client?". We use "access" as the general term for any type of access be it read, write, update, append, or delete.

Using the database of BrightStar represented by the XML tree from Figure 1 we demonstrate several options a data provider or collector should have when defining a privacy policy. To simplify the presentation we only consider purposes for a single collector. Some examples of restrictions data owners may request are: my SIN number can be accessed only if the user provides my correct name and date of birth; give an approximate address (i.e. only street name but no number) for data mining purposes instead of my exact address; use terms like permanent and temporary resident rather than social insurance numbers; for third parties asking for credit references provide amounts spent on my credit card for transactions older than a year but not the merchant or service, *etc.*

Inclusion of such conditions in the privacy model requires conditional access codes in addition to permission and denial as previously considered in security policies. The next section introduces the access types in P4A.

3.5   Access Codes

Definition 2. *[Access Code] The* access code *associated with a node in the XML tree expresses its accessibility in relation to a query purpose in a privacy concerned database. The set of access codes is $\alpha=\{yes\ (Y),\ conditional(C),\ range\ (R),\ conditional\ and\ range\ (Q),\ no\ (N)\}$.*   ∎

Providers and collectors specify access types for leaf nodes where information is stored. Table 3 depicts the proposed access codes for leaf nodes. Code No (N) means the leaf node must not be accessed while Yes (Y) allows unconditional access to it. Code Range/Perturbed value (R) permits access if a table exists

Table 3. Access specification for leaf nodes

Code	Access	XQuery representation
N	No access	-
R	Perturbed or interval value	for $x in doc ("*doc.xml*") *path* return if ($x/*item* < *value*) then \<item\>"below value"\</item\> else \<item\>"above value"\</item\>
C	Conditional access	for $x in doc ("*doc.xml*") *path* where $x/*item condition* return $x
Y	Unconditional access	for $x in doc ("*doc.xml*") *path* return $x

for this node to perturb sensitive value either by specifying interval values (i.e. age below 20, 21-40, 41-60, and above 61) or key terms (i.e. young, mature, old); otherwise the access is denied. Code Condition (C) allows access to this leaf node if the value of another node is known. The condition we suggest here is equality (or non-equality) for privacy protection. This condition should be applied to nodes that store more "private" data rather than public information. For example, it is preferable to use a condition based on SIN or date of birth rather than name. The code Q (perturbed values and condition) is for nodes where perturbed values are returned when the specified conditions are true; otherwise the access is denied. The proposed set of access codes is represented by $\alpha = \{Y, R, C, Q, N\}$, where α is a lattice based on Definition 3). The set of constraints that are associated with access code C,R, and Q is represented by Ω.

Definition 3. *[α-Order] There exists a partial order for access codes from the most permissive to the least permissive noted $>_p$ as follows: $Y >_p R >_p Q >_p N$ and $Y >_p C >_p Q >_p N$.* ■

In this approach, *operation codes* are considered in addition to the access codes to create finer and more restrictive access.

Definition 4. *[Operation Code] The operation code associated with a node in the XML schema tree expresses the permitted operations to be performed on this node in relation to a query's purpose in a privacy concerned database. The set of operation codes is $\beta = \{$no operation allowed (ϕ), read (r), append (a), update (u), delete (d), write (w)$\}$.* ■

Definition 5. *[β-Order] There exists a partial order for operations from the least permissive to the most permissive denoted $<_o$ as follows: $\phi <_o r <_o a <_o w$, $\phi <_o r <_o u <_o w$ and $\phi <_o r <_o d <_o w$.* ■

Each privacy policy specifies access using purpose of access (why is data accessed?) and operation on data (is data read, deleted, updated or just created for this purpose?). These restrictions come in addition to security policies where general user access is specified (i.e. user X is allowed to read data Y and update data Z). By including the operation code in the privacy policy, more restrictions can be imposed in addition to the security policy where the operation allowed for a data item is also according to the purpose of the query. For instance considering the example described in Section 3.2, user X from BrightStar has rights to update item *account rate*. However, depending on the purpose of X's query, X is allowed to write on *rate* when creating a new credit card (purpose *approve credit card*), and only to read this information when determining credit score (purpose *credit evaluation*).

4 Privacy Maps

A *privacy map* is proposed to store privacy preferences and practices for XML documents.

Let Λ be the set of leaf nodes from the tree associated with an XML document schema, Ψ the set of purposes for data collection, and Δ the set of data providers. The set of collectors is symbolized by Υ and includes also third party recipients that may obtain data from the original collector. In this approach we consider close privacy policies where all permissions are specified in the policy.

Definition 6. *[Privacy Practice Map (PPraM)] The privacy practice map is a function $PPraM : \Lambda \times \Psi \times \Upsilon \to \alpha \times \beta \times \Omega$.*   ∎

PPraM expresses collectors privacy practice. For each leaf node, $\lambda \in \Lambda$ an access code $a \in \alpha$ and an operation code $b \in \beta$ are specified in relation to each query purpose $\psi \in \Psi$. If the operation code is for conditional access (R, C, or Q), then conditions $\omega \in \Omega$ are specified; otherwise no condition is considered (ϕ). The traditional $r+$ and $r-$ for read allowed/denied are extended to (Y, r, ϕ), (N, r, ϕ), and $(C/R/Q, r, conditions)$.

Example 1. Two examples of practice statements from PPraM are depicted below for node SIN *when its instances are queried with purposes* data mining *and* purchase habits*:*

   PPraM (SIN, data mining, BrightStar) = (R,r, "permanent/temporary resident")
   PPraM (SIN, purchase habits, BrightStar) = (N, r, ϕ).

Definition 7. *[Privacy Preference Map (PPreM)] The privacy preference map is a function $PPreM : \Lambda \times \Psi \times \Delta \times \Upsilon \to \alpha \times \Omega$.*   ∎

PPreM is a collection of privacy preferences. It specifies the access code $a \in \alpha$ and the conditions associated with it (if any) $\omega \in \Omega$ for each leaf node $\lambda \in \Lambda$ for purposes $\psi \in \Psi$. The recipient $\upsilon \in \Upsilon$ is specified for cases where third parties query private data stored by the collector.

Example 2. An example of a preference from PPreM for an instance of node SIN *storing private information about provider John Doe when it is queried with purpose* payment *is PPreM (SIN = "123 456 789", purchase habits, John Doe, BrightStar) = (N, r, ϕ) or (N, , ϕ) where no access and, thus, no operation (space) and no condition ϕ is granted to BrightStar when querying data provided by John Doe with purpose* purchase habits*.*

The proposed privacy model P4A for XML is depicted in Figure 2. P4A extends the *Purpose constraints* table proposed in Section 3.3 by having two materializations: PPraM and PPreM. Additional privacy metadata is formed by two relations $Recipient - constraints < \Upsilon, \Psi, retention >$ and $User - constraints < U, \Upsilon >$, where U is the set of users. The first shows recipients allowed to retrieve data for different purposes, and the second depicts connections between users and collectors/recipients.

Let $\lambda \in \Lambda$ be a leaf node from an XML schema, $\psi \in \Psi$ a query purpose, and $u \in U$ a user authorized to retrieve data for recipient $\upsilon \in \Upsilon$. A data

	Privacy Practice Policy
PPraM	$< \Lambda, \Psi, \Upsilon, \alpha, \beta, \Omega >$
Recipient-constraints	$< \Upsilon, \Psi, retention >$
User-constraints	$< U, \Upsilon >$
	Provider Privacy Policy
PPreM	$< \Lambda, \Psi, \Delta, \Upsilon, \alpha, \Omega >$

Fig. 2. P4A privacy model

	T	H	E	M	P	V	S	A
clients								
client *								
clientID	N	N	N	N	N	N	N	N
personalInfo								
name	Yr	Cr	Yr	N	N	Yr	Yr	N
dateOfBirth	Yr	Rr	N	Rr	N	N	Rr	N
SIN	Yr	N	Cr	Rr	N	Yr	N	N
accountNo	N	Cr	Cr	N	Cr	Cr	N	Yw
limit	N	Yr	Qr	Rr	N	Cr	N	Yw

Fig. 3. Extras from Privacy Practice Map (PPraM)

request is expressed by the set $Q(\lambda, \psi, u, v)$. The privacy practice (PPraM, Recipient-constraints, and User-constraints) is first queried and the answer is $Q(\lambda, \psi, u, v) = (a, b, \omega)$, where $a \in \alpha$, $b \in \beta$, and $\omega \in \Omega$. If $a \in \{R, C, Q\}$ additional conditions are included in the query as *where* clauses (see Table 3) and the query becomes Q_{PPreM}. It is next performed on PPreM if $a \neq N$ with $Q_{PPreM} < \lambda, \omega_{PPraM}, \psi, v >$, where ω_{PPraM} represents the conditions specified in PPraM for leaf node λ. The answer to Q_{PPreM} is the set $< \lambda, a_i, \omega_i, \delta_i >$, where δ_i is the subset of data providers where $a_i \neq N$ in PPreM for the queried leaf node λ. Only for those the query is executed on the data document.

4.1 Privacy Practice Map (Schema Level Statements)

PPraM contains schema level authorizations defined by collector with respect to purposes for which data is collected. Figure 3 depicts an example of PPraM where access codes and operations are attached to each leaf node. The capital letters refer to access codes and the small letters to the operations allowed for each purpose. Consider the second leaf node, *name*, that has assigned the codes Yr Cr Yr N N Yr Yr N meaning that no access is allowed when querying with purposes M, P, and A, unconditional access when query purpose is T, E, V, and S, and conditional access when purpose is H. The allowed operations for purposes with permission are specified using small letters: read (r). The operation code is omitted if the access is denied and is represented by a space in Figure 3.

If the access code is C then a condition must be specified. Table 4 depicts conditional privacy statements expressed by BrightStar. For example, queries

Table 4. Some conditions associated with PPraM

Node	Purpose	Access code	Condition	Perturbed value or range interval
name	H	C	know clientID	
dateOfBirth	H, M, S	R	age < 21 /21..59 / > 59	youth / mature / elder
SIN	E	C	know name, dateOfBirth, and address	
	M	R	first digit of SIN ≠ 9 / = 9	permanent / temporary resident
limit	E	Q	know clientID and limit ≤ 500 / 500.. 2000 / > 2000	bad/ OK / good credit
	M	R	limit ≤ 500 / 500.. 2000 / > 2000	bad/ OK / good credit
	V	C	know clientID	

```
1 <privacyPolicy>
2   <purpose = "T" description = "Income Tax">
3     <recipients>
4       <recipient ="Canada Revenue" retention = "5 years"/>
5     </recipients>
6   </purpose>
7 </privacyPolicy>
```

Fig. 4. Extras from privacy extended schema: purposes, recipients, and retention time (Collector's Recipient-constraints)

```
1 <element name="clientID" type="string" access="NNNNNNNN" operation=""/>
2 <element name="personalInfo">
3   <element name="name" type="string" access="YCYNNYYN" operation="rrr--rr-">
4     <conditionID purpose="H"> 1 </conditionID>
5   </element>
6   <element name="dateOfBirth" type="string" access="YRNRNNRN" operation="rrr--rr-">
7     <rangeID purpose="H"> 1 </rangeID>
8     <rangeID purpose="M"> 1 </rangeID>
9     <rangeID purpose="S"> 1 </rangeID>
10  </element>
```

Fig. 5. Extras from privacy extended schema clients.xsd: definition of elements, access and allowed operations (Collector's Purpose-constraints)

with purpose H are executed on transaction and its subnodes only if transaction date is more than one year old. Access code R requires one or more conditions to specify the interval values (i.e., when dateOfBirth is queried with purposes H,M, or S age intervals are retrieved as in Table 4). Access codes Q combine the requirements of both codes C and R (i.e., values retrieved for card limit in queries with purpose E, when clientID is known, are bad, OK, or good credit). This means that a query with purpose E that tries to retrieve *limit* for all clients will not be executed. Instead, queries address to a specific client are performed if the correct client ID is provided.

Fragments of the XML Schema for PPraM presented in Figure 3 are depicted in Figures 4 and 5. Attributes *privacyPolicy*, *purpose*, *access*, and *operation* are added to the extended XML Schema for the collector to specify the purpose of

```
1 <conditions>
2   <condition>
3     <conditionID> 1 </conditionID>
4       <restriction>
5         for \$x in doc("clients.xml") /clients/client/personalInfo
6           where \$x/clientID=\$clientID
7           return \$x/name
8       </restriction>
9   </condition>
10 </conditions>
```

Fig. 6. Fragment from the XML presentation of the conditions in PPraM Ω

```
1 <pertubedValues>
2   <range>
3     <rangeID> 1 </rangeID>
4       <restriction>
5         for \$x in doc("clients.xml") /clients/client/personalInfo/dateOfBirth
6           return if ((\$x-\$currentDate) < 21)
7             then <age> youth </age>
8             else if ((\$x-\$currentDate) > 59)
9                 then <age> elder </age>
10                else <age> mature </age>
11      </restriction>
12  </range>
```

Fig. 7. Fragment from the XML presentation of the perturbed values in PPraM Ω

data collection, access codes, and operations allowed for data query (Figures 4 and 5). Purposes are specified once at the beginning of the XML Schema (Figure 4) in the element named *<privacyPolicy>* . Each entry specifies a purpose name (for example in line 2, *purpose = "T"*) and its description (*description = Income Tax*). The attributes "access" and "operation" are added in the nodes' description in addition to attributes name, type and max/minOccurs (Figure 5 lines 1, 3, 6). Each entry in the *access* and *operation* attributes correspond to a purpose defined in the <privacyPolicy> element and in the order specified there. The associated set Ω of conditions and restrictions is specified in Figures 6 and 7 using XQuery syntax. The value in Figure 6 for client ID identified by the XQuery variable $clientID (line 6) is required by conditions and collected through application from users. Figure 7 gives an example of a *Perturbed Values* structure where restrictions are defined for *age* to return values such as *youth, elder, mature* calculated based on the current date and the date of birth. In PPraM Purpose-restrictions, perturbed values are specified using references to data stored in *Perturbed Values* structure (see Figure 5 lines 4, 7, 8, and 9). This technique minimizes redundancy in restriction specifications as identical conditions are specified once.

4.2 Privacy Preference Map (Data Level Authorizations)

Preferences expressed by data providers are stored in PPreM. Each data provider defines their own privacy policy according to which data is accessed. A schema denial does not allow access to an attribute regardless of the data provider authorization. A schema permission allows access to data parts with data permission. In conflict resolution denials have a higher priority than permissions. Schema and data level restrictions (C, R, and Q) specified for a node must be both satisfied before allowing access to data.

For example, suppose data provider A allows access to item *limit* to queries with purpose *data mining*. Also, suppose at the schema level queries with purpose *data mining* are authorized to access attribute *limit* as an approximate value (see Figure 3). The collector's privacy policy requires only an approximate value, so data is retrieved as an interval or perturbed value. During query execution before each value of the attribute *limit* is retrieved its privacy authorization must be checked.

In P4A privacy maps, each attribute value has attached multiple access authorizations, one for each purpose defined in document schema. From this perspective, our approach is similar to polyinstantiation [13] [15]: multilevel databases provide multiple "aspects" of each data called instances; our data document provides multiple authorizations for each piece of data. In polyinstantation there are multiple access rights to each node, one access right for each clearance level (top secret, secret, public, *etc.*). Data is accessible or not depending on the user authorization and the node clearance level. In privacy, there are multiple access codes for each node, one access code for each purpose. A node is transparent or not to a query depending on the purpose and the access code assigned to it. However, in our approach there is a single "materialization" of data as oppose to multiple instantiations in multilevel databases.

```
<clients>
  <provider id="A">
  <client>
    <clientID>111</clientID>
      <personalInfo>
        <name>John Doe</name>
        <dateOfBirth>01-01-1954</dateOfBirth>
        <SIN>123 456 789</SIN>
        <address>
          <street>123 First St</street>
          <city>Calgary</city>
        </address>
      </personalInfo>
  </client>
  </providerID>
</clients>
```

Fig. 8. Data document clinets.xml

```
<clients>
  <provider id="A">
  <client>
    <clientID pref="">111</clientID>
      <personalInfo>
        <name pref="YCCNNCNN"/>
        <dateOfBirth ="YRNRNNNN"/>
        <SIN pref="YNCRNYNN"/>
        <address>
          <street pref="NNYRNNYNN"/>
          <city pref="NYYYNYNN"/>
        </address>
      </personalInfo>
  </client>
  </providerID>
</clients>
```

Fig. 9. PPreM associated with clients.xml

Figures 8 and 9 depict a fragment of the XML data file and corresponding preferences of provider A. Provider's preferences are specified through attribute *pref* automatically generated from the extended XML Schema. We suggest that privacy concerned XML editors and parsers accept attribute *pref* in XML documents without requiring its description in XML schema. Thus, privacy preferences are always portable together with data.

5   Conclusion and Future Work

Each XML database must have in place a mechanism to express and ensure privacy protection. This paper proposes a new privacy model based on an extension of XML schema that includes purposes definition and node access codes. The use of P4A gives data providers means to express their privacy preference regarding the limited use of private data. This model offers more flexibility than current approaches in that it allows unconditional and conditional access. Data providers can agree to the collector practice or impose their own privacy preferences.

We are working on implementing our proposed model and evaluate its efficiency. Further, several algorithms must be developed to reduce the privacy overhead and create compressed privacy maps. A social study should be conducted to evaluate the difficulty of expressing complex privacy constraints for non-computer related data providers. More complex or simpler conditions could be found necessary to consider in future approaches.

References

1. The Canadian Oxford Dictionary. The foremost authority on current Canadian English. Oxford University Press, Reading (1998)
2. Aggarwal, G., Bawa, M., Ganesan, P., Garcia-Molina, H., Kenthapadi, K., Mishra, N., Motwani, R., Srivastava, U., Thomas, D., Widom, J., Xu, Y.: Vision paper: Enabling privacy for paranoids. In: Proceedings of the 30th VLDB Conference, Toronto, Canada, pp. 708–719 (2004)
3. Agrawal, R.: Privacy in data systems. In: PODS 2003, p. 37 (2003)
4. Agrawal, R., Kierman, J., Srikant, R., Xu, Y.: Hippocratic databases. In: Proceedings of the 28th VLDB Conference 2002, Hong Kong, China, pp. 143–154 (2002)
5. World Wide Web Consortium. The Platform for Privacy Preferences 1.0 (P3P1.0) specification (April 16, 2002) (Last checked on July 14, 2005),
   http://www.w3.org/TR/P3P/
6. Coyle, K.: P3P: Pretty Poor Privacy? A social analysis of the Platform for Privacy Preferences (P3P) (June 1999) (Last checked on July 14, 2005),
   http://www.kcoyle.net/p3p.html
7. Elmasri, R., Navathe, S.B.: Fundamentals of database systems (2007)
8. Center for Democracy and Technology. P3P and privacy: An update for the privacy community (March 28, 2000) (Last checked July 14, 2005),
   http://www.cdt.org/privacy/pet/p3pprivacy.shtml
9. Karjoth, G., Schunter, M., Waidner, M.: The platform for enterprise privacy practices: Privacy-enabled management of customer data. In: Dingledine, R., Syverson, P.F. (eds.) PET 2002. LNCS, vol. 2482, Springer, Heidelberg (2003)

10. Kaufman, J.H., Edlund, S., Ford, D.A., Powers, C.: The social contract core. In: Proceedings of the 11th ACM International Conference on World Wide Web, Hawaii, May 2002, pp. 210–220 (2002)

11. LeFevre, K., Agrawal, R., Ercegovac, V., Ramakrishnan, R., Xu, Y., DeWitt, D.: Limiting disclosure in hippocratic databases. In: Proceedings of the 30th VLDB Conference 2004, Toronto, Canada, pp. 108–119 (2004)

12. Lorch, M., Proctor, S., Lepro, R., Kafura, D., Shah, S.: First experiences using XACML for access control in distributed systems. In: XMLSEC 2003: Proceedings of the 2003 ACM workshop on XML security, pp. 25–37. ACM Press, New York (2003)

13. Lunt, T.F., Denning, D.E., Schell, R.R., Heckman, M., Shockley, W.R.: The SeaView security model. IEEE Transactions on Software Engineering 16, 593–607 (1990)

14. Massacci, F., Mylopoulos, J., Zannone, N.: Hierarchical hippocratic databases with minimal disclosure for virtual organizations. VLDB Journal 15(4), 370–387 (2006)

15. Rjaibi, W., Bird, P.: A multi-pupose implementation of mandatory access control in relational database management systems. In: Proceedings of the Thirtieth International Conference on Very Large Data Bases, Toronto, Canada (2004)

16. Walters, G.J.: Privacy and security: An ethical analysis. ACM SIGCAS Computers and Society 31(2), 8–23 (2001)

Privacy-Aware Collaborative Access Control in Web-Based Social Networks

Barbara Carminati and Elena Ferrari

Department of Computer Science and Communication
University of Insubria
22100 Varese, Italy
{barbara.carminati,elena.ferrari}@uninsubria.it

Abstract. Access control over resources shared by social network users is today receiving growing attention due to the widespread use of social networks not only for recreational but also for business purposes. In a social network, access control is mainly regulated by the relationships established by social network users. An important issue is therefore to devise *privacy-aware* access control mechanisms able to perform a controlled sharing of resources by, at the same time, satisfying privacy requirements of social network users wrt their relationships. In this paper, we propose a solution to this problem, which enforces access control through a collaboration of selected nodes in the network. The use of cryptographic and digital signature techniques ensures that relationship privacy is guaranteed during the collaborative process. In the paper, besides giving the protocols to enforce collaborative access control we discuss their robustness against the main security threats.

Keywords: Privacy-preserving data management, Web-based Social Networks, Collaborative access control.

1 Introduction

The last few years have witnessed the explosion of Web-based Social Network (WBSN) users [1]. WBSNs make available an information space where each social network participant can publish and share information, such as personal data, annotations, blogs, and, generically, resources, for a variety of purposes. In some social networks, users can specify how much they trust other users, by assigning them a trust level. Information sharing is based on the establishment of relationships of different types among participants (e.g., colleague of, friend of). However, the availability of this huge amount of information within a WBSN obviously raises privacy and confidentiality issues. For instance, in 2006, Facebook receives the complaints of some privacy activists against the use of the News Feed feature [2], introduced to inform users with the latest personal information related to their online friends. These complaints result in an online petition, signed by over 700,000 users, demanding the company to stop this service. Facebook replayed by allowing users to set some privacy preferences. More

V. Atluri (Ed.): DAS 2008, LNCS 5094, pp. 81–96, 2008.

recently, November 2007, Facebook receives other complaints related to the use of Beacon [3]. Beacon is part of the Facebook advertising system, introduced to track users activities on more than 40 web sites of Facebook partners. Such information is collected even when the users are off from the social-networking site, and is reported to users friends without the consent of the user itself. Even in this case, the network community promptly reacts with another online petition that gained more than 50,000 signatures in less than 10 days. These are only few examples of privacy concerns related to WBSNs. All these events have animated several online discussions about security and privacy in social networking, and government organizations started to seriously consider this issue [4,5,6,7].

To partially answer the security and privacy concerns of their users, recently some social networks, e.g., Facebook (http://www.facebook.com) and Videntity (http://videntity.org), have started to enforce quite simple protection mechanisms, according to which users can decide whether their data, relationships, and, generically, resources, should be public or accessible only by themselves and/or by users with whom they have a direct relationship. However, such mechanisms are not enough, in that they enforce too restrictive and/or too simple protection policies. There is, then, the need of enforcing more flexible strategies, making a user able to define his/her own rules, denoting the set of network participants authorized to access his/her resources and personal information, even though they are not directly connected through a relationship. Additionally, since WBSN information sharing is mostly based on the relationships existing among network participants, there is the need of protecting relationship information when performing access control. For instance, a user would like to keep private the fact that he/she has a relationship of a given type with a certain user. Therefore, in [8] we have proposed a framework to enforce client-side access control to WBSN resources, according to which the requestor must provide the resource owner with a *proof* of being authorized to access the requested resource. The proposed access control is *privacy-aware* in the sense that privacy requirements referring to relationships established by WBSN users are preserved when enforcing access control. Access control requirements are expressed in terms of relationship types, depths, and trust levels. In [8], relationships are encoded through certificates and their protection requirements are expressed through a set of *distribution rules*, which basically state who can exploit a certificate for access control purposes. Relationship privacy is enforced by encrypting a certificate with a symmetric key which is delivered only to users satisfying the corresponding distribution rule. Encrypted certificates are stored at a central node, which does not receive the corresponding decryption key, and therefore it is not required to be trusted. However, the mechanism proposed in [8] has the following shortcomings:

- It relies on a central node to store relationship certificates that may become a bottleneck and may be vulnerable to DoS attacks;
- The central node must be trusted wrt certificate revocation enforcement when a relationship does not exist anymore, in that, according to the architecture proposed in [8], the central node maintains a certificate revocation list which must be updated to reflect social network topology changes;

– As pointed out in [8], one of the drawback of client-side access control is that revealing access rules regulating access to the requested resource may compromise the privacy of resource owner relationships. The reason is that, when a user requests a resource, the resource owner replies with an access rule, which contains, among other information, the relationships in which the requestor must be involved in order to gain the access. If the owner wants to keep private some types of relationships he/she has with other network nodes, this mechanism could lead to privacy breaches.

To overcome these shortcomings, in this paper, we propose an alternative way of enforcing access control wrt the solution presented in [8]. Rather than using the client-side paradigm, access control is enforced through the collaboration of selected nodes in the network. The collaboration is started by the resource owner, on the basis of the access rules regulating the access to the requested resource. The owner contacts only the nodes that satisfy its distribution rules, thus avoiding the privacy breaches related to access rules distribution discussed above. The aim of the collaboration is to provide the owner with a *path*, proving that the requestor has the relationships required to gain access to the resource. Since each node taking part in the collaboration is aware of the relationships existing among the other nodes taking part in the process, the collaborative process is driven by the specified distribution rules: a node is invited to collaborate only if it satisfies the distribution rules of the other nodes taking part in the collaboration. Encryption and signature techniques are used to avoid trust levels disclosure and forgery, as well as to make a node able to verify the correct enforcement of distribution rules.

WBSN privacy and security is a new research area. Up to now, research has mainly focused on privacy-preserving techniques to mine social network data. The main goal of this research is to avoid as much as possible the disclosure of private information about WBSN members when analyzing WBSN data for statistical purposes [9,10,11,12]. In contrast, in the field of access control (apart from [8,14]) very little work has been so far reported. The only other proposal we are aware of is the one discussed in the position paper by Hart, Johnson, and Stent [13]. The access control model presented in [13] uses existing WBSN relationships to denote authorized members, however only the direct relationships they participate in are considered, and the notion of trust level is not used in access authorizations. Resources are not denoted by their identifiers, but based on their content. Information about resources' content is derived based on users' tags and by content analysis techniques. However, [13] does not provide any information about access control enforcement, nor they consider relationship privacy protection when enforcing access control, which is the focus of the current paper.

This paper builds on some previous work we have done in the field of privacy-aware access control in WBSNs. In particular, [14] presents the access control model on which the enforcement mechanism described in this paper relies. [8] adds to the model proposed in [14] the possibility of expressing privacy requirements on relationships established by WBSN users. However, in [8] access

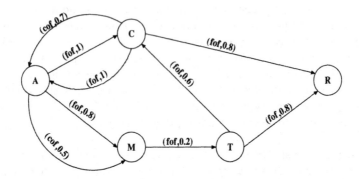

Fig. 1. A portion of a WBSN

control enforcement relies on a central node storing encrypted certificates to be used for gaining access to a resource. In the current paper, we propose an alternative enforcement mechanism, wrt the one presented in [8], where access control enforcement is obtained through a collaboration among selected nodes in the network.

The remainder of this paper is organized as follows. Next section introduces some preliminary concepts needed in the remainder of the paper. Section 3 presents our collaborative access control protocol, whereas Section 4 analyzes its security. Finally, Section 5 concludes the paper and outlines directions for future work.

2   Preliminary Concepts

In what follows, we model a WBSN $\mathcal{SN}$ as a tuple $(V_{\mathcal{SN}}, E_{\mathcal{SN}}, RT_{\mathcal{SN}}, T_{\mathcal{SN}}, \phi_{E_{\mathcal{SN}}})$, where $V_{\mathcal{SN}}$ and $E_{\mathcal{SN}}$ are, respectively, the nodes and edges of a graph, $RT_{\mathcal{SN}}$ is the set of supported relationship types, $T_{\mathcal{SN}}$ is the set of supported trust levels, and $\phi_{E_{\mathcal{SN}}}: E_{\mathcal{SN}} \rightarrow RT_{\mathcal{SN}} \times T_{\mathcal{SN}}$ is a function assigning to each edge $e \in E_{\mathcal{SN}}$ a relationship type $rt \in RT_{\mathcal{SN}}$ and a trust level $t \in T_{\mathcal{SN}}$. The number and type of relationships in $RT_{\mathcal{SN}}$ and trust levels in $T_{\mathcal{SN}}$ depend on the specific social network and its purposes. Similarly, each WBSN supports a different range and type of trust levels, corresponding either to a set of integers or rational numbers, or to Boolean values. In case a WBSN does not support trust, this means that all the nodes are equally trustworthy, and thus we assume that with each edge is associated the maximum level of trust. Given an in/direct relationship of type rel between nodes v and v', the trust level $t^{rel}_{vv'}$ denotes how much v trusts v' wrt relationship rel. We also assume the existence of a central node $\mathcal{CN}$ that is in charge of user registration and management.

Example 1. A simple example of WBSN is depicted in Figure 1. In the figure, the initial node of an edge is the node which established the corresponding relationship. Labels associated with edges denote, respectively, the type and trust level of the corresponding relationship. With reference to Figure 1, A(lex) is friend-of (fof) both C(arl) and M(ark). However, A trusts C more than M. A and T(ed) are indirect friends due to the fof relationships existing between A and M and M and T. C is also a colleague-of (cof) A, and the trust assigned to this relationship by C is 0.7.

Following the model proposed in [14], we assume that each resource rsc to be shared in the $\mathcal{SN}$ is protected by a set of *access rules*. Each access rule has the form (rid, AC), where AC is a set of *access conditions* that need to be all satisfied in order to get access to rid. An access condition is a tuple $(v, rt, d_{max}, t_{min})$, where v is the node with whom the requestor must have a relationship of type rt, whereas d_{max} and t_{min} are, respectively, the maximum depth, and minimum trust level that the relationship should have. The depth of a relationship of type rt between two nodes v and v' corresponds to the length of the shortest path between v and v' consisting only of edges labeled with rt. For instance, with reference to Figure 1, the depth of the fof relationship between A and R(obert) is 2. In contrast, the trust level associated with a path is computed by multiply all the trust levels associated with the edges in the path, even if other formulas to compute the trust level can be used as well. In this paper, we constrain the access conditions contained into an access rule by assuming that v can be only equal to the owner of the resource to be protected. As it will be clarified in what follows, this assumption makes the resource owner able to start the collaborative process needed to answer an access request. Additionally, this is not a too strong restriction because it is very common that most of the access control requirements in a $\mathcal{SN}$ are expressed by an owner in terms of the relationships it holds with other nodes in the network, rather than in terms of relationships in which it is not involved.

Like in [8], relationship privacy requirements are stated through *distribution rules*. A distribution rule on a relationship of type rt established by node A with node B, denoted in what follows as DR_{AB}^{rt}, is a triple of the form $(v, \overline{rt}, d_{max})$, stating that the only nodes authorized to be aware of the relationship of type rt established by A with B are those that have a relationship of type $\overline{rt}$ with v and maximum depth d_{max}. Similarly to access rules, in this paper we constrain distribution rules specification by assuming that v can only be A and that $\overline{rt}$ is fixed to the type of the relationship to which the distribution rule applies, that is, rt. For instance, given a relationship of type fof between A and B, the corresponding distribution rule DR_{AB}^{fof} should have the node component equal to A and the relationship type component equal to fof. Once again this restriction makes a node able to correctly enforce distribution rules when performing collaborative access control (see Section 3 for the details).

Example 2. Consider the WBSN in Figure 1. Suppose that doc_1 is a resource owned by A. Suppose that A wishes to make doc_1 accessible only to its direct or indirect friends of maximum depth three, with the constraint that their trust level must be at least equal to 0.8. These requirements can be expressed by the following access rule: $AR_1 = (doc_1, \{(A, fof, 3, 0.8)\})$. In contrast, suppose that A specifies the following distribution rule $DR_{AM}^{fof} = (A, fof, 3)$, this means that the relationship of type fof existing between A and M can be disclosed only to friends of A with maximum depth three, that is, M, T, R, and C. Finally, if M specifies the following distribution rule: $DR_{MT}^{fof} = (M, fof, 2)$, it means that the fof relationship existing between M and T can be seen only by M's direct friends and by the direct friends of M's direct friends, that is, T, R, and C.

We assume that each node n_i in a WBSN owns a key pair (SK_i, PK_i), where SK_i is the private key, whereas PK_i is the corresponding public key. We denote with $SK_i(x)$ (resp. $PK_i(x)$) the encryption of x with key SK_i (resp. PK_i). We further assume PK_i to be known by all the nodes wishing to getting in touch with n_i. Moreover, we assume that each time a node n_1 wishes to establish a relationship with another node n_2, it informs n_2 about that. Therefore, the corresponding relationship certificate is signed by both n_1 and n_2. This means that each node is aware of the relationships established with it by other nodes. We think that it is very important that a node is aware of the in-coming edges, since relationships are the basis of access control enforcement. Otherwise, a node can cheat and claim that it has a relation with others even if this is not true. For instance, if Bob is a close friend of the boss of a big company, Ann can establish a relation of type fof with him just to become an indirect friend of the boss. If Bob is not informed about that, there is no way of preventing this behaviour. However, the nodes are not aware of the trust levels of in-coming relationships, because we believe that this is a confidential information that shall be kept private (that is, a node n_1 might not want to reveal to another node n_2 how much it trusts it).

3   Collaborative Access Control

In this section, we illustrate our proposal for enforcing access control while preserving WBSN relationship privacy. We start by providing an overview of the approach, then we present the related protocols and an example of their execution.

3.1   Overview of the Approach

Differently from [8], access control is enforced through a *collaboration* among selected nodes in the $\mathcal{SN}$. The collaboration is needed to prove to the owner that the node requesting a resource satisfies the requirements (in terms of relationships it holds and corresponding trust levels and relationship depths) stated by the owner access rules. If the result of the collaboration is the identification of a path with the requirements stated by the owner access rules, then the access is granted. Otherwise, it is denied. The collaborative process is started by the owner, on the basis of the access rules regulating the access to the requested resource. This avoids the possible privacy breaches pointed out in the introduction due to distribution of access rules. In particular, the owner starts the collaboration by sending a request to its direct neighbours. More precisely, it contacts all the neighbours with which it has established a relationship of the type required by the access control rule associated with the requested resource, asking whether they have a relationship of the required type with the requestor node.

If a resource is protected by more than one access rule, the process is iterated till the access can be granted or till all the access rules have been considered. For simplicity, in the following, we assume access rules consisting only of one access condition. The protocols can be easily extended by iterating the described operations for all the access conditions contained in an access rule. Once a node different from the requestor receives a request for collaboration, it propagates the request to those of its neighbours with which it has established a relationship of the required type. This process is iterated until a node having a relationship of the required type with the requestor is reached, or until the request can no longer be propagated along the network.

To verify whether an access can be granted or not the owner must be provided not only with a path of the required type and depth, but it also must know the trust level of all the edges in the returned path. Therefore, when propagating the request for collaboration, a node forwards also the trust level of its relationship. To avoid that intermediate nodes are aware of the trust levels assigned by the nodes in the path, the trust level is encrypted with the owner's public key. Moreover, we also need a mechanism to avoid that a node can repudiate the trust level it has inserted and, therefore, to minimize as much as possible the insertion of fake trust levels. To this purpose, each node signs the encryption of the trust level it has inserted.

Since each node adds its identity to the path it receives before sending it to the subsequent node, each node in the path from the owner to the requestor is aware of the relationships existing among the nodes in the path, and this could not respect the privacy requirements that a node might have on its relationships. For this reason, the collaboration process is driven by the specified distribution rules. More precisely, a node is required by another node to participate in a collaboration only if it satisfies the distribution rules associated with *all* the relationships in the path built so far. Thus, before propagating the request for collaboration to a neighbour node, a node must verify whether the neighbour satisfies all the distribution rules associated with the relationships in the path built so far. Introducing distribution rules enforcement in collaborative access control requires to devise a mechanism avoiding untrusted nodes to require collaboration of neighbour nodes even if they do not satisfy distribution rules in the path, or at least making it possible to detect misbehaviours. To this purpose, we use signature techniques. In particular, a node attaches to the request for collaboration sent to one of its neighbours, the distribution rule for the relationship it discloses and its signature over it. Moreover, it digitally signs all the signed distribution rules contained in the received message, referring to previously disclosed relationships. As it will be clear in the following section, this sort of "*onion signature*" makes a node able to detect if all the previous nodes in the path have correctly enforced the distribution rules.

3.2   Access Control Protocol

As stated in the previous section, access control enforcement is obtained through a collaboration among nodes in the $\mathcal{SN}$. The collaboration has the aim of identifying a *path* in the $\mathcal{SN}$ satisfying the requirements stated by the access rules specified for the requested resource. The notion of path is formalized as follows.

Definition 1 (Relationship path). *Let* $\mathcal{SN} = (V_{\mathcal{SN}}, E_{\mathcal{SN}}, RT_{\mathcal{SN}}, T_{\mathcal{SN}}, \Phi_{E_{\mathcal{SN}}})$ *be a WBSN. A relationship path in* $\mathcal{SN}$ *is a pair* $(rt, node\_list)$, *where* $rt \in RT_{\mathcal{SN}}$ *is a relationship type and node_list is an ordered list* $\langle n_1, \ldots, n_k \rangle$, $n_1, \ldots, n_k \in V_{\mathcal{SN}}$ *of* $\mathcal{SN}$ *nodes such that for each pair* $n_i, n_{i+1} \in node\_list$, $i = 1, \ldots, k-1$, *there exists an edge* $(n_i, n_{i+1}) \in E_{\mathcal{SN}}$ *labeled with relationship type rt.*

In what follows, we use the dot notation to refer to specific components within a tuple.

Since the nodes to be contacted are selected on the basis of the distribution rules defined for the relationships in the path built so far, each node receiving a partial path must be aware of the corresponding distribution rules. Moreover, each node receiving a request to collaborate must be able to verify whether previous nodes in the path have correctly enforced the distribution rules for all the relationships in the path. To this purpose, each node that takes part in the collaborative process inserts in the message to be sent to the subsequent node the distribution rule associated with the relationship it inserts into the relationship path, as well as its signature. Additionally, it signs all the signatures of the distribution rules contained in the message it receives, if it verifies that they all have been correctly enforced by previous nodes. Distribution rules and corresponding signatures for the relationships in a path are stored into a data structure called *Onion signature*, defined next. In what follows, we denote with $Sign_i(x)$ the signature of node n_i over x.

Definition 2 (Onion signature). *Let* $p = (rt, node\_list)$ *be a relationship path for a social network* SN, *where* $node\_list = \langle n_1, \ldots, n_k \rangle$. *The Onion signature data structure for path p, denoted as* $Onion\_signature(p)$, *is an ordered list of pair* $(DR^{rt}_{n_i n_{i+1}}, Signature_i)$, $i = 1, \ldots, k-1$ *where* $DR^{rt}_{n_i n_{i+1}}$ *is the distribution rule specified by node* n_i *for the relationship of type rt connecting* n_i *to* n_{i+1}, *whereas* $Signature_i = Sign_k(Sign_{k-1}(\ldots Sign_i(DR^{rt}_{n_i n_{i+1}})))$.

Example 3. Consider the WBSN of Figure 1 and the distribution rules of Example 2. The following is an example of relationship path: $(\text{fof}, \langle \text{A}, \text{M}, \text{T} \rangle)$ stating that there is an indirect *fof* relationship between A and T. According to the distribution rules introduced in Example 2. The corresponding onion signature is: $\langle ((\text{A}, \text{fof}, 3), Sign_T(Sign_M(Sign_A(\text{A}, \text{fof}, 3)))), ((\text{M}, \text{fof}, 2), Sign_T(Sign_M(\text{M}, \text{fof}, 2)))\rangle$.

Enforcement of collaborative access control is performed by Algorithm 1. The resource owner, upon receiving an access request, retrieves from its Policy Base the access rules regulating the access to the requested resource (step 1). For simplicity, in the algorithm, we assume a single access rule consisting only of one access condition. The algorithm can be easily extended to more access rules, each one consisting of more than one access condition, by simply iterating the steps we are describing in what follows. Then, the owner identifies the set of

Algorithm 1. The collaborative access control protocol

INPUT: An access request (req, res) submitted to node own by req
OUTPUT: res, if req satisfies the access control requirements of own,
         an access denied message otherwise.
1. own retrieves from its Policy Base the access rule AR associated with resource res
2. Let $AC = (own, rt, d, t)$ be the access condition in AR
3. Let C_nodes be the set of nodes with which own established a relationship of type $AC.rt$
4. **Foreach** $n \in C\_nodes$:
     (a) $p := (rt, \langle own \rangle)$
     (b) $msg\_res := SendCollReq(\{req, own, p, \langle (DR^{rt}_{ownn}, Sign_{own}(DR^{rt}_{ownn})) \rangle\}, n)$
     (c) $i := msg\_res$
     (d) **While** $(i \neq \emptyset)$:
         i Let $\overline{msg}$ be the i-th received message containing a path
         ii **If** $check\_DR(\overline{msg}.path, \overline{msg}.onion\_sign) = \emptyset$:
             1. Let $depth$ be the depth of $\overline{msg}.path$
             2. Let $trust$ be the trust computed by using the trust values in $\overline{msg}$
             3. **If** $trust \geq AC.t$ and $depth \leq AC.d$: **Return** res
         EndIf
         iii $i := i$ -1
     EndWhile
endfor
5. **Return** *access denied*

---

nodes with which it has established a relationship of the type rt required by the access condition contained in the considered access rule (step 3). It iteratively considers (step 4) each node in this set and sends it a message to start the collaboration process. The message, sent by function $SendCollReq()$ in step 4.b, contains the owner and requestor identifiers, the distribution rule associated with the relationship of type rt existing between the owner and the receiving node, the signature of the distribution rule generated by the resource owner, and the path built so far (which consists only of the owner itself).

Once the message has been sent, the algorithm waits for the node reply, which consists of a null value, if no path satisfying the stated confidentiality and privacy requirements can be found, or the number of identified paths, otherwise. In case $SendCollReq()$ returns a not null value, a message containing each of the identified paths is sent to the owner (see procedure $path\_builder()$ in Figure 2 explained next). The message contains information on the identified paths (e.g., the nodes composing it, the corresponding trust levels and the onion signature). The algorithm first verifies whether all the nodes in the received path have correctly enforced the signed distribution rules contained in the message (step 4.d.ii). This is done by function $check\_DR()$, presented in Figure 3. If the check succeeds, the algorithm computes the depth of the received path and its trust level and, if they both satisfy the constraints stated in the access rule, the access is granted (step 4.d.ii.3). Otherwise the process is iterated on the next received message, until there are no more message to be processed. Then, if the access has not been granted, the collaboration is requested to the next node in the set identified in step 3, until the access is granted or all the nodes in the set have been contacted, without finding a suitable path. In this case, the access is denied (step 5).

Procedure $path\_builder(n,msg)$

1. Let $sender$ be the node from which message msg has been received
2. Let $Distr\_rules$ be the set of distribution rules contained in msg
3. **If** $check\_DR(msg.path, msg.onion\_sign) = \emptyset$:
       (a) Let TOT_msg_res be initialized to 0
       (b) Let C_nodes be the set of nodes with which n has established a relationship of type $msg.path.rt$
       (c) **If** $C\_nodes = \emptyset$:
           Send TOT_msg_res to $sender$
           Return
       endif
       (d) **Foreach** $\overline{n} \in C\_nodes$:
           i **If** $\overline{n}$ satisfies all rules in $Distr\_rules$:
               1. Let $\overline{msg}$ be a copy of msg
               2. Update $path$ in $\overline{msg}$ by adding n
               3. Add $PK_{own}(t_{n\overline{n}}), Sign(PK_{own}(t_{n\overline{n}}))$ to $\overline{msg}$
               4. Replace the onion signature in $\overline{msg}$ with $Onion\_signature(\overline{msg}.path)$
               5. **If** $\overline{n} = msg.req$:
                   (a) **If** $msg.own$ satisfies all rules in $Distr\_rules \cup DR_{\overline{n}\overline{n}}^{msg.path.rt}$:
                       i Send $\overline{msg}$ to $msg.own$
                       ii $TOT\_msg\_res := TOT\_msg\_res + 1$
                   endif
                   else
                       $msg\_res := SendCollReq(\overline{msg}, \overline{n})$
                       $TOT\_msg\_res := TOT\_msg\_res + msg\_res$
               endif
       endfor
       (e) Send TOT_msg_res to $sender$
else:
       (f) Send $msg\_res = \emptyset$ to $sender$
       (g) Send(n,msg,$check\_DR(msg.path, msg.onion\_sign)$) to $msg.own$ and CN
endif

Fig. 2. Procedure $path\_builder()$

Each time a node n receives a request for collaboration, it executes procedure $path\_builder()$, presented in Figure 2. The procedure processes the received message and decides the next action to be performed. In particular, it initializes variable TOT_msg_res to zero (step 3.a). This variable is used to store the number of identified paths. Then, the procedure identifies the nodes with which n has established a relation of the type rt of the relationship path contained into the received message (step 3.b). If this set is empty, it halts by returning TOT_msg_res to the sender, since no other path can be found (step 3.c).

Otherwise, for each node $\bar{n}$ in the computed set, it verifies whether $\bar{n}$ satisfies all the distribution rules contained into the received message (step 3.d.i). In this case, n updates the received message, by adding itself to the path, and the encrypted and signed trust level of the relationship between n and $\bar{n}$. It also updates accordingly the onion signature contained into the received message. Then, it verifies whether $\bar{n}$ is the requestor node (step 3.d.i.5). If this is the case, n verifies whether the owner satisfies all the distribution rules in the received message plus the distribution rule regulating the disclosure of the relationship existing between n and $\bar{n}$.

If this is the case, it sends the updated message to the owner and updates accordingly variable TOT_msg_res. In contrast, if $\bar{n}$ is not the requestor node, n sends it the collaboration request and updates accordingly variable TOT_msg_res. When all the possible requests of collaboration have been sent and the corresponding replies received, n sends TOT_msg_res to the sender (step 3.e).

Before processing the received message, $path\_builder()$ verifies whether all the nodes in the path received as input have correctly enforced the signed distribution rules contained into the received message (step 3). In case this check fails, n notifies the owner and the $\mathcal{CN}$ that one or more nodes have not correctly enforced the specified distribution rules contained in the received message (step 3.g). This information can be used to perform subsequent actions against the malicious nodes (e.g, notification to other nodes of their incorrect behaviours, temporary banning from the WBSN and so on).

Checking the correct enforcement of distributions rule is done by function $check\_DR()$ illustrated in Figure 3. $check\_DR()$ takes as input the path contained in the message and the corresponding onion signature and returns the set of nodes, if any, which did not correctly enforce the distribution rules. If the returned set is empty it means that all the nodes in the path have correctly enforced the corresponding distribution rules.

3.3   An Illustrative Example

Consider the $\mathcal{SN}$ shown in Figure 1 and the access and distribution rules of Example 2 and suppose that R requires doc_1 to A. According to the protocols described in Section 3, A first of all retrieves from his Policy Base the access rules regulating the access to doc_1, i.e., $AR_1 = (doc_1, \{(A, fof, 3, 0.8)\})$. According to Algorithm 1, A contacts his fof neighbours. Let us suppose it starts to contact node M by sending it a message containing the following components:

- path $p = (fof, \langle A \rangle)$;
- $req = R$, $own = A$;
- $\texttt{onion\_sign} = \langle ((A, fof, 3), Sign_A((A, fof, 3))) \rangle$, where $(A, fof, 3) = DR_{AM}^{fof}$.

Once M receives the request for collaboration message, it runs procedure $path\_builder$ (cfr. Figure 2). The procedure first checks the correct enforcement of the distribution rules in the path, by verifying the onion signature data structure through function $check\_DR()$ (see Figure 3); then, it considers the only node with

---

Function *check_DR(path, onion_sign)*

1. *Bad_nodes* := ∅
2. Let l be the length of *path.node_list*
3. **For** $i = 1$ **to** l:
   (a) *flag* := 0; k := 0
   (b) Let DR be the distribution rule in *onion_sign[i]*
   (c) Let *sign* be the signature in *onion_sign[i]*
   (d) **For** $j = l$ **to** i:
       i **If** *validate_sign(node_list[j],sign)* = 0:
          1. Add *node_list[j]* to *Bad_nodes*
          2. *flag* :=1
          3. **Break**
       endif
       ii $k := k + 1$
   endfor
   (e) **If** *flag* ≠ 1:
       i **If** $k > DR.d_{max} + 1$:
          1. **For** $y = i + DR.d_{max}$ **to** l: Add *node_list[y]* to *Bad_nodes*
endfor
4. **Return** *Bad_nodes*

Fig. 3. Function *check_DR()*

which M has a relationship of type *fof*, that is, T. It verifies whether T satisfies the distribution rules in the received message, the only one is (A,fof,3) which is satisfied by T. Therefore, it adds itself to the path and it inserts $PK_A(t_{MT}^{fof})$ in the message, that is, the encryption of the trust level M has assigned to T with the public key of the resource owner. Moreover, it updates the onion signature data structure as follows: $\langle((A,fof,3),Sign_M(Sign_A((A,fof,3)))),((M,fof,2),$ $Sign_M((M,fof,2))))\rangle$, where (M,fof,2) = DR_{MT}^{fof}. Then, since T is not the requestor node, M sends the request for collaboration to T. T first of all verifies the received onion signature. Then, it determines the set of its *fof* neighbours, that is, {C,R}. It selects one of the node in this set, suppose R, and verifies whether it satisfies all the distribution rules contained into the received message. Since the check succeeds, it updates the path by inserting itself, it updates the received message by adding $PK_A(t_{TR}^{fof})$ and it updates the onion signature data structure by adding and signing DR_{TR}^{fof}. Moreover, it signs all the distribution rules contained into the received onion signature. Since R is the requestor node, T verifies whether A satisfies all the distribution rules contained into the received message plus DR_{TR}^{fof}. In this case, A does not satisfy DR_{MT}^{fof} = (M,fof,2),[1] therefore T tries to build a valid path by contacting its other *fof* neighbour, that is, C. However, when C receives the message, it verifies that R does not satisfy one of

---

[1] According to the semantics of the distribution rules introduced in [8], A satisfies DR_{MT}^{fof} = (M,fof,2) if there exists a *fof* path of length not greater than 2, having M as source node and A as terminal node.

the distribution rules in the received message, that is, DR_{MT}^{fof}, thus it sends a null message to T.[2] Since T does not have any other node to contact, it sends a null message back to M, which in turn sends a null message back to the owner A. Therefore, A contacts its other friend, that is, C by sending it a message similar to the one sent to M and consisting of the following components:

- path $p = (fof, \langle A \rangle)$;
- $req = R$, $own = A$;
- onion_sign=$\langle((A,fof,4),Sign_A((A,fof,4)))\rangle$, where $(A,fof,4)=DR_{AC}^{fof}$;[3]

Once C receives the request for collaboration, it first checks the correct enforcement of the distribution rules in the path, then it verifies whether R satisfies DR_{AC}^{fof}. Since this is the case, it adds itself to the received path and it inserts in the message $PK_A(t_{CR}^{fof})$, that is, the encryption of the trust level C has assigned to R with the public key of the resource owner. Moreover, it updates the onion signature data structure as follows: $\langle((A,fof,4),Sign_C(Sign_A((A,fof,4)))),((C,fof,3),$ $Sign_C(C,fof,3))\rangle$, where $(C,fof,3) = DR_{CR}^{fof}$. Since R is the requestor node, C verifies whether A satisfies all the distribution rules in the updated message. Since the check succeeds, it sends the updated message to A, as well as a message containing the value 1. Upon receiving the 1 message, A processes the other message received by C. It first verifies the correctness of the contained onion signature data structure, then it computes the trust level of R on the basis of the trust levels contained into the received message. According to Figure 1, $t_{AR}^{fof} = 1 * 0.8 = 0.8$. The length of the received path is 2. Thus, $AR_1 = (doc_1, \{(A,fof,3,0.8)\})$ is satisfied and therefore R can access doc_1.

4   Security Analysis

In this section, we discuss the robustness of our system against possible attacks. As adversary model, we assume that the adversary is a node in the SN which can collude with other network nodes to attack the system. To keep the discussion simple, in this paper we have not complemented the proposed protocols with techniques generally used to protect data during transmission. However, we are aware that the current version of the proposed protocols can be subject to eavesdropping and replay attacks. These kinds of attacks can be easily avoided adopting well-know mechanisms [15]. Therefore, the main attacks that a node can perform during collaborative access control are the following:

- Learn the trust level of previous nodes in the path.
- Alter the received trust level or insert a fake one.
- Incorrectly enforce distribution rules.

---

[2] Note that, C may not be aware of the fof relationship between T and R, and therefore, by considering only the information in the received message, it deduces that DR_{MT}^{fof} is not satisfied by R.

[3] In this example, we assume that the distribution rule specified by A for the fof relationship with C is $DR_{AC}^{fof} = (A,fof,4)$, whereas the distribution rule specified by C for the fof relationship with R is $DR_{CR}^{fof} = (C,fof,3)$.

Let us consider all the above three attacks in details. Trust levels forwarded among nodes are encrypted with the public key of the resource owner. As such, provided that the computational power of a node does not make it able to break the cryptosystem, each intermediate node in the path is not able to gain access to the trust levels. The fact that each node in the path signs the trust level it sends to the next node provides non-repudiation of the inserted trust levels. Additionally, if a node alters the trust level inserted by another node it can be detected by either the owner or any node in the path, since this alteration invalidates the node's signature.

Finally, the onion signature data structure makes a node able to verify whether the previous nodes in the path have correctly enforced the distribution rules. This is performed by function $check\_DR()$ by performing two different checks for each distribution rule DR (see Figure 3 for the details). First, the function verifies whether all the nodes have properly signed DR (step 3.d.i). This makes sure the owner that all nodes are aware of distribution rule DR. If the signature of a node n fails to be validated, $check\_DR()$ informs the owner and CN that n did not have correctly performed the protocol. The second check performed by function $check\_DR()$ over DR verifies the constraint on the maximum depth specified in the distribution rule (step 3.e.i). This check makes the owner sure that the distribution rule DR, and as a consequence the corresponding relationship, have been disclosed only to nodes whose distance from the node n stating DR is less than or equal to the maximum depth stated in DR. All the nodes disclosing DR and having distance from n greater than the maximum depth in the rule are reported to the owner and CN as bad nodes.

It is relevant to note that if two or more nodes collude, they can validate the onion signature of previous nodes even if the corresponding distribution rules are not correctly enforced. However, since each node in the path verifies the distribution rules, the set of nodes that have to collude to perform the attack could be very large. Moreover, a final check on the correct distribution rule enforcement is made by the resource owner (Algorithm 1, step 4.d.ii).

5   Conclusions

In this paper we have presented a protocol on support of privacy-aware access control in WBSNs, based on a collaboration of selected nodes in the network. The protocol is based on the use of cryptographic and digital signature techniques, and ensures that relationship privacy is guaranteed during the collaborative process.

We plan to extend the work reported in this paper along several directions. First, an implementation of the collaborative access control protocol is currently under way. In the actual version of the prototype the WBSN nodes are implemented as Web services, whereas the system interface available to users is provided as an extension to the Mozilla Firefox browser. However, we plan to investigate as future work how the API defined by Google OpenSocial initiative [16] can be integrated into the current prototype. The prototype will make us able to test the feasibility of the proposed methods for different social network topologies and application domains. In particular, our techniques are not meant for general-purpose WBSNs (like for instance Facebook or MySpace). Rather, our target scenarios are social networks used at the intranet level or by virtual organizations, that is, geographically distributed organizations whose members are bound by a long-term common interest or goal, and who communicate and coordinate their work through information technology. This is in line with the emerging trend known as Enterprise 2.0 [17], that is, the use of Web 2.0 technologies, like blogs, wikis, and social networking facilities, within the Intranet, to allow for more spontaneous, knowledge-based collaboration. Therefore, we plan to test our prototype implementation in these reference scenarios.

We also plan to investigate how our collaborative access control enforcement can be deployed when access control paradigms different from the one considered in this paper are used (e.g., audit-based access control [18]).

Acknowledgements

The work reported in this paper is partially funded by the European Community under the QUATRO Plus project (SIP-2006- 211001).

References

1. Staab, S., Domingos, P., Mika, P., Golbeck, J., Ding, L., Finin, T.W., Joshi, A., Nowak, A., Vallacher, R.R.: Social networks applied. IEEE Intelligent Systems 20(1), 80–93 (2005)
2. Chen, L.: Facebook's feeds cause privacy concerns. the amherst student (October 2006), http://halogen.note.amherst.edu/ astudent/2006-2007/issue02/news/01.html
3. Berteau, S.: Facebook's misrepresentation of beacon's threat to privacy: Tracking users who opt out or are not logged in. Security Advisor Research Blog (2007), http://community.ca.com/blogs/securityadvisor/archive/2007/11/29/facebook-s-misrepresentation-of-beacon-s-threat-to-privacy-tracking-users-who-opt-out-or-are-not-logged-in.aspx
4. Canadian Privacy Commission: Social networking and privacy (2007), http://www.privcom.gc.ca/information/social/index_e.asp
5. EPIC: Social networking privacy (2008), http://epic.org/privacy/socialnet/default.html
6. Federal Trade Commission: Social networking sites: A parents guide (2007), http://www.ftc.gov/bcp/edu/pubs/consumer/tech/tec13.shtm
7. Hogben, G.: Security issues and recommendations for online social networks. Position Paper 1, European Network and Information Security Agency (ENISA) (2007), http://www.enisa.europa.eu/doc/pdf/deliverables/enisa_pp_social_networks.pdf
8. Carminati, B., Ferrari, E., Perego, A.: Private relationships in social networks. In: ICDE 2007 Workshops Proceedings, pp. 163–171. IEEE CS Press, Los Alamitos (2007)

9. Backstrom,C.D.L., Kleinberg, L.: Wherefore art thou r3579x? anonymized social networks, hidden patterns, and structural steganography. In: Proceedings of the World Wide Web Conference (2007)
10. Frikken, K.B., Golle, P.: Private social network analysis: How to assemble pieces of a graph privately. In: Proceedings of the 5th ACM Workshop on Privacy in Electronic Society (WPES 2006), pp. 89–98 (2006)
11. Hay, M., Miklau, G., Jensen, D., Weis, P., Srivastava, S.: Anonymizing social networks. Technical Report 07-19, University of Massachusetts Amherst, Computer Science Department (2007)
12. Zheleva, E., Getoor, L.: Preserving the privacy of sensitive relationships in graph data. In: Proceedings of the 1st ACM SIGKDD International Workshop on Privacy, Security, and Trust in KDD (PinKDD 2007) (2007)
13. Hart, R.J.M., Stent, A.: More content - less control: access control in the web 2.0. In: Proceedings of the Web 2.0 Security and Privacy Workshop (2007)
14. Carminati, B., Ferrari, E., Perego, A.: Rule-Based Access Control for Social Networks. In: Meersman, R., Tari, Z., Herrero, P. (eds.) OTM 2006 Workshops. LNCS, vol. 4278, pp. 1734–1744. Springer, Heidelberg (2006)
15. Stallings, W.: Network security essentials: applications and standards. Prentice Hall, Englewood Cliffs (2000)
16. OpenSocial, G.: Opensocial api v0.7,
    http://code.google.com/apis/opensocial/articles/persistence.html
17. McAfee, A.: Enterprise 2.0: The dawn of emergent collaboration. MITSloan Management Review 47(3), 21–28 (2006)
18. Cederquist, J., Corin, R., Dekker, M., Etalle, S., den Hartog, J., Lenzini, G.: Audit-based compliance control. International Journal of Information Security 6(2-3), 133–151 (2007)

A Privacy-Preserving Ticketing System

Kristof Verslype[1], Bart De Decker[1], Vincent Naessens[2],
Girma Nigusse[1], Jorn Lapon[2], and Pieter Verhaeghe[1]

[1] Katholieke Universiteit Leuven, Department of Computer Science,
Celestijnenlaan 200A, 3001 Heverlee, Belgium
firstname.lastname@cs.kuleuven.be
[2] Katholieke Hogeschool Sint-Lieven, Department of Industrial Engineering
Gebroeders Desmetstraat 1, 9000 Gent, Belgium
firstname.lastname@kahosl.be

Abstract. Electronic identity (eID) cards are deployed in an increasing number of countries. These cards often provide digital authentication and digital signature capabilities, but have at the same time serious privacy shortcomings. We can expect that ordering and issuing tickets for events (e.g. soccer matches) will be increasingly done using eID cards, hence, severely threatening the user's privacy. This paper proposes two alternative ticketing systems that are using the eID card in a bootstrap procedure, but still are providing a high degree of privacy to the user.

Keywords: Privacy, Anonymity, Security, Ticketing, Electronic Identity cards.

1 Introduction

Tickets are used for an innumerable number of events: soccer matches, music festivals, exhibitions, etc. These tickets are ever more bought electronically. An increasing number of countries issue electronic identity cards to their citizens. Examples are Belgium, Estonia and Austria. These eID cards usually allow the holder to authenticate and to digitally sign documents, but often, they are very privacy unfriendly. For example, authentication using the Belgian eID card will usually lead to the divulgement of important personal data such as your national registration number (NRN). Despite these privacy dangers, the use of the eID card is promoted by the governments. We can thus expect that in the near future, electronic ticketing systems will arise based on the eID card. A trivial solution is easy to devise. However, this solution is not acceptable because it further endangers the card holder's privacy as profiles can easily be compiled, linked to each other and to the identity of the card holder. An advantage of the use of eID cards is that it is straightforward to impose restrictions on the maximum number of tickets that can be bought by one user, hence, thwarting sales on black markets. Sometimes, special offers are available for buyers under or over a certain age or living in the region where the event is organized. Here too, eID cards can help in securely conveying (proving) that these conditions

V. Atluri (Ed.): DAS 2008, LNCS 5094, pp. 97–112, 2008.

are satisfied for the buyer. However, the use of these cards will usually disclose more information than is required.

For big events with thousands of attendants, the police would be helped if tickets were not anonymous, but could be linked to the identity of the attendants, or at least to the identity of the buyers of these tickets. Especially, when rows or riots occur, it would make it easier to identify and prosecute the instigators. However, the use of tickets attributable to individuals poses severe privacy risks and brings us closer to a "Big Brother" state.

This paper proposes two solutions where the eID card is needed to obtain an anonymized permit, allowing a user to obtain tickets in a privacy friendly way. The role of the eID card is thus reduced to a bootstrapping role. A first solution is based on pseudonym certificates, i.e. X.509 certificates containing a user's nym instead of a real identity. A second solution is based on the more enhanced anonymous credential systems, which allow to anonymously disclose only a subset of the personal attributes (or properties thereof) embedded in the credential. Both solutions are validated and compared with the trivial solution and with each other.

The main requirements are given in section 2. Section 3 introduces the required technologies. Section 4 explains notations and specifies the assumptions. Sections 5, 6 and 7 discuss the trivial protocol and two privacy friendly alternatives and are followed by a comparison in section 8. Sections 9 and 10 examine the related work, draw the conclusions and describe future work.

2   Requirements

The requirements are now summed up. F4 and F5 are optional.

Functional/Security Requirements

F1. Every event may have a policy that limits the number of tickets obtainable by one buyer. The policy may discriminate between different groups of buyers.

F2. Event organizers may choose to offer a subscription for a series of events.

F3. Every event can have a pricing policy that differentiates between different groups of buyers (e.g. youngsters or elderly people).

F4. When abuse is detected or when serious incidents happen during the event, it should be possible to identify the buyer of the ticket(s) involved, but only with a court order.

F5. Individuals who have been imposed a banning order for a particular event type, should not be able to buy tickets for this kind of events.

Privacy Requirements

P1. Buyers of tickets should not directly be identifiable.

P2. Except when subscriptions are used, it should not be possible to compile buyer's profiles.

P3. It should not be possible to identify an individual on a blacklist.

3   Technologies

The main technologies required in this paper are pseudonym certificates, anonymous credentials, commitment schemes and provable one-way functions.

3.1   Pseudonym Certificates

Pseudonym certificates [1] are traditional certificates where the identity information is replaced by a pseudonym. The certificate states that the identity of the user referred to by that pseudonym and the properties certified in the certificate have been verified by the issuer. Different shows of the same certificate are linkable, which can undermine anonymity.

The relevant functions for both classical and pseudonymous certificates are:

- $U \leftrightarrows I$: $Cert \leftarrow$ issueCertificate($attributes$). I issues a certificate $Cert$ to U. I knows the certificate $attributes$, but not the private key corresponding to $Cert$. Pseudonyms, ids, expiry date, etc. are also considered attributes.
- $U \rightarrow V$: authenticate($Cert$). U proves possession of $Cert$ to verifier V. As a result, V gets to know all the attribute values embedded in $Cert$.

Enhanced Pseudonymous Certificates. We further extend the privacy without requiring considerable computational capabilities by replacing each certificate attribute att that contains personal properties (date of birth, social security number, etc.) by $H(att, \text{RANDOM})$. Showing such an enhanced pseudonym certificate thus only reveals personal data if the owner of the certificate also discloses the corresponding (att, RANDOM) tuple to the verifier. Evidently, the linkability issue persists.

3.2   Anonymous Credentials

Anonymous credential systems ([2], [5], [6]) allow for anonymous yet accountable transactions between users and organizations and allow for *selective disclosure* by showing properties of credential attributes (e.g. $age > 18$) while hiding all the other credential attribute information. In the Idemix system [5], different usages of the same credential are *unlinkable* (except when unique attribute values are revealed). Credentials can have features such as an expiry date, the allowed number of times it can be shown and the possibility to be revoked. A mix network ([10], [11]) is required to provide for anonymity at the network layer.

The (simplified) anonymous credential protocols relevant in this paper are:

- $U \leftrightarrows O$: $(Nym, Sig) \leftarrow$ generateSignedNym($Cert$). One can establish multiple non-transferable pseudonyms (i.e. nyms) with the same organization. Here, the user signs the established Nym giving O a provable link between the nym and the identity certified in $Cert$.
- $U \leftarrow I$: $Cred \leftarrow$ issueCredential(Nym, $attributes$). A credential is issued by I on a pseudonym Nym. The credential is known only to the user and cannot be

shared. Also, a number of attributes, not necessarily known by I, is embedded into the credential.

- $U \leftrightarrows V$: *transcript* $\leftarrow$ authenticate(*Cred, properties,* [*DeanCond*], [*Msg*]). A user U authenticates to verifier V by proving possession of a valid credential *Cred*. U can selectively reveal credential attributes or properties thereof. The resulting transcript for V may be deanonymizable upon fulfillment of condition *DeanCond* (cfr. the deanonymize()). U may decide to sign a message *Msg* with his credential by a provable link between the transcript and the message. Different transcripts for the same credential are unlinkable (unless the value of a unique attribute is proved).
- $U \rightarrow V$: prove(*properties*). Simplified notation of the above function. *Properties* will refer to the credential used in the proof.
- D: (*Nym, DeanProof*) $\leftarrow$ deanonymize(*transcript, condition*). If a credential show is deanonymizable, the pseudonym *Nym* on which the credential was issued can be revealed by a trusted deanonymizer D. *DeanProof* proves the link between the transcript and the nym. D is only allowed to perform the deanonymization when *condition* fulfills *DeanCond* (included in the transcript).

3.3 Commitments

A commitment [7,14] hides one (or more) values. Later the committer can open the commitment, or prove properties of the committed value(s). The following (simplified) commitment methods are relevant:

- (*Com, OpenInfo*) $\leftarrow$ commit(*attribute*). A new commitment containing a single attribute is generated as well as the opening info required to prove properties about the commitment (or to open it).
- $U \rightarrow V$: prove(*Com, properties, OpenInfo*). Prove properties of commitments.

3.4 Provable One-Way Functions

We define a provable one-way function $out \leftarrow f(in)$ as a one-way function whereof the one knowing in can prove that he knows a in such that $out = f(in)$ in a zero-knowledge proof. Multiple arguments are possible as well.

As an example, according to the DL assumption, $out \leftarrow g^{in} \bmod p$ is such a function for p prime and g a generator of a multiplicative group with order q with $q|p-1$ and p and q sufficiently large.

4   Assumptions and Notation

The general assumptions and notation w.r.t. the protocols are now summed up.

4.1   Assumptions

- For every protocol, a server always first authenticates to U using a classical X.509 certificate. Also, an integrity and confidentiality preserving connection

is established during a protocol. Anonymity at the network layer is added
when necessary.

- A ticketing server can service multiple events. However, for each event, there
  is only one ticketing server.
- Tickets do only contain a ticket identifier (e.g. event name, date and seat
  number) and are unforgeable.

4.2 Notation

- Each protocol requires the following roles: user U (client), ticket server T
  (issues tickets to users), event organizer E and the court of justice J.
- $U \leftrightarrows B \leftrightarrows T$: (PayProof$_U$, PayProof$_T$) ← pay($price$, Msg). U pays an
  amount of money, via an intermediary bank B, to T. A message can be
  linked to the payment. The bank can deliver proofs of the payment to both
  parties. The payment protocols can preserve U's privacy.
- $U \leftrightarrows T$: ($desc[]$, $price$, [$Proof$]) ← negotiate($Cert \vee Cred$, $Nym \vee Id$, $event$,
  $eventPolicy$, $\#tickets$, $specification$) allows U and T to agree on the exact
  seat numbers as well as on the total price. Therefore, U gives an identifier (Nym or Id), shows (properties of) credential/certificate attributes. The
  event policy can state e.g. that people younger than 18 get reductions. Evidently, the number and (general) specification of the tickets are given as
  well. The restrictions on the blacklists can further constrain the possibilities
  of the user. U can give T a proof of the agreement (signed by $Cert$ or $Cred$).
- O: Nym ← retrieveOrGenerateNym($Id \vee Nym^*$) returns a newly generated
  nym if the user refered to by Id or Nym^* does not yet have a nym with O.
  However, if that user already has been given a nym in the past, it is simply
  retrieved from O's local storage system.
- T: Restrictions ← retrieveRestrictions($Blacklist$, $Nym \vee Id$). T looks up in a
  blacklist the restrictions of a person referred to by Nym or Id.
- G: Restriction[] ← getRestrictionBooleans(Id) implicitly uses all blacklists,
  and returns for each event type whether or not the user is blacklisted or not.
- Other, self explaining methods are: add(), lookup(), store (), update () and
  generateTickets().

5   Trivial eID-Based Solution

Without alternatives, this protocol will most likely be implemented in Belgium
as the government is really promoting the use of the eID card in commercial
applications. However, this protocol has serious privacy drawbacks.

U uses his eID card to authenticate to T, revealing a lot of personal data
to T. A government agency G maintains a blacklist containing identifiable user
ids. This blacklist is checked by T before issuing tickets.

The user authenticates to T using his eID card. T first checks whether the
user is blacklisted. Based on the user's id and personal attributes, the user can
be given the possibility to buy a number of tickets as a result of the negotiation
phase. After the payment and ticket issuance, T finally stores ticket selling info.

Identification in case of abuse is straight forward since T knows the *link* between the seat (or ticket) and the user's id.

The functional/security requirements are trivially fulfilled. However for the privacy requirements, this protocol fails completely. T knows the user's id and all other attributes contained in the eID certificate (P1). User profiling is trivial for T as well as sharing and linking of profiles (P2). The users' NRNs are on the blacklist (P3). In addition, many countries simply forbid blacklists on which users are identifiable due to privacy legislation. Deployment will often thus result in omitting the F5 requirement.

6 Solution Based on Enhanced Pseudonym Certificates

6.1 Introduction

This approach improves the privacy of the user by introducing pseudonymous permits. First, each user is issued a unique pseudonymous root certificate by the government. This allows the user to obtain pseudonymous permit certificates from different permit servers. One permit server could for instance be responsible for one event type (e.g. soccer matches). With such a pseudonymous permit a user can buy tickets for events that happen in a small (permit specific) time period[1]. The user will thus most likely need multiple permits. The blacklists no longer contain user identifiers, but pseudonyms.

6.2 Roles

Besides the already defined U, T and E, a government agency G is needed to issue root certificates and a permit server PS issues permit certificates.

6.3 Assumptions

- All certificates contain a unique serial number, a pseudonym or id, a public key and an expiry date.
- There can be many pseudonym servers (PS) and many ticket servers (T).
- For every event, the ticket server (T) accepts permits issued by a limited set of pseudonym servers. However, the user sets of different pseudonym servers do not overlap (necessary for requirement F1).
- Only one entity G can issue valid pseudonymous root certificates.
- Nyms that are no longer valid, are forgotten by the permit server.

High Level Description and Data Structures. The user receives a pseudonymous root certificate (Cert^R), which contains a rootnym (Nym^R) and possibly other attributes (such as year of birth, citizenship, place of residency, ...). Cert^R is used to authenticate to the permit server PS.

---

[1] The fixed time period is introduced to minimize linkabilities.

The user can apply to the PS for a pseudonym (Nym^P) that is valid during a predefined time period. Nym^P will be certified in a (pseudonymous) permit certificate ($Cert^P$). Each certificate also contains a public key used to verify authentications with $Cert^P$, and possibly (properties of) other attributes that were copied from the root certificate ($Cert^R$). Using permit certificates with non-overlapping time-slots, each user can have at most one valid $Cert^P$ to order tickets for a particular event. The PS can refuse permits to users who have been sentenced to a banning order for events supported by the PS.

6.4 Protocols

Getting a Root Certificate. A governmental instance G assigns to each citizen one root pseudonym Nym^R. The first time U requests a root certificate $Cert^R$, a new Nym^R is generated and included in $Cert^R$. In case the user was already assigned a Nym^R in the past, that pseudonym is retrieved from G's local storage instead. G finally stores the user's NRN and $Cert^R$s (which include Nym^R).

Getting a Permit Certificate. U authenticates with a valid root certificate $Cert^R$ to the PS. PS will issue a number of permit certificates $Cert^P$s which have to be used before a (user specified) date (validThru). For instance, the user can request permit certificates that allow him to buy soccer tickets for the upcoming year. PS generates a set of nyms (Nym^R) or retrieves them (if they were already assigned in the past): one nym per time period[2]. Each nym Nym^P is also certified in a permit certificate $Cert^P$ which also contains a validity period (for Nym^P), possibly a set of attributes, and an encryption of the user's root pseudonym Nym^R. The validity periods of Nym^Ps are non-overlapping. Hence, users cannot buy tickets for the same event using different nyms. Also, when a user requests a new permit for the same period (e.g. because the previous one was lost or the private key was stolen), PS will always use the same nym (Nym^P). Each $Cert^P$ contains a probabilistic encryption of Nym^R with the public key of J. This allows law enforcement to eventually identify the user involved in case of abusive behavior (see further). PS finally updates the list of $Cert^P$s that are issued to Nym^R. PS can derive the time intervals for which a Nym^R has obtained a valid $Cert^P$ from that list.

Buying Tickets for an Event. The user first authenticates to the ticket server T using the permit certificate $Cert^P$ that is valid for that specific event and specifies the number of tickets he wants to order. T then obtains the restrictions associated with Nym^P on the blacklist. The user and the ticket server agree on the price of the tickets and the seats, based on the user's nym, allowing to limit the number of tickets for that user. The limitations and price can depend on certain attributes that are embedded in the permit certificate (such as the user's age) and on the restrictions on the blacklist. Finally, the ticket server updates the number of tickets that are sold to Nym^P for that event.

---

[2] The length of the non-overlapping time periods is chosen by the PS in such a way that the number of events that fall in each period is limited.

Updating Anonymous Blacklists. To fulfill requirement F4, anonymous blacklists are used. Four entities are involved in updating blacklists (see table 2).

A law enforcement entity J forwards the court orders (NRN, Restrictions) to G. G substitutes the NRNs with the corresponding Nym^{R}s and forwards the list to the permit server PS. PS can then add Nym^R to a blacklist for certain event types (i.e. PS will no longer issue Cert^{P}s to Nym^R for the event types that are specified in the blacklist).

Finally, PS retrieves the valid Nym^{P}s for each Nym^R with a banning order, substitutes every Nym^R-record in the blacklist with a number of Nym^P-records and forwards the new list to the ticket server T. T no longer issues tickets to pseudonyms in the blacklist. Note that the ticket service can even revoke tickets that were already issued to pseudonyms in the blacklist.

Identifying Buyer of a Ticket. To reveal the identity of a participant with a specified seat number, the ticket service T looks up the Nym^P of the user that ordered the ticket. The corresponding permit certificate Cert^P is kept by the ticket server and is passed to J. The latter can link Cert^P to Nym^R (as Nym^R is encrypted with the public key of J in Cert^P). G can reveal the user behind Nym^R (as G knows the mapping between NRN and Nym^R).

Increasing Privacy with Enhanced Pseudonym Certificates. For each personal attribute *att* in Cert^R, G can include the hash value $H(att, rand_G)$ in Cert^R instead, where $rand_G$ is a random value. Each $rand_G$ is sent to U as part of the issuance of Cert^R. After authentication by U to a PS with Cert^R, the user sends to PS the $rand_G$ value of those attributes of Cert^R that need to be included in the Cert^P certificate. In a similar way, PS includes hash values using freshly generated $rand_{PS}$ values in the new Cert^P. This allows U to selectively disclose personal attributes to T. More complex constructions are possible as well, but are not discussed in this paper.

6.5   Evaluation

F1. This requirement is easily fulfilled as each user has only one Nym^{P}to buy tickets for a particular event.

F2. If Nym^P can be used to order tickets for multiple events (e.g. multiple soccer games during a World Cup contest), T can even restrict the total number of tickets that can be bought for the whole contest (i.e. a set of events).

F3. A user can get a lower price for some tickets based on the attribute values of Cert^P. However, tickets can be passed on. Hence, T should be careful with price reductions.

F4. Fulfilled (cfr. *"Identifying buyer of a ticket"* protocol).

F5. Three entities are needed to ban a user from event types for which a user already has a permit certificate, namely G, PS and T. Two entities are needed to ban a user from event types for which a user does not yet have a permit certificate, namely G and PS.

Table 1. Protocols with pseudonym certificates

(1.a) Getting a pseudonymous root certificate Cert^R

(1) U → G	:	authenticate(eID)
(2) G	:	$\text{Nym}^R \leftarrow$ retrieveOrGenerateNym(eID.NRN)
(3) U ← G	:	$\text{Cert}^R \leftarrow$ issueCertificate({Nym^R, attributes ... })
(4) G	:	store [eID.NRN, Cert^R]

(1.b) Getting a permit certificate Cert^P

(1) U → PS	:	authenticate(Cert^R)
(2) U → PS	:	validThru, *attributes to include*
(3) PS	:	$\forall$ [from,till], from $\leq$ validThru:
(4) PS	:	$\text{Nym}^P \leftarrow$ retrieveOrGenerateNym($\text{Cert}^R.\text{Nym}^R$, [from,till])
(5) U ← PS	:	$\text{Cert}^P \leftarrow$ issueCertificate({Nym^P, [from,till], *attributes*,
		enc_{pk_J}(RANDOM $\|$ $\text{Cert}^R.\text{Nym}^R$)})
(6) PS	:	store [$\text{Cert}^R.\text{Nym}^R$. [from,till], Cert^P]

(1.c) Buying tickets

(1) U → T	:	authenticate(Cert^P)
(2) U → T	:	event, #tickets, specification
(3) T	:	Restrictions $\leftarrow$ retrieveRestrictions($\text{Cert}^P.\text{Nym}^P$, EventType)
(4) U ⇆ T	:	(SeatNb[], price) $\leftarrow$ negotiate($\text{Cert}^P.\text{Nym}^P$, event, #tickets,
		eventPolicy, Cert^P.attr, specification, [Restrictions])
(5) U, T	:	if (SeatNb[] = ⊘) **abort**
(6) U ⇆ B ⇆ T	:	pay(price, Hash(SeatNb[], ...))
(7) U ← T	:	tickets[] $\leftarrow$ generateTickets(SeatNb[])
(8) T	:	update [Cert^P, event, tickets[]]

P1. As discussed in *"Identifying buyer of a ticket"*, four entities are needed to reveal the user's identity. Moreover, G (and maybe PS) are governmental instances. Hence, users can trust that players in the commercial sector (such as E and T) cannot identify users without help of governmental instances.

P2. Each Nym^P only has a limited validity period. The number of tickets that is issued to the same Nym^P is restricted. Hence, T and E can only compile limited profiles. PS can link all Nym^Ps to the same Nym^R. However, multiple pseudonym servers PS can be used. If each PS can only issue permit certificates for specific types of events, the one PS cannot link multiple interests of the same Nym^R. Moreover, no PS obtains more personal attributes than needed. Only a subset of the attributes in Cert^P are revealed to T by U when the latter wants to buy a ticket. Evidently, different Ts affiliated with the same PS can collaborate in order to get hold of more personal attribute values.

P3. Only Nym^Rs and Nym^Ps are kept in blacklists.

Table 2. Protocols with pseudonym certificates (bis)

(2.a) anonymizing the blacklists		
(1) $J \to G$	:	[NRN, Restrictions, eventType]
(2) G	:	$\text{Nym}^R \leftarrow \text{lookupNym}(\text{NRN})$
(3) $G \to PS$	:	[Nym^R, Restrictions, eventType]
(4) PS	:	$\text{Nym}^P \leftarrow \text{lookupNym}(\text{Nym}^R, \text{eventType})$
(5) $PS \to T$	:	[Nym^P, Restrictions, eventType]
(2.b) Identifying buyer of a ticket		
(1) $J \leftarrow E$	:	complaint, seatNb
(2) $J \to T$	:	event, seatNb
(3) $J \leftarrow T$	:	[Cert^P, event, ticket] $\leftarrow$ lookup(event, seatNb)
(4) J	:	(RANDOM $\|$ Nym^R) $\leftarrow$ $\text{dec}_{prk_J}(\text{Cert}^P.\text{enc})$
(5) $J \to G$	:	Nym^R
(6) $J \leftarrow G$	:	NRN $\leftarrow$ lookup(Nym^R)

7   A Ticketing System Based on Anonymous Credentials

7.1   Introduction

We further increase the user's privacy. The user needs a single permit - issued by a government agency - which allows the user to buy tickets for every event. In case of abuse, the transcript resulting from the permit show can be deanonymized. For each event type, there is a privacy-preserving blacklist, summing up the user's rights restrictions.

7.2   Roles

Besides U, E, T, and J, we define G as a government agency that issues permits and manages blacklists.

7.3   Assumptions

In the ticketing system based on anonymous credentials, we assume the following:

- The anonymous credential system provides the unlinkability property to permits. The user does not reveal identifiable permit attribute properties.
- All Es and all Ts and G have a unique, publicly available provable one-way function; $f^E()$ for E, $f^T()$ for T and $f^G(.\,,\,.)$ for G. Note that the latter requires two arguments. These functions could for instance be included in their X.509 certificate.

- The opening info generated by a commit method does not reveal any information about the content contained in the commitment. This is easily achieved using a symmetric key K:
  $Com^{new} \leftarrow (Com, enc_K(OpenInfo))$ and $OpenInfo^{new} \leftarrow K$ combined with integrity preserving measures (e.g. MACs).

7.4   High Level Description

The permit is an anonymous credential containing a set of personal attributes, a boolean value for each event type indicating whether or not the user is blacklisted, and two nyms. One nym (Nym^R) is known to G and used to blacklist persons. The other nym (Nym^P), is not known to G, but is used to generate an event specific nym, allowing T to keep track of the number of tickets sold to that person for that specific event.

Per event type, a blacklist is maintained by G. This blacklist contains user pseudonyms (Nym^Rs). These nyms are converted to event specific nyms (Nym^Es) before the blacklist is sent to a specific T in order to avoid linkabilities.

7.5   Protocols

Getting an Anonymous Permit Certificate. The actual issue of the permit (3.a.5) includes a subset of the user's personal attributes (*attributes*) contained in the user's eID. These can be selectively disclosed during a credential show protocol.

The permit contains for each event type a boolean Restrictions[EventType] stating whether or not the user is blacklisted. G can easily extract this information out of the blacklists it manages (cfr. below).

Each permit contains two user unique pseudonyms Nym^R and Nym^P. Nym^R is known to both U and G and is the nym under which the permit is issued by G. G possesses a provable link Sig^R between the U's id and his Nym^R. This can be used in case of disputes.

The second pseudonym in the permit, Nym^P, is known to the user U only and is included in the permit as an attribute that is not known to G. This is done using a commitment, whereof U proves that he knows the corresponding *UserSecret* and Nym^P (underlined in table 3) such that $Nym^P \leftarrow f^G(Nym^R, UserSecret)$.

To obtain a new permit, after the previous one was lost, step 6 changes. After recalculating $Nym^P \leftarrow f^G(Nym^R, UserSecret)$ and generating a new commitment $Com2 \leftarrow \text{commit}(Nym^P)$ (Step 4 and 5), U decrypts c, resulting in the opening info of the previous commitment. This allows U to prove that $Com.Nym^P = Com2.Nym^P$ (corresponds to step 6), convincing G that the same Nym^P was used.

Buying a Ticket. For each ticket order, U sends $Nym^E \leftarrow f^E(Nym^P)$ to T and proves possession of the corresponding Nym^P (3.b.1,2). The use of one-way functions gives the user for each event a different, but event-unique nym. This gives T the possibility to limit the number of tickets per user while at the same time, this function avoids linking of T's customers to the customers of other Ts. Collusion with G does not help, because G does not even know Nym^P.

When ordering a ticket, the user proves that he is not blacklisted by showing Restrictions[EventType]. If U is blacklisted, he sends $\mathrm{Nym}^T \leftarrow f^T(\mathrm{Nym}^R)$ to T and proves that Nym^T is correctly formed with $\mathrm{Cred}^P.\mathrm{Nym}^R$. T now looks up the exact restrictions associated with Nym^T on the blacklist (3.b.3). This limits linking possibilities and possible collusion with G. The latter can only be done for blacklisted Us.

The negotiation phase (3.b.4) requires the user's permit as input, such that RequestProof can be generated. RequestProof is a proof for G that U did request the negotiated tickets at the negotiated price. This proof is also deanonymizable by J which provably reveals Nym^R.

Blacklist Maintenance and Retrieval. A law enforcement entity J forwards the court orders (NRN, Restrictions) to G. G substitutes the NRNs with the

Table 3. Protocols with anonymous credentials

(3.a) Getting the first anonymous permit certificate Cred^P		
(1) U → G	:	authenticate(eID)
(2) G ⇆ U	:	$(\mathrm{Nym}^R, \mathrm{Sig}^R) \leftarrow$ generateSignedNym(eID.NRN)
(3) G	:	Restriction[] ← getRestrictionBooleans(eID.NRN)
(4) U ⇆ G	:	$\mathrm{Nym}^P \leftarrow f^G(\mathrm{Nym}^R, \mathit{UserSecret})$
(5) U → G	:	$(\mathit{Com}, \mathit{OpenInfo}) \leftarrow$ commit(Nym^P)
(6) U → G	:	Com, prove($\underline{\mathit{Com}.\mathrm{Nym}^P} = f^G(\mathrm{Nym}^R, \underline{\mathit{UserSecret}}))$,
		$c \leftarrow enc_{H(\mathit{UserSecret})}(\mathit{OpenInfo})$
(7) U ⇆ **G**	:	$\mathrm{Cred}^P \leftarrow$ issueCredential(Nym^R, {$\mathit{Com}.\mathrm{Nym}^P$,
		Restriction[], $\mathit{attributes}$})
(8) G	:	store [eID.NRN, Nym^R, Sig^R, Com, c]

(3.b) Buying tickets		
(1) U → T	:	$\mathrm{Nym}^E \leftarrow f^E(\mathrm{Cred}^P.\mathrm{Nym}^P)$, event
(2) U → T	:	authenticate(Cred^P, {$\mathrm{Cred}^P.\mathrm{Nym}^P \simeq \mathrm{Nym}^E$,
		$\mathrm{Cred}^P.\mathrm{Restriction[EventType]}$})
(3) T	:	if($\mathrm{Cred}^P.\mathrm{Restriction[EventType]}$ == true) do
(3.a) U → T	:	$\mathrm{Nym}^T \leftarrow f^T(\mathrm{Cred}^P.\mathrm{Nym}^R)$
(3.b) U → T	:	prove($\mathrm{Nym}^T \simeq \mathrm{Cred}^P.\mathrm{Nym}^R$)
(3.c) T	:	Restrictions ← retrieveRestrictions($\mathrm{Blacklist}_T$, Nym^T)
(3.d) T	:	end if
(4) U ⇆ T	:	(SeatNb[], price, RequestProof) ← negotiate(Cred^P, event,
		Nym^E, #tickets, eventPolicy, [Restrictions])
(5) U ⇆ B ⇆ T	:	(PayProof$_U$, PayProof$_T$) ← pay(price, Hash(SeatNb[], ...))
(6) U ← T	:	tickets[] ← generateTickets(SeatNb[])
(7) T	:	update [event, Nym^E, RequestProof, tickets[]]

corresponding Nym^Rs. Each Nym^R is further converted to $\text{Nym}^T \leftarrow f^T(\text{Nym}^R)$ before the blacklist is sent to a specific T to avoid linkabilities and profiling by T (4.b).

Misbehaviour and Deanonymization. Protocol 4.c illustrates how the collaboration of E, T and G is required in order to obtain a (provable) link between the ticket and the user's id. The proof is (RequestProof, deanProof, Sig^R). If someone is put on a blacklist for EventType, his permit Cred^P is revoked. U can obtain a new Cred^P, with the updated restrictions booleans Restriction[EventType], immediately.

Table 4. Protocols with anonymous credentials (bis)

	(4.a) Maintaining the blacklists	
(1) $J \to G$	:	Nym^R, Restrictions, EventType
(2) G	:	Blacklists[EventType].add(Nym^R, Restrictions)
(3) $J \to G$	:	revokeCert(Nym^R)
	(4.b) Obtaining a blacklist	
(1) G	:	for each (Nym^R, Restrictions) in Blacklists[EventType]:
		Blacklist$_T$.add($f^T(\text{Nym}^R)$, Restrictions)
(2) $T \leftarrow G$	:	Blacklist$_T$
	(4.c) Identifying buyer of a ticket	
(1) $J \leftarrow E$	:	complaint, seatNb
(2) $J \to T$	:	event, seatNb
(3) $J \leftarrow T$	:	RequestProof $\leftarrow$ lookup(event, seatNb)
(4) J	:	Nym^R, deanProof $\leftarrow$ deanonymize(RequestProof, *complaint*)
(5) $J \to G$	:	(NRN, Sig^R) $\leftarrow$ lookup(Nym^R)

7.6 Evaluation

We now evaluate by checking the requirements

Functional and Security Evaluation

F1. $\text{Nym}^E \leftarrow f^E(\text{Nym}^P)$ enables T to link ticket orders of the same U for the same event.

F2. A subscription can be issued by T or a coordinating organization. It can be an anonymous credential that contains Nym^P, Nym^R, the Restriction[EventType] booleans and information about the subscription. It can be pseudonymously shown to a ticketing service in order to obtain tickets without a payment phase. Alternatively, a multiple-use ticket with an expiry date can be issued.

F3. The user can selectively disclose properties in the permit.

F4. is explained in section 7.5.

F5. is done using the anonymized blacklists. Revocation of tickets issued to persons that were blacklisted after the ticket order is possible if Nym^{R} is systematically shown to T. However, the price is an increase in linkabilities.

Privacy Evaluation

P1. Deanonymization requires the collaboration of T, G and J as we argued in *Misbehaviour and Deanonymization*.

P2. We argued that a user has for each E a different $\text{Nym}^{\text{E}} \leftarrow f^{\text{E}}(\text{Nym}^{\text{P}})$. Different Es thus should know the user's Nym^{P} – which remains hidden – to do linking. For blacklisted users, G can link Nym^{R} and Nym^{T}. Collusion of T and G is then possible.

P3 G knows the links between nyms on a blacklist and the user's id. However, such convictions are publicly available. Collusion of T and G can reveal the identity associated with Nym^{T}.

8   Comparison and Feasibility

Table 5 compares the three approaches; the main functional/security requirements can be fulfilled while boosting privacy. To maintain user-friendliness, the interactions with e.g. *PS* can be done transparently to the user. The proposed solutions disallow a banned person to buy tickets for someone else (e.g. father for his children) and it is still possible that a person buys tickets and gives them to a banned person.

Estimates of the feasibility on the server side where done on an Intel 1.83GHz CPU. In the case of pseudonym certificates, steps 2.a.3 and 2.b.5, i.e. key generation, will be dominant if RSA is used; on average 377ms for 1024 bits and 4110 ms for 2048 bits. For the anonymous credential based protocols, issueCred and showCred/prove are dominant (steps 4.a.6, 4.a.7, 4.b.2 and optionally 4.b.3.b). showCred will require less than 400ms and less than 1,500ms for 1024 and 2048 bits respectively, while issuing lasts less than 600 ms and 2000 ms. Happily, obtaining (one or more) permit certificates will usually be spread in time.

9   Related Work

Ticketing framework [8], hybrid electronic ticketing [15] and ticket for mobile user and communication [3] [13] are valuable contributions for building future ticketing systems. However, except for [15], all fall short in properly addressing user privacy. In comparison, we propose two solutions that preserve the user's privacy and avoid arbitrary blacklisting.

Heydt-Benjamin et al. [15] propose a hybrid electronic ticketing system which uses passive RFID transponders and higher powered computing devices such as smart phones or PDAs. Their hybrid ticketing system framework takes the advantage of e-cash, anonymous credentials and proxy re-encryption [9] to alleviate the concern of privacy in public transportation ticketing systems.

Table 5. Comparison of the three approaches

	Trivial	Pseudonym certs.	Anon. creds.
F1 - # Tickets	✓	✓	✓
F2 - Subscription	✓	✓	✓
F3 - Pricing	✓	✓	✓
F4 - Deanon.	✓	✓ - *J* interacts with *E, T, PS, G.*	✓ - *J* interacts with *E, T, G.*
F5 - Ban	—	✓ + ticket revocability	✓ (2)
P1 - User anon.	T knows user id	If no collusion of E, T, PS, G. *T* knows permit atts.	✓
P2 - User profiles	*T* can link everything.	Linkability during limited, fixed period.	✓ (1)
P3 - Anon. blacklists	—	If no collusion *PS, G.*	only *G* can identify. *U.*

(1): If the user is blacklisted, *G* can collude with one or more *T*s.
(2): Ticket revocability is possible at the cost of increased linkabilites.

In general, anonymous credential protocols as described in [5], [4] commonly use a Trusted Third Party (TTP) to selectively deanonymize (or link) misbehaving users. However, Patrick et al. [12] strongly argued that deanonymizing a user with the help of TTP is a too heavy measure against a misbehaving user in a privacy-preserving system. Some applications might not necessarily need deanonymization to discourage misbehaving users, they can simply blacklist user pseudonyms, to block a user without actually revealing that user's identity. Thus, the authors propose a scheme where user misbehaviour is judged *subjectively* and blacklisted by each individual service provider (SP) without the need for TTP. Although subjective blacklisting reduces the size of a blacklist in comparison with the usual centralized blacklisting approach, it can empower a SP to arbitrarily discriminate (or freely blacklist) among its ticket users. In comparison, our protocols do not allow SPs to blacklist a user or to maintain its own blacklist. As discussed previously, in our protocols the blacklist is centrally managed by a *trusted* government instance and forwarded to the SPs. Moreover, arbitrary user blacklisting is forbidden without a judicial verdict.

10   Conclusions and Future Work

Two privacy preserving ticketing systems were proposed; one based on pseudonym certificates and one on anonymous credentials. We showed that it is possible to offer the user a high degree of privacy, while the other requirements remain fullfilled. Still the privacy unfriendly eID card is used as bootstrap.

A prototype implementation will be made, using an applet for registration and ticket ordering. Entering the event can be done using a bar code reader. The influence of mix networks on the overall performance must be examined.

Acknowledgements. This research is a contribution to the European PRIME project and is partially funded by the Interuniversity Attraction Poles Programme Belgian State, Belgian Science Policy, the Research Fund K.U.Leuven and the IWT-SBO project (ADAPID) "Advanced Applications for Electronic Identity Cards in Flanders".

References

1. Asokan, N., van Herreweghen, E., Steiner, M.: Towards a framework for handling disputes in payment systems. Technical Report RZ 2996 (1998)
2. Brands, S.: A technical overview of digital credentials (1999)
3. Buttyn, L., Hubaux, J.P.: Accountable anonymous access to services in mobile communication systems. In: Proceedings of the 18th IEEE Symposium on Reliable Distributed Systems (1999)
4. Camenisch, J., Herreweghen, E.V.: Design and implementation of the idemix anonymous credential system. In: ACM Computer and Communication Security (2002)
5. Camenisch, J., Lysyanskaya, A.: An Efficient System for Non-transferable Anonymous Credentials with Optional Anonymity Revocation. In: Pfitzmann, B. (ed.) EUROCRYPT 2001. LNCS, vol. 2045, pp. 93–118. Springer, Heidelberg (2001)
6. Chaum, D.: Security without identification: transaction systems to make big brother obsolete. Commun. ACM 28(10), 1030–1044 (1985)
7. Damgard, I., Pedersen, T., Pfitzmann, B.: Statistical secrecy and multi-bit commitments (1996)
8. Fujimura, K., Nakajima, Y.: General-purpose digital ticket framework. In: Proceedings of the 3rd USENIX Workshop on Electronic Commerce, pp. 177–186 (1998)
9. Green, M., Ateniese, G., Fu, K., Hohenberger, S.: Improved proxy re-encryption schemes with applications to secure distributed storage. In: Proceedings of the 12th Annual Network and Distributed System Security Symposium (NDSS) (2005)
10. Hooks, M., Miles, J.: Onion routing and online anonymity. CS182S (2006)
11. Goldschlag, D.M., Syverson, P.F., Reed, M.G.: Anonymous connections and onion routing. In: SP 1997: Proceedings of the 1997 IEEE Symposium on Security and Privacy, p. 44. IEEE Computer Society, Washington (1997)
12. Kapadia, A., Tsang, P.P., Au, M.H., Smith, S.W.: Blacklistable anonymous credentials: blocking misbehaving users without TTPs. In: CCS 2007: Proceedings of the 14th ACM conference on Computer and communications security, pp. 72–81. ACM Press, New York (2007)
13. Patel, B., Crowcroft, J.: Ticket based service access for the mobile user. In: Proceedings of Mobicom (1997)
14. Pedersen, T.P.: Non-interactive and Information-Theoretic Secure Verifiable Secret Sharing. In: Feigenbaum, J. (ed.) CRYPTO 1991. LNCS, vol. 576, pp. 129–140. Springer, Heidelberg (1992)
15. Defend, B., Heydt-Benjamin, T.S., Chae, H., Fu, K.: Privacy for Public Transportation. In: Danezis, G., Golle, P. (eds.) PET 2006. LNCS, vol. 4258. Springer, Heidelberg (2006)

The Analysis of Windows Vista Disk Encryption Algorithm

Mohamed Abo El-Fotouh and Klaus Diepold

Institute for Data Processing (LDV)
Technische Universität München (TUM)
80333 Munich Germany
{mohamed,kldi}@tum.de

Abstract. Windows Vista Enterprise and Ultimate editions use Bit-locker Drive Encryption as its disk encryption algorithm, and at its heart is the AES-CBC + Elephant diffuser encryption algorithm (ELE-PHANT). In this paper we present our analysis of ELEPHANT using statistical tests. Our analysis has explored some weaknesses in its diffusers, thus we propose new diffusers to replace them. The new diffusers overcome the weaknesses of the original ones, and offer better and faster diffusion properties. We used the new diffusers to build variants of ELE-PHANT, that possess better diffusion properties.

Keywords: Disk encryption, Windows Vista disk encryption algorithm.

1 Introduction

Data security on lost or stolen PCs is a growing concern among security experts and corporate executives. The data stored on the PC asset is often significantly more valuable to a corporation than the asset itself, and the loss, theft or unwanted disclosure of that data can be very damaging. Thus, this data should be encrypted to minimize that loss. Disk encryption applications are used to encrypt all the data on the hard disk, where all the hard disk is encrypted with a single/multiple key(s) and encryption/decryption are done on the fly, without user interference.

Disk encryption usually encrypts/decrypts a whole sector at a time. There exist dedicated block ciphers, that encrypts a whole sector at once. Bear, Lion, Beast and Mercy [1, 1, 2, 3] are examples of these ciphers. Bear, Lion and Beast are considered to be slow, as they pass the data multiple times and Mercy was also broken in [4]. The other method is to let a block cipher like the AES [5] (with 16 bytes block size) to process the data within a mode of operation. The most used mode of operation is CBC [6], but it is subjected to manipulation attacks. There exist other modes of operations dedicated to solve this problem XTS, XCB, CMC and EME [7, 8, 9, 10] are to name a few.

The Enterprize and Ultimate editions of Windows Vista contain a new feature called Bitlocker Drive Encryption which encrypts all the data on the system

V. Atluri (Ed.): DAS 2008, LNCS 5094, pp. 113–126, 2008.

volume [11]. Bitlocker uses existing technologies like the AES in the CBC mode and TPM [12], together with two new diffusers.

In this paper, we study the current implementation of AES-CBC + Elephant diffuser (ELEPHANT) and propose new diffusers to replace its diffusers. The proposed diffusers possess better and faster diffusion properties than the current ones. We used the proposed diffusers to construct two variants of ELEPHANT. Our study shows that the proposed diffusers and variants of ELEPHANT, possess better diffusion properties.

In section 2, we describe ELEPHANT with its current diffusers (CURDIFF). In section 3, we propose new diffusers (NEWDIFF) and two variants of ELEPHANT which we name NEWELF and NEWELFRED. In section 4, we tried to answer the following questions: Does the cipher/diffuser behave randomly as expected with different patterns of plaintexts and tweaks? How sensitive is the cipher/diffuser to a change in the plaintext/tweak? We examined different data-sets against randomness to answer these questions. In section 5, we tried to answer the following questions: Can the cipher be reduced to CBC? Is the tested cipher correlated with CBC? Does the cipher/diffuser suffer from the bit-flipping attack? We designed statistical test to answer these questions. In section 6, we tried to answer the following questions: Does the cipher possess the avalanche effect in the encryption direction? Does the cipher possess poor man's authentication property [11]? We designed statistical test to answer these questions. In section 7, we tried to answer the following questions: Does each bit in ciphertext depend on all the bits in the plaintext? Does each bit in plaintext depend on all the bits in the ciphertext? We designed statistical test to answer these questions. We present a performance analysis of the ciphers/diffusers in section 8, and our discussion in section 9 and finally we conclude in section 10.

2   Current Implementation

2.1   ELEPHANT

Figure 1 shows an overview of ELEPHANT [11]. There are four steps to encrypt a sector:

1. The plaintext is xored with a sector key K_s (1).
2. The result of the previous step run through diffuser A.
3. The result of the previous step run through diffuser B.
4. The result of the previous step is encrypted with AES in CBC mode using IV_s (2), as the initial vector.

$$K_s = E(K_{sec}, e(s)) \parallel E(K_{sec}, e'(s)) \tag{1}$$

$$IV_s = E(K_{AES}, e(s)) \tag{2}$$

Where E() is the AES encryption function, K_{sec} is a key used to generate K_s, K_{AES} is the key used to generate the sector IV_s and used in the AES-CBC process, e() is an encoding function that maps each sector number s into a unique

16-byte value. The first 8 bytes of the result are the byte offset of the sector on the volume. This integer is encoded in least-significant-byte first encoding. The last 8 bytes of the result are always zero and e'(s) is the same as e(s) except that the last byte of the result has the value 128.

Note that the plaintext and key are parameterized. In our study we used the following parameters:

1. Plaintext of size 4096-bits (the current standard sector size).
2. Tweak-Key of size 384-bits (the first 128-bits serves as the IV_s "Sector Initial Vector" for the AES-CBC and the other 256-bits serve as K_s "Drive Sector Key").
3. We examined the 256-bits key version of the AES (that provides maximum security), that means both K_{sec} and K_{AES} are of size 256-bits.

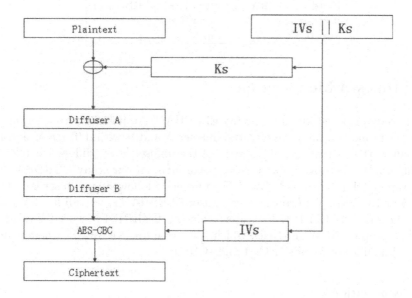

Fig. 1. Overview of AES-CBC with Elephant Diffuser

2.2 The Diffusers

The current diffusers (CURRDIFF) are very similar. The following notations are used to define the diffusers:

1. d_i is the ith 32-bits word in the sector, if i falls outside the range then d_i =$d_{i \bmod n}$, where n is the number of the 32-bits in the sector.
2. AC and BC are the number of cycles of diffuser A and B, they are defined to be 5 and 3 respectively.

3. RA = [9, 0, 13, 0] and RB = [0, 10, 0, 25] hold the rotation constants of diffuser A and B respectively.
4. $\oplus$ is the bitwise xor operation.
5. << is the integer 32-bit left rotation operation, where the rotation value is written on its right size.
6. - is integer subtraction modulo 2^{32}.

Table 1 presents the description of the CURRDIFF (diffuser A and diffuser B).

Table 1. Current diffusers

Diffuser A:	Diffuser B:
for j=1 to AC	for j=1 to BC
for i=n-1,...,2,1,0	for i= n-1,...,2,1,0
t=(d_{i-5} << $RA_{i \bmod 4}$)	t=(d_{i+5} << $RB_{i \bmod 4}$)
t=t $\oplus$ d_{i-2}	t=t $\oplus$ d_{i+2}
d_i= d_i - t	d_i= d_i - t

3   Proposed Modification

The novelty of this study is to modify ELEPHANT to possess better and faster diffusion properties, we have replaced diffuser A and B with diffuser A' and B'. We named the current implementation of the diffuser layer (diffuser A followed by diffuser B, where AC=5 and BC=3) thorough out our study CURDIFF and our proposed diffuser layer NEWDIFF (diffuser A' followed by diffuser B', where AC=5 and BC=3). We propose a variant of ELEPHANT, we call it NEWELF. It is the same as ELEPHANT after replacing CURRDIFF with NEWDIFF. We also propose NEWELFRED, which is a variant of NEWELF, where it uses reduced number of rounds (AC=1 and BC=2).

3.1   Motivation

From studying the current diffusers, three undesired properties have been found:

1. If their input is of all zeros or of all ones, their output will be identical to their input. This is true for both the encryption and decryption directions. This is due to the fact, that the result of the xor operations (in diffuser A and diffuser B) will always be zero and the diffusers are bypassed (i.e. that sector will be encrypted with CBC only). This is due to the absence of any confusion operations.
2. The current diffusers are completely linear functions, that do not offer any form of non-linearity. Due to the absence of confusion operations.
3. The current diffusers updates only a single word (in the inner loop), thus the diffusion is slow.

3.2   Proposed Diffusers

The main objectives of the proposed diffusers are to overcome the limitations of the current diffusers. Table 2 presents the description of the NEWDIFF (diffuser A' and diffuser B'), where SBOX[X] returns 8-bits from the AES SBOX, using the least significant 8-bits of X as the index.

Table 2. Proposed diffusers

Diffuser A':	Diffuser B':
for j=1 to AC	for j=1 to BC
for i=n-1,...,2,1,0	for i= n-1,...,2,1,0
$d_{i-5} = d_{i-5} \oplus \text{SBOX}[d_i]$	$d_{i+5} = d_{i+5} \oplus \text{SBOX}[d_i]$
$d_{i-5} = d_{i-5} << RA_{i \bmod 4}$	$d_{i+5} = d_{i+5} << RA_{i \bmod 4}$
$d_{i-5} = d_{i-5} \oplus d_{i-2}$	$d_{i+5} = d_{i+5} \oplus d_{i+2}$
$d_i = d_i - d_{i-5}$	$d_i = d_i - d_{i+5}$

3.3   Discussion

The proposed diffusers possess the following properties:

1. They can not be easily bypassed, like the current diffusers. Thanks to the SBOX which offers confusion.
2. The confusion operation is well studied (AES SBOX) and they offer good confusion properties. Note that, all the non-linearity of the AES is offered by its SBOX [13].
3. Two 32-bits words are updated in the inner loop of the diffusers, thus providing faster diffusion properties (see Sect. 8), for example for diffuser A':
   (a) d_{i-5} is first xored with the result of SBOX of d_i, that means the last 8-bits of d_{i-5} depends on each bit in the last 8-bits of d_i.
   (b) Then the rotation performs diffusion within d_{i-5}, which reflect the effect of the previous step.
   (c) Then d_{i-5} is xored with d_{i-2}, so each corresponding bit of d_{i-5} depends of that of d_{i-2}.
   (d) Finally d_{i-5} is subtracted from d_i, which means that each corresponding bit of d_i depends of that of d_{i-5} (reflecting the effects of all the previous steps).

In the next sections we are going to present different statistical tests and their corresponding results . We divide these tests into four different categories, each category tries to answer specific questions, to help us better understand the behavior of the tested ciphers/diffusers.

4   Randomness Tests

One of the criteria used to evaluate block ciphers is their demonstrated suitability as random number generators. That is, the evaluation of their outputs utilizing statistical tests should not provide any means by which to computationally distinguish them from truly random sources [14]. In [15], the randomness of the final five candidates of the AES algorithms were tested. Another study [16], which we applied here, applies the NIST statistical tool [17] to the disk encryption modes of operation, where eleven data-sets are subjected to 188 statistical tests each. These tests try to explore the behavior of the ciphers/diffusers for different patterns of tweak and plaintext values, these data-sets are:

1. Random plaintext / random tweak.
2. Random plaintext / low density tweak.
3. Random plaintext / high density tweak.
4. Low density plaintext / random tweak.
5. Low density plaintext / low density tweak.
6. Low density plaintext / high density tweak.
7. High density plaintext / random tweak.
8. High density plaintext / low density tweak.
9. High density plaintext / high density tweak.
10. Plaintext avalanche.
11. Tweak avalanche.

For more details about these data-sets please refer to [16]. In table 3 we reported the number of failed tests (out of 188) for each cipher/diffuser for the eleven data sets, where a test fails when either the cipher/diffuser failed that test too often or the output is uniform. These tests try to answer the following questions: *Does the cipher/diffuser behave randomly as expected with different patterns of plaintexts and tweaks? How sensitive is the cipher/diffuser to a change in the plaintext/tweak?* ELEPHANT, NEWELF and NEWELFRED possess a good random profile, while CBC possesses an acceptable random profile (it has problems with plaintext avalanche test, which is expected as it pass the data only once). The proposed NEWDIFF possesses a good random profile, however CURRDIFF possesses a weak one (CURRDIFF fails completely when the plaintext is

Table 3. Number of failed statistical tests for the eleven data-sets

Data set #	1	2	3	4	5	6	7	8	9	10	11
CBC	10	13	11	15	22	19	16	16	18	**166**	30
ELEPHANT	15	10	9	20	7	17	12	12	12	12	15
	12	7	17	22	17	15	14	12	14	12	33
CURRDIFF	18	18	18	**185**	**187**	**187**	**173**	**187**	**187**	9	**186**
	18	18	18	**185**	**187**	**187**	**174**	**187**	**187**	9	**186**
NEWDIFF	8	6	13	16	12	17	10	14	16	6	13
	9	7	7	20	12	15	12	11	15	8	34
NEWELF	18	10	9	8	16	12	9	12	19	10	8
	9	10	12	15	14	15	9	15	15	12	33
NEWELFRED	8	9	10	8	12	15	18	13	17	8	30
	12	7	13	11	11	8	15	16	12	7	13

a repeated pattern and it is not so sensitive to a tweak change). Note that as the tweak (K_s) can not be all zero or all ones, refer to(1), to produce a tweak that is low/high density. We ran the tests two time, one with the first half low/high density and the rest random, the second time with the first half random and the second half with low/high density.

5   Correlation Tests

5.1   CBC-Correlation Function

As ELEPHANT, NEWELF and NEWELFRED are based on CBC, we measured their correlation with CBC, using the nine combinations of all zero, all one, and all random bits between the plaintext and the tweak. This function is called

Table 4. Nomenclatures for some test functions

GenRndKey(X)	Generates a random key X with length 256-bits.
No_of_Bits	The number of bits in the sector.
Samplesize	Number of random samples used for each bit location, we used 1539 samples.
Init(R)	Initialize the array R with zeros.
GenerateSector(P)	Generates a sector P of size 4096-bits, for the first 513 calls it returns low density plaintext, for the next 513 calls it returns high density plaintext and for the last 513 calls it returns random plaintext.
GenTweak(K2,x)	Generates a 384-bits tweak. If x equals zero then all the tweak is filled with zero bits, if x equals ones then all the tweak is filled with one bits, otherwise the tweak is filled with random bits.
Encrypt(P,C,A,B)	Encrypts the plaintext P to the ciphertext C, using A as the encryption key and B as the tweak.
ChangeBit(C,i,C2)	Flips the bit number i in the text C and put the result in C2.
Decrypt(C,P,A,B)	D ecrypts the ciphertext C to the plaintext P, using A as the encryption key and B as the tweak.
Xor(R,P,T)	Xors P with T and puts the results in R.
Add(R,Y)	Adds the values in the array Y to that in the array R.
Analyze(R,Matrix[i])	Calculates the minimum, maximum, average and standard deviation of the R array. The above four values as stored in Matrix[i]. Note: any one added to the R array represents that this bit has changed as a result of changing the bit number i in the ciphertext/plaintext.
Summarize(Matrix)	Calculates the normalized minimum of minimums (**Min**), maximum of the maximums (**Max**), average of the averages (**AVG**) and average of the standard deviations (**SD**) in Matrix.

CBC-Correlation. This function tries to answer the following question: *Can the cipher be reduced to CBC?* NEWELF and NEWELFRED succeeded to pass **CBC-Correlation** function, while ELEPHANT failed to pass the test for two inputs:

1. When the tweak is all zeros and the plaintext is all zeros.
2. When the tweak is all zeros and the plaintext is all ones.

In both cases the diffuser layer has **no effect** on the plaintext. Although with the current design of the tweak, it is impossible to get a tweak with all zeros refer to (1), it is still possible to bypass the CURRDIFF in those two cases:

1. When the encrypted sector contains the repetitions of K_s (i.e. the xor operation will result in all zero plaintext and the diffuser layer will be bypassed).
2. When the encrypted sector contains the repetitions of the negation of K_s (i.e. the xor operation will result in all ones plaintext and the diffuser layer will be bypassed).

These failures are due to the absence of non-linear operations in CURRDIFF and that the result of the xor operations in CURRDIFF will result always with zero (the identity element of subtraction), when the input is all zeros or all ones. In these two cases ELEPHANT is reduced to CBC.

5.2   Bit-Flipping Attack

We applied the Bit-Flipping-Attack function three times each with a different parameter x, $(0 \leq x \leq 2)$ that determines the pattern of the used plaintext and tweak, the function is listed in table 5 and its nomenclatures are in table 4.

Table 5. Bit-Flipping-Attack function

```
Function Bit-Flipping-Attack(x)
double Martrix[No_of_Bits][Samplesize];
GenRndKey(K1);
GenTweak(K2,x);
For (i=0;i<No_of_Bits;i++)
{     Init(R);
        For(j=0;j<Samplesize;j++)
           {GenSector(P);
            Encrypt(P,C,K1,K2);
            ChangeBit(C,I,C2);
            Decrypt(C2,T,K1,K2);
            Xor(Y,P,T);
            Add(R,Y) ;}
        Analyze(R,Matrix[i]);
}
Summarize(Matrix);
```

Table 6. Bit-Flipping-Attack results

ELEPHANT				CBC			
x	Min	Max	AVG	SD	Min	Max	AVG	SD
0	0.23	0.76	0.5	0.05	0	1	0.02	0.09
1	0.24	0.76	0.5	0.05	0	1	0.02	0.09
2	0.24	0.78	0.5	0.05	0	1	0.02	0.09
CURRDIFF				NEWDIFF			
x	Min	Max	AVG	SD	Min	Max	AVG	SD
0	0.24	0.78	0.5	0.05	0.25	0.77	0.5	0.05
1	0.22	0.76	0.5	0.05	0.24	0.78	0.5	0.05
2	0.24	0.75	0.5	0.05	0.24	0.79	0.5	0.05
NEWELF				NEWELFRED			
x	Min	Max	AVG	SD	Min	Max	AVG	SD
0	0.24	0.78	0.5	0.05	0.24	0.79	0.5	0.05
1	0.22	0.77	0.5	0.05	0.25	0.75	0.5	0.05
2	0.25	0.76	0.5	0.05	0.25	0.77	0.5	0.05

Bit-Flipping-Attack function tests if changing any bit in the ciphertext will be associated with changing a specific bit(s) in the plaintext. This function tries to answer the following question: *does the cipher/diffuser suffer from the bit-flipping attack ?* If the maximum returned by the "Summary" function is equal to the sample size, that means there is at least one bit that changes whenever a specific bit in the ciphertext is changed, and that means bit-flipping attack [18] is applicable on the tested cipher/diffuser. The results of the Bit-Flipping-Attack in table 6, show that ELEPHANT, NEWELF, NEWELFRED, CURRDIFF, NEWDIFF pass these tests, while CBC fails these tests as it is subjected to the bit-flipping attack.

6   Avalanche Tests

This category consists of six tests, where two functions are applied three times with a different parameter x, ($0 \leq x \leq 2$), that determines the pattern of the used plaintext and tweak, these two functions are:

- **Avalanche-Encryption(x):** Measures avalanche effect [19] in the encryption direction (the effect of changing one bit of plaintext on the ciphertext), a good cipher will have roughly half the bits of the ciphertext changed due to a single bit change in plaintext. It tries to answer the following question: *does the cipher possess the avalanche effect in the encryption direction?*
- **Avalanche-Decryption(x):** Measures avalanche effect in the decryption direction (the effect of changing one bit of ciphertext on the plaintext), this is to possess poor man's authentication, that is changing one bit in the ciphertext will lead that the plaintext will be scrambled. It tries to answer the following question: *does the cipher possess poor man's authentication property?*

Table 7. Avalanche-Encryption results

x	ELEPHANT				CBC			
	Min	Max	AVG	SD	Min	Max	AVG	SD
0	0.46	0.54	0.5	0.01	0.01	0.99	0.5	0.28
1	0.46	0.54	0.5	0.01	0.01	0.99	0.5	0.28
2	0.47	0.54	0.5	0.01	0.01	0.99	0.5	0.28
x	CURRDIFF				NEWDIFF			
	Min	Max	AVG	SD	Min	Max	AVG	SD
0	0.46	0.53	0.5	0.01	0.46	0.53	0.5	0.01
1	0.47	0.54	0.5	0.01	0.46	0.54	0.5	0.01
2	0.46	0.54	0.5	0.01	0.46	0.53	0.5	0.01
x	NEWELF				NEWELFRED			
	Min	Max	AVG	SD	Min	Max	AVG	SD
0	0.46	0.54	0.5	0.01	0.46	0.54	0.5	0.01
1	0.46	0.54	0.5	0.01	0.46	0.54	0.5	0.01
2	0.46	0.53	0.5	0.01	0.46	0.54	0.5	0.01

Table 8. Avalanche-Decryption results

x	ELEPHANT				CBC			
	Min	Max	AVG	SD	Min	Max	AVG	SD
0	0.46	0.54	0.5	0.01	0.01	0.99	0.49	0.48
1	0.47	0.54	0.5	0.01	0.01	0.99	0.5	0.48
2	0.46	0.54	0.5	0.01	0.01	0.99	0.5	0.48
x	CURRDIFF				NEWDIFF			
	Min	Max	AVG	SD	Min	Max	AVG	SD
0	0.46	0.53	0.5	0.01	0.46	0.53	0.5	0.01
1	0.46	0.53	0.5	0.01	0.47	0.54	0.5	0.01
2	0.46	0.53	0.5	0.01	0.46	0.54	0.5	0.01
x	NEWELF				NEWELFRED			
	Min	Max	AVG	SD	Min	Max	AVG	SD
0	0.46	0.54	0.5	0.01	0.46	0.54	0.5	0.01
1	0.46	0.54	0.5	0.01	0.46	0.54	0.5	0.01
2	0.46	0.54	0.5	0.01	0.47	0.54	0.5	0.01

The results in tables 7 and 8 show that ELEPHANT, NEWELF, NEWELFRED, CURRDIFF, NEWDIFF all have good avalanche effect in both encryption and decryption directions, on the other hand CBC failed to pass these tests.

7   Bit Dependency Tests

This category consists of two tests:

- **BD-Encryption()** is passed, when each bit in the ciphertext depends on every bit in the plaintext. It tries to answer: *does each bit in ciphertext depend on all the bits in the plaintext?*

- **BD-Decryption()** is passed, when each bin in the plaintext depends on every bit in the ciphertext. It tries to answer: *does each bit in plaintext depend on all the bits in the ciphertext?*

The Bit-dependency functions are measured as following:

1. A dependency matrix M is constructed of size B × B (where B is the number of bits in the plaintext/ciphertext, here B = 4096).
2. The diagonal is initialized by 1 and all other bits are set to zero, as initially each bit depends only on itself.
3. Depending on the applied operations the matrix M is updated, BD-Encryption applies the operation in the encryption direction and BD-Decryption applies them in the decryption direction.
4. If an output bit is dependent on an input bit(s), the column of the output bit is ORed with that (those) of the input bit(s). For example:
   (a) Xor operation: each output bit is dependent on the corresponding input bit.
   (b) Addition and subtraction modulo 2^{32} operations are approximated to an xor operation for simplicity and generality.
   (c) AES operation: each bit in the input 128-bits is dependent on the other 127 bits.
   (d) 32-bit rotation: the columns change there order depending on the rotation amount and direction.
   (e) SBOX look up: each bit of the output depends on every bit of the input.
5. All the operation of the tested function/cipher are applied and the matrix M is updated.
6. At the end the sum of all ones in the matrix is calculated and is divided by B^2.
7. If the returned value in the previous step is 1, this means that each bit of the output bits depends on all the bits of the input and the function succeeds, it fails otherwise.

The results of applying **BD-Encryption** and **BD-Decryption** functions are found in table 9, where we reported the minimum values of AC and BC each algorithm needs to pass these tests (under columns AC' and BC'), together

Table 9. BD-Encryption and BD-Decryption results

	Pass	AC'	BC'	AC	BC	SF	DP	Speed
							Performance	
CBC	false	NA	NA	NA	NA	NA	NA	16530
ELEPHANT	true	2	1	5	3	2.7	NA	22147
CURDIFF	true	2	3	5	3	1.6	1.6	6847
NEWDIFF	true	1	2	5	3	2.7	7.3	11580
NEWELF	true	0	1	5	3	8	NA	26820
NEWELFRED	true	0	1	1	2	4	NA	20860

with the current used values. The results show that all the ciphers but CBC succeeded these tests. CURDIFF needs at least three rounds of diffuser B and two rounds of diffuser A, on the other hand ELEPHANT which uses it needs only at least AC=2 and BC=1 to pass it, this is because the CBC layer does the rest of the diffusion. NEWDIFF needs at least AC=1 and BC=2, while NEWELF and NEWELFRED needs only BC=1 and the CBC layer does the rest of the diffusion.

8   Performance

We studied the performance of the optimized C versions of the ciphers/diffusers. For the diffusers we used the loop unrolling mechanism [20] and for the AES we used optimized Gladmann's implementation [21]. The results are listed in table 9 under column speed, note that the reported measurements are done on a PIV 3 GHz processor running on Windows Vista, where the programming environment was Microsoft VC++ 6. Here we reported the number of clock cycles needed by each algorithm, which is the minimum of 100 iterations to remove any initial overheads or cache misses. These results show that NEWDIFF is about 70% slower than CURRDIFF, NEWELF is about 20% slower than ELEPHANT and NEWELFRED is about 6% faster than ELEPHANT.

We define the Safety Factor (SF) with (3), which is the ratio between the total number of used diffusers' cycles over the minimum required. SF represents how safe is the current number of diffusers' cycles, under any circumstances this ratio should not be less than one. In (4), we defined the Diffusion Power (DP) , of a diffuser layer , to be the ratio between the number of bits updated per cycle (NC) over the total number of bits (TN) times SF. DP shows how fast the diffusion layer diffuse the plaintext/ciphertext. The values of SF and DP are reported in table 9. These values show that CURRDIFF possesses less SF and DP as NEWDIFF, and ELEPHANT possesses less SF that both NEWELF and NEWELFRED.

$$SF = (AC + BC) \div (AC' + BC') \tag{3}$$

$$DP = (NC) \div (TN) \times SF \tag{4}$$

From [11], suppose an attacker is attacking two identical hard drives, one encrypted with ELEPHANT and the other one encrypted with CBC. We are going to give the attacker the tweak key (K_{sec}), this means the attacker can now perform the diffusion layer for any plaintext. In other words, the diffuser layer becomes transparent to the attacker. All what is left now for the attacker is to attack the CBC layer, which is the same problem that he has when attacking the other hard drive (encrypted only using CBC). Although we helped the attacker significantly by providing him with the tweak key, he still has to attack the CBC layer. This shows that attacking ELEPHANT is not easier than attacking just CBC, and ELEPHANT is at least as secure as CBC. Note that the previous security proof is valid for any diffuser, that means NEWELF and NEWELFRED are also at least secure as CBC.

9 Discussion

CBC failed a lot of tests, as it is a narrow-block mode of operation [22], it possesses no avalanche effect at all and it is subjected to bit-flipping attack.

CURRDIFF is sensitive to repeated patterns, where its output can be distinguished from a random text and it is not so sensitive to the tweak change. We discovered also two cases where it will not change the input at all. It diffuses the plaintext/ciphertext slowly as at least five diffuser cycles, to pass **BD-Encryption** and **BD-Decryption** functions. It possesses also low SF and DP.

Due to the shortcomes of CURRDIFF, we designed NEWDIFF to replace it, the design of CURRDIFF was changed to update more bits each cycle and we added SBOX lookup operation to add non-linearity to the diffusers. NEWDIFF overcomes the shortcomes of CURRDIFF with good random profile, high SF and DP, but it is about 70% slower than CURRDIFF.

ELEPHANT is a wide-block mode of operation [22] that uses CURRDIFF together with CBC. Our analysis shows that it is superior than CBC, but the drawbacks of CURRDIFF can affect it, for example when CURRDIFF does not change the plaintext, ELEPHANT is reduced to CBC (although this may happen with a very low probability, it is still a problem, as we can not restrict the plaintext). ELEPHANT possesses low SF.

NEWELF is a proposed variant of ELEPHANT, where we replaced CURRDIFF with NEWDIFF, it possesses good random profile and high SF, but it is about 20% slower than ELEPHANT.

NEWELFRED is a variant of NEWELF, where we reduced the number of diffuser cycles. Although it uses less number of cycles as NEWELF, it possesses a good random profile, with a higher SF than ELEPHANT and is about 6% faster than ELEPHANT.

10 Conclusion

We present a couple of statistical tests, that can be used to evaluate the behavior of ciphers that uses a diffuser followed by a mode of operation. We used these tests to study Windows Vista's disk encryption algorithm ELEPHANT. The algorithm provides better statistical and random behavior than CBC. Our study discovered some weaknesses in its diffusers, so we proposed new diffusers to replace them. Our proposed diffusers overcome the drawbacks of the current ones. We used the proposed diffusers to build a new variant of ELEPHANT called NEWELF, that possesses better properties than ELEPHANT with only 20% increase in its total running time. If performance is an issue, we proposed NEWELFRED that uses NEWDIFF with reduced number of cycles, it is faster than ELEPHANT and it possesses better properties than ELEPHANT.

References

[1] Anderson, R., Biham, E.: Two practical and provable secure block ciphers: BEAR and LION. In: Gollmann, D. (ed.) FSE 1996. LNCS, vol. 1039. Springer, Heidelberg (1996)

[2] Lucks, S.: BEAST: A fast block cipher for arbitrary blocksizes. In: Horster, P. (ed.) Communications and Multimedia Security II, Proceedings of the IFIP TC6/TC11 International Conference on Communications and Multimedia Security (1996)

[3] Crowley, P.: Mercy: A Fast Large Block Cipher for Disk Sector Encryption. In: Schneier, B. (ed.) FSE 2000. LNCS, vol. 1978. Springer, Heidelberg (2001)

[4] Fluhrer, S.: Cryptanalysis of the Mercy Block Cipher. In: Matsui, M. (ed.) FSE 2001. LNCS, vol. 2355. Springer, Heidelberg (2002)

[5] Nechvatal, J., Barker, E., Bassham, L., Burr, W., Dworkin, M., Foti, J., Roback, E.: Report on the Development of the Advanced Encryption Standard (AES). Technical report (2000)

[6] Menezes, A., van Oorschot, P., Vanstone, S.: Handbook of Applied Cryptography. CRC Press, Boca Raton (1996)

[7] Rogaway, P.: Efficient Instantiations of Tweakable Blockciphers and Refinements to Modes OCB and PMAC,
http://citeseer.ist.psu.edu/rogaway03efficient.html

[8] McGrew, D., Fluhrer, S.: The Extended Codebook (XCB) Mode of Operation. Cryptology ePrint Archive, Report 2004/278 (2004)

[9] Halevi, S., Rogaway, P.: A tweakable enciphering mode,
http://eprint.iacr.org/2003/148

[10] Halevi, S., Rogaway, P.: A parallelizable enciphering mode,
http://eprint.iacr.org/2003/147

[11] Ferguson, N.: AES-CBC + Elephant diffuser: A Disk Encryption Algorithm for Windows Vista (2006),
http://download.microsoft.com/download/0/2/3/0238acaf-d3bf-4a6d-b3d6
-b3d6-0a0be4bbb36e/BitLockerCipher200608.pdf

[12] Trusted Computing Group. TCG TPM Specification Version 1.2,
http://www.trustedcomputinggroup.org

[13] Daemen, J., Rijmen, V.: AES Proposal: Rijndael,
http://citeseer.ist.psu.edu/daemen98aes.html

[14] Soto, J.: Randomness Testing of the Advanced Encryption Standard Candidate Algorithms (1999),
http://citeseer.ist.psu.edu/article/soto99randomness.html

[15] Soto, J., Bassham, L.: Randomness Testing of the Advanced Encryption Standard Finalist Candidates. Computer Security Division,National Institute of Standards and Technology (2000)

[16] El-Fotouh, M., Diepold, K.: Statistical Testing for Disk Encryption Modes of Operations. Cryptology ePrint Archive, Report 2007/362 (2007)

[17] NIST statistical Suite, http://csrc.nist.gov/rng/rng2.html

[18] Fruhwirth, C.: New Methods in Hard Disk Encryption (2005),
http://clemens.endorphin.org/nmihde/nmihde-A4-ds.pdf

[19] Webster, F., Tavares, S.E.: On the Design of S-boxes. In: Williams, H.C. (ed.) CRYPTO 1985. LNCS, vol. 218. Springer, Heidelberg (1986).

[20] Davidson, J., Jinturkar, S.: An aggressive approach to loop unrolling. Technical report, Department of Computer Science. University of Virginia. Charlottesville (1995)

[21] Gladman, B.: AES optimized C code (June 2006),
http://fp.gladman.plus.com/AES/index.htm

[22] IEEE P1619 homepage on Wikipedia,
http://en.wikipedia.org/wiki/IEEE_P1619

Shared and Searchable Encrypted Data for Untrusted Servers*

Changyu Dong, Giovanni Russello, and Naranker Dulay

Department of Computing, Imperial College London
180 Queen's Gate, London, SW7 2AZ, UK
{changyu.dong,g.russello,n.dulay}@imperial.ac.uk

Abstract. Current security mechanisms pose a risk for organisations that outsource their data management to untrusted servers. Encrypting and decrypting sensitive data at the client side is the normal approach in this situation but has high communication and computation overheads if only a subset of the data is required, for example, selecting records in a database table based on a keyword search. New cryptographic schemes have been proposed that support encrypted queries over encrypted data but all depend on a single set of secret keys, which implies single user access or sharing keys among multiple users, with key revocation requiring costly data re-encryption. In this paper, we propose an encryption scheme where each authorised user in the system has his own keys to encrypt and decrypt data. The scheme supports keyword search which enables the server to return only the encrypted data that satisfies an encrypted query without decrypting it. We provide two constructions of the scheme giving formal proofs of their security. We also report on the results of a prototype implementation.

1 Introduction

Data growth is inevitable for nearly all organisations. According to Forrester Research, enterprise storage needs grow at 52 percent per year [1]. To reduce the increasing costs of storage management, many organisations choose to outsource their data storage to third party service providers. Recent research from TheInfoPro shows that nearly 20% of Fortune 1000 organisations outsource at least some portion of their storage management activities [2].

One of the biggest challenges raised by data storage outsourcing is security and trust. Business data is a valuable asset for many companies. While companies may trust a Storage Service Provider's (SSP) reliability, availability, fault-tolerance and performance, they cannot trust that an SSP is not going to use the data for other purposes, especially when the value of the data is high. Traditional access controls which are used to provide confidentiality are mostly designed for in-house services and depend greatly on the system itself to enforce authorisation

---

* This research was supported by the UK's EPSRC research grant EP/C537181/1. The authors would like to thank the members of the Policy Research Group at Imperial College for their support.

V. Atluri (Ed.): DAS 2008, LNCS 5094, pp. 127–143, 2008.

policies, effectively relying on a trusted infrastructure. In the absence of trust, traditional security models are no longer valid. Another common approach to provide data confidentiality is cryptography. Server side encryption is not appropriate when the server is not trusted. The client must encrypt the data before sending it to the SSP and later the encrypted data can be retrieved and decrypted by the client. This could ease a company's concern about data leakage, but introduces a new problem. Because the encrypted data is not meaningful to the servers, many useful data management functionalities are not possible. For example, if a client wants to retrieve documents or records containing certain keywords, how can this request be processed? Can we keep the data incomprehensible to servers and their administrators while efficiently retrieving the data? Consider the following scenarios:

Scenario 1. *Company A is considering outsourcing its data processing centre to a service provider B. This will cut its annual IT cost by up to 25%. But the CIO is concerned about data security. The company's databases contain valuable production data and customer information. It would be unacceptable if competitors got hold of the data. Administrative controls such as formal contracts, confidential agreements and continuous auditing provide a certain level of assurance, but the CIO would also like to encrypt the sensitive data and have fast searches over it.*

Scenario 2. *Bob subscribes to a Personal Health Record service from company C. The service allows Bob to maintain his electronic medical records and share them with his doctors through a web interface. Bob wants to encrypt his records, ensuring the staff of company C will not be able to know what is inside.*

A trivial solution is to download all the data to the client's computer and decrypt it locally. This does not scale to large datasets. Recently, several innovative schemes have been proposed to address the above problems. The basic idea is to divide the cryptographic component between the client and server. The client performs the data encryption/decryption and manages the keys. The server processes search queries by carrying out some computation on the encrypted data. The server knows nothing about the keys or the plaintexts of the data nor the queries, but is still able to return the correct results.

These schemes also have an important limitation. The operations, e.g. encryption, decryption and query generation, more or less rely on some secret keys. This implies that the operations can only be executed by one user, or by a group of users who share the secret keys somehow. A single user is usually not an adequate assumption for data outsourcing. Perhaps the biggest problem for supporting multiple user access to encrypted data is key management. Sharing keys is generally not a good idea since it increases the risk of key exposure. In response to this, keys must be changed regularly. The keys must also be changed if a user is no longer qualified to access the data. However, changing keys may result in decrypting all the data and re-encrypting it using the new keys. For large data sets, this is not practical.

In this paper, we propose a scheme for multi-user searchable data encryption. Our scheme does not require a fully trusted server. The server can search an encrypted keyword on the encrypted data. More importantly each authorised user in the system has his own unique keys which simplifies key revocation and avoids data re-encryption. All the authorised users can insert encrypted data, decrypt the data inserted by other users and search encrypted data without knowing the other users' keys. The keys of one user can easily be revoked without affecting other users or the encrypted data at the server.

2   Related Work

Song et al. [3] introduced the first practical scheme for searching on encrypted data. The scheme enables clients to perform searches on encrypted text without disclosing any information about the plaintext to the untrusted server. The untrusted server cannot learn the plaintext given only the ciphertext, it cannot search without the user's authorisation, and it learns nothing more than the encrypted search results. The basic idea is to generate a keyed hash for the keywords and store this information inside the ciphertext. The server can search the keywords by recalculating and matching the hash value. Yang et al. [4] proposed an elegant scheme for performing queries on encrypted data and also provided a secure index to speed up queries by two-step mapping. Goh's scheme [5] enables searches on encrypted data by constructing secure indexes based on bloom filter.

In the *bucketization* approach for searching encrypted databases [6,7,8,9], an attribute domain is partitioned into a set of buckets each of which is identified by a tag. These bucket tags are maintained as an index and are utilised by the server to process the queries. Bucketization has relatively small performance overhead and enables more complex queries such as range queries and comparison queries at the cost of revealing more information about the encrypted data.

All the schemes above rely on secret keys however, which implies single user access or sharing keys among a group of users. Boneh et al. [10] presented a scheme for searches on encrypted data using a public key system that allows mail gateways to handle email based on whether certain keywords exist in the encrypted message. The application scenario is similar to [3], but the scheme uses identity-based encryption instead of symmetric ciphers. Using asymmetric keys allows multiple users to encrypt data using the public key, but only the user who has the private key can search and decrypt the data. Curtmola et al. [11] partly solved the multi-user problem by using broadcast encryption. The set of authorised users share a secret key r (which is used in conjunction with a trapdoor function). Only people who know r will be able to access/query the data. A user can be revoked by changing r, and using broadcast encryption to send the new key r' to the set of authorised users. The revoked user does not know r', and hence cannot search. In this scheme, the database is searchable, but is read-only and cannot be updated. In our scheme, any authorised user can read, search and update the database.

3   Multi-user Searchable Data Encryption Scheme: Basic Construction

In this section, we introduce the basic construction of the multi-user searchable data encryption scheme which is built upon *proxy encryption*. The scheme does not require sharing keys among the users. We also formalise the notions of security and provide proofs later in this section.

3.1   An RSA-Based Proxy Encryption Scheme

The notion of proxy encryption was first introduced in [12]. In a proxy encryption scheme, a ciphertext encrypted by one key can be transformed by a proxy function into the corresponding ciphertext for another key without revealing any information about the keys and the plaintext. Proxy encryption schemes can be built on top of different cryptosystems such as El Gamal [13] and RSA [14]. Applications of proxy encryption include: secure email lists [15], access control systems [16] and attribute based publishing of data [17]. A comprehensive study on proxy cryptography can be found in [18].

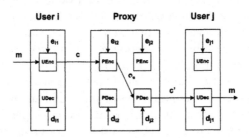

Fig. 1. Encryption/Decryption in Our RSA-based Proxy Encryption Scheme

Our scheme uses an RSA-based proxy encryption scheme. Let's use $\mathcal{E} = (IGen,$ $UGen, UEnc, UDec, PEnc, PDec)$ to denote the proxy encryption scheme. Fig. 1 shows the encryption/decryption process in the proxy encryption scheme.

- *IGen* is the master key generation algorithm which is identical to the key generation algorithm in the standard RSA. It takes a security parameter k and generates $(p, q, n, \phi(n), e, d)$. *IGen* needs only to be run once at the beginning of the system setup. All the outputs except n must be kept secret. In the rest of the paper, we assume all arithmetic to be *mod n* unless stated otherwise.
- *UGen* is the algorithm for generating the key pairs for the users and the proxy. For each user i, *UGen* takes the output of *IGen* and finds $e_{i1}, e_{i2}, d_{i1},$ d_{i2} such that $e_{i1}e_{i2} \equiv e \mod \phi(n)$ and $d_{i1}d_{i2} \equiv d \mod \phi(n)$. This can be efficiently done. Take the e_{i1}, e_{i2} pair for example, we can pick $e_{i1} < \phi(n)$ randomly, where e_{i1} is relatively prime to $\phi(n)$, i.e. $gcd(e_{i1}, \phi(n)) = 1$. Since

$e_{i1}x \equiv 1 \ mod \ \phi(n)$ always has a solution, then $e_{i2} \equiv ex \ mod \ \phi(n)$ always satisfies $e_{i1}e_{i2} \equiv e \ mod \ \phi(n)$. Note that knowing only a is not sufficient for solving the two variable equation $ax \equiv y \ mod \ n$. Therefore by knowing only e_{i1} or e_{i2}, one cannot compute its counterpart (e_{i2} or e_{i1} respectively) and e. The user's key pair is $(K_{uei}, K_{udi}) = (e_{i1}, d_{i1})$. The proxy's corresponding key pair for the user i is $(K_{pei}, K_{pdi}) = (e_{i2}, d_{i2})$. The lower bound of the number of valid key pairs is $\phi(\phi(n)) > \sqrt{\phi(n)}$.

- $UEnc$ is the algorithm for user encryption. For a message m, user i encrypts it using his encryption key $K_{uei} = e_{i1}$. The resulting ciphertext is $c = m^{e_{i1}}$.
- $PEnc$ is the algorithm for proxy encryption. When the proxy receives a ciphertext c from user i, it re-encrypts it using the corresponding encryption key $K_{pei} = e_{i2}$ as $c^* = c^{e_{i2}}$.
- $PDnc$ is the algorithm for proxy decryption. Before sending the ciphertext to user j, the proxy decrypts it using the corresponding decryption key $K_{pdj} = d_{j2}$ as $c' = (c^*)^{d_{j2}}$.
- $UDec$ is the algorithm for user decryption. When a user j receives a ciphertext c' from the proxy, he decrypts it using his decryption key $K_{udj} = d_{j1}$. He will be able to recover the plaintext $m = (c')^{d_{j1}}$.

Note that in the system, for any user i and any user j, $e_{i1}e_{i2} \equiv e_{j1}e_{j2} \equiv e \ mod \ \phi(n)$ and $d_{i1}d_{i2} \equiv d_{j1}d_{j2} \equiv d \ mod \ \phi(n)$. Therefore $c^* = c^{e_{i2}} = m^{e_{i1}e_{i2}} = m^e$, $c' = (c^*)^{d_{j2}} = m^{ed_{j2}}$ and the user j can correctly decrypt c' because $(c')^{d_{j1}} = m^{ed_{j2}d_{j1}} = m^{ed} = m$.

In our system, we use a trusted key management server (KMS) controlled by the data owner to manage the keys. First, the KMS runs $IGen$ to generate a master key pair (e, d) and publishes the only public parameter n. When a new user is enrolled into the system, the KMS runs $UGen$ to generate a unique tuple $((e_{i1}, d_{i1}), (e_{i2}, d_{i2}))$ and sends (e_{i1}, d_{i1}) to the user and (e_{i2}, d_{i2}) to the data server through secure channels. If the user is removed from the system at a later stage, the KMS can send a instruction to the data server to remove the key pair (e_{i2}, d_{i2}) at the server side. We will see in the following sections, without the server side key pairs, the user cannot search and decrypt the data.

Although requiring a trusted KMS seems at odds with using an untrusted data storage service, we can argue that the KMS requires less resources and less management effort. Securing the KMS is much easier since a very limited amount of data needs to be protected and the KMS can be kept offline most of time.

3.2 Data Encryption

In our system, each data item D_x is associated with a set of searching keywords $\{W_1, W_2, ..., W_n\}_x$. The encryption algorithm is shown in Fig. 2. The data item could be a document, an email, or a data cell in a database etc..

The data encryption is done at the client side using a semantically secure [19] symmetric encryption algorithm E. For each data item D_x, the user i picks a key K_x uniformly randomly from the key space of E and encrypts D_x under the

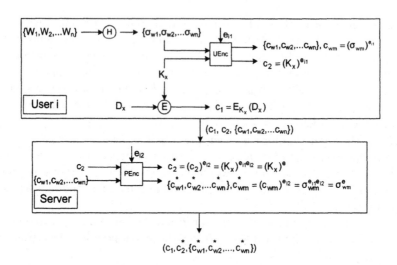

Fig. 2. Basic Data Encryption Scheme

key which generates a ciphertext $c_1 = E_{K_x}(D_x)$. K_x is then encrypted by the user's piece of RSA encryption key as $c_2 = (K_x)^{e_{i1}}$.

For each search keyword W_m, the client uses a hash function H to compute $\sigma_{wm} = H(W_m)$ and computes $c_{wm} = (\sigma_{wm})^{e_{i1}}$. The client then sends the tuple $(c_1, c_2, \{c_{w1}, c_{w2}, ..., c_{wn}\})$ to the server.

After receiving the tuple, the server first computes $c_2^* = c_2^{e_{i2}}$. For each encrypted keyword c_{wm}, the server computes $c_{wm}^* = c_{wm}^{e_{i2}}$. The final cipher stored on the server is a tuple $(c_1, c_2^*, \{c_{w1}^*, c_{w2}^*, ...c_{wm}^*\})$.

3.3 Keyword Search

A user j may want to retrieve all the documents on the server which contain a keyword W. To do so, j first computes the hash value of the keyword $\sigma = H(W)$. Then j encrypts σ as $Q = \sigma^{e_{j1}}$ and sends Q to the server.

The server re-encrypts Q as $Q^* = Q^{e_{j2}}$. Then it tests each ciphertext: in the encrypted keywords set $\{c_{w1}^*, ..., c_{wm}^*\}_x$, if there exists a c_{wm}^* such that $c_{wm}^* = Q^*$, then adds this ciphertext into the result set.

Recall that $e_{i1}e_{i2} \equiv e_{j1}e_{j2} \equiv e \bmod \phi(n)$, so $Q^* = (H(W))^e$ and $c_{wm}^* = (H(W_m))^e$ are equal if and only if $W = W_m$. If the server cannot find the corresponding key for the user j, it cannot correctly compute the searching keyword. Therefore an unauthorised user cannot perform searching on the data.

3.4 Data Decryption

If an authorised user j wants to retrieve D_x, the server gets the tuple $(c_1, c_2^*, \{c_{w1}^*, c_{w2}^*, ...c_{wm}^*\})$ from the data storage, computes $c_2' = (c_2^*)^{d_{j2}}$ and sends c_1, c_2' to j. The user j then computes $(c_2')^{d_{j1}} = (c_2^*)^d = (K_x)^{ed} = K_x$ and can decrypt the data item $D_x = E_{K_x}^{-1}(c_1)$. An unauthorised user cannot decrypt the data because the server does not have the corresponding proxy decryption key.

3.5   Attack Model

We focus the scope of our scheme on protecting data confidentiality, therefore we will not consider attacks on data integrity and availability which can be handled by other mechanisms. For the scheme, we assume that the KMS and the authorised users are fully trusted. We also assume they can properly protect their secrets, for example, the key pairs and the parameters for generating keys. The server is modelled as "honest-but-curious", i.e. we trust it to correctly execute the instructions from the clients, but do not want it to access the plain data. An adversary Adv is an attacker (or a software agent) that gains privileged access to the data storage: either an outsider or a untrustworthy employee in the data centre. The adversary can also intercept the communications between clients and the server, but it is computationally bounded. In addition, the adversary is restricted to only perform passive attacks, i.e. attacks are based upon observed data. This restriction is reasonable because: (1) in most cases Adv is physically isolated from the users; (2) most communications between the clients and the server are one-round and initialised by the client, i.e. query-reply. The goal of the adversary is to gather direct or indirect information about the stored data.

3.6   Security Analysis

We now give the formal notions of security and proof of security for our system. Note that in the basic construction, the ciphertexts are encrypted by two different schemes. In such situations, the security of the whole system depends on the individual scheme. We assume that the symmetric key scheme is semantically secure, and will prove our proxy encryption scheme is One-Way secure.

Readers who are familiar with RSA may have concerns because there are several known attacks on RSA, e.g. common modulus attack [20,21], which enables an attacker to recover the plaintext. Because our proxy encryption scheme is RSA-based, readers may be curious about how secure it is. We will prove in lemma 1 that if an attacker can recover a plaintext encrypted under our proxy encryption scheme, then he can recover any message encrypted by any arbitrary RSA key by knowing only the ciphertext and the modulus n. This contradicts the RSA assumption, therefore our scheme should be secure against all such attacks.

Definition 1. *Let* $\mathcal{E} = (IGen, UGen, UEnc, UDec, PEnc, PDec)$ *be the proxy encryption scheme.* $\mathcal{E}$ *is said to be One-Way secure against any PPT attacker* $\mathcal{A}$ *if* $Succ_{\mathcal{A},\mathcal{E}}$ *is negligible.* $Succ_{\mathcal{A},\mathcal{E}}$ *is defined as follows:*

$$
Succ_{\mathcal{A},\mathcal{E}} = Pr \left[m' = m \left| \begin{array}{l} (p,q,n,\phi(n),e,d) \leftarrow IGen(1^k), \\ (\mathcal{K}_u, \mathcal{K}_p) \leftarrow UGen(\phi(n),e,d), \\ m' \leftarrow \mathcal{A}(\mathcal{K}_p,n,m^\varepsilon), \varepsilon \in \mathcal{K}_u \end{array} \right. \right]
$$

Loosely speaking, the proxy encryption scheme is one-way secure if by knowing the public parameter n, all the key pairs on the server side, ciphertexts encrypted under an authorised user's encryption key and any information can be derived from above, e.g. intermediate ciphertexts calculated using the server side keys, but without knowing any key pairs in the authorised user key pair set $\mathcal{K}_u$, no PPT adversary can find the corresponding plaintext.

Lemma 1. *Under the RSA assumption, the proxy encryption scheme is One-Way secure against Adv.*

Proof. We will show that if Adv can break the proxy encryption scheme, i.e. $Succ_{\mathcal{A},\mathcal{E}}$ is not negligible, then there is an attacker $\mathcal{B}$ who can solve the RSA problem with non-negligible probability.

Given an RSA ciphertext $c = m^e$ where the corresponding key pair is (e, d), the goal of $\mathcal{B}$ is to decrypt it, i.e. to find m. $\mathcal{B}$ can pick x pairs of random primes $\frac{n}{2} < (e_\mathcal{B}, d_\mathcal{B})_i < n - 2^{161}$. The primes are relatively prime to $\phi(n)$ because $\frac{\phi(n)}{2} < (e_\mathcal{B}, d_\mathcal{B})_i < \phi(n)$. $\mathcal{B}$ then sends $c, n, (e_\mathcal{B}, d_\mathcal{B})_i, i = 1, ..., x$ to Adv.

Adv can computes $c_1 = c^{e_{\mathcal{B}1}}$, $c_2 = c_1^{d_{\mathcal{B}1}}$. Next we will show that c, c_1, c_2, n, $(e_\mathcal{B}, d_\mathcal{B})_i, i = 1, ..., x$ can correctly simulate adv's knowledge in the proxy encryption scheme. First we will show that c, c_1, c_2 are valid ciphertexts for the proxy encryption scheme. The ciphertexts are valid if there exists a d' such that $e_2^{d'} = m$, i.e. $ee_{\mathcal{B}1}d_{\mathcal{B}1}d' \equiv 1 \mod \phi(n)$. Because $e_{\mathcal{B}1}, d_{\mathcal{B}1}$ are relatively prime to $\phi(n)$, we can always find y such that $e_{\mathcal{B}1}d_{\mathcal{B}1}y \equiv 1 \mod \phi(n)$. Therefore there always exists $d' \equiv dy \mod \phi(n)$ such that $ee_{\mathcal{B}1}d_{\mathcal{B}1}d' \equiv ee_{\mathcal{B}1}d_{\mathcal{B}1}dy \equiv (ed)(e_{\mathcal{B}1}d_{\mathcal{B}1}y) \equiv 1 \mod \phi(n)$. We also need to show that $(e_\mathcal{B}, d_\mathcal{B})_i, i = 1, ..., x$ are valid server side key pairs, this can be easily proved using the similar method as above therefore is omitted.

Now with the message from $\mathcal{B}$, Adv can find m with probability $Succ_{\mathcal{A},\mathcal{E}}$ and returns the result to $\mathcal{B}$. This means $\mathcal{B}$ can solve the RSA problem with non-negligible probability $Succ_{\mathcal{A},\mathcal{E}}$, which contradicts the RSA assumption.

Theorem 1. *The basic construction is One-Way secure against Adv.*

This is quite straightforward. The ciphertext is encrypted disjointedly by two encryption schemes. The symmetric encryption scheme is semantically secure, i.e. ciphertext indistinguishable, which implies it is One-Way secure against Adv. Since the proxy encryption scheme has been proved to be One-Way secure, overall, the basic construction is One-Way secure against Adv.

One-Way secure is sufficient to protect a data item, since an adversary cannot recover the symmetric key and then decrypt the data item. But it does leak some information about the keywords. Because the proxy encryption is deterministic, the ciphertexts of keywords are not indistinguishable. All the occurrences of the same keyword generate the same ciphertext. The adversary can make inferences from the keyword distribution by observing the encrypted data service.

In the following section, we will show a enhanced scheme which is semantically secure and makes the above attack impossible.

4   Enhanced Construction

The problem with the basic construction comes from the fact that the keyword encryption is not semantically secure. Using some probabilistic padding schemes can solve the problem, but then the encrypted keywords are no longer searchable. In this section, we will show a enhanced construction with a new keyword encryption scheme which is both semantically secure and searchable.

4.1 Keyword Encryption Scheme

In the new construction, to avoid the problem discussed in section 3.6, the keywords are no longer encrypted under the proxy encryption scheme. Instead, we encrypt each keyword as a non-interactive zero-knowledge proof style witness. An additional key pair is generated for encrypting the keywords and in the queries. The new keyword encryption scheme is based on Discrete Logarithms.

Let $\mathcal{E}' = (IGen', UGen', UEnc', PEnc')$ denote the keyword encryption scheme.

- $IGen'$ is the algorithm for generating the public parameters and the master key. It takes a security parameter k and generates $\{p', q', g, x, h, a, g^a h^a\}$. p' and q' are two large prime numbers such that q' divides $p' - 1$. g is a generator of $G_{q'}$, the unique order-q' subgroup of $Z_{p'}^*$. $h \equiv g^x \bmod p'$ where x is chosen uniformly randomly from $Z_{q'}$. a is also a random number from $z_{q'}$. $p', q', g, h, g^a h^a$ are publicised and x, a must be kept secret. The reason why we publish $g^a h^a$ instead of g^a is that if g^a is available to the adversary, then it can generate search queries of any chosen keywords.
- $UGen'$ is the algorithm for generating the key pairs for the users and the proxy. For a user i, it finds $a_{i1} a_{i2} \equiv a \bmod q'$. The user's keyword encryption key is a_{i1}, and the proxy's share is a_{i2}. The number of key pairs is at least $\phi(q') = q' - 1$.
- $UEnc'$ is the client-side encryption algorithm.
- $PEnc'$ is the server-side encryption algorithm.

Note that there is no decryption algorithm for this keyword encryption scheme. This is because the ciphertexts of the keywords are only used for testing whether there is a match and do not need to be decrypted.

4.2 Data Encryption/Decryption

The new encryption scheme is shown in Fig. 3. The data item encryption/ decryption is the same as in the basic construction. Although plain RSA can sufficiently protect the symmetric keys used to encrypt the data items, it cannot make the ciphertexts indistinguishable and may leak some information. If the adversary can somehow distinguish the encrypted keys and uses the keys as tags, he can distinguish the data items. To prevent such attacks, we pad the keys with OAEP (Optimal Asymmetric Encryption Padding) [22], a probabilistic padding scheme, before encryption. RSA-OAEP has been proved to be indistinguishable under adaptive chosen ciphertext attack in the random oracle model [23]. Now the symmetric key is encrypted by the user's piece of the RSA encryption key

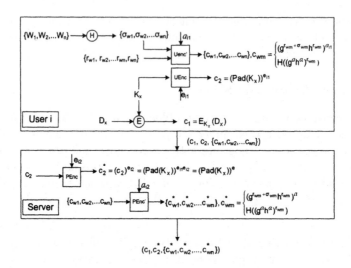

Fig. 3. Data Encryption Algorithm 2

as $c_2 = (Pad(K_x))^{e_{i1}}$. The server side proxy encryption/decryption algorithms remain the same, i.e. modular exponentiation.

The keywords are now processed as follows: for each keyword W_m, the user i computes $\sigma_{wm} = H(W_m)$ using a hash function H. The user also picks a random number $r_{wm} \in Z_{q'}$ and computes $c_{wm,1} = (g^{r_{wm}+\sigma_{wm}} h^{r_{wm}})^{a_{i1}} \bmod p'$, $c_{wm,2} = H((g^a h^a)^{r_{wm}})$, where $g, h, g^a h^a, p'$ are public parameters in the system and a_{i1} is the user's keyword encryption key. The user then sends the tuple $(c_1, c_2, \{c_{w1}, c_{w2}, ..., c_{wn}\})$ to the server, where c_{wm} is the tuple $(c_{wm,1}, c_{wm,2})$.

The server re-encrypts the data encryption key as in the basic construction. Then it processes the keywords information. For each c_{wm}, the server computes $c^*_{wm,1} = c^{a_{i2}}_{wm1} = (g^{r_{wm}+\sigma_{wm}} h^{r_{wm}})^{a_{i1}a_{i2}} = (g^{r_{wm}+\sigma_{wm}} h^{r_{wm}})^a \bmod p'$, $c^*_{wm,2} = c_{wm,2}$. The final cipher stored is a tuple $(c_1, c^*_2, \{c^*_{w1}, c^*_{w2}, ...c^*_{wm}\})$, where $c^*_{wm} = (c^*_{wm,1}, c^*_{wm,2})$.

4.3 Keyword Search

To search for a keyword W, the user j computes $\sigma = H(W)$. The user then computes the encrypted query $Q = g^{(-\sigma)a_{j1}} \bmod p'$ and sends it to the server. The server computes $Q' = Q^{a_{j2}} \bmod p' = g^{(-\sigma)a} \bmod p'$. For each c^*_{wm}, the server computes:

$$y_1 = c^*_{wm,1} Q' = (g^{r_{wm}+\sigma_{wm}} h^{r_{wm}})^a g^{(-\sigma)a} = (g^{ar_{wm}+a\sigma_{wm}} h^{ar_{wm}}) g^{(-a\sigma)} \bmod p'$$
$$y_2 = H((y_1))$$

We can see that if $a\sigma_{wm} - a\sigma = 0$, i.e., $W_m = W$, then $y_1 = (g^{ar_{wm}} h^{ar_{wm}}) = (g^a h^a)^{r_{wm}} \bmod p'$ and therefore $y_2 = H((g^a h^a)^{r_{wm}}) = c^*_{wm,2}$. Then by comparing y_2 and $c^*_{wm,2}$, the server can decide whether the keyword matches the query.

4.4   Security Analysis

We first prove that the keyword encryption is semantically secure. Semantic security means that the ciphertexts are indistinguishable to the adversary, therefore the adversary learns nothing by looking at the ciphertext.

Lemma 2. *Let the keyword encryption* $\mathcal{KE} = (Pub\_para, Sec\_para, \mathcal{K}_u, \mathcal{K}_p,$ *Enc) where Pub_para is the public parameter set, Sec_para is the secret parameter set, $\mathcal{K}_u, \mathcal{K}_p$ are the user and proxy key sets respectively, Enc, Dec are the encryption/decryption algorithms. It is semantically secure against any PPT attacker (i.e. $Succ_{\mathcal{A},\mathcal{KE}}$ is negligible) where*

$$Succ_{\mathcal{A},\mathcal{KE}} = Pr\left[b' = b \left| \begin{array}{c} m_0, m_1 \in \{0,1\}^l, \\ b \overset{R}{\leftarrow} \{0,1\}, \\ b' \leftarrow \mathcal{A}(Pub\_para, \mathcal{K}_p, Enc_k(m_b)), k \in \mathcal{K}_u \end{array} \right. \right] - \frac{1}{2}$$

Proof. The ciphertext of a keyword m_b in the form of $c_{m_b} = ((g^{r_{m_b}+\sigma_{m_b}} h^{r_{m_b}})^{a_{i1}},$ $H((g^a h^a)^{r_{m_b}}))$. It's easy to see that if r_{m_b} is selected uniformly randomly from $Z_{q'}$, then $g^{r_{m_b}+\sigma_{m_b}} h^{r_{m_b}}$ is distributed uniformly in $G_{q'}$. We will show that if $Succ_{\mathcal{A},\mathcal{KE}}$ is non-negligible, then there is an attacker $\mathcal{B}$ who can win the following game with a non-negligible probability $Succ_{\mathcal{B},\mathcal{C}}$, which contradicts the fact that r is random.

$$Succ_{\mathcal{B},\mathcal{C}} = Pr\left[b' = b \left| \begin{array}{c} m_0, m_1 \in \{0,1\}^l, \\ b \overset{R}{\leftarrow} \{0,1\}, r \overset{R}{\leftarrow} Z_{q'}, \sigma_{m_b} = H(m_b) \\ b' \leftarrow \mathcal{A}(p', q', g, h, H, g^{r+\sigma_{m_b}} h^r) \end{array} \right. \right] - \frac{1}{2}$$

$\mathcal{B}$ first sends m_0, m_1 to the encryption oracle and receives $g^{r+\sigma_{m_b}} h^r$. Then it chooses a random number $a \in Z_{q'}$ and generates n pairs of (a_{i1}, a_{i2}) such that $a_{i1}a_{i2} \equiv a \bmod p'$. It also computes $\sigma_{m_0} = H(m_0)$ and $\theta = g^{r+\sigma_{m_b}} h^r g^{-\sigma_{m_0}}$, it is clear that $Pr[\theta = g^r h^r] = \frac{1}{2}$. Then $\mathcal{B}$ sends $(m_0, m_1, p', q', g, h, g^a h^a,$ $(g^{r+\sigma_{m_b}} h^r)^{a_{11}}, (g^{r+\sigma_{m_b}} h^r)^a, H(\theta^a), a_{12}, ..., a_{n2})$ to $\mathcal{A}$. If $\theta = g^r h^r$, then $\mathcal{A}$ can output $b' = b$ with probability $Succ_{\mathcal{A},\mathcal{KE}}$. Therefore the probability of $\mathcal{B}$ winning the game is $Succ_{\mathcal{B},\mathcal{C}} = Succ_{\mathcal{A},\mathcal{KE}}/2$, which is non-negligible.

The semantically secure definition for searchable encryption is tricky because searching leaks information inevitably. As long as the searching algorithm is correct, it always returns the same result set for the same query. Although the queries and the result sets are encrypted, the adversary can still build up search patterns. Therefore the security definition for searchable encryption should be modified to reflect the intuition that nothing should be leaked beyond the outcome and the pattern of a sequence of searches. Here we adapt the definition from [11] and prove our scheme is non-adaptive semantically secure. Informally, non-adaptive semantic security means that given two non-adaptively generated query histories with the same length and outcome, no PPT adversary can distinguish one from another with non-negligible probability. Non-adaptive means the adversary cannot choose queries based on the prior queries and results. This is acceptable because in our setting, only the authorised user can generate queries.

We first introduce some notions to be used in the definition. Δ is the set of all possible data items, i.e. documents. $\mathcal{D} = \{D_1, ..., D_n\}$ denotes an arbitrary subset of Δ, i.e. $\mathcal{D} \in \mathcal{P}(\Delta)$, and each D_i is a document. $\mathcal{W} = \{w_1, ..., w_d\}$ is a dictionary which contains all the possible words can be used in the queries. Each document in $\mathcal{D}$ is associated with a local unique identifier $id(D_i)$, and a set of keywords $kw(D_i)$ which is a subset of $\mathcal{W}$. The result set of a search query w on a document set is denoted by $rs(w)$, which is the set of document identifiers of all the documents in $\mathcal{D}$ that contain the keyword, i.e. $\{id(D)|D \in \mathcal{D} \wedge w \in kw(D)\}$. A *history* is defined in terms of a sequence of queries made on a document set.

Definition 2 (History). *A history $H_q \in \mathcal{P}(\Delta) \times \mathcal{W}^q$ is an interaction between a client and a server over q queries on a document set $\mathcal{D}$, i.e. $H_q = (\mathcal{D}, w_1, ..., w_q)$.*

During the interaction, the adversary cannot directly see the history because the documents, keywords and queries are encrypted. What the adversary can see is a *view*, i.e. the encrypted version of the history. Let E be the symmetric key encryption scheme, $\mathcal{E}$ be the proxy encryption scheme and $\mathcal{KE}$ be the keyword encryption scheme, Q_i be an encrypted query, the view of the adversary is then defined as:

Definition 3 (View). *Given a document set $\mathcal{D}$ with n documents and a history over q queries $H_q = (\mathcal{D}, w_1, ..., w_q)$, an adversary's view of H_q is defined as:*
$V(H_q) = (id(D_1), ..., id(D_n), E_{k_1}(D_1), ..., E_{k_n}(D_n), \mathcal{E}(k_1), ..., \mathcal{E}(k_n), \mathcal{KE}(kw(D_1)), ...,$
$\mathcal{KE}(kw(D_n)), Q_1, ..., Q_q).$

As we have stated above, searching leaks information. The maximum information we have to leak is captured by *trace*. In our settings, a trace contains information from three sources: the encrypted file stored on the server, e.g. the id, length and number of keywords of each document, the result set and the query pattern.

Definition 4 (Trace). *Given a document set $\mathcal{D}$ with n documents and a history over q queries H_q, the trace of H_q is defined as:*
$Tr(H_q) = (id(D_1), ..., id(D_n), |D_1|, ..., |D_n|, |kw(D_1)|, ..., |kw(D_n)|, rs(w_1), ..., rs(w_q), \Pi_q).$
Π_q is the search pattern over the history which is a symmetric binary matrix where $\Pi_q[i, j] = 1$ if $w_i = w_j$, and $\Pi_q[i, j] = 0$ otherwise, for $1 \leq i, j \leq q$.

The security definition is then based on the idea that the scheme is secure if no more information is leaked beyond what the adversary can get from the traces. This intuition is formalised by defining a game where the adversary has to distinguish two histories, possibly on two different document sets, which have the same trace. Since the traces are identical, the adversary cannot distinguish the two histories by the traces, i.e. the knowledge he already has. He must extract additional knowledge from what he can see during the interactions, i.e. the views. The negligible probability of the adversary successfully distinguishing the two histories implies that he cannot get extra knowledge and in consequence the scheme is secure.

Definition 5 (Non-Adaptive Semantic Security). *Our searchable data encryption is Non-Adaptive Semantically Secure if for all $q \in \mathbb{N}$, for all (H_0, H_1) which are histories over q queries and $Tr(H_0) = Tr(H_1)$, and any PPT adversary $\mathcal{A}$, $Succ_{\mathcal{A}}$ is negligible:*

$$Succ_{\mathcal{A}} = Pr \left[b' = b \left| \begin{array}{c} Pub\_para, Sec\_para, \mathcal{K}_u, \mathcal{K}_p \leftarrow SETUP(1^k), \\ H_0, H_1 \in \mathcal{P}(\Delta) \times \mathcal{W}^q, \\ b \xleftarrow{R} \{0,1\}, \\ b' \leftarrow \mathcal{A}(Pub\_para, \mathcal{K}_p, V(H_b)) \end{array} \right. \right] - \frac{1}{2}$$

Theorem 2. *The enhanced construction is non-adaptive semantically secure.*

Proof. Let's examine each part of the view.

Document identifiers $id(D_1), ..., id(D_n)$: Because $Tr(H_0) = Tr(H_1)$, this part of the view must be identical for the two histories. So the adversary cannot distinguish the two histories by the document identifiers.

Encrypted documents $E_{k_1}(D_1), ..., E_{k_n}(D_n)$: The adversary cannot distinguish because E is semantically secure.

Encrypted symmetric keys $\mathcal{E}(k_1), ..., \mathcal{E}(k_n)$: $\mathcal{E}$ is based on RSA-OAEP which is IND-CCA2 secure. Therefore is also indistinguishable.

Encrypted keywords $\mathcal{KE}(kw(D_1)), ..., \mathcal{KE}(kw(D_n))$: We have proved they are indistinguishable to the adversary in lemma 2.

Encrypted queries $Q_1, ..., Q_q$: Because $Tr(H_0) = Tr(H_1)$, we don't need to consider the query pattern and can reduce the problem to distinguish any two sequences of distinct queries: $(Q_{01}, ..., Q_{0m}), (Q_{11}, ..., Q_{1m}), m \leq q$. For each $Q_{ij}, i \in 0, 1, 1 \leq j \leq m$, it is a pseudorandom number $g^{a_1 H(w_{ij})} \bmod p'$. Therefore the queries are not distinguishable as long as the discrete logarithm problem is hard.

5   Other Considerations

Access to encrypted data involves both client-side and server-side keys. So revoking a user's access is quite simple. The KMS can send an instruction to the server to let it remove the user's corresponding keys on the server side. After the keys have been removed, the user cannot access the data unless the KMS generates new keys for him. Even a revoked user can masquerade as an authorised user, his requests cannot be processed correctly if he does not know the authorised user's keys.

Each authorised user has his own RSA key pair (e_{i1}, d_{i1}) and the server holds the corresponding key pair (e_{i2}, d_{i2}). Because $e_{i1}d_{i1}e_{i2}d_{i2} \equiv ed \equiv 1 \bmod \phi(n)$, $k_1 = e_{i1}d_{i1}$ and $k_2 = e_{i2}d_{i2}$ form another RSA key pair. This key pair can be used for public key based mutual authentication and to establish a secure channel e.g. SSL. This adds another layer of protection against unauthorised users.

The main concern with proxy encryption schemes comes from a collusion attack. If a user colludes with adversary Adv, who knows all the server side keys, they can easily recover the master keys by combining their keys. Although some work has been done in [16] using bilinear map to prevent the colluded parties from recovering the master key, the colluded parties are still able to decrypt the ciphertext with a weak secret they can recover. Theoretically, the design of collusion-resistant proxy encryption schemes is an open problem. But in practice, we can lower the risk to an acceptable level by implementing other mechanisms. For example, we can limit the access to the keys by using tamper-proof devices.

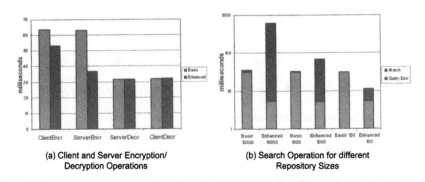

(a) Client and Server Encryption/   (b) Search Operation for different
       Decryption Operations   Repository Sizes

Fig. 4. Performance of the Operations

We can also split the master keys into multiple shares and introduce additional servers, making collusion more difficult. Monitoring and auditing to detect collusion can also help to mitigate the risk.

6   Implementation and Performance

We implemented a prototype in Java using the packages provided in the standard Java 1.5 distribution. We use our encryption scheme to encrypt a single table database. We chose AES as the symmetric cipher which encrypts the actual data and SHA-1 as the hash function. For the RSA-based proxy encryption scheme, we used 1024-bit keys. For the keyword encryption scheme, q' was 160-bit and p' was 1024-bit. The tests were executed on a Intel Pentium IV 3.2 GHz (dual core) with 1 GB of RAM.

The first evaluation consists of measuring for each scheme the execution time of the following operations: (1) **Client Encryption**: that consists of encrypting a data item using the symmetric cipher, encrypting the symmetric key and encrypting the keywords; (2) **Server Encryption**: re-encryption of the symmetric key and the keywords using the server side keys; (3) **Server Decryption**: pre-decryption of the symmetric key; (4) **Client Decryption**: decryption of the symmetric key and the data item.

The graph in Fig. 4-(a) shows the performance for the execution of encryption and decryption operations for each construction. The time in the Y-axis is given in milliseconds. The graph provides the average time for 10,000 executions. The data item we used in the experiments was a 16-byte string with one associated keyword. The result shows that the enhanced construction has better performance than the basic construction in encryption. Since the data encryption and key encryption are nearly identical in both constructions, the difference is due to the fact that they encrypt the keywords using different schemes. The enhanced construction encrypts the keywords using a Discrete Logarithm based scheme and the basic construction uses an RSA-based scheme. The exponent used in the DL scheme is smaller than that of the RSA scheme, therefore the keyword encryption of the DL scheme is faster than the RSA scheme. The decryption part of both constructions are almost the same, so we can see from the figure that the two constructions have nearly the same performance in decryption.

We also measured the time for processing a search query on the server side in both constructions, the result is shown in Fig. 4-(b). Processing a search query involves two operations: query re-encryption (Query Encr) and matching (Match). The graph shows the time (in milliseconds) for a search operation (the time scale is logarithmic) executed on several databases with different sizes in both constructions. We used three databases containing 100, 1,000 and 10,000 keywords each. The graph shows that for the basic construction, the query encryption dominates the overall searching time. This is easy to understand since the matching operation in the basic construction is simply string comparison. Therefore the size of the database has little effect on the searching time in the basic construction. In contrast, the time spent on the matching operation is much more significant in the enhanced construction. And when the database becomes large, the time increases linearly. As a result, the basic construction has better performance than the enhanced construction when searching large databases.

7   Conclusion and Future Work

In this paper, we presented a new data encryption scheme that does not require a trusted data server. In the scheme the server can perform searches and updates on the encrypted data without knowing the plaintext or the decryption keys. Unlike previous searchable data encryption schemes that require a shared key for multi-user access, each user in our system has a unique set of keys. The data encrypted by one user can be correctly decrypted by all the authorised users in the system. Moreover the keys can be easily revoked without any overhead, i.e. without having to re-encrypt the stored data. We provided two constructions for the scheme built on top of proxy encryption schemes. For each construction, we gave the formal definitions and proofs of security. We also implemented them in Java and compared the performance.

One aspect of our future work is to investigate and integrate our scheme with Private Information Retrieval (PIR) schemes. PIR schemes [24,25,26] allow a user to retrieve some items from a database without revealing to the database which items were queried. A weakness of our scheme is that it allows statistical attacks on the queries. By combining PIR techniques, we could potentially make our scheme more secure. Secure indexes [4,5] is another promising technique that is used to improve the performance and decrease the storage overhead of searchable encryption schemes. We will investigate current schemes and develop a new index scheme for the multi-user system.

References

1. Blackwood, J.: Is storage outsourcing a viable alternative? http://techupdate. zdnet.com/techupdate/stories/main/0,14179,2851289,00.html
2. Connor, D.: Storage outsourcing on the rise, http://www.networkworld.com/ news/2007/012207-storage-outsourcing-rises.html

3. Song, D.X., Wagner, D., Perrig, A.: Practical techniques for searches on encrypted data. In: IEEE Symposium on Security and Privacy, pp. 44–55 (2000)
4. Yang, Z., Zhong, S., Wright, R.N.: Privacy-Preserving Queries on Encrypted Data. In: Gollmann, D., Meier, J., Sabelfeld, A. (eds.) ESORICS 2006. LNCS, vol. 4189, pp. 479–495. Springer, Heidelberg (2006)
5. Goh, E.J.: Secure indexes. Cryptology ePrint Archive, Report 2003/216 (2003), http://eprint.iacr.org/2003/216/
6. Hacigümüs, H., Iyer, B.R., Li, C., Mehrotra, S.: Executing sql over encrypted data in the database-service-provider model. In: SIGMOD Conference, pp. 216–227 (2002)
7. Damiani, E., di Vimercati, S.D.C., Jajodia, S., Paraboschi, S., Samarati, P.: Balancing confidentiality and efficiency in untrusted relational dbmss. In: ACM Conference on Computer and Communications Security, pp. 93–102 (2003)
8. Agrawal, R., Kiernan, J., Srikant, R., Xu, Y.: Order-preserving encryption for numeric data. In: SIGMOD Conference, pp. 563–574 (2004)
9. Hore, B., Mehrotra, S., Tsudik, G.: A privacy-preserving index for range queries. In: VLDB, pp. 720–731 (2004)
10. Boneh, D., Crescenzo, G.D., Ostrovsky, R., Persiano, G.: Public Key Encryption with Keyword Search. In: Cachin, C., Camenisch, J.L. (eds.) EUROCRYPT 2004. LNCS, vol. 3027, pp. 506–522. Springer, Heidelberg (2004)
11. Curtmola, R., Garay, J.A., Kamara, S., Ostrovsky, R.: Searchable symmetric encryption: improved definitions and efficient constructions. In: ACM Conference on Computer and Communications Security, pp. 79–88 (2006)
12. Blaze, M., Bleumer, G., Strauss, M.: Divertible Protocols and Atomic Proxy Cryptography. In: Nyberg, K. (ed.) EUROCRYPT 1998. LNCS, vol. 1403, pp. 127–144. Springer, Heidelberg (1998)
13. Elgamal, T.: A public key cryptosystem and a signature scheme based on discrete logarithms. IEEE Transactions on Information Theory 31(4), 469–472 (1985)
14. Rivest, R.L., Shamir, A., Adleman, L.M.: A method for obtaining digital signatures and public-key cryptosystems. Commun. ACM 21(2), 120–126 (1978)
15. Khurana, H., Slagell, A.J., Bonilla, R.: Sels: a secure e-mail list service. In: SAC, pp. 306–313 (2005)
16. Ateniese, G., Fu, K., Green, M., Hohenberger, S.: Improved proxy re-encryption schemes with applications to secure distributed storage. In: NDSS (2005)
17. Kapadia, A., Tsang, P.P., Smith, S.W.: Attribute-based publishing with hidden credentials and hidden policies. In: NDSS (2007)
18. Ivan, A.A., Dodis, Y.: Proxy cryptography revisited. In: NDSS (2003)
19. Goldreich, O.: Foundations of Cryptography: Basic Applications, vol. II. Cambridge University Press, Cambridge (2004)
20. Simmons, G.J.: A "weak" privacy protocol using the rsa crypto algorithm. Cryptologia 7(2), 180–182 (1983)
21. Delaurentis, J.M.: A further weakness in the common modulus protocol for the rsa cryptoalgorithm. Cryptologia 8(3), 253–259 (1984)
22. Bellare, M., Rogaway, P.: Optimal Asymmetric Encryption. In: De Santis, A. (ed.) EUROCRYPT 1994. LNCS, vol. 950, pp. 92–111. Springer, Heidelberg (1995)
23. Fujisaki, E., Okamoto, T., Pointcheval, D., Stern, J.: RSA-OAEP Is Secure under the RSA Assumption. In: Kilian, J. (ed.) CRYPTO 2001. LNCS, vol. 2139, pp. 260–274. Springer, Heidelberg (2001)

24. Chor, B., Goldreich, O., Kushilevitz, E., Sudan, M.: Private information retrieval. In: FOCS, pp. 41–50 (1995)
25. Cachin, C., Micali, S., Stadler, M.: Computationally Private Information Retrieval with Polylogarithmic Communication. In: Stern, J. (ed.) EUROCRYPT 1999. LNCS, vol. 1592, pp. 402–414. Springer, Heidelberg (1999)
26. Gentry, C., Ramzan, Z.: Single-Database Private Information Retrieval with Constant Communication Rate. In: Caires, L., Italiano, G.F., Monteiro, L., Palamidessi, C., Yung, M. (eds.) ICALP 2005. LNCS, vol. 3580, pp. 803–815. Springer, Heidelberg (2005)

Secure Construction of Contingency Tables from Distributed Data

Haibing Lu, Xiaoyun He, Jaideep Vaidya, and Nabil Adam

MSIS Department and CIMIC, Rutgers University, USA
{haibing,xiaoyun,jsvaidya,adam}@cimic.rutgers.edu

Abstract. Contingency tables are widely used in many fields to analyze the relationship or infer the association between two or more variables. Indeed, due to their simplicity and ease, they are one of the first methods used to analyze gathered data. Typically, the construction of contingency tables from source data is considered straightforward since all data is supposed to be aggregated at a single party. However, in many cases, the collected data may actually be federated among different parties. Privacy and security concerns may restrict the data owners from free sharing of the raw data. However, construction of the global contingency tables would still be of immense interest. In this paper, we propose techniques for enabling secure construction of contingency tables from both horizontally and vertically partitioned data. Our methods are efficient and secure. We also examine cases where the constructed contingency table may itself leak too much information and discuss potential solutions.

1 Introduction

Contingency tables have been widely used in a number of application domains, including social science [11] , epidemiology [8] , experimental studies of economics [9], etc. Simply put, a contingency table is a table of frequency counts (i.e., Figure 2), which is often used to analyze the relationship or infer the association between two or more variables. The construction of contingency tables from a source data is considered straightforward - i.e., in the two variable case, listing all the levels of one variable as rows and the levels of the other variables as columns in a table, then finding the joint frequency for each cell. The underlying assumption of such computation is that the original data is centralized at one site or owned by a single party.

However, there are many situations where we may want to construct contingency tables from multiple data sources and/or ownerships. For example, in the health care domain, each hospital holds its patients' medical records. Consider a scenario where doctors are trying to find out the relationship between a certain rare disease and the effectiveness of different treatments. Given the small number of instances, it is beneficial for all the hospitals to start with constructing contingency tables from their combined medical records. However, in these circumstances, the privacy of the patients is a major concern, which may prevent the eventual collaboration between hospitals. Similar conflicts have been observed in other domains, such as financial services, telecommunications, and government agencies ([3], [6]). Therefore, how to solve such problems in

V. Atluri (Ed.): DAS 2008, LNCS 5094, pp. 144–157, 2008.

a privacy-preserving way is an emerging issue. In this regard, privacy-preserving data mining is a very closely related area, and the work in this area is quite relevant.

During the past years, privacy-preserving data mining [24] has attracted much attention from the research community since the seminal papers by Agrawal and Srikant [2] and Lindell and Pinkas [18]. Primarily the focus has been on creating privacy-preserving variants of different data mining tasks. Two main solution approaches have been followed. In the randomization approach, "noise" is added to the data before the data mining process, and then reconstruction techniques are used to mitigate the impact of the noise from the data mining results[1,2,10,22]. However, there is some debate about the security properties of such algorithms[15,17]. On the other had, cryptographic solutions following the secure multiparty computation framework ([13], [14], [25]) aim to achieve "perfect" privacy and limit disclosure only to information that can be inferred from each participant's own input and the results. Given that the general method for secure multiparty computations does not scale well to large dataset problems, a number of efficient methods (i.e., secure sum, secure size of set intersection, secure scalar product, etc.) have been developed ([7], [12]). These methods demonstrate provable privacy on individual information and bounds on information released. Another important fact is their applicability - we can use them as primitive tools to develop secure solutions for some specific applications. We follow this approach for our work.

In this paper, we present solutions to construct a general n-way contingency tables from distributed data in a privacy-preserving way. Two solutions are presented. The first solution assumes that the data is horizontally partitioned between parties, where different data objects with the same attributes are owned by each party. For this approach, we follow the underlying idea of secure sum protocol discussed in [7]. The second one focuses on the vertically partitioned data, in which different attributes for the same set of data objects are owned by each party. This solution is based on the secure scalar protocol [12]). In the horizontal partition case, we assume that there are three or more parties involved. Clearly, in the two-party case, one can first construct its local contingency table. Subtraction of the local table from the global contingency table reveals the other party's contingency table. Therefore much of the information we try to protect is revealed even though we follow a completely secure protocol to compute the global result. Clearly, at least three parties are necessary for security. There is no such constraint for the vertically partitioned case.

The remainder of this paper is organized as follows. We first formally define the problem in Section 2. In Section 3 we present the proposed algorithms for secure contingency tables computation. The solutions are presented for horizontally partitioned data as well as vertically partitioned data. Along with the algorithms, a detailed computation cost analysis and security analysis is provided. Finally, Section 4 concludes the paper and provides directions for future work.

2 Problem Definition

Consider data such as shown in Figure 1, where A_j denotes the jth attribute, R_i denotes the ith record, and v_{ij} denotes the value of the jth attribute for the ith record. We assume that each attribute is categorical. Therefore, each value v_{ij} is a nominal value.

	A_1	A_2	...	A_n
R_1	v_{11}	v_{12}	...	v_{1n}
R_2	v_{21}	v_{22}	...	v_{2n}
...	...	...	...	...
R_m	v_{m1}	v_{m2}	...	v_{mn}

Fig. 1. Categorical Data Table

In itself, this table is sufficient to construct a contingency table which can be used for information processing, like extraction of association rules or statistical analysis. However, consider that several parties collectively gather this data. Thus, each party independently possesses only part of the data – either several rows or several columns. Due to privacy/security concerns, the parties are not willing to release their raw data to the other parties or to any outside third party. However, they may wish to perform global data analysis using contingency tables or even be willing to allow a third party to do such analysis as long as it only gets the data analysis results as opposed to the raw data. Though the parties could compute their local contingency tables, clearly these could be very different from the global table and thus lead to quite inaccurate results. Therefore, they wish to compute the global contingency table in a privacy-preserving fashion. We denote this as the problem of **Secure Integration**. Specifically, this problem can be divided as **Secure Horizontal Integration**, where each party owns several rows, and **Secure Vertical Integration**, where each party owns several columns.

In this paper, we assume that all attributes are categorical – thus all values are nominal. In general, it is easily possible to discretize numerical data to form categorical attributes as well. Now to compute the contingency table of Figure 1, we only need to count the number of records having the same attributes values. Formally, assume attribute A_i has d_i distinct values, denoted by $\{a_{i,1}, a_{i,2}, ..., a_{i,d_i}\}$. Thus, the contingency table resulting from the integral table in Figure 1 is a n-dimensional matrix $C_{d_1 \times d_2 ... \times d_n}$, where cell $c_{j_1, j_2, ..., j_n}$ denotes the count of records in the table having the value $\{a_{1,j_1}, a_{2,j_2}, ..., a_{n,j_n}\}$. Obviously, the sum of all of the cells is the total number of records.

We now illustrate this with an example. Figure 2 shows data records on shopping lists, along with its corresponding contingency table. The shopping list collects data on two attributes, the drinks and fruits that are bought. Here, Drink has distinct values "Beer" and "Coke", and Fruit has distinct values "Apple" and "Orange". After counting the records having the same values, we have its contingency table, which is a 2×2 table shown on the right.

In the following, we will give the formal definition of contingency table and the corresponding secure integration problems as well.

Definition 1 (Contingency Table). *Given a dataset of m records and n attributes (as shown in Figure 1), where the distinct values of attribute A_i are denoted by $\{a_{i,1}, a_{i,2}, ..., a_{i,d_i}\}$, its contingency table is defined as a n-dimensional matrix $C_{d_1 \times d_2 ... \times d_n}$, where cell $c_{j_1, j_2, ..., j_n}$ denotes the count of records having the value $\{a_{1,j_1}, a_{2,j_2}, ..., a_{n,j_n}\}$.*

	Drink	Fruit
R_1	Beer	Apple
R_2	Coke	Apple
R_3	Coke	Orange
R_4	Beer	Apple

	Beer	Coke
Apple	2	1
Orange	0	1

Fig. 2. A Shopping List Table and its Contingency Table

Definition 2 (Construct Contingency Table on Horizontally Partitioned Data). *The global dataset (such as shown in Figure 1) is shared by many parties separately, each of whom owns different set of data objects with the same set of attributes. The parties want to construct the contingency table of the whole table together securely without letting others know the detailed data they own.*

Definition 3 (Construct Contingency Table on Vertically Partitioned Data). *The global dataset (such as shown in Figure 1) is shared by many parties separately, each of whom owns different set of attributes but for the same set of data objects. The parties want to construct the contingency table of the whole table together securely without letting others know the detailed data they own.*

The complete n-way contingency table can also be used to compute smaller contingency tables (for example, a 2-way contingency table looking at the correlation of two attributes) simply by summing up over the cells of all the other attributes. However, it might be useful to directly compute the smaller contingency tables. This can easily be done by using the same protocols but on a reduced subset of the data.

3   Secure Construction of Contingency Tables

As we have mentioned earlier, a contingency table is basically a table of counts. The count in a cell with respect to two or more attribute values is computed as the total number of co-occurrences of these values in a dataset. This seems simple for the centralized data. For computing the contingency tables from distributed data, a global view of the data needs to be composed by combining all the individual data belonging to different parties. However, these parties may not be willing to share/reveal their own data for reasons discussed in Section 1. The proposed approaches in this section enable computation of the contingency tables from the distributed data without requiring parties to reveal any details about their own data.

In a distributed environment, different models for data partitioning have been proposed (i.e.,[16], [24]). Here, we consider the two most common and practical models - horizontal partitioning and vertical partitioning of data. In each case, we present secure protocols for the general case of computing n-way contingency tables in a decentralized manner. In the following, we describe each of the protocols in more detail and illustrate them with examples.

3.1   On Horizontally Partitioned Data

Algorithm. In the horizontally partitioned data case, each party owns different set of data objects with the same set of attributes. The protocol for secure computation of contingency tables from horizontally partitioned data is depicted in Algorithm 1. This protocol is run by all k parties. We assume there are n attributes, namely, A_1, A_2, ..., A_n, in common for all the parties. Each attribute can take a number of distinct values, i.e., for A_i, these values are denoted by $a_{i,1}, a_{i,2}, \ldots, a_{i,d_i}$, that is, there are a total of d_i distinct values for A_i. Hence, the general contingency tables from such data can be represented as n-way $d_1 \times d_2 \times \cdots \times d_n$ contingency table, denoted by CT.

Given that the data is horizontally partitioned among the parties, it is possible for each party P_i first locally computes a n-way contingency table LCT_i from its own data. LCT_i is equivalent to CT in dimension but only includes the count of the attribute values co-occurring in the data owned by P_i. Then, the next step is to securely sum the counts of the corresponding cells in all LCT_i along each dimension. The spirit of the performed secure operations follows that of the secure sum protocol presented in [7]. The basic idea is to designate P_1 as the master site. P_1 generates a n-way matrix of random numbers R, uniformly chosen from $[0 \ldots z - 1]$ (we assume that this is the range in which all the cell count values fall). Then, for any given cell count c in LCT_1, P_1 adds the corresponding random number r to it - $(r+c) \bmod z$, and sends its therefore randomized local contingency table RCT_1 to the next party, say P_2. P_2 will learn nothing about the actual cell counts in LCT_1. This is because P_1 has uniformly at random chosen r from range $[0 \ldots z - 1]$, and all of the randoms are different for each cell. Therefore, for each cell, the number $(r + c) \bmod z$ is also uniformly distributed across the range.

From P_2 to P_{k-1}, each party does the same operations as follows. Party P_i receives RCT_{i-1} from P_{i-1}, and adds the cell counts in this randomized contingency table to the corresponding cell counts in its local contingency table LCT_i, resulting in RCT_i. Again, since all the cell values in RCT_{i-1} are uniformly distributed over the range $[0 \ldots z - 1]$, P_i learns nothing from it. Then, P_i passes RCT_i to next party P_{i+1}.

After receiving RCT_{k-1} from P_{k-1}, P_k performs the same sum mentioned above and sends the resulting table RCT_k back to P_1. Finally, P_1, knowing the random matrix R, subtracts each corresponding r from the cell of RCT_k to get the actual contingency table CT.

Example. In this section, we will give an example to illustrate Algorithm 1. The tables on the left of Figures 3, 4 and 5 are patient treatment response tables possessed by three different hospitals, where each record represents a patient and their identifications are suppressed. The tables on the right are their associated contingency tables. For the convenience of reading, we display 3-dimensional tables in a 2-dimensional way.

Now, we show how to employ Algorithm 1 to construct a contingency table on these three separated tables. First, the holder of Figure 3 generates a random table. Suppose it is as the table on the left of Figure 6. Then the holder of Figure 3 adds the random data to his original data and passes the result to the holder of Figure 4. As the holder of Figure 4 knows that the received data having been masked, he cannot figure out the real table. Then according to the protocol, he adds his data to the received table and passes it to the holder of Figure 5. Then, the holder of Figure 5 does the same thing and passes the result to the first person. The returned table is the table on the right of of Figure 6. Finally, the first person subtracts the returned table by the random table generated by him and gets the final contingency table.

Algorithm 1. Secure Construction of Contingency Tables for Horizontally Partitioned Data

Require: k parties $P_1, \ldots, P_k$.
Require: n attributes $A_1, \ldots, A_n$. For each attribute A_i, there is a set of distinct values $a_{i,1}, a_{i,2}, \ldots, a_{i,d_i}$ $(i = 1, 2, \ldots, n)$.
Require: The counts in the computed contingency tables lie in the range $[0..z]$
Require: OUTPUT: n-way $d_1 \times d_2 \times \cdots \times d_n$ contingency table CT.

1: **for** $i \leftarrow 1 \ldots k$ **do**
2:    At P_i: Compute the local n-way $d_1 \times d_2 \times \cdots \times d_n$ contingency table LCT_i.
3: **end for**
4: P_1 generates a n-way $(d_1 \times d_2 \times \cdots \times d_n)$ matrix of random numbers r, uniformly chosen from $[0..z]$.
5: At P_1: Given any local cell value c in LCT_i, add the corresponding random number r from the random matrix to compute the sum $(r + c) \bmod z$, resulting in the contingency table RCT_1
6: P_1 sends RCT_1 to P_2
7: **for** $i \leftarrow 2 \ldots k - 1$ **do**
8:    At P_i: Sums each cell's count in its local LCT_i with the corresponding cell count in RCT_{i-1}, resulting in the contingency table RCT_i.
9:    P_i passes RCT_i to P_{i+1}.
10: **end for**
11: P_k performs the above sum operation and sends the resulting contingency table RCT_k to P_1.
12: P_1 subtracts the corresponding r (of the random matrix) from each cell in RCT_k and gets the result CT.
13: **return** CT

3.2 On Vertically Partitioned Data

Algorithm. When the data is vertically partitioned among k parties, it is assumed that each party owns different set of attributes but for the same set of data objects. Let the overall naturally ordered attribute set be $\{A_1, \ldots, A_n\}$, and for each attribute A_i, there is a set of distinct values $\{a_{i,1}, a_{i,2}, \ldots, a_{i,d_i}\}$ $(i = 1, 2, \ldots, n)$. For simplicity, we assume that P_1 owns the consecutive attributes $\{A_1, \ldots, A_{p_1}\}$, P_2 owns $\{A_{p_1+1}, \ldots, A_{p_2}\}$, $\ldots$, P_k owns $\{A_{p_{k-1}+1}, \ldots, A_n\}$. Let the number of participating data objects be m. Indeed, this is not a restriction, since, for a large dataset, we can divide the data into chunks of size m, and invoke the protocol on the chunks. Then, we can sum the resulting sub-contingency tables. In the end, the result is a n-way $d_1 \times d_2 \times \cdots \times d_n$ contingency table CT.

In order to compute the count in cell $c_{j_1,j_2,\ldots,j_n}$ of $CT(1 \leq j_1 \leq d_1, 1 \leq j_2 \leq d_2, \ldots, 1 \leq j_n \leq d_n)$, each party P_i first needs to perform the following local computations in order to get a representative vector X_i. The first step is that, for each of its attributes A_s $(p_{(i-1)} + 1 \leq s \leq p_i)$, P_i transforms the corresponding attribute values in its data into a binary vector $V_s = \{v_{s,1}, \ldots, v_{s,m}\}$. Specifically, $v_{s,t}$ is set to 1 if the t-th data value of A_s equals $a_{s,j_s}(1 \leq t \leq m)$; otherwise 0. Then, for all V_s, P_i locally computes their product such that $X_i = \{x_{i,1}, \ldots, x_{i,m}\}$ and $x_{i,t} = \prod_{s=p_{(i-1)}+1}^{p_i} v_{s,t}$.

	Center	Treatment	Response
R_1	1	1	2
R_2	2	1	1
R_3	2	2	2

Center	Treatment	Response 1	Response 2
1	1	0	1
1	2	0	0
2	1	1	0
2	2	0	1

Fig. 3. Treatment Response Data and Contingency Table I

	Center	Treatment	Response
R_4	2	1	2
R_5	1	1	2
R_6	2	2	1

Center	Treatment	Response 1	Response 2
1	1	0	1
1	2	0	0
2	1	0	1
2	2	1	0

Fig. 4. Treatment Response Data and Contingency Table II

After the above local computations, all the parties engage in a secure k-vector product protocol, as described in algorithm 3, with their respective input vector $X_i(i = 1, \ldots, k)$. The result of the secure k-vector product protocol is the count in cell $c_{j_1, j_2, \ldots, j_n}$. All the other cells' count of CT can be done in the same way. Clearly, the security of the protocol completely depends on that of the secure k-vector product protocol, which we shall elaborate below.

Secure k-Vector Product Protocol. In this section, we discuss and present the solutions for securely computing the vector product problem.

First, let us consider $k = 2$ case, which is also known as scalar or dot product. Assume that party P_1 has vector X while party P_2 has vector Y, and each vector has the cardinality n. Let $X = (x_1, \ldots, x_n)$, $Y = (y_1, \ldots, y_n)$. The scalar product of vectors X and Y is defined as:

$$\sum_{i=1}^{n} x_i * y_i$$

The goal of the secure computation is that, at the end of the protocol, each party would get $X \cdot Y$ while knowing nothing about the other party's vector. The protocol proposed by Goethals et al. [12] is quite simple and provably secure. The main idea behind the protocol is to use a homomorphic encryption system including the Benaloh cryptosystem [4], the Naccache-Stern cryptosystem [19], the Paillier cryptosystem [21], the Okamoto-Uchiyama cryptosystem [20], and the Goldwasser-Micali cryptosystem [5]. Besides the standard guarantees, homomorphic encryption, as a semantically-secure public-key encryption, has the additional property that given any two encryptions $E(A)$ and $E(B)$, there exists an operation $\otimes$ such that $E(A) \otimes E(B) = E(A * B)$, where $*$ is either addition or multiplication (in some abelian group). The cryptosystems mentioned above are additively homomorphic (thus the operation $*$ denotes addition, and the operation $\otimes$ denotes multiplication). Using such a system, it is quite simple to create a secure scalar product protocol. The key is to note that $\sum_{i=1}^{n} x_i \cdot y_i = \sum_{i=1}^{n} (x_i + x_i + \cdots + x_i)$

	Center	Treatment	Response
R_7	1	1	2
R_8	1	1	2
R_9	2	2	2

Center	Treatment	Response 1	Response 2
1	1	0	2
1	2	0	0
2	1	0	0
2	2	0	1

Fig. 5. Treatment Response Data and Contingency Table III

Center	Treatment	Response 1	Response 2
1	1	1	1
1	2	2	0
2	1	2	0
2	2	1	2

Center	Treatment	Response 1	Response 2
1	1	1	5
1	2	2	0
2	1	3	1
2	2	2	4

Fig. 6. Generated Random Table and Returned Table

(y_i times). If P_1 encrypts her vector and sends in encrypted form to P_2, P_2 can use the additive homomorphic property to compute the scalar product.

In the following, we extend the idea behind the above secure scalar product protocol to securely compute k-vector product ($k \geq 3$), which is defined as follows.

Assume that there are k parties ($P_1, P_2, \ldots, P_k$), where each party P_i has a $(0, 1)$ vector X_i of cardinality n. Let $X_i = \{x_{i,1}, \ldots, x_{i,n}\}$ ($i = 1, \ldots, k$). Our goal here is to securely compute $\sum_{j=1}^{n} \prod_{i=1}^{k} x_{i,j}$ without requiring each party to disclose its vector.

The key to computing this securely lies in the fact that each row contributes a 1 to the final answer, if and only if, each party has a 1 for that row. The key is to keep this information secure. The protocol starts with one party, say P_1, who first generates a private and public key pair (sk, pk) for a semantically secure homomorphic encryption system and sends pk to other parties. Then, P_1 encrypts each of its vector elements $x_{1,j}$ and sends the encrypted value $w_{1,j} = E_{pk}(x_{1,j})$ ($j = 1, \ldots, n$) to P_2. For each j, if $x_{2,j} = 0$, P_2 sends to P_3, $E_{pk}(0)$; otherwise, it sends to P_3 $E_{pk}(x_{1,j}) \cdot E_{pk}(0)$ – this effectively hides the value it has received from its neighbor. To see how this gives the right answer, recall that the vectors contain values of either 0 or 1. If P_2 has 0 as the current value of $x_{2,j}$, then no matter what values the other parties have, $\prod_{i=1}^{k} x_{i,j} = 0$. Therefore, P_2 can send out $E_{pk}(0)$. On the other hand, if P_2 has 1 as the current value, then $\prod_{i=1}^{k} x_{i,j} = x_{1,j} \cdot \prod_{i=3}^{k} x_{i,j}$, and, based on the additive homomorphic property, $E_{pk}(x_{1,j}) \cdot E_{pk}(0) = E_{pk}(x_{1,j})$. That is, it doesn't affect the final result. However, this way makes the computations secure and prevents collusion (i.e., between P_1 and P_3, since it hides the value sent by P_1 to P_2). In both cases, P_2 sends out different encrypted values from those of P_1. Therefore, the other parties will be unable to figure out the actual values, even when they collude.

The above operations done by P_2 are repeated on by the following party P_i ($i = 3, \ldots, k_1$), one following the other, on its own vector. Finally, P_k, who finally decides on $w_{k,j}$, computes $w = \prod_{j=1}^{n} w_{k,j}$ sends w back to P_1. P_1 decrypts it using her private key and, again, based on additive homomorphic property, gets the result of $\sum_{j=1}^{n} \prod_{i=1}^{k} x_{i,j}$.

Algorithm 2. Secure Construction of Contingency Tables for Vertically Partitioned Data

Require: k parties $P_1, \ldots, P_k$
Require: n attributes $A_1, \ldots, A_n$. For each attribute A_i, there is a set of distinct values $\{a_{i,1}, a_{i,2}, \ldots, a_{i,d_i}\}$ $(i = 1, 2, \ldots, n)$. The number of data objects is m.
Require: For simplicity, we assume that P_1 owns $\{A_1, \ldots, A_{p_1}\}$, P_2 owns $\{A_{p_1+1}, \ldots, A_{p_2}\}$, $\ldots, P_k$ owns $\{A_{p_{k-1}+1}, \ldots, A_n\}$.
Require: OUTPUT: n-way $d_1 \times d_2 \times \cdots \times d_n$ contingency table CT.
1: For any given cell $c_{j_1, j_2, \ldots, j_n}$ of $CT (1 \le j_1 \le d_1, 1 \le j_2 \le d_2, \ldots, 1 \le j_n \le d_n)$, its count is computed as follows:
2: **for** $i \leftarrow 1 \ldots k$ **do**
3:    At P_i: encode the data values of its attribute A_s $(p_{(i-1)} + 1 \le s \le p_i)$ into a binary vector V_s of size m such that $V_s = \{v_{s,1}, \ldots, v_{s,m}\}$ and $v_{s,t} = 1$ if the t-th data value of A_s equals $a_{s,j_s} (1 \le t \le m)$; otherwise 0.
4:    At P_i: Locally compute the product X_i of all V_s such that $X_i = \{x_{i,1}, \ldots, x_{i,m}\}$ and $x_{i,t} = \prod_{s=p_{(i-1)}+1}^{p_i} v_{s,t}$.
5: **end for**
6: $P_1, \ldots, P_k$ invoke the secure vector product protocol (algorithm 3) to compute $VP = \sum_{t=1}^{m} \prod_{i=1}^{k} x_{i,t}$, which is the count for cell $c_{j_1, j_2, \ldots, j_n}$.
7: Compute all the other cells' count of CT in the same way.
8: **return** CT

The specific details of the protocol are given in Algorithm 3. One problem lies with collusion. Since P_1 owns the secret key corresponding to the public key, it can easily decrypt any of the intermediate messages. Thus, P_1 can collude with other parties to breach the security of the protocol. However, this can be avoided by using threshold encryption. In threshold encryption, all parties own the public key, but the decryption key is split between all parties so that at least a certain number of parties (over a threshold) are required to successfully decrypt a message. This can effectively remove the problem of collusion.

Example. In this section, we will give an example to illustrate Algorithm 2. The table on the left of Figure 7 is the global table. There are three parties, each of whom holds one attribute (i.e., one column). To get the contingency table, they follow Algorithm 2 exactly. For illustration , we show the procedures of calculating the count of records having value (center=1, treatment=1, response=1). For that particular value, three parties have the corresponding vectors $\{1, 0, 0, 0, 1, 0, 1, 1, 0\}$, $\{1, 1, 0, 1, 1, 0, 1, 1, 0\}$ and $\{0, 1, 0, 0, 0, 1, 0, 0, 0\}$ respectively. The product of these three vectors is the count. According to Algorithm 3, party one generates a pair of public key pb and private key pv and passes the encrypted message $\{E_{pb}(1, r_{11}), E_{pb}(0, r_{12}), \ldots, E_{pb}(0, r_{19})\}$ to party two. Party two receives the message and executes the operations associative with its own values by Algorithm 3. For example, for the first component, as the value is 1, encrypt $E_{pb}(1, r'_{21})$ and multiply with $E(1, r_{11})$ to get $E(1, r_{21})$. For the second component, as the value is 0, generate $E_{pb}(0, r_{22})$ directly. Following this algorithm, party two passes the data to party three finally. Party three does the same operations and gets $\{E_{pb}(0, r_{31}), E_{pb}(0, r_{32}), \ldots, E_{pb}(0, r_{39})\}$. Then multiply them together to get

---

Algorithm 3. Secure k-Vector Product Protocol

Require: k parties $P_1, \ldots, P_k$.
Require: Each party P_i has input vector $\boldsymbol{X_i} = \{x_{i,1}, \ldots, x_{i,n}\}$ $(i = 1, \ldots, k)$
Require: $P_1, P_2, \ldots, P_k$ get the output $VP = \sum_{j=1}^{n} \prod_{i=1}^{k} x_{i,j}$
  1: P_1 generates a private and public key pair (sk, pk) for a semantically secure homomorphic
     encryption system.
  2: P_1 broadcasts pk to $P_2, \ldots, P_k$.
  3: **for** $j = 1 \ldots n$ **do**
  4:     P_1 sends to P_2 $w_{1,j} = E_{pk}(x_{1,j})$.
  5: **end for**
  6: **for** $i = 2 \ldots k - 1$ **do**
  7:     At P_i:
  8:     **for** $j = 1 \ldots n$ **do**
  9:         **if** $x_{i,j} = 0$ **then**
 10:             $w(i, j) = E_{pk}(0)$.
 11:         **else**
 12:             $w(i, j) = E_{pk}(w_{i-1,j}) \cdot E_{pk}(0)$
 13:         **end if**
 14:         P_i sends to P_{i+1} $w_{i,j}$
 15:     **end for**
 16: **end for**
 17: At P_k:
 18: **for** $j = 1 \ldots n$ **do**
 19:     **if** $x_{i,j} = 0$ **then**
 20:         $w(k, j) = E_{pk}(0)$.
 21:     **else**
 22:         $w(k, j) = E_{pk}(w_{i-1,j}) \cdot E_{pk}(0)$
 23:     **end if**
 24: **end for**
 25: P_k computes $w = \prod_{j=1}^{n} w_{k,j}$
 26: P_k sends w to P_1
 27: P_1 computes $VP = D_{sk}(w) = \sum_{j=1}^{n} \prod_{i=1}^{k} x_{i,j}$.

$E_{pb}(0, r'')$ and send it back to party one. Party one uses his private key to decrypt it and gets the final product value 0. The same operations are repeated for the other cells of the contingency table. The final result is the table on the right of Figure 7.

3.3 Communication and Computation Costs

We now give cost estimates for constructing contingency tables using the protocols we have presented. Let the number of participating parties be k. The total number of cells in the resulting contingency table is $d = d_1 \times d_2 \times \cdots \times d_n$.

First, we analyze the cost for the horizontal partition case. The dominating cost for algorithm 1 is communication cost. Let u be the number of bits in representing the count values in cells of the contingency table. Then, the total bits in order to pass the whole contingency table is $(d * u)$. In the protocol, there are k passes of the contingency table around the parties. Therefore, the protocol requires $(d * u * k)$ bits of communication.

	Center	Treatment	Response
R_1	1	1	2
R_2	2	1	1
R_3	2	2	2
R_4	2	1	2
R_5	1	1	2
R_6	2	2	1
R_7	1	1	2
R_8	1	1	2
R_9	2	2	2

Center	Treatment	Response 1	Response 2
1	1	0	4
1	2	0	0
2	1	1	1
2	2	1	2

Fig. 7. Vertically Partitioned Table and Resulting Contingency Table

Clearly, the cost mainly depends on the dimension of the contingency table. We can see there is a tradeoff here. If a higher dimension contingency table is needed, it would incur higher communication cost. Computation cost is not significant since the only computation carried out are a series of sums.

For the protocol on the vertically partitioned data, we analyze the cost in terms of the following actual operations: encryptions, multiplications, and decryptions. This is because these are the dominating factors in the protocol. As we have mentioned in the above section, the secure construction of contingency tables on vertically partitioned data makes use of the secure vector product protocol given in algorithm 3, which is also the only part involving the secure computations for computing a cell count. Given the k parties, each has a vector of size m after some local computations. Then, for each cell in the contingency table, all the parties engage in the k-vector product protocol, which requires $m * k$ encryptions, $m * (k * p + 1)$ multiplications (where p is the percentage of 1's in the vectors), and 1 decryption. Therefore, for constructing the contingency table with d cells, the total number of encryptions required to be performed is $m * k * d$, while the total number of multiplications required is $m * (k * p + 1) * d$ and the total number of decryptions is d. Essentially, the cost of the encryptions dominate the overall cost.

We ran tests on a SUN Blade 1000 workstation with a 900 Mhz processor and 1 gigabyte of RAM. A C implementation of the Okamoto-Uchiyama [20] encryption system was used. The key size was fixed at 1152 bits, which is more than sufficient for most applications. With this setup, 1000 encryptions require on average around 13s. Also, the time for encryption/decryption cost increases approximately linearly with the number of encryptions. Thus, it is very easy to estimate the actual time required for different number of parties, different vector sizes, and different contingency table sizes. For example, 5 parties with vectors of size 1000 and contingency tables of size 25 would require approximately 28 minutes. The time required would be significantly lower with smaller key sizes and with use of special purpose encryption hardware. Secondly, it is also possible to use a much more efficient size of set intersection protocol[23] to compute the k party scalar product. While this is orders of magnitude more efficient, the downside is the increased disclosure – the size of the intersection sets of all of the subsets is also revealed. If this is acceptable, the more efficient protocol should definitely be used.

3.4   Security Analysis

In the above sections, we gave secure protocols for integrating contingency tables securely in both the horizontal and vertical partitioning case. However, do these protocols really protect each participating party's privacy? In this section, we will discuss the security of the protocols. Further, the discussion considers two factors, the protocols themselves and the specific concerns in the context of contingency tables.

First, consider the multi-party secure sum protocol for horizontal partitioning. This protocol is as secure as figuring out the random data added by the first party. As the random data is generated only by one party, it can be proven that the protocol is secure. However, this conclusion is based on the assumption that no parties collude. If party $i - 1$ and party $i + 1$ collude, they can get the value of party i by subtracting, without knowing the added random data. To against this type of attacks, we may apply the method proposed by [26]. First, divide the sub-contingency table that each party holds into multiple parts. Second, for each party, put all users into a ring randomly and use the same multi-party secure sum protocol to get the sum of parts. Finally, party one sums up all the sums to get the final result. Since at each time, the order of parties is random, it avoids the collusion of some parties at the cost of extra computation. People may argue that if there are only three parties, this method dose not work. Considering the real cases of integrating contingency table, it is fair to assume there are more than 3 parties involved. Thus, multi-party secure sum protocol is secure in terms of the protocol itself.

There are other concerns from the domain of contingency table itself. Suppose one party has data A and the final sum is A also. This means that party can infer that all other parties hold empty tables, without knowing the added random data. In our paper, we assume it is not a threat. This assumption meets our experience in practice. A contingency table is trying to catch the count of every combination of attribute values. The cells of zero do not interest any party. Actually, in the case of sparse contingency table, each party can even assume all the cells are zero. Another possibility is to not remove the final randoms from the sum. Instead the first and the last party (P_1 and P_k) can perform a secure addition and comparison to check if the actual value of the cell is above a certain threshold. If so, the value can be computed. If not, the value is discarded. Now, the parties may simply infer that the actual value is below a threshold without knowing exactly how much it is. However, this could become quite expensive in terms of computation cost.

Now, let us consider the protocol for vertical partitioning of data. It uses the key property of semantic security encryption systems that $E_{pb}(1, r1)$ and $E_{pb}(0, r2)$ are indistinguishable. While this is true, the protocol itself is quite secure. However, the domain of contingency table brings some specific concerns. In our problem, the message that each party sends out is a 0-1 vector. One concern is that if one party has a vector of m cells of 1 and the final multi-vector product is m, this party can infer that the cells of all other parties at the same coordinates are 1. However, that may happens rarely in a large database. Even it happens, that party can at most infer a small part of data. In terms of this, we assume this type of threat is not harmful. As earlier, we can cause the parties to see random splits of the scalar product and use secure comparisons to find out if the actual result should be shared, though this again would be computationally expensive. Another concern is that of collusion among the parties. As discussed earlier, using threshold encryption systems can solve this problem. Also, to overcome this, we may borrow the method for horizontally partitioned data. For each count, put all parties in a ring randomly. Thus, each time the party generating keys is different and the colluded person do not stay together. Another way dealing with potential privacy leak is to generate contingency tables for fewer attributes, like every two or three. Thus, get a set of lower-dimensional tables instead of a whole high-dimensional data. This way will improve the privacy of all parties significantly, while at the cost of loosing lots of information. The generated tables would not help people learn the relationship among all attributes. This is a tradeoff. Its selection may depend on the data self and the real goals for the contingency table. We intend to carefully examine this tradeoff in the future.

4   Conclusion

In this paper, we have presented the problem of secure construction of contingency tables from distributed data and suggested some solutions. Our methods are reasonably efficient and secure. More work is still required to figure out how much information can be inferred from the contingency table itself. It may even be unnecessary to compute the entire contingency table depending on what you would like to learn from it. In the future, we intend to propose secure methods to perform basic analysis on the contingency table such as the chi square test or Fisher's exact test directly without computing the entire table.

References

1. Agrawal, D., Aggarwal, C.C.: On the design and quantification of privacy preserving data mining algorithms. In: Proceedings of the Twentieth ACM SIGACT-SIGMOD-SIGART Symposium on Principles of Database Systems, pp. 247–255 (2001)
2. Agrawal, R., Srikant, R.: Privacy-preserving data mining. In: Proceedings of the 2000 ACM SIGMOD Conference on Management of Data, pp. 439–450 (2000)
3. Bedi, R.: Money Laundering - Controls and Prevention, 1st edn. ISI Publications (2004)
4. Benaloh, J.C.: Secret Sharing Homomorphisms: Keeping Shares of a Secret Secret. In: Odlyzko, A.M. (ed.) CRYPTO 1986. LNCS, vol. 263, pp. 251–260. Springer, Heidelberg (1987)
5. Blum, M., Goldwasser, S.: An efficient probabilistic public-key encryption that hides all partial information. In: Blakely, R. (ed.) Advances in Cryptology – Crypto 84 Proceedings. Springer, Heidelberg (1984)
6. L. Cauley.: Nsa has massive database of americans' phone calls (May 2006) (USA Today).
7. Clifton, C., Kantarcioglu, M., Lin, X., Vaidya, J., Zhu, M.: Tools for privacy preserving distributed data mining. SIGKDD Explorations 4(2), 28–34 (2003)
8. Cornfield, J.: A method of estimating comparative rates from clinical data: Applications to cancer of the lung, breast, and cervix. Journal of the National Cancer Institute 11, 1269–1275 (1951)
9. Dellaportas, P., Tarantola, C.: Model determination for categorical data with factor level merging. Journal of the Royal Statistical Society 67, 269–283 (2005)
10. Evfimievski, A., Srikant, R., Agrawal, R., Gehrke, J.: Privacy preserving mining of association rules. In: The Eighth ACM SIGKDD International Conference on Knowledge Discovery and Data Mining, pp. 217–228 (2002)

11. Fienberg, S.E.: The Analysis of Cross-classified Categorical Data, 2nd edn. M.I.T. Press, Cambridge (1980)
12. Goethals, B., Laur, S., Lipmaa, H., Mielikäinen, T.: On Secure Scalar Product Computation for Privacy-Preserving Data Mining. In: Park, C.-s., Chee, S. (eds.) ICISC 2004. LNCS, vol. 3506, pp. 104–120. Springer, Heidelberg (2005)
13. Goldreich, O.: General Cryptographic Protocols. In: The Foundations of Cryptography, vol. 2. Cambridge University Press, Cambridge (2004)
14. Goldreich, O., Micali, S., Wigderson, A.: How to play any mental game - a completeness theorem for protocols with honest majority. In: 19th ACM Symposium on the Theory of Computing, pp. 218–229 (1987)
15. Huang, Z., Du, W., Chen, B.: Deriving private information from randomized data. In: Proceedings of the 2005 ACM SIGMOD International Conference on Management of Data, Baltimore, MD, June 13-16 (2005)
16. Jagannathan, G., Wright, R.N.: Privacy-preserving distributed k-means clustering over arbitrarily partitioned data. In: KDD 2005: Proceeding of the eleventh ACM SIGKDD international conference on Knowledge discovery in data mining, pp. 593–599. ACM Press, New York (2005)
17. Kargupta, H., Datta, S., Wang, Q., Sivakumar, K.: On the privacy preserving properties of random data perturbation techniques. In: Proceedings of the Third IEEE International Conference on Data Mining (ICDM 2003) (2003)
18. Lindell, Y., Pinkas, B.: Privacy Preserving Data Mining. In: Bellare, M. (ed.) CRYPTO 2000. LNCS, vol. 1880, pp. 36–54. Springer, Heidelberg (2000)
19. Naccache, D., Stern, J.: A new public key cryptosystem based on higher residues. In: Proceedings of the 5th ACM conference on Computer and communications security, pp. 59–66. ACM Press, San Francisco (1998)
20. Okamoto, T., Uchiyama, S.: A New Public-Key Cryptosystem as Secure as Factoring. In: Nyberg, K. (ed.) EUROCRYPT 1998. LNCS, vol. 1403, pp. 308–318. Springer, Heidelberg (1998)
21. Paillier, P.: Public-Key Cryptosystems Based on Composite Degree Residuosity Classes. In: Stern, J. (ed.) EUROCRYPT 1999. LNCS, vol. 1592, pp. 223–238. Springer, Heidelberg (1999)
22. Rizvi, S.J., Haritsa, J.R.: Maintaining data privacy in association rule mining. In: Proceedings of 28th International Conference on Very Large Data Bases. VLDB, Hong Kong, August 20-23, pp. 682–693 (2002)
23. Vaidya, J., Clifton, C.: Secure set intersection cardinality with application to association rule mining. Journal of Computer Security 13(4) (November 2005)
24. Vaidya, J., Clifton, C., Zhu, M.: Privacy-Preserving Data Mining, 1st edn. Advances in Information Security. Springer, Heidelberg (2005)
25. Yao, A.C.: Protocols for secure computation (extended abstract). In: Proceedings of the 23th IEEE Symposium on Foundations of Computer Science, pp. 160–164. IEEE, Los Alamitos (1982)
26. Yu, H., Vaidya, J.: Secure matrix addition (UIOWA Technical Report) (2004)

Web Services Security: Techniques and Challenges
(Extended Abstract)

Anoop Singhal

Computer Security Division
National Institute of Standards and Technology (NIST), Gaithersburg, MD 20899, USA
anoop.singhal@nist.gov

Abstract. Web services-based computing is currently an important driver for the software industry. While several standards bodies (such as W3C and OASIS) are laying the foundation for Web services security, several research problems must be solved to make secure Web services a reality. This talk will present techniques for Web services security and some of the challenges and recommendations for secure web services. This paper is based on our experience in developing the National Institute of Standards and Technology (NIST) Special Publication SP 800-95, "Guide to Secure Web Services". Some of the challenges for secure web services are

1. End to End Quality of Service and Protection
2. Availability of Service
3. Protection from Command Injection Attacks
4. Identity Management

To adequately support the needs of Web services-based applications, effective risk management and appropriate deployment of alternate countermeasures are essential. Defense-in-depth through security engineering, secure software development, and architecture risk analysis can provide the robustness and reliability required by these applications.

Reference

1. Singhal, A., Winograd, T., Scarfone, K.: NIST Special Publication 800-95, Guide to Secure Web Services (August 2007), http://csrc.nist.gov/publications/nistpubs/800-95/SP800-95.pdf

V. Atluri (Ed.): DAS 2008, LNCS 5094, pp. 158, 2008.

Empirical Analysis of Certificate Revocation Lists*

Daryl Walleck[1], Yingjiu Li[2], and Shouhuai Xu[1]

[1] University of Texas at San Antonio, 6900 North Loop 1604,
West San Antonio, TX 78249
[2] Singapore Management University, 80 Stamford Road, Singapore 178902
dwalleck@cs.utsa.edu, yjli@smu.edu.sg, shxu@cs.utsa.edu

Abstract. Managing public key certificates revocation has long been a central issue in public key infrastructures. Though various certificate revocation mechanisms have been proposed to address this issue, little effort has been devoted to the empirical analysis of real-world certificate revocation data. In this paper, we conduct such an empirical analysis based on a large amount of data collected from VeriSign. Our study enables us to understand how long a revoked certificate lives and what the difference is in the lifetime of revoked certificates by certificate types, geographic locations, and organizations. Our study also provides a solid foundation for future research on optimal management of certificate revocation for different types of certificates requested from different organizations and located in different geographic locations.

Keywords: public key infrastructure, certificate revocation, empirical analysis.

1 Introduction

With the rapid growth of the Internet over the last decade, new challenges appear daily. Of these challenges, perhaps none is more important than the need for protecting sensitive transactions. By means of digital certificates, public key infrastructures provide a degree of authentication to protect sensitive transactions. However, digital certificates must be revoked if the corresponding private keys have somehow become compromised, perhaps due to attacks launched by worms or viruses. Thus, managing certificate revocation efficiently has become a major issue in public key infrastructures [14].

Previous research on certificate revocation management has primarily focused on the tradeoffs that can be made among different revocation mechanisms [6,15], including certificate revocation list (CRL) [5], certificate revocation system (CRS) [12], certificate revocation tree (CRT) [7], and on-line certificate status protocol (OCSP) [11]. Though various tradeoffs have been studied, little effort has been made toward understanding the distribution of certificate

---

* The work of Shouhuai Xu was supported in part by ARO, NSF and UTSA CIAS.

V. Atluri (Ed.): DAS 2008, LNCS 5094, pp. 159–174, 2008.

revocations, especially from real-world data. Understanding the distribution of certificate revocations would enable certificate authorities to optimize their operations over time.

Our Contributions. We collected five real-world certificate revocation files from VeriSign for different types of certificates, and conducted an in-depth empirical study to understand the distribution of certificate revocations from different perspectives. This paper reports the major findings of our empirical study, which can be summarized as follows.

- The types of certificate revocation files, which are used for different purposes, do not appear to be a fundamental factor regarding the behavior of certificate revocation distributions. This is so because all the five individual certificate revocation files exhibit exponential distribution patterns, so is the merged dataset. Nevertheless, different types of certificates can still be clustered into two groups based on their mean certificate lifetimes, where each certificate's lifetime is defined to be the difference between its revocation date and its issue date. This may suggest that certain classes of certificate-enabled systems (e.g., code signing and financial applications) are better protected than others under the assumption that other factors that affect the certificate lifetimes remain similar in the comparison.

- Although certificate revocations in different geographic locations still exhibit exponential distributions, the distribution parameters vary significantly. This implies that different strategies should be used to disseminate certificate revocation information for different countries or continents. Moreover, the average certificate lifetimes may serve as a measure for the security levels of certificate-enabled systems in different geographic locations provided that no other factors that affect the certificate lifetimes are significantly different in comparison.

- The number of revoked certificates is bouncing on a daily basis. In particular, many certificate revocations occur during weekdays, whereas few occur during weekends. This indicates that an attacker who compromises a public key certificate during weekends may have a better opportunity to conduct unlawful activities before the compromised private key (i.e., the corresponding certificate) is effectively revoked. We also observed that the numbers of revoked certificates in January and February in both 2005 and 2006 are always significantly lower than their respective counterparts in other months of the same year. This is not because the certificate-enabled systems are better protected, but because fewer certificates are requested and issued due to seasonal reasons.

- Different organizations exhibit different characteristics in terms of their certificate lifetimes. Although the certificate lifetimes still follow exponential distributions, the average certificate lifetimes vary widely among different organizations, even within the same industry group such as financial institutions. This result may stimulate organizations to improve their security levels and security awareness in a competitive market.

Limitations of this Paper. The nature of empirical study restricts us from extrapolating our results to the whole universe. In particular, the following limitations of the present study are identified for possible future improvements.

- The major findings of this paper are based on a number of CRL data sets collected from VeriSign only. Though considered to be representative for commercial use of public key certificates, VeriSign's data may not demonstrate the same revocation patterns as other data sets. In addition, our findings cannot be extrapolated to OCSP responders.
- We do not have access to the certificates that are issued by VeriSign but never revoked. While it is meaningful to investigate the ratio of revoked certificates to the certificates that are never revoked, we experience difficulties in collecting such data from VeriSign or any other resources in the public domain (in most cases, only the information regarding the revoked certificates is available to the public).
- We do not investigate why the certificates are revoked. Understanding various revocation reasons will definitely help us understand the relationship between certificate revocation and the security levels of certificate-enabled systems. For example, one can suspect that no one cares too much about their SSL certificates if they lose the private keys, as they can get new certificates minted, maybe from someone cheaper than VeriSign. For another example, it is very important to revoke public key certificates if someone loses his company's smart cards. Unfortunately, it is very difficult to obtain such information as the revocation reasons are often considered sensitive in commercial applications (to some extent, this is similar to the situation in which financial organizations are disinclined to publish any security breaches to the public).
- We do not consider many other factors in certificate revocations except the security factor on which we focus. There could be a host of other factors affecting certificate revocations: (i) the errors made in data entries, (ii) the purposes of the certificates being used, (iii) the reasons of the certificates being revoked, (iv) the administration policies for certificate revocation, and (v) the fraction of all issued certificates that get revoked. We assume that all these factors are similar when we make connections between certificate revocations and security levels in certificate-enabled systems.

Related Work. The work most closely related to this work is the paper "On the Release of CRLs in Public Key Infrastructure" by Ma, Hu, and Li [9], which builds analytical models on how often a certificate authority should release CRLs in order to minimize its operational cost based on empirical analysis on real-world data. However, their analysis of the data gathered from certificates is not as in depth as what is proposed in this paper. In particular, they did not consider the impact of geographic location and organization to the distribution of certificate revocations. Another difference is that they proposed optimal CRL releasing strategies, while the main purpose of our study is to characterize certificate revocations based on real empirical data.

Except [9], most of previous researches are not based on any empirical analysis of real-world data; instead, they focus on theoretical aspects of certificate revocation including the meaning of revocation [3,4], the model of revocation [2], communication cost of revocation [12], tradeoffs in certificate revocation schemes [16], and risk management in certificate revocation [8]. Rivest has once proposed to use short-lived certificates so as to eliminate certificate revocations [13]. However, his approach places a high burden on certificate servers which need to sign more certificates as compared with traditional certificate revocation solutions; it also creates the problem of key compromise which cannot be addressed without using a separate mechanism [10].

Paper Organization. The rest of this paper is organized as follows. In Section 2, we discuss the methodology we used to collect and analyze real-world data from VeriSign. In Section 3, we analyze the VeriSign data from various perspectives including differences in certificate revocation between certificate classes, geographic factors in certificate revocation, trends in certificate revocation rates over time, and trends in certificate revocation rates by organizations. We also discuss how to derive optimal certificate revocation policies based on our empirical results. Finally, in Section 4, we summarize our research and point out possible future directions.

2   Methodology and Data Collection

To investigate certificate revocation, we used VeriSign's Certificate Revocation Lists (CRLs) to find certificates that have been revoked over the last several years. After gathering a large sample of revoked certificates, VeriSign's database was queried using its web interface to determine relevant information about each certificate such as when the certificate was issued, what organization requested the certificate, and its country of origin. However, not all of their certificate data is publicly accessible. Though VeriSign allows users to determine the status of some certificates through a web interface, we could not find information about certificates from all CRL files through it. Because of this, our analysis is limited to the data we could gather from the files mentioned later.

We also encountered similar problems when considering analyzing data from other certificate authorities such as Thawte and GeoTrust. Since the CRL file contains the revoked date for each certificate, we would require some way to determine the date a certificate was issued to determine its lifetime. Though both certificate authorities do publish CRLs, neither of them offers an interface to search their certificate database, making any analysis of their CRL files impossible.

We were also interested in discovering the number of active certificates (including those never revoked) so that it would be possible to compare the number of revoked certificates to the number of active certificates at a given time.

Unfortunately, aside from searching the Internet to find live VeriSign certificates, there is no easy way to determine this. Though VeriSign's web interface does allow users to search its database by organization name which does return some valid certificates, organizations can also request that their certificates not be viewable through that interface. Because of this, even if we had attempted to build a list of valid certificates, there would be no guarantees of its completeness.

Using the CRLs available, we were able to analyze the data gathered to characterize certificate lifetimes by different sub-fields. In this paper, we will try to characterize the lifetime of revoked certificates by the following criteria:

- The lifetime of certificates over time
- The difference in the lifetime of certificates by type
- The difference in the lifetime of certificates by geographic location
- The characteristics of certificate lifetimes by organization

Table 1. Breakdown of the Composite Data Set by CRL File

File Name	Issue Date	# Certificates	Dates Covered	Purpose
SVRIntl	3/26/2007	21192	2/15/2005-3/26/2007	Global Server certificates
RSA	3/13/2007	10100	12/18/2004-3/13/2007	Secure Server certificates; also a root CA
Secure	3/26/2007	11898	12/18/2004-3/26/2007	Secure Server certificates
Financial	3/26/2007	326	5/7/2002-3/26/2007	OFX certificates
Code signing	3/13/2007	1413	9/28/2004-3/13/2007	Code signing and object signing certificates for use with Netscape browsers, Microsoft Internet Explorer browsers, Microsoft Office, Sun Java Signing, Macromedia, and Marimba

For the purpose of this paper, five CRL files were used to find revoked certificates which were used to create our data pool. The files chosen for this research are described in Table 1. Since VeriSign removes most certificates from its CRLs after they expire [1] (most certificates have a one to two years issued lifespan before their expiration), most of the certificates contained in the lists cover the past two years. Between these five CRL files, 44,929 certificates were gathered. Since each CRL file only includes the serial number and revocation date for each certificate, a Ruby script was used to search VeriSign's database for each certificate's issue date, country of origin, and the organization that requested the certificate.

3   Empirical Analysis

First, we would like to examine the trend of certificate lifetimes for revoked certificates from all of the CRL files. The lifetime of a certificate can be defined as follows:

Actual Lifetime = Date Revoked − Date Issued

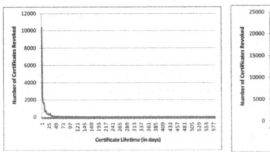 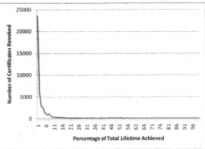

Fig. 1. Number of Certificates Revoked vs. Certificate Lifetime

Fig. 2. Number of Certificates Revoked vs. Percentage of Lifetime Achieved

We begin our analysis by plotting the lifetime of a certificate against the amount of certificates revoked for that lifetime. As can be seen in Figure 1, the lifetime of a revoked certificate is fairly short. In fact, the average lifetime for certificates in the composite data set is 28 days. However, this plot does not take into account the fact that certificates expire at different rates. While some certificates may only be valid for a year, the issued lifetime of other certificates may be two or three years. The issued lifetime of a certificate can be calculated as:

Issued Lifetime = Expiration Date − Date Issued

To see what kind of difference this might have, in Figure 2 we take this into account by plotting the percent of a certificate's normal lifetime against the number of certificates that were revoked after that percentage. As can be seen, the trends displayed in Figure 1 still hold. We discovered that the mean percent lifetime of any given certificate is 4.8%.

By using the `dfittool` and `expfit` functions of Matlab, it was determined that this data follows an exponential distribution. The common form of the probability density function (PDF) for the exponential distribution is as follows:

$$R(t) = ke^{-kt}$$

However, Matlab uses an alternate form of the exponential distribution. This form is:

$$f(x) = \frac{1}{\mu}e^{-\frac{x}{\mu}}$$

The composite data set was discovered to follow the exponential distribution with the parameter μ being 27.56 at a 95% confidence interval. When testing the percent lifetime view, it was also determined to follow the exponential distribution with $\mu = 0.0479$ at a 95% confidence interval. This is an interesting finding: most revoked certificates have lifetimes shorter than a month, or 4% of their issued lifetimes, even though they have one to two years issued lifetimes. As it is mentioned earlier, our research is restricted to the certificates that get revoked.

3.1   Differences between Certificate Classes

Now that we have examined the characteristics of the data set as a whole, we were also interested in breaking down the data into the individual files and seeing how well the distribution holds. Table 2 shows the mean lifetime for the revoked certificates from each CRL file. While the International, RSA, and Secure server certificates have relatively similar mean lifetimes, the mean lifetime for Code Signing and Financial certificates is nine to ten days (or about 25%) longer than the others.

Table 2. Mean Certificate Actual Lifetime by CRL File

CRL File	μ (mean)
International	26.83
RSA	27.12
Secure	27.99
Code Signing	35.72
Financial	37.08

Figure 3 plots each of the five CRL files separately to see how well the distribution holds. Though there is some difference in scale, the data from each file still follows the exponential distribution with the parameter μ shown in Table 2, all at a 95% confidence interval.

This result indicates that the type of certificates is not a fundamental factor regarding the distribution of certificate revocations. An exponential distribution is observed for each of the five certificate revocation files and for the merged dataset. The difference in the mean value of certificate lifetimes may suggest that certain classes of certificate-enabled systems (e.g., code signing and financial) are better protected than others under the assumption that all other factors affecting certificate lifetimes are similar in comparison. It should be noted that the protection levels are not the only factor affecting the certificate lifetimes. For instance, the differences in certificate lifetimes in different certificate-enabled systems could suggest that the administrators of certain systems such as financial servers (for which certificates get revoked slowly) work in environments in which it takes longer to get authorization for revocation. On the other hand, some certificates get revoked quickly because errors were made in data entries, or because

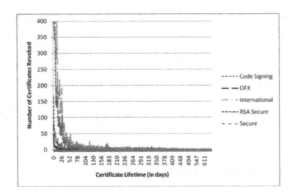

Fig. 3. Certificate Actual Lifetime by CRL File

the certificates were for tests or experimental systems. To get a comprehensive understanding about protection levels, one needs to know about all these factors that affect certificate lifetimes, which may include the purposes of the certificates being used, the reasons of the certificates being revoked, the administration policies for certificate revocation, and the fraction of all issued certificates that get revoked. The certificate lifetime in a certificate-enabled system can be considered as a multivariate function of many variables; in our discussions, we focus on the variable of protection levels while assuming that the other variables are fixed. A more comprehensive study on all such variables is an obvious topic for future work if sufficient data is available.

3.2   Geographic Factors

Now that a standard has been created to compare against, we would first like to discover if geographic location has any influence on the lifetime of a revoked digital certificate. In all, 136 countries were identified in the CRL files we used. To begin, we first investigated CRL usage of the country with the most total certificates revoked, the United States, and plotted the results in Figure 4.

Considering that certificates from the United States make up a large portion of the composite data, it is not surprising that Figure 4 is very similar to Figure 1. Before coming to any conclusions, we then plotted the results for four of the other leading certificate holders in Figure 5. The difference in the amount of certificates used by these countries is significantly smaller than that of the United States, so a smaller scale will be used to display these graphs.

We also examined the behavior of certificate lifetimes over the first 30 days more clearly, Figure 6 shows the same data from Figure 5 on an even smaller scale (i.e., Figure 6 is a "zoom in" of a portion of Figure 5).

Like the composite data set, when divided by country these data sets also follow the exponential distribution. Table 3 gives the parameter μ for each of the data sets (all at a 95% confidence interval). Interestingly enough, the trends shown in the initial results hold true when the data is broken down by geographic

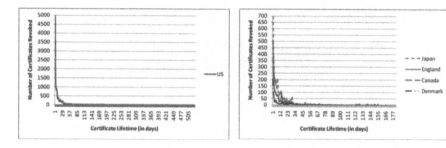

Fig. 4. Number of Certificates Revoked vs. Lifetime (United States)

Fig. 5. Number of Certificates Revoked vs. Lifetime (Remaining Countries)

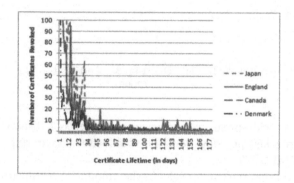

Fig. 6. Number of Certificates Revoked vs. Lifetime (Remaining Countries - magnified)

region. In all cases, a large number of certificates are revoked within the first month before falling off to a few revocations per day after that. By these results, it can be inferred that location plays only a minor role in certificate revocation rates. However, it is also of interest to note that the average lifetime of a revoked certificate in Japan is less than half that of any of the other countries shown here. Since the average certificate lifetimes vary significantly for different geographic locations, different strategies may be used to disseminate certificate revocation information for different countries or continents. Moreover, the average certificate lifetimes may serve as a metric for the security levels of certificate-enabled systems in different geographic locations provided that all other factors that affect the certificate revocation are the same.

3.3   Trends in Revocation Rates over Time

Another view of the data we were interested in was tracking certificate revocation rates over time. If surges in revoked certificates could be found, we would expect that these surges could be traced back to the occurrence of major security

Table 3. Mean Certificate Lifetime by Country (in days)

US	JP	GB	CA	AU	DE
29.48	13.15	25.18	37.26	30.62	29.36

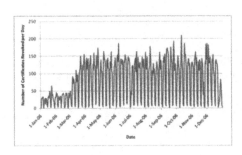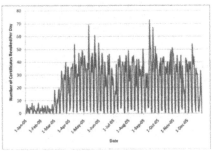

Fig. 7. Certificates Revoked Per Day (2006)   **Fig. 8.** Certificates Revoked Per Day (2005)

incidents such as widespread worms or viruses. Figure 7 displays the amount of certificates revoked per day from the composite data during the period of 1/1/2006 to 12/31/2006.

Though we did observe small peaks in the amount of certificates revoked per day, there were no extraordinarily large spikes in certificate revocations like we thought there might possibly be. What we did notice was the wave-like bouncing pattern that certificate revocations follow. Upon further investigation, we found that nearly all certification revocations happened between Monday and Friday, with only minimal revocations occurring on weekends. To make sure that this trend did not only occur in 2006, we also investigated the data from 2005 in Figure 8 and compared the trends between 2006 and 2005 in Figure 9.

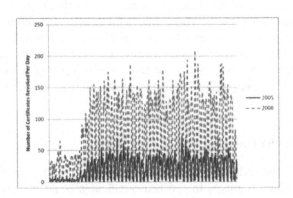

Fig. 9. Number of Certificates Revoked Per Day (2006 compared to 2005)

Surely enough, the pattern still holds. From these two figures, we observed that the number of certificates revoked per day in January and February is significantly smaller than the number of certificates revoked per day in other months. Another observation is that the number of certificates revoked per day increases significantly from 2005 to 2006. These changes are primarily due to the changes in the total number of certificates being issued at different times. To make this clear, we also investigated the percentage of the valid certificates revoked each day. Since we did not have access to VeriSign's database to determine the true number of certificates active at a given time, we instead used the certificates from the CRL files to determine the number of not-yet-revoked certificates daily. Figure 10 below plots the percentage of certificates revoked daily (over the total number of certificates that have not been revoked at the beginning of the day, which would vary on a daily basis) for the period of 1/3/2005 through 3/26/2007.

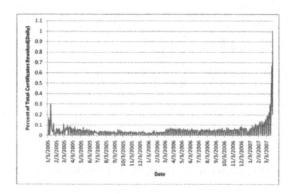

Fig. 10. Percentage of Certificates Revoked Daily

Because every certificate in a CRL file is eventually revoked, the end of the curve in Figure 10 is skewed because at the end of the time period, 100% of the certificates are revoked. However, this is artificial and does not affect the data before it. On average, 4% of the total revoked certificates were revoked daily. From this plot it can be seen that no matter how many total revoked certificates are in existence, the percentage of certificates revoked daily stays fairly constant with some small growth over time. Next, we were interested in seeing how the number of not-yet-revoked certificates plots over time. In Figure 11, we plot the number of not-yet-revoked certificates over the same period of time.

Since these CRL files contain only certificates that were eventually revoked, the number of certificates active at the end becomes zero. Other than the rise and decline at the starting and ending periods, there is only one sharp change in active certificates, as the number of active certificates double in number in March, due to expired certificates being removed from the CRLs. Even with this large increase of active certificates, the percent of certificates revoked daily only gradually rises. This implies that the number of revoked certificates changes in

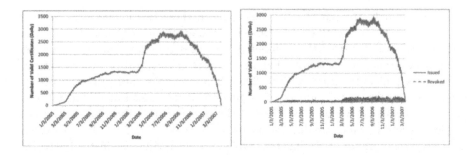

Fig. 11. Number of Not-Yet-Revoked Certificates over Time

Fig. 12. # Not-Yet-Revoked Certificates Compared to # Revoked Certificates

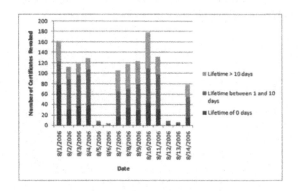

Fig. 13. Number of Certificates Revoked Per Day - Breakdown by Length of Lifetime

a similar trend as the number of active certificates does and this similarity in trend is illustrated in Figure 12 on a daily basis.

In Figure 13, we take a different approach to viewing the actual lifetime of revoked certificates. In this chart, we take the number of certificates revoked over a two week period and break down the certificates revoked each day by the lifetime of certificate before it was revoked. We observed that almost one third of certificates were revoked within one day after they were issued, and that only about one third of certificates enjoyed lifetime greater than 10 days. Since we do not have access to the reasons why these certificates are revoked, we cannot further interpret this result.

3.4   Trends by Organization

From the files collected, 15,341 organizations were identified. However, due to differences in how the company name was placed on the certificate, it is likely that there are fewer than that amount. To make our data as correct as possible, records that had similar names but only differed by punctuation (ex. Verisign Inc. and Verisign, Inc.) were modified and merged into one standard name. We began

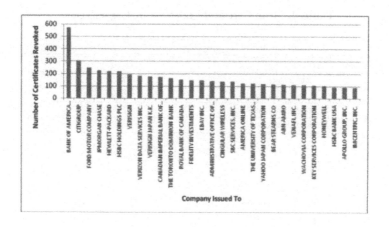

Fig. 14. Number of Certificates Revoked by Organization (Top 30)

our analysis by visualizing the amount of certificates used by each organization. Since it would be impossible to list the number of certificates revoked for every company, we decided to instead focus on a smaller portion of the organizations. Figure 14 shows the top 30 organizations by certificates revoked.

Another one of the ways we would have liked to examine the data is from a per certificate perspective, judging the distance between when a given certificate is revoked and when the next certificate for the organization is issued. Since each company uses multiple certificates at any given time, it is impossible to determine the average time between when a certificate is revoked and when its replacement is issued. Instead, we will have to use other methods to try to measure the security of an organization. First, we determine the mean certificate lifetime for each company in Table 4.

For these top five companies, the means vary widely. It is interesting to note that the mean lifetime for certificates issued to Bank of America and Citigroup, both financial institutions, differ by almost 45 days. While this may not for certain say that one company is more secure than the other, it does show that these organizations have either mishandled their certificates or possibly have had breaches in their security.

Since these numbers vary so widely, we next decided to fit the lifetime data for each of the above organizations to a probability distribution. We determined that when the data is divided by organization, it still follows the exponential distribution, as shown in Figure 15. The parameter μ for each organization is given by the mean listed in Table 4, all at a 95% confidence interval.

Clearly, different organizations exhibit different characterizations in terms of their certificate lifetimes. While the certificate lifetimes still follow exponential distributions, the average certificate lifetimes change from organization to organization, even within the same industry group such as financial institutions. If

Table 4. Mean Certificate Lifetime by Organization

Organization	Mean Certificate Lifetime (in days)
Bank of America Corporation	15.92
Citigroup	60.32
Ford Motor Company	42.28
JPMorgan Chase	50.00
Hewlett-Packard	14.34

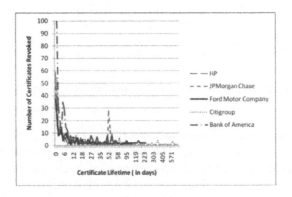

Fig. 15. Number of Certificates Revoked vs. Lifetime (By Top 5 Organizations with Revoked Certificates)

the average certificate lifetimes are treated as a reflection of the organizations' security level or security awareness, those organizations in a competitive market should investigate why their certificates are revoked more or less frequently than their competitors and how to improve their certificate lifetimes at organizational levels. It is imaginable that the publication of more empirical analysis on certificate lifetimes would stimulate organizations to increase their security levels or security awareness, especially in a competitive market.

3.5   Discussion on Optimal Management of Certificate Revocation

Our empirical analysis provides a solid foundation for optimal management of certificate revocation for different types of certificates requested from different organizations located in different geographic locations. The reason is that our study enables us to understand the distribution of certificates being newly revoked and the distribution of certificates being cumulatively revoked both on a daily basis. Given these distributions, a certificate authority (CA) can minimize its operational cost for any type of certificates based on the analytical models proposed in [9], where the CA's operation cost consists of three parts: (i) the expected liability cost per certificate revocation if CA delays publishing the revocation for one day; (ii) the fixed cost for CA to publish a CRL regardless of its size; and (iii) the variable cost for CA to include each individual certificate into a CRL. The CA needs to balance between the liability cost of not releasing CRL on time and the fixed and variable costs of releasing CRL too often for optimal management of certificate revocation.

We should note that the distribution of certificates being newly revoked and the distribution of certificates being cumulatively revoked are not derived directly from empirical data in [9]; instead, they are deduced from the exponential distribution of certificate lifetimes. Consequently, these distributions become constant after the time reaches the issued lifetime. However, as it is shown in our paper, these distributions may fluctuate over time in reality. The analytical models proposed in [9] therefore need to be revised so as to capture this phenomenon.

4   Conclusion and Future Work

The certificate revocation is a very complicated issue and is affected by many factors. This paper analyzes the influence of these factors empirically from the Verisign's data. Our research represents the first step towards linking empirical observations to mathematical models in description of the complicated problem of certificate revocation. We have focused on the empirical part in this study. In the future, we plan to conduct extended research on optimal management of certificate revocation based on our empirical analysis. We also hope to conduct a more thorough examination of the per organization data from a larger and more continuous data pool.

Acknowledgement

The authors would like to thank the anonymous referees for their helpful comments, including a suggestion to revise the title of this paper to be more appropriate.

References

1. VeriSign certification practice statement, version 3.4. Internet proposed standard RFC 2560 (April 2007),
   http://www.verisign.com/repository/CPS/VeriSignCPSv3.4.pdf
2. Cooper, D.A.: A model of certificate revocation. In: ACSAC 1999: Proceedings of the 15th Annual Computer Security Applications Conference, pp. 256–264. IEEE Computer Society (1999)
3. Fox, B.L., LaMacchia, B.A.: Certificate revocation: Mechanics and meaning. In: Hirschfeld, R. (ed.) FC 1998. LNCS, vol. 1465, pp. 158–164. Springer, Heidelberg (1998)
4. Gunter, C.A., Jim, T.: Generalized certificate revocation. In: Symposium on Principles of Programming Languages, pp. 316–329 (2000)
5. Housley, R., Ford, W., Polk, W., Solo, D.: RFC 2459: Internet X.509 public key infrastructure certificate and CRL profile, Status: Proposed standard (January 1999)

6. Jain, G.: Certificate revocation: A survey,
   http://citeseer.ist.psu.edu/511985.html
7. Kocher, P.C.: On certificate revocation and validation. In: Hirschfeld, R. (ed.) FC 1998. LNCS, vol. 1465, pp. 172–177. Springer, Heidelberg (1998)
8. Li, N., Feigenbaum, J.: Nonmonotonicity, user interfaces, and risk assessment in certificate revocation (position paper). In: Syverson, P.F. (ed.) FC 2001. LNCS, vol. 2339, pp. 166–177. Springer, Heidelberg (2002)
9. Ma, C., Hu, N., Li, Y.: On the release of crls in public key infrastructure. In: Proceedings 15th USENIX Security Symposium, Vancouver, Canada, pp. 17–28 (2006)
10. McDaniel, P., Rubin, A.: A response to can we eliminate certificate revocation lists? In: Frankel, Y. (ed.) FC 2000. LNCS, vol. 1962, pp. 245–258. Springer, Heidelberg (2001)
11. Myers, M., Ankney, R., Malpani, A., Galperin, S., Adams, C.: X.509 internet public-key infrastructure — online certificate status protocol (OCSP). Internet proposed standard RFC 2560 (June 1999)
12. Naor, M., Nissim, K.: Certificate revocation and certificate update. In: Proceedings 7th USENIX Security Symposium, San Antonio, Texas (1998)
13. Rivest, R.L.: Can we eliminate certificate revocations lists? In: Hirschfeld, R. (ed.) FC 1998. LNCS, vol. 1465, pp. 178–183. Springer, Heidelberg (1998)
14. Stubblebine, S.: Recent-secure authentication: Enforcing revocation in distributed systems. In: Proceedings 1995 IEEE Symposium on Research in Security and Privacy, May 1995, pp. 224–234 (1995)
15. Wohlmacher, P.: Digital certificates: a survey of revocation methods. In: Multimedia 2000: Proceedings of the 2000 ACM workshops on Multimedia, pp. 111–114. ACM Press, New York (2000)
16. Zheng, P.: Tradeoffs in certificate revocation schemes. Computer Communication Review 33(2), 103–112 (2003)

Using New Tools for Certificate Repositories Generation in MANETs

Candelaria Hernández-Goya[1], Pino Caballero-Gil[1], Oscar Delgado-Mohatar[2],
Jezabel Molina-Gil[1], and Cándido Caballero-Gil[1]

[1] Dpto. Estadística, I.O. y Computación. Universidad de La Laguna
38271 La Laguna, Tenerife, Spain
{mchgoya,pcaballe}@ull.es, {jezabelmiriam,candido.caballero}@gmail.com
[2] Instituto de Física Aplicada, Consejo Superior de Investigaciones Científicas
Serrano, 144, 28006, Madrid, Spain
oscar.delgado@iec.csic.es

Abstract. This paper includes a new proposal for the generation of certificates repositories in MANETs. The described process is based on the combination of the self-organized key management model together with the MultiPoint Relay (MPR) technique, generally used in the Optimized Link State Routing protocol. The main objective is to reduce the cost of generating and updating local certificate repositories by selecting those certificates that allow to reach the maximum number of nodes. This goal is just achieved by applying low-cost operations carried out locally by the nodes themselves.

Keywords: Public-key management, MANETs.

1 Introduction

Due to the lack of centralized infrastructure when dealing with Mobile Ad-hoc NETworks (MANETs) almost any task related to management or security services depend on network members themselves. It conveys that a significant amount of their restricted resources are spent on self-organization duties. Hence, special attention to nodes overload should be paid when designing new management mechanisms such as public-key management. In particular, the design of public-key management schemes may be catalogued as one of the hardest tasks when providing MANETs with security. The existent approaches to solve this problem are mainly based on one of two alternatives: distributed certification authorities or self-organized key management model.

In this paper the self-organized approach to public-key management is chosen as base in order to guarantee identical roles for all the network nodes. Therefore, nodes are in charge not only of creating, storing, distributing and revoking their public keys but also they should perform other classical management tasks such as packet routing.

The proposal here described tries to improve the performance of key management in the well-known web of trust model. In order to achieve this aim, we face

V. Atluri (Ed.): DAS 2008, LNCS 5094, pp. 175–189, 2008.

the problem by combining typical authentication elements with common ideas used in routing protocols. In this way, we seek a reduction in resource consumption while undertaking the verification process associated to authentication.

The structure of this paper is as follows. Section 2 provides an insight into routing protocols used in MANETs, paying special attention to the Optimized Link State Routing (OLSR) protocol from which some ideas regarding the use of the MPR technique have been borrowed in order to improve key management tasks. Since our proposal is specifically designed to be deployed in the self-organized key management model, section 3 deals with the details of that approach. Both the Multipoint Relay technique described in Section 2 together with the graph-based public-key certification protocol described in Section 3 constitute the keystones of the proposal, which is described from an algorithmic point of view in this latter section. Finally, Section 4 closes the paper with the conclusions that may be extracted from this work and some questions that deserve further research.

2   Routing in MANETs: OLSR and MPR

In the last years one of the areas in MANETs where more research has been developed is that of routing algorithms [1]. Due to the lack of centralized infrastructure, routing in MANETs is one of the innumerable tasks that are in charge of the nodes themselves. This is just one of the reasons why cooperation among the members of the network is essential.

Some basic concepts referring to routing protocols used in MANETs and the information handled by them are here gathered in order to understand later how they are used to help in the authentication process.

There is a first basic classification used when talking of routing protocols that distinguish between proactive and reactive protocols. Protocols in the first category are characterized because each node should store a route for each reachable member of the network although such a path may not be required at that precise moment whilst regarding reactive protocols, it should be stressed that only when a request for communication between two nodes exists, a route discovery procedure is initiated. Due to this feature, these protocols are referred to as on-demand routing protocols.

Proactive algorithms are also known as table-driven routing protocols since local routing information defining the different paths is organized according a table stored by each node. The information contained in such a table defines an entry associated to each reachable node containing the next node in the path to the destination and a metric or distance, among another data. The metric can be defined in function of several criteria such as the hop distance, the total delay or the cost of sending messages. In networks with high mobility these routing protocols have a good behaviour since the paths are calculated in advance, and so the nodes do not have to wait until they are computed.

When comparing proactive and reactive protocols, it is important to point out that in the first set certain overload is originated in the network due to the continuous updates produced in routing information while those routing algorithms belonging to the second set have to face the delay due to the execution of routing discovery procedures produced any time a new path is defined.

In this work, we use certain elements of the proactive routing protocol known as Optimized Link State Routing (OLSR) protocol, which is one of the four basic protocols adopted for MANETs, in order to improve the construction of certificate repositories defined in the key management scheme when adopting the web of trust model.

In the OLSR proactive routing there are two stages clearly differentiated. Firstly, a reliable map of the network is built. In order to obtain such an accurate map, all the network nodes must exchange messages regarding the state of their connections links. In the second stage, and based on the map built, the optimum route among the nodes is generated. The main obstacle this protocol has to skip is the high number of messages to be exchanged among nodes. However, thanks to these messages the network configuration is known by all its members.

This routing algorithm has been extensively analyzed in the bibliography, and recently, some works devoted to improve it by integrating security tools [2] have been developed.

Thinking of reducing the overhead and message redundancy and trying to avoid the storm problem [3], a specific technique was defined in OLSR. In this technique each node selects a particular neighbour subset (nodes at one-hop distance) whose members will be in charge of broadcasting the information related to topology control. By doing so, the number of messages exchanged is considerably reduced, [4].

Roughly speaking, it can be said that this technique allows determining the minimum number of nodes needed for reaching the whole network when it is recursively applied. This procedure is named as the MultiPoint Relay (MPR) technique. The way we will utilise the basics of this technique in the key management proposal as well as its relationship with Graph Theory problems are included below.

The MPR technique was originally deployed for reducing the duplicity of messages at local level when broadcasting information in a proactive MANET [5]. In general, the number of redundant packets received by a node may be equal to the number of neighbours a node has. In the OLSR protocol only a subset of nodes will be in charge of retransmitting the received packets. In this way, every node u must define among its direct neighbours a set of transmitters (here denoted by $MPR(u)$) that will be the only ones in charge of retransmitting the messages emitted by the initial node.

According to this method, the choice of the set MPR should guarantee that all the nodes in a two-hop distance of the initial node receive the messages. In order to fulfil this requirement every node in a two-hop distance of u must have a neighbour belonging to $MPR(u)$.

In routing models the network is usually represented with a graph whose vertex set $V = \{u_1, u_2, \ldots, u_n\}$ symbolizes the set of nodes of the network. In this way, for any node u, $N^i(u)$ denotes the set of u's neighbours in a

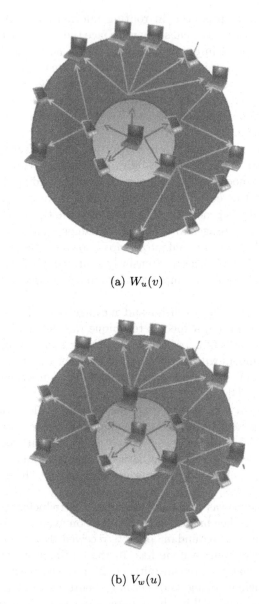

(a) $W_u(v)$

(b) $V_w(u)$

Fig. 1. Defining some vertex subsets

i-hop distance from u. Consequently, $N^1(u)$ stands for u's direct neighbours and $|N^1(u)|$ corresponds to vertex u degree. These sets are defined by using the shortest path and in such a way that $N^i(u)$ and $N^{i+1}(u)$ are disjoint sets.

Following the notation defined in [6] jointly with the one previously introduced in this paper it is feasible to formally define the MPR set for a vertex u as $MPR(u) \subseteq N^1(u) | \forall w \in N^2(u) \exists v \in MPR(u) | w \in N^1(v)$.

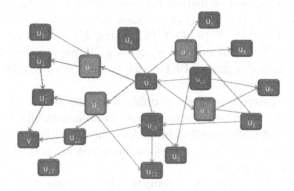

(a) Stage 1: Isolated nodes in $N^2(u)$ are analyzed

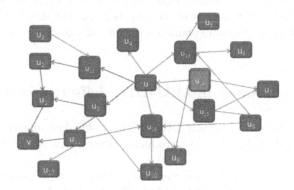

(b) Stage 2: Nodes of maximum degree are included in $MPR(u)$

Fig. 2. Stages in MPR-OLSR

Through this definition, decision and optimization problems associated may be defined. According to the Computational Complexity hierarchy such problem belongs to the $NP - hard$ class. The heuristic defined in the OLSR routing procedure uses a greedy approach handling the vertex degree as parameter. The idea is to select the neighbours of the original vertex u which cover the highest number of vertices in u's two-hop vicinity that have not been previously covered.

In order to calculate $MPR(u)$ we need to define several vertex subsets that are specified below. First, for each node v in a one-hop distance from u it is required to consider a new vertex subset $W_u(v)$ formed by those vertices that simultaneously belong to the order 2 u's neighbourhood and are direct neighbours of v (see figure 1(a)). This set may be calculated by the following intersection $W_v(u) = N^2(u) \cap N^1(v)$. Vertices in this set have in common the fact that they are candidates to be covered by vertex v.

A second vertex subset is defined for each vertex w belonging to u's two-hop neighbourhood $V_w(u)$. In this case, such a subset may be obtained through the intersection $V_w(u) = N^1(w) \cap N^1(u)$ (figure 1(b)). This new set gathers those vertices in $N^1(u)$ that may cover vertex w. When transferring the MPR computation to the self-organized PKI model, $V_w(u)$ is calculated by using $N_1(w)$ this means the set of predecessors of vertex w.

Analyzing the description of the problem from the Graph Theory point of view, it can be concluded that the node being examined and its MPR set must form a dominant set in its level 2 vicinity. A dominant set in a graph is a vertex subset such that any node in the corresponding graph has and edge linking it to a vertex in the dominant set.

The greedy heuristic algorithm is composed by two main stages stages. In the first one those vertices w in $N^2(u)$ which have an only neighbour v in $N^1(u)$ are examined, in order two include in $MPR(u)$ the vertex v to which is connected. In case there are remaining nodes without covering in $N^{(}u)$, in the second stage, those vertices in $N^1(u)$ which cover more vertices in that situation are also included in $MPR(u)$. A graphic explanation of how the algorithm works is included in figure 2.

3   Key Management in MANETs: Self-organized Model

In this section the main characteristics of the public-key management model that we use are described before introducing several new ideas that form our proposal.

In the bibliography we may find two main alternatives for the deployment of Public-Key Infrastructures (PKIs) in MANETs: distributed certification authorities, and self-organized public-key management model.

In the first case the certification procedure relays on distributed Certification Authorities (CAs) that thanks to a (t,n) threshold signature scheme issue and renew nodes's certificates [7], [8].

The main drawbacks of this model are the computational intensive operations required by the threshold application when signing a certificate, and the definition of additional procedures such as share refreshing [9]. Also, when dealing with certificate validation, nodes should locate a correct coalition but, depending on the actual network topology and conditions, it might result infeasible.

In this work we decided to follow the self-organized key management model based on the web of trust approach. Several are the reasons that justify the choice of this option. First, this model demands less maintenance overhead. Secondly, it is well worth remarking that on the one hand the self-organized approach eases the use of a simple bootstrap mechanism and on the other hand all the nodes perform equal roles.

The self-organized model in MANETs was initially described in [10]. Its authors put forward the substitution of the centralized certification authority by a self-organized scenario where certification is carried out through chains of certificates which are issued by the nodes themselves. Such a scheme is based on the information stored by each node and the trust relationship among neighbour nodes.

In this model public keys and certificates are represented as a directed graph $G = (V, A)$, known as *certificate graph*. Each vertex u in this graph defines a public key linked to a node, and each arc (u, v) symbolizes a certificate associated to v's public key, signed by using u's private key. Each node u has a public key, a private key, and two certificate repositories, the updated and the non-updated repositories. Initially the updated certificate repository will contain the list of certificates on which each node trust (out-bound list) and the list of certificates of all the nodes that trust on u (in-bound list).

A sequence $P_{uv} = \{(u, u_0), (u_0, u_1), ..., (u_m, v)\}$ of certificates where the vertices are all different is called a chain of certificates from u to v.

The tasks that a member of the network has to develop in this public-key management scheme are the following [10]:

1. Certificate Management:
   (a) Key generation: The node generates its keys by itself.
   (b) Certificate issue: The node issues certificates that bind public keys of other nodes to their identities.
   (c) Certificate exchange: The node exchange certificates with other nodes and builds its non-updated repository.
   (d) Updated certificate repository construction: The node builds its updated repository.
2. Public-Key Verification:
   (a) Finding a certificate chain.
   (b) Verifying the certificates in the chain.

Next we describe how certificate management and public-key verification are carried out in the self-organized model.

Each node u generates by its own the pair formed by its public key and its secret key. Then a request for signing the generated public key is sent to u's neighbours. Since these nodes are in a one-hop distance from u, they can use any trusted mechanisms such as side channels in order to assure the binding established between the corresponding public key and the node's identity.

Apart from that, in order to ease certificate revocation, each certificate issued will be valid for a certain period of time. This parameter may be chosen depending on the mobility characteristics of the underlying MANET.

Since the certificates issued by a node are stored in its local repository, one of the tasks that a node may perform during idle periods is the renewal of certificates issued by it to those nodes that might still be considered as trusted. Otherwise, certificate renewal may be developed on demand. It means that when an expired certificate is included in the non-updated repository of a node, such a node should request a renewal for that certificate.

When a certificate for a node u is issued by a node v the edge (v, u) is added to the certificate graph and each node u and v stores it in its in-bound and out-bound list, respectively.

Note that the speed in the creation of the certificate graph and its density depend on the motivation of the users for distributing certificates, and on nodes' mobility. In particular, the more mobility the nodes have, the more complete the repositories will be. The same happens with other aspects related to MANETs cooperation.

As in any PKI-based system, certificate revocation should also be taken into account. When revocation is initiated due to key compromise or misbehaviour of the corresponding node, the certificate issuer sends a message to all nodes stating that such a certificate has been revoked. This can be accomplished thanks to that each node maintains a list containing the members of the network that have contacted him to request updates of the certificates he has issued. Hence, in fact it is not necessary to send the revocation message to all the members of the network. The last proposals related to revocation policies in MANETs defend the creation of schemes based in reputation systems [11], [12]. When revocation is due to the fact that the expiration time has been reached, such a revocation can be deduced directly by all nodes since the expiration date is contained in the certificate.

Certificate exchange is a low-cost procedure because it only involves one-hope distance nodes. It allows to share and to distribute the issued and stored certificates. A description of this procedure is as follows:

1. Every node u retransmits the hash values of the certificates stored in the repositories G_u and G_u^N to its neighbours. The recipient nodes answer with the hash values of the certificates contained in its repositories.
2. Every node contrasts the received value with the one he already has and requests to its neighbours only the certificates that are new.
3. If the local memory of a node is not enough, the expired certificates are deleted from the non-updated repository, starting by the oldest ones.
4. In this way, after a short period of time the non-updated repository G_u^N contains almost all the certificate graph G. Afterwards, the only task to be carried out by the nodes is to exchange the new certificates.

In the original proposal two ways of building the updated certificate repository G_u of a node u were described:

1. Node u communicates with its neighbours in the certificate graph.
2. Node u applies over G_u^N an appropriate algorithm in order to generate G_u after checking the validity of every single certificate.

The selection of the certificates stored by each node in its repository should be done carefully in order to satisfy at the same time two requirements: limitation in storing requirements, and usefulness of the repository in terms of ability to find chains for the largest possible number of nodes. This problem, known as optimal dispersal of certificate chains, has lately received particular attention in the bibliography [13].

The algorithm used in the construction of the updated repositories will influence in the efficiency of the scheme, so it should be carefully designed. The simplest algorithm for that construction is the so-called Maximum Degree Algorithm (MDA) (see algorithm 3.1), where the criterion followed in the selection of certificates is the degree of the vertices in the certificate graph.

Algorithm 3.1. MDA-$G_{out}(G, u, l_{out}, c)$

Step 0: $V_{out} = \emptyset, A_{out} = \emptyset, D_{out} = \emptyset, i \leftarrow 1$
Step 1: $e_{out} = min\{deg_{out}(u), c\}$
Step 2: $l \leftarrow deg_{out}(u)$
Step 3: $N^1(u) = S_{out}(N^1(u)) = \{v_1, v_2, \ldots, v_l\}$
Step 4: $D_{out} = \{v_1, v_2, \ldots, v_{e_{out}}\}$
Step 5: $V_{out} = V_{out} \cup \{u\} \cup D_{out}, A_{out} = A_{out} \cup \{(u, v_i)\}, \ i = 1, 2, \ldots, e_{out}$
Step 6: $i \leftarrow 1, l_i \leftarrow 1$
Step 7: while $i < e_{out}$ **and** D_{out} **not** $= \emptyset$

do
{
  Step 7.1: if $l_i = l_{out}$
  then Step 7.1.1: $i \leftarrow i + 1$

  else
  {
    Step 7.2.1: $v_i = get(D_{out})$
    Step 7.2.2: $N^1(v_i) = S_{out}(N^1(v_i))$
    Step 7.2.3: $w_i = get(N^1(v_i))$
    Step 7.2.4: while $w_i \in D_{out}$ **and** $N^1(v_i)$ **not** $= \emptyset$
    do Step 7.2.4.1: $w_i = get(N^1(v_i))$
    Step 7.2.5: if $N^1(v_i) = \emptyset$
    then Step 7.2.5.1: $i \leftarrow i + 1$

    else
    {
      Step 7.2.6.1: if $w_i \notin D_{out}$
      then
      {
        Step 7.2.6.1.1: $put(w_i, D_{out})$
        Step 7.2.6.1.2: $A_{out} = A_{out} \cup \{(v_i, w_i)\}$
        Step 7.2.6.1.3: $V_{out} = V_{out} \cup \{w_i\}$
        Step 7.2.6.1.4: $l_i = l_i + 1$
        Step 7.2.6.1.5: $i \leftarrow i + 1$
      }
    }
  }

  Step 7.3: if $i \bmod e_{out} = 0$
  then Step 7.3.1: $i \leftarrow 0$
}

There is a more sophisticated algorithm, called Shortcut Hunter Algorithm, in which certificates are chosen taking into account that when they are deleted, the length of the minimum path between the nodes connected through that certificate is increased in more than two units.

When using the MDA, every node u builds two subgraphs, the out-bound subgraph and the in-bound subgraph, which when joined generate the updated certificate repository G_u. The out-bound subgraph is formed by several disjoint paths with the same origin vertex u while in the in-bound subgraph u is the final vertex. In the description of the algorithm that follows, the starting node is u

and $deg_{out}(u)$, $deg_{in}(u)$ stands for the in-degree and the out-degree respectively of node u. The number of paths to be found is represented by c.

A bound on the number of disjoint paths starting at u, as well as a bound on the number of disjoint paths to be built with u as final node are given by e_{out} and e_{in}, respectively.

Algorithm 3.2. MPR-$G_{out}(G, u)$

Step 0: *Initialization* : $MPR(u) = \emptyset$
Step 1: $N^1(u) = \{v_1, v_2, \ldots, v_l\}$
Step 2: $N^2(u)$
comment: First stage

Step 3: **for** $i \leftarrow 1$ **to** l

do $\begin{cases} \textbf{Step 3.1: } N^1(v_i) \\ \textbf{Step 3.2: } W_{v_i}(u) = N^1(v_i) \cap N^2(u) = \{w_1, w_2, \ldots, w_k\} \\ \textbf{Step 3.3: if } k \neq 0 \\ \quad \text{then} \begin{cases} \textbf{Step 3.3.1: for } j = 1 \text{ to } k \\ \quad \text{do} \begin{cases} \textbf{Step 3.3.1.1: } N_1(w_j) \\ \textbf{Step 3.3.1.2: } V_{w_j}(u) = N^1(u) \cap N_1(w_j) \\ \textbf{Step 3.3.1.3: if } |V_{w_j}(u)| = 1 \\ \quad \text{then} \begin{cases} \textbf{Step 3.3.1.3.1: } MPR(u) = MPR(u) \cup \{v_i\} \\ \textbf{Step 3.3.1.3.2: } N^2(u) = N^2(u) \setminus W_v(u) \end{cases} \end{cases} \end{cases} \end{cases}$

Step 4: $N(u) = N(u) \setminus MPR(u)$
Step 5: $l = l - |MPR(u)|$
comment: Second stage

Step 6: **while** $N^2(u) \neq \emptyset$

do $\begin{cases} \textbf{Step 6.1: for } i = 1 \text{ to } l \\ \quad \text{do} \begin{cases} \textbf{Step 6.1.1: } N(v_i) \\ \textbf{Step 6.1.2: } W_{v_i}(u) = N^1(v_i) \cap N^2(u) \\ \textbf{Step 6.1.3: } d_u^+(v_i) = |W_{v_i}(u)| \end{cases} \\ \textbf{Step 6.2: } d_{max}(u) = \max d_u^+(v_i), i = 1, 2, \ldots, l \\ \textbf{Step 6.3: for } i = 1 \text{ to } l \\ \quad \text{do Step 6.3.1: if } d_u^+(v_i) = d_{max}(u) \\ \qquad \text{then} \begin{cases} \textbf{Step 6.3.1.1: } MPR(u) = MPR(u) \cup \{v_i\} \\ \textbf{Step 6.3.1.2: } N^2(u) = N^2(u) \setminus W_{v_i}(u) \end{cases} \\ \textbf{Step 6.4: } N^1(u) = N^1(u) \setminus MPR(u) \end{cases}$

Step 7: $MPR(u) = \{v_1, v_2, \ldots, v_k\}$
Step 8: **for** $i = 1$ **to** k

do $\begin{cases} \textbf{Step 8.1: if } v_i \notin V_{out} \begin{cases} \textbf{Step 8.1.1: } V_{out} = V_{out} \cup \{v_i\} \\ \textbf{Step 8.1.2: } A_{out} = A_{out} \cup \{(u, v_i)\} \\ MPR - G_{out} \{G, v_i\} \end{cases} \end{cases}$

Another important input parameter is s, which represents the maximum number of vertices to be included in the subgraph generated when the in-bound and the out-bound subgraphs are combined. This parameter may be also controlled by defining as $l_{out} = \lceil s/(2e_{out}) \rceil$ the length of the chains generated when building the out-bound subgraph and $l_{in} = \lceil s/(2e_{in}) \rceil$ for the in-bound one.

In order to apply the greedy criterion, $S_{out}(N)$ and $S_{in}(N)$, where N consists of a set of vertices, include the sorted vertices of N into descending order according to $deg_{out}(u)$ and $deg_{in}(u)$, respectively.

Note that the process to build the in-bound subgraph is equivalent to it except for the fact that in this case the edges to be chosen are always incoming edges.

In the first stage of the MDA, $deg_{out}(u)$ outgoing arcs from u are included. The final vertices of these arcs are then included in D_{out}. This set is implemented as a typical queue where the insertion (put) and the extraction (get)operations are used. Henceforth, e_{out} arcs are chosen in such a way that the formed paths are disjoint. This is accomplished by selecting their origin belonging to D_{out} and checking that neither the origin nor the final vertices were previously used in another path.

The main contribution introduced in this paper consists in substituting the MDA proposed for the updated repository construction by a new algorithm that uses the MPR technique described in 2. In this way, for each vertex in the certificate graph we have to define a re-transmitter set. Hence, the smallest number of vertices required for reaching the whole certificate graph will be obtained.

The MPR heuristic adapted to the certificate graph is described below (algorithm 3.2). First, node u starts by calculating $MPR(u) = \{v_1, v_2, \ldots, k\}$. Then, these vertices are included in G_{out} together with the edges $(u, v_i), i = 1, 2, \ldots, k$. Henceforth, nodes v_i in $MPR(u)$ apply recursively the same procedure of retransmitting backwards the result $MPR(v_i)$.

In order to extend the notation used in the introduction of the MPR greedy heuristic described in section 2, which is required to be used in the certificate graph, we denote by $N_i(u)$ the set of predecessors of node u that may be found in an i-hop distance.

This means that the smallest number of certificate chains required in order to reach the remaining nodes will be obtained as well. The algorithm proposed is an iterative scheme that may be described in the following way:

1. Every vertex $u \in G$ locally determines its re-transmitter set ($MPR(u)$), which include the certificates associated to the corresponding edges.
2. This vertex contacts all the nodes in $MPR(u)$. At this stage, every node $v \in MPR(u)$ has previously obtained its re-transmitters set $MPR(u)$, and consequently it may send to node u the certificates associated to such a set.

Since each node knows from whom is a re-transmitter, the G_{in} subgraph is generated by applying first the reverse process and then adding in-going arcs.

The certificate chains required in the authentication are built by using the arcs $(u, MPR(u))$. After that, $\forall v \in MPR(u)$ and $\forall w \in MPR(v)$ the arcs (v, w) are also added after having checked that they have not been added in previous updates.

Note that the procedure every node $u \in G$ has to develop in order to build $MPR(u)$ takes $1 + ln(N^2(u))$ steps when no bound is defined on the length of the chains to be built. Otherwise, the number of iterations to be carried out is given by the number of hops to explore in the certificate graph. As for the definition of the aforementioned bound, it has to be remarked that such a parameter may be dynamically adjusted in function of the changes experienced by the certificate graph. This may be justified by the fact that as the network evolves, the information contained in each node's repository is more complete.

Thanks to this substitution the generated procedure is easier and more efficient, guaranteeing in this way that each node has a set of neighbours that allows it to reach the biggest number of public keys.

Although this work is in its inital stage, a first implementation has been developed. It has been carried out using Java and the open source library JUNG 2.0 [14] (Java Universal Network/Graph Framework) which provides the basic tools for representing and dealing with graphs. Apart from this, JUNG allows generating random graphs with the small-world property, which is fulfilled by certificate graphs [15]. When a graph holds this characteristic, most nodes may be reached by a small number of hops from any source node. This kind of graphs has received special attention in several scientific disciplines including MANETs. The particular small-world model used in the simulation developed was proposed by Kleingberg [16]. When generating a graph with n^2 vertices according to this model, the first step is to create an nxn toroidal lattice. Then each node u is conected to four local neighbours, and in addition one long range connection to some node v, where v is chosen randomly, according to a probability proportional to $d^{-\alpha}$. d denotes the lattice distance between u and v and α stands for the clustering coefficient. This coefficient α is defined as the average over all the nodes in the network of the relationship between the maximum number of edges that may be deifned and the number of edges that actually exist. Generating the graphs following this model guarantees that the shortest paths may be determined using local information, what makes them particularly interesting for the networks we are dealing with.

Some of the data gathered from the computational experience are shown below (table 1). The number of nodes in the graph (n), the rate of certificates contained in the repository (R_c), the clustering coefficient (α), the maximum length in the chains generated (C_l) and the time consumption while the execution (t) expressed in seconds are the marameters that have been measured. From this experience, it may be remarked that the certificate rate finally contained in the local repository increases as the size of the graph increases as well as the clustering coefficient increases. This phenomenon may be better apreciated in figure 3. Additionally, the maximum length in the chains obtained are kept at reasonable values, what makes the chain verification process lighter. Finally, the rate of certificates stored in the repository surpasses 95% in more than 75% of the executinos while time consumption corresponds to sensible values. These first experiments shown promising results.

Table 1. Computational Experience

n	$\alpha = 0.1$			$\alpha = 0.4$			$\alpha = 0.8$		
	R_c	C_l	t	R_c	C_l	t	R_c	C_l	t
9	42.93	4	0.24	37.03	3	0.27	37.78	3	0.18
16	82.08	3	0.49	86.67	3	0.41	84.17	3	0.46
25	93.13	3	0.64	96.00	3	0.59	96.00	3	0.69
36	98.70	3	0.81	99.63	3	0.83	99.44	3	0.8
49	99.73	4	1.24	99.18	4	1.2	99.59	4	0.92
64	99.59	3	0.68	100.00	4	0.68	99.48	3	0.64
81	99.92	4	0.77	99.92	4	0.81	99.82	4	0.84
100	99.93	4	0.91	99.93	4	0.97	99.80	4	0.96

One of the main advantages of the proposal is that all the information gathered for the construction of the chains is locally obtained by each node.

After obtaining the in-bound and out-bound subgraphs, both subgraphs are merged and the initial repository is generated so that the authentication process may start.

When a node u needs to check the validity of the public key of another node v, it has to find a certificate chain P_{uv} from itself to v in the graph that results from combining its own repository with v's repository.

If this chain is not found there, the search is extended to $G_u \cup G_u^N$, what implies the inclusion of u's non-updated repository in the search. If this second exploration is successful, u should request the update of those certificates that belong exclusively to G_u^N. When no path is found, the authentication fails.

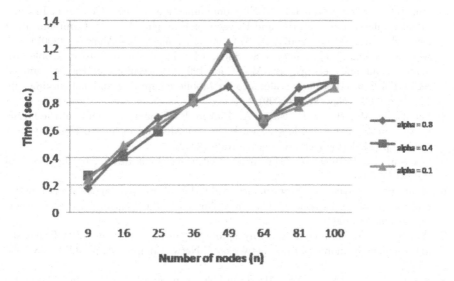

Fig. 3. Time consumption

Once the path P_{uv} is determined, u should validate every certificate included in it. This is done as follows:

1. The first certificate in the chain (u, u_0) is directly checked by u since it was signed by u himself.
2. Each one of the remaining certificates (u_i, u_{i+1}) in the chain may be checked using the public key of the previous node u_{i-1}.
3. The last arc (u_m, v) corresponds to the certificate issued by u_m that binds v with its public key.

4   Conclusions and Further Research

This work proposes the application of the Multipoint Relay Technique in the computation of certificate repositories included in the self-organized public-key management model proposed by [10]. Our proposal is supported by the good results obtained when using the MPR procedure in the $OLSR$ routing algorithm in MANETs and a prelimiar computational experience. Through this improvement we provide the public-key management scheme with simplicity and efficiency.

The computational implementation of the proposal is part of a work in progress. Consequently, a future version of this paper will include an extended simulation experiment.

References

1. Royer, E., Toh, C.K.: A review of current routing protocols for ad-hoc mobile wireless networks. IEEE Personal Communications Magazine 6(2), 46–55 (1999)
2. Vilela, J.P., Barros, J.: A feedback reputation mechanism to secure the optimized link state routing protocol. In: IEEE Communications Society/CreateNet International Conference on Security and Privacy for Emerging Areas in Communication Networks (Securecomm 2007). IEEE Computer Society, Los Alamitos (2007)
3. Ni, S.Y., Tseng, Y.C., Chen, Y.S., Sheu, J.P.: The broadcast storm problem in a mobile ad hoc network. In: MobiCom 1999: Proceedings of the 5th annual ACM/IEEE international conference on Mobile computing and networking, pp. 151–162. ACM, New York (1999)
4. Laouti, A., Mhlethaler, P., Najid, A., Plakoo, E.: Simulation results of the OLSR routing protocol for wireless network. In: 1st Mediterranean Ad-Hoc Networks workshop (Med-Hoc-Net), Sardegna, Italy (2002)
5. Clausen, T., Jacquet, P.: RFC 3626: Optimized Link State Routing Protocol (OLSR) (2003)
6. Mans, B., Shrestha, N.: Performance evaluation of approximation algorithms for multipoint relay selection. In: The Third Annual Mediterranean Ad Hoc Networking Workshop (2004)
7. Wu, B., Wu, J., Fernandez, E.B., Ilyas, M., Magliveras, S.: Secure and efficient key management in mobile ad hoc networks. J. Netw. Comput. Appl. 30(3), 937–954 (2007)
8. Saxena, N., Tsudik, G., Yi, J.H.: Threshold cryptography in P2P and MANETs: The case of access control. Comput. Networks 51(12), 3632–3649 (2007)

9. Narasimha, M., Tsudik, G., Yi, J.: On the utility of distributed cryptography in P2P and MANETs: The case of membership control. In: Proceedings of the 11th IEEE International Conference on Network Protocols (ICNP 2003), pp. 336–345. IEEE, Los Alamitos (2003)
10. Capkun, S., Buttyan, L., Hubaux, J.P.: Self-organized public key management for mobile ad hoc networks. Mobile Computting and Communication Review 6(4) (2002)
11. Arboit, G., Crepeau, C., Davis, C.R., Maheswaran, M.: A localized certificate revocation scheme for mobile ad hoc networks. Ad Hoc Networks (2006), doi:10.1016/j.adhoc.2006.07.003
12. Moore, T., Clulow, J., Nagaraja, S., Anderson, R.: New strategies for revocation in ad-hoc networks. In: Stajano, F., Meadows, C., Capkun, S., Moore, T. (eds.) ESAS 2007. LNCS, vol. 4572, pp. 232–246. Springer, Heidelberg (2007)
13. Jung, E., Elmallah, E.S., Gouda, M.G.: Optimal dispersal of certificate chains. IEEE Transactions on Parallel and Distributed Systems 18(4), 474–484 (2007)
14. JUNG 2.0 (Java Universal Network/Graph framework)
15. Capkun, S., Buttyan, L., Hubaux, J.P.: Small worlds in security systems: an analysis of the PGP certificate graph. In: Proceedings of The ACM New Security Paradigms Workshop 2002, Norfolk, Virginia Beach, USA, September 2002, p. 8 (2002)
16. Kleinberg, J.: The small-world phenomenon: An algorithmic perspective. In: Proceedings of the 32nd ACM Symposium on Theory of Computing (2000)

Exclusive Strategy for Generalization Algorithms in Micro-data Disclosure

Lei Zhang[1], Lingyu Wang[2], Sushil Jajodia[1], and Alexander Brodsky[1]

[1] Center for Secure Information Systems
George Mason University
Fairfax, VA 22030, USA
{lzhang8,jajodia,brodsky}@gmu.edu
[2] Concordia Institute for Information Systems Engineering
Concordia University
Montreal, QC H3G 1M8, Canada
wang@ciise.concordia.ca

Abstract. When generalization algorithms are known to the public, an adversary can obtain a more precise estimation of the secret table than what can be deduced from the disclosed generalization result. Therefore, whether a generalization algorithm can satisfy a privacy property should be judged based on such an estimation. In this paper, we show that the computation of the estimation is inherently a recursive process that exhibits a high complexity when generalization algorithms take a straightforward *inclusive strategy*. To facilitate the design of more efficient generalization algorithms, we suggest an alternative *exclusive strategy*, which adopts a seemingly drastic approach to eliminate the need for recursion. Surprisingly, the data utility of the two strategies are actually not comparable and the exclusive strategy can provide better data utility in certain cases.

1 Introduction

The dissemination and sharing of information has become increasingly important to our society. However, such efforts may be hampered by the lack of security and privacy guarantees. For example, when a healthcare organization releases tables of diagnosis information, explicit identifiers such as names will be removed. However, an adversary may still identify a patient from the released table if, say, the combination of the patient's race, date of birth, and Zip code can be linked to a unique record in a publicly available voter list [20,24,25].

Existing solutions to the micro-data release problem are largely based on randomization or generalization. This paper considers generalization techniques. At an abstract level, a micro-data table can be considered as a mapping between quasi-identifiers (for example, the combination of race, date of birth, and Zip code) and sensitive values (such as diagnosis result). A generalization can be regarded as a partition on this mapping, which divides quasi-identifiers and corresponding sensitive values into disjoint groups. By hiding the detailed mapping inside each group, each quasi-identifier is *blended* with others in the same group. The amount of privacy protection achieved through such a generalization can be measured under various privacy properties, such as l-diversity[2].

V. Atluri (Ed.): DAS 2008, LNCS 5094, pp. 190–204, 2008.

However, a major limitation of most existing solutions is to assume a disclosed table to be the only source of information available to an adversary. Unfortunately, this is not always the case. An adversary usually knows the fact that a generalization algorithm will maximize the utility function in addition to satisfying the privacy property (relying on the secrecy of such information is an example of *security by obscurity*). As recently pointed out in [30], this extra knowledge may allow the adversary to obtain a more precise estimation of the secret table, on which the privacy property may no longer be satisfied. An apparent solution is to anticipate what the adversary will do, that is to estimate the secret table based on both the disclosed table and public knowledge about the generalization algorithm. Once the estimation is obtained, the privacy property can be evaluated to decide the safety of the generalization algorithm.

In this paper, we study the computation of an adversary's estimation of the secret table, which can be modeled as a set of possible instances of the unknown secret table, namely, *disclosure set*. We show that a given sequence of generalization functions can be combined into different strategies in releasing generalized tables. We first consider generalization algorithms designed under a straightforward *inclusive strategy*. We show that the computation of disclosure sets under the inclusive strategy is inherently a recursive process and exhibits a high complexity. To facilitate the design of efficient generalization algorithms, we then suggest an alternative *exclusive strategy*, which adopts a seemingly more drastic approach to generalization in order to avoid the need for a recursive process. Surprisingly, we show that the data utility of those two strategies are actually incomparable, and the exclusive strategy can provide better data utility in certain cases. First of all, we motivate further discussions with an example.

Motivating Example. Table 1 shows our running example as a table containing patient information. The table has three attributes: Name, Age, and Patient's Condition. The attribute Name is an identifier. We assume the Age attribute forms a quasi-identifier, and the Condition attribute is sensitive.

Table 2 shows three possible generalizations, G_1, G_2 and G_3, together with the original table, in an abstract way. We denote as ID the identifier (that is, Name), QI the quasi-identifier (that is, Age), and S the sensitive attribute (that is, Condition). Each generalization G_1, G_2 and G_3 includes a group quasi-identifier $QI_i (i = 1, 2, 3)$ and the sensitive attribute S (notice the identifier ID has been removed). For simplicity, we omit the details of each group quasi-identifier and sensitive value in the remainder of this paper.

We assume the generalization algorithm to be public knowledge. This knowledge has several aspects. First, the generalization algorithm defines a sequence of generalization functions sorted in a non-increasing order of data utility. In Table 2, the three generalizations are results of applying g_1, g_2, and g_3 to the original table G_0, respectively. We assume the three generalizations have non-increasing data utility (for example, average group size). The assumption of given aggregation functions is a common practice of most existing generalization techniques. Although the number of possible generalization functions may grow quickly, say, in the number of attributes, the issue of choosing suitable aggregation functions among all possibilities is beyond the scope of this paper. Our assumption of non-increasing utility in the sequence of functions is also a common practice, and also notice that functions with equal or incomparable utilities

Table 1. An Example of Patient Information Table

Name	Age	Condition
Alice	21	flu
Bob	27	tracheitis
Clark	31	pneumonia
Diana	36	tracheitis
Ellen	43	gastritis
Fen	49	gastritis
George	52	cancer
Henry	58	enteritis
Ian	63	cancer
Jason	67	heart disease

Table 2. An Example of Three Generalization Functions

Original Table G_0			Generalization G_1		Generalization G_2		Generalization G_3	
ID	QI	S	QI_1	S	QI_2	S	QI_3	S
A	$g_0^1(21)$	c_1	g_1^1	c_1	g_2^1	c_1	g_3^1	c_1
B	$g_0^2(27)$	c_2	$(20 \sim 29)$	c_2	$(20 \sim 29)$	c_2	$(20 \sim 34)$	c_2
C	$g_0^3(31)$	c_3	g_1^2	c_3	g_2^2	c_3		c_3
D	$g_0^4(36)$	c_2	$(30 \sim 39)$	c_2	$(30 \sim 44)$	c_2	g_3^2	c_2
E	$g_0^5(43)$	c_4	g_1^3	c_4		c_4	$(35 \sim 54)$	c_4
F	$g_0^6(49)$	c_4	$(40 \sim 49)$	c_4	g_2^3	c_4		c_4
G	$g_0^7(52)$	c_6	g_1^4	c_6	$(45 \sim 59)$	c_6		c_6
H	$g_0^8(58)$	c_5	$(50 \sim 59)$	c_5		c_5	g_3^3	c_5
I	$g_0^9(63)$	c_6	g_1^5	c_6	g_2^4	c_6	$(55 \sim 69)$	c_6
J	$g_1^{10}(67)$	c_7	$(60 \sim 69)$	c_7	$(60 \sim 69)$	c_7		c_7

can be treated in the same way in our discussions. Second, the generalization algorithm defines a privacy property. In this paper, we consider a particular privacy property, namely, recursive $(2, 2)$-diversity (basically, among all possible sensitive values that any record can take, the highest ratio of any value X, denoted as $r_{DS}(X)$, should satisfy $r_{DS}(X) < 2(1 - r_{DS}(X))$, or equivalently, $r_{DS}(X) < 2/3$) [2]. Third, the generalization algorithm applies the sequence of generalization functions to the original table, and returns the first generalization on which the privacy property evaluates to true. Clearly, this approach aims to maximize the data utility while satisfying the privacy property.

However, the above knowledge about the generalization algorithm may allow an adversary to deduce more information than what is directly disclosed in the generalization. For example, in Table 2, consider two cases. First, suppose an adversary does not know about the generalization algorithm, but only sees the second generalization G_2. In guessing the original table G_0, the adversary cannot discriminate the sensitive values in each group with respect to their association with each ID. For example, the ID A can be associated with either c_1 or c_2 in the group g_2^1. Therefore, to the adversary, all tables obtained by permuting the sensitive values within each group can potentially be the original table. Second, suppose an adversary knows about the generalization algorithm in addition to seeing G_2. The adversary can then deduce that G_1 must not satisfy the recursive $(2, 2)$-diversity because otherwise G_1 will be returned instead of G_2 due to better data utility. Although the adversary cannot see G_1 (more precisely, the sensitive values of G_1), based on the relationship between the groups in G_1 and G_2, he/she can still conclude that both E and F must be associated with c_4 in the original table. Clearly, between the above two cases, the recursive $(2, 2)$-diversity is satisfied in the first but not satisfied in the second.

The above example shows that it is insufficient to evaluate a privacy property based on a generalization itself when the generalization algorithm is publicly known. Unfortunately, this is indeed the approach adopted by most existing generalization algorithms. Those algorithms may thus produce results that actually violate the given privacy property (we say such algorithms are *unsafe*). To develop *safe* generalization algorithms, a critical question is: *What exactly can an adversary deduce about the original table, when he/she knows about the generalization algorithm?* In this paper, we first show how to exactly compute an adversary's knowledge about the original table, namely, the *disclosure set*. Second, as a consequent, we obtain a safe version of the traditional approach to generalization by evaluating the privacy property on the disclosure set instead of the generalization. Later in this paper, we shall show that by applying the safe version of the generalization algorithm to the above example, we would reach the counter-intuitive conclusion that neither G_2 nor G_3 can be safely disclosed.

Organization. The remainder of the paper is organized as follows. Section 2 shows how to compute a disclosure set and reveals the inherent complexity of such a process. Section 3 introduces the *exclusive strategy* and studies the complexity and data utility of the corresponding generalization algorithms. Section 4 reviews related work. Section 5 finally concludes the paper.

2 Computing Disclosure Sets under the Inclusive Strategy

Section 2.1 first introduces the concept of *disclosure set*. Section 2.2 then studies the computation of disclosure sets under the *inclusive strategy*.

2.1 Disclosure Set

We consider the following micro-data disclosure problem. An *original table* $G_0(ID, QI, S)$ is given where ID, QI, and S denote the identifier attribute, quasi-identifier attribute(s), and sensitive attribute, respectively. A *generalization algorithm* $\mathbb{G}$ is given, which defines a sequence of *generalization functions* $g_1, g_2, \ldots, g_n$. The algorithm $\mathbb{G}$ applies each g_i in the given order to G_0 to obtain a *generalization* $G_i(QI_i, S)$ where QI_i is the group quasi-identifier attribute. We assume the last generalization function g_n always yields an empty set, indicating that nothing should be disclosed. The algorithm $\mathbb{G}$ always returns a generalization G_i that satisfies a given *privacy property* CHK.

The above discussion, however, does not address a critical issue, that is how the given privacy property CHK should be evaluated when a generalization G_i is to be disclosed. Generally, CHK should be evaluated based on an adversary's knowledge about the original table G_0. Such knowledge can be characterized as follows. The adversary attempts to guess G_0 based on the disclosed generalization G_i and the public information about the generalization algorithm $\mathbb{G}$. Any table that contradicts the information available to the adversary will be eliminated. The adversary will end up with a set of *possible instances*, which represents the best guess the adversary can make about G_0, namely, his/her knowledge about G_0. We call such a set the *disclosure set* corresponding to the generalization function g_i, denoted as DS_i. Clearly, the privacy property CHK should be evaluated on DS_i, when the generalization G_i is to be disclosed.

If a disclosed generalization is the only source of information available to the adversary, then the disclosure set DS_i is simply the collection of tables to which applying g_i will yield the generalization G_i. Such a collection of tables can be obtained by fixing an order on the attribute ID and QI while permuting the sensitive values within each group of G_i. We denote the collection of tables as $PER(G_i)$. For example, in Table 2, $PER(G_1)$ includes $2 \times 2 \times 1 \times 2 = 16$ tables since every group except g_1^3 has two permutations.

As illustrated in Section 1, we cannot simply evaluate CHK on $PER(G_i)$ when the generalization algorithm $\mathbb{G}$ is publicly known. The reason is that an adversary may eliminate some possible instances from $PER(G_i)$ due to a conflict with the fact that G_i is disclosed by $\mathbb{G}$. More precisely, the adversary can apply $\mathbb{G}$ to each possible instance in $PER(G_i)$. If $\mathbb{G}$ returns any $G_j (j < i)$, then the adversary knows this possible instance cannot be the original table G_0, and hence it should not be included in DS_i. In this way, the adversary can derive DS_i as a subset of $PER(G_i)$.

Example 1. In Table 2, DS_1 is simply $PER(G_1)$ because generally the original table will not satisfy CHK, so the adversary cannot eliminate any instance from $PER(G_1)$. Although we shall delay the computation of DS_2, we can see that any possible instance in $PER(G_2)$ that has two different sensitive values associated with the ID E and F will cause $\mathbb{G}$ to return G_1 instead of G_2, and thus will not be included in DS_2.

We formalize the concept of disclosure set in Definition 1.

Definition 1. *The disclosure set DS_i corresponding to a generalization G_i is a set of possible instances that satisfy*

- $DS_i \subseteq PER(G_i)$
- $\forall X \in DS_i$ *the generalization algorithm $\mathbb{G}$ will not return G_j for any $j < i$.*

2.2   The Computation of Disclosure Set

Table 3 shows two algorithms. $\mathbb{G}$ on the left-hand side is a generalization algorithm and $\mathbb{DS}$ on the right-hand side is an algorithm for computing the disclosure set of a given generalization. $\mathbb{G}$ simply returns the first generalization G_i whose disclosure set (computed by the other algorithm $\mathbb{DS}$) satisfies a given privacy property CHK. On the other hand, $\mathbb{DS}$ computes the disclosure set of G_i by eliminating from $PER(G_i)$ any instance X for which the algorithm $\mathbb{G}$ returns a generalization that appears before G_i.

Table 3. Algorithms $\mathbb{G}$ and $\mathbb{DS}$

Algorithm $\mathbb{G}$
Input: An original table G_0,
    generalization functions $g_1, g_2, \ldots, g_n$,
    and a privacy property CHK
Output: A generalization $G_i(1 \leq i \leq n)$ or ϕ
Method:
1.   **For** $i = 1$ to n
2.   **If** $\mathbb{DS}(g_i(G_0))$ satisfies CHK
3.   **Return** $g_i(G_0)$
4.   **Return** ϕ

Algorithm $\mathbb{DS}$
Input: A generalization G_i
Output: The disclosure set DS_i
Method:
1.   **Let** $DS_i = PER(G_i)$
2.   **For each** $X \in DS_i$
3.   **If** $\mathbb{G}(X) = G_j$ for some $j < i$
4.   **Let** $DS_i = DS_i \setminus \{X\}$
5.   **Return** DS_i

The algorithms in Table 3 show that the computation of disclosure sets is inherently a recursive process. In the algorithm $\mathbb{DS}$, to compute the disclosure set of a generalization G_i, we must test every possible instance X in $PER(G_i)$ to determine whether X should be included in DS_i. More specifically, we first assume X to be the original table, then we apply the generalization algorithm $\mathbb{G}$. Each call to $\mathbb{G}$ will then involve $i - 1$ calls to the algorithm $\mathbb{DS}$ for computing the disclosure set of the generalizations $g_j(X)(j = 1, 2, \ldots, i - 1)$ (each such computation will again involve multiple calls to the generalization algorithm). One subtlety here is that we are actually using a modified version of $\mathbb{G}$ since it only uses the first $i - 1$ generalization functions. This is in accordance with Definition 1, and it also guarantees the recursive process to always terminate.

Example 2. In Table 2, to compute DS_2, the algorithm $\mathbb{DS}$ will call the algorithm $\mathbb{G}$ with each of the possible instances as the input. In this simple case, only g_1 is applied to each instance, and DS_1 is simply equal to $EXP(G_1)$. Clearly, for any instance in which E and F are not both associated with c_4, the disclosure set DS_1 will satisfy the $(2, 2)$-diversity, and hence the instance is not included in DS_2. On the other hand, all instances in which both E and F are associated with c_4 (such as the original table G_0) form the disclosure set DS_2, which clearly does not satisfy $(2, 2)$-diversity, either.

The computation of disclosure sets has another complication as follows. Recall that to compute DS_i, we apply the algorithm $\mathbb{G}$ to each $X \in PER(G_i)$. The algorithm $\mathbb{G}$ will then compute a disclosure set for each generalization $g_j(X)(1 \leq j \leq i - 1)$. It may seem that we can then reuse previous results since the disclosure sets $g_j(X)(1 \leq j \leq i - 1)$ should normally have been computed before we compute DS_i (refer to the algorithm $\mathbb{G}$). However, this is not the case. The two sets $PER(G_{i-1})$ and $PER(G_i)$ are generally not comparable. Some instance X may appear in $PER(G_i)$ (for example, $g_2(X) = g_2(G_0)$) but not in $PER(G_{i-1})$ (for example, $g_1(X) \neq g_1(G_0)$). For such an instance X, the disclosure sets for $g_j(X)(1 \leq j \leq i - 1)$ must be computed from scratch.

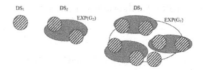

Fig. 1. Computing Disclosure Sets

Figure 1 illustrates this situation. The left-hand side denotes the disclosure set DS_1, which is equal to $EXP(G_1)$. In the middle is DS_2 where the shaded oval represents $EXP(G_2)$. Each of the two small circles denotes a set $PER(X)$ that satisfies CHK for some $X \in EXP(G_2)$. All the instances in $EXP(G_2) \setminus PER(X)$ should thus be excluded from DS_2. Notice that while all instances in $PER(G_2)$ yield the same generalization under g_2, they may yield different results under g_1, as indicated by the two disjoint circles (there may certainly be more than two different results under g_1). One subtlety here is that when we compute DS_2 we typically assume DS_1 does not satisfy CHK, so none of the small circles could be DS_1.

Example 3. In Table 2, any instance $X \in PER(G_2)$ in which E and F are not both associated with c_4 will not appear in $PER(G_1)$. The disclosure set DS_1 must thus be re-computed for each such X while computing DS_2. On the other hand, for any such instance X, $PER(X)$ will satisfy the $(2, 2)$-diversity. If we represent those instances as small circles to be subtracted from $EXP(G_2)$, as in Figure 1, there would be $3 \times 3 - 1 = 8$ such circles (in $PER(G_2)$, E and F can each be associated with three different values so totally nine different generalizations are possible under g_1 among which only G_1 does not satisfy the $(2, 2)$-diversity).

The situation of computing DS_3 is similar but more complicated, as illustrated in the right-hand side of Figure 1. The ellipse depicts $PER(G_3)$. We first consider how the algorithm $\mathbb{DS}$ will compute DS_3. For each $X \in PER(G_3)$, the algorithm $\mathbb{G}$ may return g_1 if CHK is satisfied on the disclosure set of $g_1(X)$ (that is, $PER(g_1(X))$), as represented by the small circle. If CHK is not satisfied, the algorithm $\mathbb{G}$ will continue to compute the disclosure set for $g_2(X)$, which again involves computing a disclosure set for the generalization under g_1 on each instance in $PER(g_2(X))$. If CHK is satisfied on the disclosure set of $g_2(X)$, then the algorithm $\mathbb{G}$ returns g_2. When $\mathbb{G}$ returns either g_1 or g_2, the algorithm $\mathbb{DS}$ will exclude the instance X from DS_3. As illustrated in the right-hand side of Figure 1, an instance X in $PER(G_3)$ can satisfy one (and only one) of the following conditions.

1. CHK holds on the disclosure set of $g_1(X)$ (illustrated as small circles in Figure 1)
2. CHK holds on the disclosure set of $g_2(X)$ (illustrated as shaded areas)
3. CHK does not hold on the disclosure set of $g_1(X)$ or $g_2(X)$ (illustrated as unfilled areas)

Example 4. In addition to the original table G_0 in Table 2, Table 4 shows two other possible instances in $PER(G_3)$. The left-hand side table G_a is an example of instances that satisfy the first condition since $PER(g_1(G_1))$ clearly satisfies $(2, 2)$-diversity. Both the original table G_0 in Table 2 and the right-hand side table G_b in Table 4 are examples of instances that satisfy the third condition.

In Example 4, although both G_0 in Table 2 and G_b in Table 4 satisfy the third condition, they clearly do so in different ways. More specifically, CHK does not hold on $PER(g_1(G_b))$ or $PER(g_2(G_b))$; CHK does not hold on $PER(G_1)$ but it does hold on $PER(G_2)$. The reason that G_0 does not satisfy the second condition but the third is that CHK does not hold on DS_2. Referring to Figure 1, $PER(g_2(G_b))$ will be a shaded oval; $DS(G_2)$ will be a shaded oval (that is, $PER(G_2)$) subtracted by some small circles (that is, $PER(g_1(X))(X \in PER(G_2)$) on which CHK holds.

Table 4. Two Possible Instances in $PER(G_3)$

Table G_a			Table G_b		
ID	QI	S	ID	QI	S
A	g_0^1	c_1	A	g_0^1	c_1
B	g_0^2	c_2	B	g_0^2	c_3
C	g_0^3	c_3	C	g_0^3	c_2
D	g_0^4	c_4	D	g_0^4	c_2
E	g_0^5	c_2	E	g_0^5	c_4
F	g_0^6	c_6	F	g_0^6	c_4
G	g_0^7	c_4	G	g_0^7	c_6
H	g_0^8	c_5	H	g_0^8	c_6
I	g_0^9	c_6	I	g_0^9	c_5
J	g_0^{10}	c_7	J	g_0^{10}	c_7

We are now ready to consider which instances in $PER(G_3)$ should be included in DS_3. Clearly, according to Definition 1, any instance that satisfies the first two conditions should be excluded, whereas instances satisfying the last condition should be included. Although the third condition can be satisfied in two different ways, we do not need to treat the two cases differently with the generalization algorithm $\mathbb{G}$ (however, we shall see the need for doing so in next section). In Figure 1, DS_3 corresponds to the unfilled area formed as the complement of all the small circles and shaded ovals.

Example 5. Both G_0 in Table 2 and G_b in Table 4 will be included in DS_3, although they fail $(2, 2)$-diversity in different ways (we shall see another case in next section).

In this special case, DS_3 can actually be computed more easily since there does not exist any $X \in PER(G_3)$ that can satisfy the above second condition (that is, $(2, 2)$-diversity is satisfied on the disclosure set of $g_2(X)$). Informally, any such X must first allow the $(2, 2)$-diversity to satisfy on $PER(g_2(X))$ but not on $PER(g_1(X))$ (for example, G_0 meets this requirement). However, we have that $g_1^1 = g_2^1$, $g_1^5 = g_2^4$, and

g_2^2 and g_2^3 can satisfy $(2, 2)$-diversity only if they each includes three different values. Therefore, the only possibility is that g_1^3 has two identical values, such as in the case with G_0. However, we already know that in this case the disclosure set of $g_2(X)$ will not satisfy $(2, 2)$-diversity since both E and F must be associated with the same value. We conclude that the second condition cannot be satisfied by any instance in $PER(G_3)$, and DS_3 can thus be computed by excluding from $PER(G_3)$ any instance X with $(2, 2)$-diversity satisfied on $PER(g_1(X))$.

In Figure 1, a confusion may arise about the instances in $PER(G_{i-1}) \setminus PER(G_i)$, such as those inside the small circles but outside the shaded ovals. When we compute the disclosure set for G_2, for any instance $X \in PER(G_2)$, we evaluate CHK on the disclosure set of $g_1(X)$. It seems those instances in $PER(g_1(X)) \setminus PER(G_2)$ should be excluded during such an evaluation because we know those instances are not possible. However, this is not the case. The algorithm $\mathbb{DS}$ simulates what an adversary will do to eliminate an instance X from $PER(G_2)$, he/she aims to prove that X cannot be the original table. For this purpose, the adversary will first assume that X is the original table and then attempt to show that CHK is already satisfied on $PER(g_1(X))$. If this is indeed the case, then $g_1(X)$ would have been released, and thus the adversary would not have any knowledge about $g_2(X)$ at all.

3   Exclusive Strategy

The generalization algorithm $\mathbb{G}$ in Table 3 adopts a straightforward strategy in using the sequence of generalization functions $g_1, g_2, \ldots, g_n$. That is, each function is applied in the given order, and the first generalization whose disclosure set satisfies the privacy property will be returned. Although this strategy is a natural choice and has been adopted by most existing generalization algorithms, it is not necessarily the only choice, neither is it an optimal choice in terms of data utility or computational complexity. By adopting different strategies, we may develop different generalization algorithms from the same sequence of generalization functions. In this paper, we do not intend to give a comprehensive study of possible strategies. Instead, we only present one strategy that is more efficient and may lead to more data utility in some cases.

Recall that in Example 4, G_0 in Table 2 and G_b in Table 4 are both included in DS_3. However, the difference lies in that CHK does not hold on $PER(g_2(G_b))$ but it does on $PER(G_2)$. An important observation is that we know G_b should be included in DS_3 without computing any disclosure sets, whereas we do not know whether G_2 should be included in DS_3 until we compute DS_2 (and know it does not satisfy CHK). Such a recursive computation of DS_2 within that of DS_3 brings high complexity, and should be avoided if possible. We thus propose a different strategy in handling instances like G_0. That is, we simply do not include it in DS_3, regardless whether DS_2 satisfies CHK (notice that if DS_2 does satisfy CHK then G_2 will also be excluded from DS_3). If we were to represent this situation using Figure 1, then the shaded oval will correspond to any $PER(g_2(X))$ that satisfies CHK (and the small circles remain to have the same meaning), regardless whether the corresponding disclosure set satisfies CHK. More generally, we exclude any instance $X \in EXP(G_i)$ from DS_i, if only $EXP(G_j)$

Table 5. Algorithms $\mathbb{G}_e$ and $\mathbb{DS}_e$

Algorithm $\mathbb{G}_e$
Input: An original table G_0,
      generalization functions $g_1, g_2, \ldots, g_n$,
      and a privacy property CHK
Output: A generalization $G_i (1 \leq i \leq n)$ or ϕ
Method:
1.   **For** $i = 1$ to n
2.   **If** $PER(g_i(G_0))$ satisfies CHK
3.   **If** $\mathbb{DS}(g_i(G_0))$ satisfies CHK
4.   **Return** $g_i(G_0)$
5.   **Else**
6.   **Return** ϕ
7.   **Return** ϕ

Algorithm $\mathbb{DS}_e$
Input: A generalization G_i;
Output: The disclosure set DS_i;
Method:
1.   **Let** $DS_i = PER(G_i)$;
2.   **Foreach** $X \in DS_i$
3.   **For** $j = 1$ to $i - 1$
4.   **If** $PER(g_j(X))$ satisfies CHK
5.   **Let** $DS_i = DS_i \setminus \{X\}$
6.   **Return** DS_i

---

satisfies CHK. We present this *exclusive* strategy as Algorithm $\mathbb{G}_e$ in Table 5. On the other hand, we shall refer to Algorithm $\mathbb{G}$ in section 2 as the *inclusive* strategy from now on.

In Table 5, it can be noticed that both the algorithm for generalization and that for computing disclosure sets in the exclusive strategy are different from those in the inclusive strategy. This fact is a reflection of the inter-dependency between the two algorithms, or equivalently, the inter-dependency between the approach to generalization and adversary's knowledge. More specifically, the generalization algorithm $\mathbb{G}_e$ simply refuse to disclose anything, if the given original table yield a generalization G_i for which $PER(G_i)$ satisfies CHK but DS_i does not. An adversary also knows this fact since the algorithms are publicly known. In guessing the original table after seeing G_i released, the adversary will test each instance $X \in PER(G_i)$ to see whether X can be the original table. However, different from the inclusive strategy, the exclusive strategy makes such a testing fairly simple. That is, any instance X for which $PER(g_j(X))$ satisfies CHK for some $j < i$ can be immediately eliminated from further consideration, because if X were indeed the original table, then the algorithm $\mathbb{G}_e$ would have either returned $g_j(X)$ (if its disclosure set satisfies CHK) or nothing (if the disclosure set does not satisfy CHK) instead of releasing G_i.

Example 6. Consider applying the exclusive strategy to G_0 in Table 2. Clearly, the three generalizations G_1, G_2, and G_3 do not change, because we are still using the same generalization functions as before (but in a different way). The disclosure sets DS_1 and DS_2 also remain the same (note that $PER(G_1) = DS_1$). When the algorithm $\mathbb{G}_e$ sees that $PER(G_1)$ does not satisfy CHK, it continues to the next generalization function g_2 as with the inclusive strategy. However, when $\mathbb{G}_e$ sees $PER(G_2)$ satisfies CHK but DS_2 does not, it simply returns ϕ indicating that nothing can be disclosed (recall that with the inclusive strategy, $\mathbb{G}$ will continue to g_3).

In contrast to the inclusive strategy, the exclusive strategy may seem to be a more drastic approach that may result in less data utility. Example 6 may seem to support this statement. However, this is in fact not the case. Due to space limitation, we cannot show DS_3 computed from Table 2 under the inclusive strategy, but we calculate the ratio of the association between E and c_4 in Example 7.

Example 7. As mentioned in Section 2.2, for this special case, DS_3 can be computed by excluding any instance X for which $EXP(g_1(X))$ satisfies CHK. The instances in DS_3 must thus fall into following three sets. First, both E and F have c_4. Second, both C and D have c_2, and only one of E and F may have c_4 (the other will have c_6). Third, both G and H have c_6, and only one of E and F may have c_4 (the other will have c_2). These three sets are clearly disjoint. Moreover, by counting the number of permutations, we can see that the cardinality of the first set is $6 \times 2 \times 6 = 72$ (A, B, and C can have 6 different permutations; D and G can have 2, etc.) among which all have E associated with c_4. Similarly, the second and third set each has $2 \times 6 = 12$ instances in which E is associated with c_4, and the other 12 instances in which E is associated with c_6 and c_2, respectively. We can thus conclude that the ratio of E associated with c_4 is $(72 + 12 + 12)/(72 + 24 + 24) = 0.8$.

By applying the inclusive strategy, the $(2,2)$-diversity is not satisfied on DS_3. Therefore, nothing can be disclosed under the inclusive strategy, either. That is, for the given original table G_0 (and also the substantialized table in Table 1), the two strategies yield the same data utility. Besides, there also exist other cases where the exclusive strategy will provide more data utility. Suppose now G_b in Table 4 is given as the original table. Clearly, the inclusive strategy will disclose nothing because none of the generalizations through G_1, G_2 and G_3 can satisfy $(2,2)$-diversity. For exclusive strategy, neither $PER(g_1(G_b))$ nor $PER(g_2(G_b))$ can satisfy $(2,2)$-diversity. For $PER(g_3(G_b))$, again we calculate the ratio that c_4 is associated with E among all conditions in Example 8.

Example 8. Following Example 7, DS_3 under the exclusive strategy can be obtained by eliminating any instance X for which $PER(g_2(X))$ satisfy $(2,2)$-diversity from the previous result of DS_3 under the inclusive strategy. For the first set, D and G must now have c_2 and c_6, respectively, so we are left with 36 instances. Moreover, C and H must have 2 and 6, respectively, leaving totally 20 instances all with E associated with c_4. For the second and third set, nothing need to be eliminated. The ratio of E associated with c_4 is thus now $(20 + 12 + 12)/(20 + 24 + 24) = 0.647$. And this is also the maximal ratio of a single condition among all IDs.

Surprisingly, under the exclusive strategy, we can now disclose G_3 for the original table G_b in Table 4 (a substantialized example is shown in Table 6). In another word, the exclusive strategy actually provides more data utility in this case. The reason lies in the fact that the privacy property (that is, $(2,2)$-diversity) is not set-monotonic [30], neither is the sequence of sets of possible instances $PER(G_i)$ ($i = 1, 2, \ldots, n$). Generally, the data utility of the two strategies will be incomparable. Their performances depend on specific problem settings.

Table 6. Another Example of Patient Information Table

NAME	AGE	Condition
Alice	21	flu
Bob	27	pneumonia
Clark	31	tracheitis
Diana	36	tracheitis
Ellen	43	gastritis
Fen	49	gastritis
George	52	cancer
Henry	58	cancer
Ian	63	enteritis
Jason	67	heart disease

However, the exclusive strategy has an important advantage over the inclusive strategy, that is, a significantly lower complexity. In Table 5, unlike under the inclusive strategy, the algorithms under the exclusive strategy are not recursive because we do not call G_e within DS_e. Denote x_i the complexity for computing the disclosure set DS_i under the inclusive strategy, and y_i the cardinality of $PER(G_i)$. We have that $x_i = (\sum_{j=1}^{i-1} x_j) \cdot y_i$ and $x_1 = |G_0|$. By solving this recursive function, we can estimate the worst case complexity of the inclusive strategy to be $O((|PER(G_{max})|)^n)$ where G_{max} is a generalization with the maximum cardinality of possible instances. In contrast, the complexity of the exclusive strategy is $O(n^2 \cdot |PER(G_{max})|)$. By avoiding a recursive process, the exclusive strategy reduces the complexity from exponential to polynomial.

Other strategies are certainly possible, although their discussion is out of the scope of this paper. One complication is that the definition of disclosure sets given in Definition 1 should be generalized to accommodate the fact that the given sequence of generalization functions is not necessarily evaluated in the given order. The evaluation of those functions may actually happen in any order as defined in a strategy, and may vary depending on the given original table. For example, the exclusive strategy may directly jump to the last function (that returns ϕ) from any step. One way to keep the Definition 1 valid in this particular case is to have multiple copies of the last function and place a copy in front of each generalization function in the given sequence. In each step, if the algorithm chooses to either return the current generalization or to use the copy of the last function to return ϕ, then the current instance will be eliminated from the next disclosure set, which is in accordance with Definition 1.

4   Related Work

Micro-data disclosure has been extensively studied [1,3,10,16,17] where the security issue discussed in this paper is largely ignored. In particular, data swapping [9,23,28] and cell suppression [18] both aim to protect micro-data released in census tables. However, the amount of privacy is usually not measured in those earlier work. Miklau et. al presents an interesting measurement of information disclosed through tables based on the perfect secrecy notion by Shannon [8]. The important notion of k-anonymity is a model of privacy requirement [25] that received extensive studies in recent years. To achieve optimal k-anonymity (with the most utility) is shown to be computationally infeasible [21].

A model based on the intuition of blending individuals in a crowd is recently proposed in [27]. Personalized requirement for anonymity is studied in [29]. In [11], the authors approach the issue from a different perspective where the privacy property is based on generalization of the protected data and can be customized by users. Much efforts have been made around developing efficient k-anonymity algorithms [5,7,15,20,24,25,26], whereas the security of the k-anonymity model is assumed. Two exceptions are the l-diversity notion proposed in [2] and the t-closeness notion proposed in [19], which address the deficiency of k-anonymity of allowing insecure groups with a small number of sensitive values. Algorithms developed for k-anonymity can be extended to l-diversity and t-closeness, but they still do not take into account an adversary's knowledge about generalization algorithms. In [30], the authors pointed out the above problem and proposed a model for the adversary's knowledge, but did not give any efficient solution for the general micro-data disclosure problem.

In contrast to micro-data disclosure, aggregation queries are the main concern in statistical databases [10,13,22]. The main challenge is to answer aggregation queries without allowing an adversary to deduce secret individual values. The auditing methods in [6,4] address this problem by determining whether each new query can be safely answered based on previously answered queries. The authors of [6,12,14] consider the same problem in more specific settings of off-line auditing and online auditing, respectively. Closest to our work, the authors of [14] consider knowledge about the decision algorithm itself. However, it only applies to a limited case of aggregation queries and does not consider the current state of the database in determining the safety of a query.

5   Conclusion

Armed with knowledge about a generalization algorithm used for computing disclosed data, an adversary may deduce more information to violate a desired privacy property. We have studied this issue in the context of generalization-based micro-data disclosure algorithms. We showed that a naive solution to address this issue demands prohibitive computational cost. We then introduced an alternative *exclusive strategy* for generalization algorithms. Compare to the naive exponential algorithms based on the traditional *inclusive strategy*, algorithms based on *exclusive strategy* have much better efficiency (polynomial in the size of the table), and also, provide even better data utility in certain cases.

Acknowledgements. This material is partially supported by the National Science Foundation under grants CT-0716567, CT-0627493, IIS-0242237, and IIS-0430402; by the Army Research Office under the grant W911NF-07-1-0383; by the MITRE Technology Program; by the Natural Sciences and Engineering Research Council of Canada under Discovery Grant N01035; and by Fonds de recherche sur la nature et les technologies. The authors thank the anonymous reviewers for their valuable comments.

References

1. Dobra, A., Feinberg, S.E.: Bounding entries in multi-way contingency tables given a set of marginal totals. In: Foundations of Statistical Inference: Proceedings of the Shoresh Conference 2000, Springer, Heidelberg (2003)
2. Machanavajjhala, A., Gehrke, J., Kifer, D., Venkitasubramaniam, M.: l-diversity: Privacy beyond k-anonymity. In: Proceedings of the 22nd IEEE International Conference on Data Engineering (ICDE 2006) (2006)
3. Slavkovic, A., Feinberg, S.E.: Bounds for cell entries in two-way tables given conditional relative frequencies. Privacy in Statistical Databases (2004)
4. Dobkin, D.P., Jones, A.K., Lipton, R.J.: Secure databases: Protection against user influence. ACM TODS 4(1), 76–96 (1979)
5. Du, Y., Xia, T., Tao, Y., Zhang, D., Zhu, F.: On multidimensional k-anonymity with local recoding generalization
6. Chin, F.: Security problems on inference control for sum, max, and min queries. J.ACM 33(3), 451–464 (1986)
7. Aggarwal, G., Feder, T., Kenthapadi, K., Motwani, R., Panigrahy, R., Thomas, D., Zhu, A.: k-anonymity: Algorithms and hardness. Technical report, Stanford University (2004)
8. Miklau, G., Suciu, D.: A formal analysis of information disclosure in data exchange. In: SIGMOD (2004)
9. Duncan, G.T., Feinberg, S.E.: Obtaining information while preserving privacy: A markov perturbation method for tabular data. In: Joint Statistical Meetings, Anaheim, CA (1997)
10. Fellegi, I.P.: On the question of statistical confidentiality. Journal of the American Statistical Association 67(337), 7–18 (1993)
11. Byun, J., Bertino, E.: Micro-views, or on how to protect privacy while enhancing data usability: concepts and challenges. SIGMOD Record 35(1), 9–13 (2006)
12. Kleinberg, J., Papadimitriou, C., Raghavan, P.: Auditing boolean attributes. In: PODS (2000)
13. Schlorer, J.: Identification and retrieval of personal records from a statistical bank. Methods Info. Med. (1975)
14. Kenthapadi, K., Mishra, N., Nissim, K.: Simulatable auditing. In: PODS (2005)
15. LeFevre, K., DeWitt, D., Ramakrishnan, R.: Incognito: Efficient fulldomain k-anonymity. In: SIGMOD (2005)
16. Cox, L.H.: Solving confidentiality protection problems in tabulations using network optimization: A network model for cell suppression in the u.s. economic censuses. In: Proceedings of the Internatinal Seminar on Statistical Confidentiality (1982)
17. Cox, L.H.: New results in disclosure avoidance for tabulations. In: International Statistical Institute Proceedings (1987)
18. Cox, L.H.: Suppression, methodology and statistical disclosure control. J. of the American Statistical Association (1995)
19. Li, N., Li, T., Venkatasubramanian, S.: t-closeness: Privacy beyond k-anonymity and l-diversity. In: ICDE (2007)
20. Sweeney, L.: k-anonymity: a model for protecting privacy. International Journal on Uncertainty, Fuzziness and Knowledge-based Systems 10(5), 557–570 (2002)
21. Meyerson, A., Williams, R.: On the complexity of optimal k-anonymity. In: ACM PODS (2004)
22. Adam, N.R., Wortmann, J.C.: Security-control methods for statistical databases: A comparative study. ACM Comput. Surv. 21(4), 515–556 (1989)
23. Diaconis, P., Sturmfels, B.: Algebraic algorithms for sampling from conditional distributions. Annals of Statistics (1998)

24. Samarati, P.: Protecting respondents identities in microdata release. In: IEEE TKDE, pp. 1010–1027 (2001)
25. Samarati, P., Sweeney, L.: Protecting privacy when disclosing information: k-anonymity and its enforcement through generalization and suppression. Technical report, CMU, SRI (1998)
26. Bayardo, R.J., Agrawal, R.: Data privacy through optimal k-anonymization. In: ICDE (2005)
27. Chawla, S., Dwork, C., McSherry, F., Smith, A., Wee, H.: Toward privacy in public databases. In: Theory of Cryptography Conference (2005)
28. Dalenius, T., Reiss, S.: Data swapping: A technique for disclosure control. Journal of Statistical Planning and Inference 6, 73–85 (1982)
29. Xiao, X., Tao, Y.: Personalized privacy preservation. In: SIGMOD (2006)
30. Zhang, L., Jajodia, S., Brodsky, A.: Information disclosure under realistic assumptions: Privacy versus optimality. In: ACM Conference on Computer and Communications Security (CCS) (2007)

Protecting the Publishing Identity in Multiple Tuples

Youdong Tao, Yunhai Tong, Shaohua Tan, Shiwei Tang, and Dongqing Yang

Key Laboratory of Machine Perception (Peking University),
Ministry of Education,
100871 Beijing, China
{taoyd,yhtong,shtan,tsw,dqyang}@pku.edu.cn

Abstract. Current privacy preserving methods in data publishing always remove the individually identifying attribute first and then generalize the quasi-identifier attributes. They cannot take the individually identifying attribute into account. In fact, tuples will become vulnerable in the situation of multiple tuples per individual. In this paper, we analyze the individually identifying attribute in the privacy preserving data publishing and propose the concept of identity-reserved anonymity. We develop two approaches to meet identity-reserved anonymity requirement. The algorithms are evaluated in an experimental scenario, demonstrating practical applicability of the approaches.

Keywords: Privacy preservation, Data publishing, Anonymity, Identity.

1 Introduction

In recent privacy preserving data publishing research, k-anonymity principle [8,9,10] is of importance. It first removes the individually identifying attribute, then generalizes the quasi-identifier attributes and divides the tuples into different groups. It guarantees that each group has at least k tuples and the tuples in one group share the same quasi-identifier attribute values after generalization. Other enhanced principles, such as l-diversity [7], (α,k)-anonymity [12], extend this basic idea. All these methods have a default precondition that each individual has at most one tuple in the data set. In some real circumstances, that precondition doesn't meet.

For example, in a patient dataset published by a hospital (Table 1), some persons may appear more than one time for different diseases. In Table 1, Mike appears twice for two diseases: hypertension and hyperlipemia. If a number of people get both diseases at the same time, we may draw a conclusion that these two diseases are related. If the individually identifying attribute is removed, we can't make such a conclusion.

Current methods first remove the Name attribute and then generalize the quasi-identifier attributes. If we set k=2 in k-anonymity (or l=2 in l-diversity or α=0.5, k=2 in (α,k)-anonymity), we will get the result table as Table 2. From Table 1, we notice the first 2 rows will be grouped together since they share

V. Atluri (Ed.): DAS 2008, LNCS 5094, pp. 205–218, 2008.

the same quasi-identifier attribute values and have different diseases. According the k-anonymity assumption, if an adversary notices that Mike belongs to the Group 1, the probability that the adversary reveals the Mike's disease should be 50%. In fact, whatever disease the adversary judges, it is true and probability of privacy breach is 100%. This defect appears because they ignore the condition that one person may appear several times in a dataset.

Table 1. A patient table in which someone appears more than once

No	Name	Sex	Postcode	Disease
1	Mike	M	10085	hypertension
2	Mike	M	10085	hyperlipemia
3	Emily	F	10075	diabetes
4	Tim	M	10075	heart
5	Jane	F	10086	cancer
6	Ella	F	10087	flu

Table 2. Published table after common generalization

Group id	Sex	Postcode	Disease
1	M	10085	hypertension
1	M	10085	hyperlipemia
2	*	10075	diabetes
2	*	10075	heart
3	F	1008*	cancer
3	F	1008*	flu

This paper analyzes this situation and proposes an identity-reserved anonymity method. It modifies the current anonymity principles and reserves more information. The contributions of this paper are:

- We propose 3 identity-reserved anonymity principles. These principles reserve more information inside the dataset while protecting the individual privacy. The current anonymity principles don't take the multiple tuples per individual into account.
- We implement two algorithms to achieve identity-reserved anonymity principles. Global recoding algorithm extends the Incognito [4] to solve this problem. For less distortion, we adopt the domain generalization with tuple suppression. We also propose a local recoding algorithm and achieve less distortion. The algorithms are evaluated in an experimental scenario, demonstrating practical applicability of the approaches.

The remainder of this paper is organized as follows. In section 2, we review the related work before. In section 3, we propose the identity-reserved anonymity principles. In section 4, we discuss algorithms to implement these principles. We present experimental result in section 5 and conclude in section 6.

2 Related Work

In recent years, privacy preserving data publishing has gotten widely researched. Samarati and Sweeney proposed a principle called k-anonymity [8,9,10]. That requires each tuple in the table should be indistinguishable from at least (k-1) other tuples with respect to every set of quasi-identifier attributes. Beyond the k-anonymity, Machanavajjhala et al. proposed l-diversity principle [7]. That requires each quasi-identifier group should have at least l "well-represented" sensitive values. That principle extends the k-anonymity and diversifies the sensitive attribute values. They provided multiple interpretations on "well-represented". A simple interpretation on "well-represented" is that each quasi-identifier group has l distinct sensitive attribute values. Wong et al. proposed (α,k)-anonymity [12]. That requires each sensitive value in a quasi-identifier group should appear no more than a fixed frequency α besides k-anonymity. Li et al. proposed t-closeness principle which requires that distribution of sensitive attribute in groups should be close [6]. All these methods first remove the individually identifying attribute and generalize quasi-identifier attributes. Xiao and Tao proposed a personalized anonymity [13]. When they analyzed the probability of privacy breach, they distinguished two cases. One is the primary key scenario which each individual appears at most once. The other is the non-primary key scenario which each individual may appear an arbitrary number of times.

Generalization and suppression are the main approaches to achieve anonymity principles. Generalization is to replace a detailed value by a general value. Suppression is to delete some tuples. In generalization processing, suppression may be adopted. Suppression helps to decrease the generalization degree.

There are two main models in the algorithm of anonymity. One is global recoding [3,4,8,9], and the other is local recoding [1,9]. In global recoding, all values of an attribute should be generalized to the same domain level in hierarchy. But it always suffers from over-generalization and loses much information. In local recoding, values of an attribute may be generalized to different levels in hierarchy. For example, Table 2 is a result table of local recoding because some values of SEX attribute keep unchanged while some are generalized to the unknown value (*). If a recoding model divides an attribute into a set of non-overlapping intervals, it is called a single-dimensional recoding [3,4,8,9]. On the other hand, multidimensional recoding [5] divides the domain into a set of non-overlapping multidimensional regions. Besides generalization, Xiao and Tao proposed an "anatomy" method to meet the privacy requirement [14]. They published a quasi-identifier table (QIT) and a sensitive table (ST). These two tables share the same group-id attribute. In fact, it is a lossy join of database table.

3 Conceptions and Ideas

3.1 Identity Processing

The attributes of original table are classified to 3 types: (1) Individually identifying attribute (ID), that explicitly indicates an individual, such as name, SSN and mobile number. (2)Quasi-identifier attribute (QI), that can be exploited for linking and of k-anonymity as characterizing the degree of data protection with respect to inference by linking, such as sex, age and zip code. (3) Sensitive attributes (ST), that describe the privacy information of an individual, such as disease or income.

Removal of the ID attributes is the first step in common methods. But that processing loses individual information and may lead to the privacy breach, as shown before. We propose to recode and reserve the ID attribute for publishing. Recoding the ID attribute values is simply to replace it by a randomized number or string.

Reserving the ID attribute dramatically improves the utility of data set. For example in Table 2, reserving the ID attribute could help the research of complicating diseases which often appear together such as hypertension and hyperlipemia.

Individually identifying attributes may be specified by the publisher. We recode one of them and discard other individually identifying attributes since they are of redundancy.

3.2 Identity-Reserved Anonymity

We reserve the individually identifying attribute and propose identity-reserved anonymity. In common k-anonymity, there are at least k tuples in every set of quasi-identifier attribute values. Similarly, in identity-reserved k-anonymity, there are at least k individuals in every set of quasi-identifier attribute values.

Definition 1 (Identity-reserved k-anonymity requirement). *Every release version of data must be such that every combination of values of quasi-identifiers can be indistinctly matched to at least k different individuals.*

This definition is the same as the notion in [8]. But in [8], it takes it regarded that each tuple links with a distinct individual. So it removes the explicit ID attribute at first. With ID attribute recoded, we define a data requirement based on individuals.

In the previous papers, published table's format is $T(QI, ST)$. QI is the combination of quasi-identifier attributes and ST is the sensitive attribute. In this paper, published table's format is $T(ID, QI, ST)$. ID is the recoded identifier, QI is the combination of quasi-identifier attributes and ST is the sensitive attribute. Let A= $\{a_1, a_2, \ldots, a_b\}$ be the individual set of T.ID and S=$\{s_1, s_2, \ldots, s_t\}$ be the distinct sensitive values set of T.ST. For each a_i, $S(a_i)$ is the sensitive attribute value set associated with the individual a_i. For each s_j, $A(s_j)$ is the individual set associated with the sensitive value s_j. QI consists of one or several quasi-identifier attributes. The tuples shared the same combination of values of quasi-identifiers after generalization form a QI group. In a QI group Q, let $m = |\bigcup_{a_i \in Q.ID} S_{a_i}|$ and $n = |\bigcup_{s_j \in Q.ST} A_{s_j}|$.

Definition 2 (Identity-reserved k-anonymity). *Let T(ID, QI, ST) be a published table and QI be a quasi-identifier associated with it. ID is the recoded identifier, ST is the sensitive attribute. T is said to satisfy identity-reserved k-anonymity with regard to QI if each sequence of values in T.QI appears at least with k distinct occurrences in T.ID. That is in any QI group Q, $n = |\bigcup_{s_j \in Q.ST} A_{s_j}| \geq k$.*

For protecting the sensitive attributes, *l*-diversity is proposed. A naive interpretation of *l*-diversity requires that each QI group should have *l* different sensitive values. *l*-diversity principle doesn't take the situation into account that an individual may correspond to several tuples in the published table.

Definition 3 (Identity-reserved (k,l)-diversity). *Let T(ID,QI,ST) be a published table and QI be a quasi-identifier associated with it. ID is the recoded identifier, ST is the sensitive attribute. T is said to satisfy identity-reserved (k,l)-diversity if any QI group Q satisfies $m = |\bigcup_{a_i \in Q.ID} S_{a_i}| \geq l$ and $n = |\bigcup_{s_j \in Q.ST} A_{s_j}| \geq k$.*

(α,k)-anonymity takes the sensitive attribute value frequency into account. It requires that in each QI group, every sensitive value frequency should be no more than α and the size of each QI group should be no less than k. In our context, we propose identity-reserved (α,β)-anonymity. (α,β)-anonymity requires the frequency of sensitive and individually identifying attribute value in a QI group. Since it requires the frequency of individually identifying attribute, parameter k is abandoned.

Definition 4 (Identity-reserved (α,β)-anonymity). *Let T(ID,QI,ST) be a published table and QI be a quasi-identifier associated with it. ID is the recoded identifier, ST is the sensitive attribute. T is said to satisfy identity-reserved (α,β)-anonymity if in any QI group , each individual frequency is no more than α, and each sensitive value frequency is no more than β, $0 < \alpha, \beta < 1$.*

3.3   Privacy Breach Probability

In this section, we analyze the probability of privacy breach. In [13] the situation was discussed that an adversary has an external database for linking without any other background knowledge. Now we only discuss the situation that the adversary confirms someone (called "T") in the published table and knows T's QI attribute values. So the adversary knows the group that T belongs to (called group "G").

In group G, let individual set be $\{a_1, \ldots, a_n\}$. a_i appears c_i times in G, i=1,...,n. Assume $c_1 \geq c_2 \geq \ldots \geq c_n$. In group G, let sensitive value set be $\{s_1, \ldots, s_t\}$. s_j appears d_j times in G, j=1,...,t. Assume $d_1 \geq d_2 \ldots \geq d_t$. In identity-reserved k-anonymity ($n \geq k$), we don't consider the distribution and background knowledge on sensitive attribute. So the probability of recognizing a_i is $c_i/\sum_{i=1}^{n} c_i$. If $c_1 = 1$, the probability is $1/n$. That is the case of the common k-anonymity. If $c_1 \gg (c_2 + \ldots + c_n)$, the most of tuples in G correspond to a_1 and a_1 is easy to leakage of private information. This situation is similar to "homogeneity attack" discussed in [7].

In identity-reserved (k,l)-anonymity, we consider the diversity of sensitive attribute values. If we don't consider the distribution on ID attribute and other background knowledge, the probability of s_j is $d_j/\sum_{j=1}^{n} d_j$. These two principles simply take into account the diversity of ID or sensitive attribute, but they don't consider the frequency of these two attributes.

Identity-reserved (α,β)-anonymity confines the frequency of individual and sensitive value avoiding "homogeneity attack". If we only consider the identity or sensitive attribute respectively, the probability is no more than α or β.

3.4 Applicability

The identity-reserved anonymity takes the situation of multiple tuples per individual into account. We define the records per individual (rpi) of dataset to evaluate this situation, that is $rpi = (the\ size\ of\ dataset)/(the\ number\ of\ individuals)$. If $rpi = 1$, each individual appears only once in the dataset. It's appropriate to use common anonymity. If $rpi > 1$, it's appropriate to use our anonymity for avoiding the privacy breach described before.

The identity-reserved anonymity holds the information between sensitive values of an individual that is discarded in common anonymity. The information is meaningful in researches, such as the market basket analysis or related diseases research.

4   Implementing

In common anonymity, generalization and suppression are the main approaches to meet the anonymity principles [8]. In fact generalization with suppression reduces the generalization height, but removal of the tuples also reduces the utility of the published table. In this paper, we also apply generalization to achieve identity-reserved anonymity.

Before generalization, we first recode an individually identifying attribute. Recoded individually identifying value is just a randomized numeric symbol to discriminate different individuals.

4.1   Global Recoding

Global recoding requires that all values of an attribute should generalize to the same domain level in the generalization hierarchy. For example, all values in Birth date are generalized to year and month in the format "mm/yyyy". The algorithm is similar to existing global-recoding algorithm in [4,7]. It makes use of monotonicity property in generalization lattice space. The generalization doesn't stop until the result table meets the privacy requirement. If a certain number of suppression is allowed, the generalization processing finishes with suppressing. If suppression isn't allowed, suppression threshold is set as 0. Algorithm1 is a single-dimensional global recoding algorithm.

Algorithm 1. global recoding algorithm

Input : Table T, Suppression threshold S
Output: Published table PT
1. PT=the relation after recoding individually identifying attribute on T;
2. while (tuples that don't meet identity-reserved anonymity on PT>S) do
2.1   choose a QI attribute on PT;
2.2   generalize the chosen QI attribute on PT;
3. Remove the tuples that don't meet identity-reserved anonymity in PT;
4. return PT;

4.2 Local Recoding

Global recoding may generate excessive distortion to data set. Local recoding applies generalization on tuples not attributes. In local recoding, we adopt generalization without suppression. Wong et al. [12] proposed a top-down local-recoding algorithm. This approach first generalizes all tuples completely into one equivalence class. Then tuples are specialized in iterations while maintaining the anonymity principle. The process continues until specialization can't take place.

Table 3. A patient table needing publishing

Tuple-No	ID	Zip	Disease
1	1318	10085	Hypertension
2	1318	10085	Hyperlipemia
3	5072	10086	Diabetes
4	8634	10087	Heart
5	7437	10075	Hypertension
6	7437	10075	Diabetes
7	3582	10076	Heart
8	5629	10077	Flu
9	4713	10050	Heart

In this section, we propose a bottom-up approach. In our approach, we first check all tuples and mark the tuples that meet the requirement with group-id. Then we generalize a QI attribute on tuples without group-id in iterations. In every step of generalization, those tuples that meet the identity-reserved anonymity requirement are marked with a group-id. At last, a few tuples may be left without group-id, which are called "orphans". These orphans can't be

Table 4. A published table satisfying identity-reserved 2-anonymity

Group-No	ID	Zip	Disease
1	1318	1008*	Hypertension
1	1318	1008*	Hyperlipemia
1	8634	1008*	Heart
2	7437	1007*	Hypertension
2	7437	1007*	Diabetes
2	3582	1007*	Heart
2	5629	1007*	Flu
3	4713	100**	Heart
3	5072	100**	Diabetes

Table 5. A published table satisfying identity-reserved 3-anonymity

Group-No	ID	Zip	Disease
1	1318	100**	Hypertension
1	1318	100**	Hyperlipemia
1	8634	100**	Heart
1	5072	100**	Diabetes
1	4713	100**	Heart
2	7437	1007*	Hypertension
2	7437	1007*	Diabetes
2	3582	1007*	Heart
2	5629	1007*	flu

grouped as a group whatever they are generalized to (For example, 5 tuples are left without group-id while k=7). To group these orphans, we first move some tuples from other groups which could lend some tuples while maintaining the anonymity. If all other groups have no additional tuples to lend, we merge each orphan into a neighbor group and generalize them to form a QI group at last.

Let us illustrate with an example in Table 3. Suppose the QI contains only zipcode and ID is the recoded randomized number. The individual "1318" appears twice as tuple 1 and 2, and the individual "7437" appears twice as tuple 5 and 6. Other 5 individuals appear once in the table. We require identity-reserved k-anonymity and set k=2. First we check the table and find no tuples can be marked in a group. So zipcode attribute generalizes once (such as 1008*). Then tuple 1-4 can be marked with group-id 1, and tuple 5-8 can be marked with group-id 2. Now each group has 3 distinct individuals and 4 tuples. Tuple 9 is left, which is called "orphan". So we first search whether a group can lend some tuples while maintaining the anonymity. If we only require identity-reserved k-anonymity and set k=2, we move a tuple (such as Tuple-No=3) to join the orphan and form the group 3. That result is showed on Table 4. If we require identity-reserved 3-anonymity (or identity-reserved (0.5,0.5)-anonymity), we can't move any tuple to join the orphan. So we could merge the orphan to a group(such as Group 1) and generalize tuples in that group. That result is showed on Table 5. Algorithm2 is a single-dimensional local recoding algorithm.

Algorithm 2. local recoding algorithm

Input : Table T
Output: Published table PT
1. PT=the relation after recoding individually identifying attribute on T;
2. Check and mark the tuples on PT which meet the identity-reserved anonymity;
3. While (tuples without marking the group-id on PT) >0 and (not generalize to the top of hierarchy) do
3.1   choose a QI attribute of PT;
3.2   generalize the chosen QI attribute for tuples without group-id on PT;
3.3   check and mark the tuples on PT which meet the identity-reserved anonymity;
4. if (tuples without marking the group-id on PT) >0 then
4.1   move tuples from other group;
4.2   check and mark;
5. if (tuples without marking the group-id on PT) >0 then
5.1   merge left tuples to other group;
6. return PT;

---

5   Experiments

In this section, we evaluate the identity-reserved anonymity principles in an experimental scenario, demonstrating practical applicability of the approaches. First we check the vulnerable QI group ratio in the situation of multiple tuples per individual. Then we evaluate the distortion ratio between the common k-anonymity and identity-reserved k-anonymity. At last we compare the global recoding and local recoding methods.

Experimental data come from the Adult database of UCI Machine Learning Repository [11]. The Adult database contains 45,222 tuples from US census data. We remove tuples with missing values. Since we check the identity-reserved anonymity effect, we add an attribute "Id-number". We fill in id-number so that a certain frequency of individuals appear several tuples. Description of other attributes is the same as [2].

We first choose 40,000 tuples and fill in distinct id-number. We partition these tuples to three disjoint subsets, called A, B, C. For each tuple in subset B, we duplicate it with the same id-number and QI values, and generate a different sensitive value. So each individual in subset B corresponds to 2 tuples. For each tuple in subset C, we duplicate it twice with the same id-number and QI values, and generate a distinct sensitive value respectively. So each individual in subset C corresponds to 3 tuples. Subset A is directly added to the final relation. Thus we get $|A| + 2|B| + 3|C|$ tuples in the relation. According to the rpi definition in section 3.4, $rpi = (|A| + 2|B| + 3|C|)/(|A| + |B| + |C|) = Ratio_A + 2Ratio_B + 3Ratio_C$. We set test datasets with 4 different rpis according to Table 6.

Table 6. Description of test datasets size and rpi

rpi	A ratio	B ratio	C ratio	Dateset Size
1.2	0.85	0.1	0.05	48,000
1.4	0.70	0.2	0.10	56,000
1.6	0.55	0.3	0.15	64,000
1.8	0.40	0.4	0.20	72,000

First we check the vulnerable QI group ratio in the situation of multiple tuples per individual. We adopt common k-anonymity method by ignoring the id-number and get the anonymized table PT. In PT, we define the vulnerable group as the group which contains at least k tuples and at most (k-1) individuals, that is it meets the common k-anonymity but cannot meet identity-reserved k-anonymity. So the vulnerable group ratio is defined as (the number of vulnerable groups)/(the number of all groups). When k increase or rpi decreases, the number of individual in a QI group increases. So the vulnerable group ratio decreases. Fig. 1 shows this trend.

Especially, some groups in PT only contain one individual. We call them single value group. Single value group only exists when k is no more than the maximum tuple number per individual. Fig. 2 shows that single value group ratio decreases as k increase or rpi decreases.

We evaluate information loss of anonymized table in terms of distortion ratio. Distortion ratio is defined to describe the cost of recoding of the dataset. In [12], distortion ratio is equal to the distortion of generalized dataset divided by the distortion of the fully generalized dataset. The distortion of a value is the height of generalized value. The distortion of a tuple is the sum of its each attribute value generalization height. Let $height_i$ be the height of the ith tuple. Let Height be the height of the fully generalized tuple. So the distortion ratio of dataset is defined as:

$$distortion\ ratio = \frac{\sum_{i=1}^{TupleCount} height_i}{TupleCount \times Height}$$

We compare the common k-anonymity and identity-reserved k-anonymity in Fig. 3 (rpi=1.2) and Fig. 4 (rpi=1.4). We notice that common k-anonymity achieves less distortion ratio, but the difference is slight.

At last we compare local recoding and global recoding in identity-reserved anonymity. Figure 5 shows the distortion ratio of identity-reserved k-anonymity. When k increases, the distortion ratio increases slowly because more individuals have been generalized together. Since the global recoding algorithm generalizes the values to the same level on the hierarchy, the local recoding algorithm

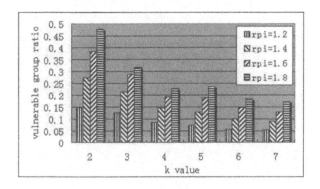

Fig. 1. Vulnerable group ratio with rpi and k

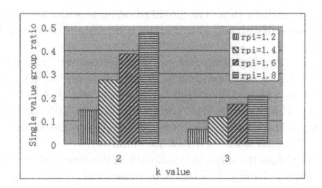

Fig. 2. Single value group ratio with rpi and k

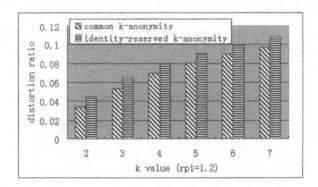

Fig. 3. Distortion ratio between common k-anonymity and identity-reserved k-anonymity when rpi=1.2

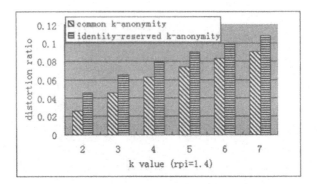

Fig. 4. Distortion ratio between common k-anonymity and identity-reserved k-anonymity when rpi=1.4

achieves much lower distortion. The global recoding algorithm with suppression achieves a bit lower distortion than that without suppression since it removes several outliers.

Figure 6 shows the distortion ratio of identity-reserved (k,l)-anonymity. In the experiments, l is usually less than k. When l increases with k fixed ($l \leq k$), the distortion ratio of global recoding keeps steady and that of local recoding increases slowly. The reason is that parameter l affects little compared to the parameter k when the number of all distinct sensitive values is larger than the parameter k and sensitive values distribute uniformly.

Figures 7 and 8 show the distortion ratio of identity-reserved (α,β)-anonymity using local recoding. In Fig. 7, when β increases with α=0.5, distortion ratio decreases remarkably. When β is smaller, a QI group needs more distinct sensitive values. So it needs higher generalization level and distortion ratio. When β is large enough (such as 0.5) to match α, distortion ratio keeps steady because the table satisfying α usually satisfies that value of β at that time. In Fig. 8, when α increases with β=0.5, distortion ratio decreases similar to Fig. 7. Since the number of distinct identity values is much larger than that of sensitive value, the distortion ratio of Fig. 7 decreases steeper than that of Fig. 8.

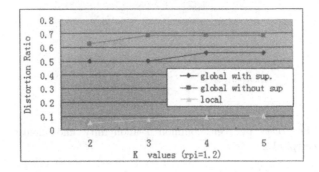

Fig. 5. Distortion ratio of identity-reserved k-anonymity

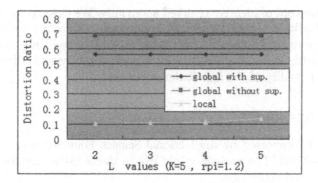

Fig. 6. Distortion ratio of identity-reserved (k, l)-anonymity

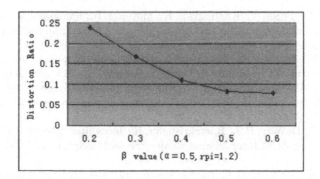

Fig. 7. Distortion ratio of identity-reserved (α, β)-anonymity

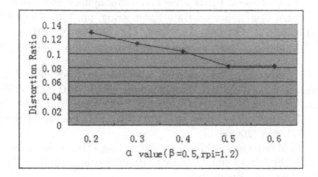

Fig. 8. Distortion ratio of identity-reserved (α, β)-anonymity

6   Conclusion

The current anonymity methods are inadequate since they can't take the individually identifying attribute into account. In this paper, we analyze the individually identifying attribute in the privacy preserving data publishing and

propose the concept of identity-reserved anonymity. We develop two approaches to achieve identity-reserved anonymity requirement. In local recoding, we propose a bottom-up algorithm which solves the orphan tuples by moving and merging. The algorithms are evaluated in an experimental scenario, demonstrating practical applicability of the approaches.

Acknowledgements

This work was supported by the National Science Foundation of China under Grant No.60403041. The authors would like to thank the anonymous reviewers for their insightful comments.

References

1. Aggarwal, G., Feder, T., Kenthapadi, K., Motwani, R., Panigrahy, R., Thomas, D., Zhu, A.: Anonymizing Tables. In: Proceedings of the 10th International Conference on Database Theory, pp. 246–258 (2005)
2. Bayardo, R., Agrawal, R.: Data privacy through optimal k-anonymization. In: the 21st International Conference on Data Engineering, pp. 217–228 (2005)
3. Fung, B.C.M., Wang, K., Yu, P.S.: Top-down Specialization for Information and Privacy Preservation. In: the 21st International Conference on Data Engineering, pp. 205–216 (2005)
4. LeFevre, K., DeWitt, D.J., Ramakrishnan, R.: Incognito: Efficient Full-domain K-anonymity. In: ACM International Conference on Management of Data, pp. 49–60 (2005)
5. LeFevre, K., DeWitt, D.J., Ramakrishnan, R.: Mondrian Multidimensional K-Anonymity. In: the 22nd International Conference on Data Engineering, pp. 25–35 (2006)
6. Li, N., Li, T.: t-Closeness: Privacy Beyond k-Anonymity and l-Diversity. In: the 23rd International Conference on Data Engineering, pp. 106–115 (2007)
7. Machanavajjhala, A., Gehrke, J., Kifer, D.: l-diversity: Privacy beyond K-anonymity. In: the 22nd International Conference on Data Engineering, pp. 24–35 (2006)
8. Samarati, P.: Protecting Respondents' Identities in Microdata Release. IEEE Transactions on Knowledge and Data Engineering 13, 1010–1027 (2001)
9. Sweeney, L.: Achieving K-anonymity Privacy Protection Using Generalization and Suppression. International Journal on Uncertainty, Fuzziness and Knowledge Based Systems 10, 571–588 (2002)
10. Sweeney, L.: K-anonymity: A Model for Protecting Privacy. International Journal on Uncertainty, Fuzziness and Knowledge Based Systems 10, 557–570 (2002)
11. UCI Machine Learning Repository, www.ics.uci.edu/~mlearn/MLRepository.html
12. Wong, R.C., Li, J., Fu, A.W., Wang, K. (α,k)-anonymity: an Enhanced K-anonymity Model for Privacy-preserving Data Publishing. In: the 12th ACM SIGKDD, pp. 754–759 (2006)
13. Xiao, X., Tao, Y.: Personalized Privacy Preservation. In: ACM International Conference on Management of Data, pp. 229–240 (2006)
14. Xiao, X., Tao, Y.: Anatomy: Simple and Effective Privacy Preservation. In: the 32nd international conference on Very large data bases, pp. 139–150 (2006)

Panel Session:
What Are the Key Challenges in Distributed Security?

Steve Barker[1], David Chadwick[2], Jason Crampton[3],
Emil Lupu[4], and Bhavani Thuraisingham[5]

[1] Dept. of Computer Science, King's College London, UK
[2] Computing Laboratory, University of Kent, UK
[3] ISG, Royal Holloway, University of London, UK
[4] Dept. of Computing, Imperial College London, UK
[5] University of Texas at Dallas, USA
steve.barker@kcl.ac.uk, d.w.chadwick@kent.ac.uk,
jason.crampton@rhul.ac.uk, e.c.lupu@imperial.ac.uk,
bhavani.thuraisingham@utdallas.edu

Abstract. The principal motivation for organizing a panel session at DBSEC'08 was to invite a number of distinguished researchers in data security to present their thoughts and to stimulate conference debate on a question of major importance: what are the key future challenges in distributed data security? The thoughts of the panellists on this issue are summarized in this article.

Steve Barker, the session moderator, opened the discussion by commenting that the term "distributed data security" describes a very wide-ranging space of issues that are often quite loosely related. For example, in terms of technologies, "distributed security" is applicable at the levels of the minute (e.g., hand-held devices) and the massive (e.g., the Internet). Barker noted that although there are common challenges (e.g., dealing with incomplete, contradictory, non-contemporary, and unreliable distributed sources) specific distributed systems present specific challenges. Barker also noted that the term "security" in "distributed data security" is also very general and covers privacy and integrity issues that present particular challenges in the distributed context. Barker concluded by observing that the contributions of the panellists revealed that the key challenges in distributed security remain many and varied.

David Chadwick argued that security will be increasingly policy-based with common policies being distributed to many sites so that a consistent approach to security can be developed throughout the system. Chadwick predicted that there would be significant advances in user-friendly tools for creating security policies and that these will be based on natural language so that humans will be able to understand clearly the policies they create. Many systems will have multiple stakeholders, each of whom will want to express their own security policies for (some of) the data in the system. Consequently there will be conflicting policies from the different stakeholders, which will require automated mechanisms for the resolution of policy conflicts. Chadwick suggested that federated identity management will increase in prominence, with single sign-on and attribute-based authorization, with the attributes coming from a variety of authorities.

V. Atluri (Ed.): DAS 2008, LNCS 5094, pp. 219–221, 2008.
© IFIP International Federation for Information Processing 2008

Trusted platform modules will be utilized to increase trust between the federated systems. Users will become more aware of protecting their privacy as losses from identity theft increase. National ID-based schemes will be increasingly rolled out throughout Europe and will tend to be used for valuable transactions. Biometrics will be used more frequently for authentication. Biometric databases of entire populations will become more prevalent and will lead to increased fears of privacy leaks. (We already have the biometrics of 4 million people on the UK police database). Furthermore, networks will be patrolled by governments, police and the security services, and all traffic on the Internet will be routinely analysed. (Either legislation will be introduced to enforce ISPs to record all traffic, or it will be done surreptitiously at key gateways.) Chadwick noted that these developments will increase users concerns about privacy, making them turn to OpenID or similar systems, in which the users choose their own globally unique pseudonyms. There will be advances in anonymized data access for medical and other applications that require access to large distributed data stores of personal information, and intelligent history-based protection mechanisms will stop users from trawling and aggregating output in order to flout privacy rules.

Jason Crampton observed that access control models for closed, centralized environments assume the existence of components that are responsible for authenticating users, for intercepting requests and enforcing authorization decisions, and for deciding whether a request is authorized or not. Moreover, Crampton noted that, in the centralized case, it is assumed that mutual trust relationships exist between these components and that they share a common "vocabulary" for authentication and authorization.

Crampton expressed the view that implementing access control in open distributed environments can be very challenging because the assumptions that hold in the centralized case do not necessarily apply to decentralized systems. For example, prior trust relationships may not necessarily exist between components; indeed, they may not even be aware of each other's existence. Crampton suggested that five challenges emerge:

1. To be able to *map* a user in one domain to one or more principals defined in the authorization policy of another domain without any prior agreement between the domains.
2. To be able to *identify* all of the user attributes that are required to make an authorization decision.
3. To be able to *collect* all of the statements about user attributes that are required to make an authorization decision.
4. To develop a language to *encode* statements about user attributes in a common format with a universal semantics.
5. To be able to *verify* the authenticity of statements binding user identifiers to user attributes.

Emil Lupu suggested that the trend towards "pervasive systems" leads us to envisage a world that includes mobile devices such as phones and PDAs, body area sensor-networks (e.g., for health monitoring), autonomous vehicles and instrumented environments such as smart-homes, autonomous buildings and watchful urban environments. Lupu noted that, in such environments, data is continuously acquired, aggregated and proactively exchanged amongst devices and amongst infrastructure services. Beyond access control, data protection requires privacy, dissemination and usage controls. Decisions regarding data protection, retention and disclosure need to be made in the presence of uncertain and partial authentication information and are often context dependent. Data exchanges are subject to regulations derived from legislation, organizational procedures and data sharing agreements between organizations. Expressing these, deriving operational policies, and deploying those policies to enforcement mechanisms close to the data remains a significant challenge. Policy analysis algorithms to detect and resolve conflicts between policies are also necessary. Frameworks in which data can be protected beyond the originator's domain need to cater for a variety of protection requirements and threat models. On smaller scale devices this needs to be achieved with limited computational resources. Yet the same techniques that are used for data protection may be abused to ensure its survival and proliferation.

Bhavani Thuraisingham observed that many technologies are being developed for distributed information management and that security and privacy issues have to be investigated in relation to these emerging technologies. Thuraisingham suggested that one of the main challenges in distributed information management is to support social networking algorithms and, for this, work on the integration of the information in disparate and diverse data sources is needed. In addition, the knowledge that is extracted from these information sources has to be integrated so that the manager(s) of them can make effective decisions. Today we see an explosion of social networks such as My Space and Face Book. Ensuring the security of access and privacy of individuals for such networks are critical issues. Thuraisingham reported that research at the University of Texas at Dallas (UTD) is focusing on developing novel and secure semantic web technologies for effective knowledge management and social networking. (Sponsors of this work include the Air Force Office of Scientific Research, the Intelligence Advanced Research Projects Activity, the National Science Foundation, the National Geospatial Intelligence Agency and Raytheon Corporation.) More specifically, a secure framework, based on the service oriented architecture paradigm, is being developed at UTD and is based on a three-level model that includes: The RDF Graph Manager, The Ontology Heuristics Reasoner and the Entity Extractor. Thuraisingham explained that novel dependable and secure semantic web technologies are being employed to realize this framework of connected layers. For example, the ontology-based heuristics reasoner will rely on the RDF graph manager to provide efficient storage and retrieval of RDF graphs. The entity extractor will depend on both the RDF graph manager and ontology-based heuristics reasoner to structure and reason about the graphs so that the entity extractor component can effectively carry out its task. All of the layers combined will provide the infrastructure support for distributed algorithms for social network analysis and knowledge management. Thuraisingham stated that one of the main focus areas for this work is security and privacy so that secure and private social networks can be supported. Thuraisingham noted that although research in secure distributed systems and distributed databases systems began in the 1980s, there remain many aspects of information distribution for which specific solutions for secure distributed networks, middleware, databases, information sources and applications are still needed. Thuraisingham concluded by suggesting that secure semantic web technologies will form the glue to secure various aspects of future distributed systems.

On the Applicability of Trusted Computing in Distributed Authorization Using Web Services

Aarthi Nagarajan[1], Vijay Varadharajan[1], Michael Hitchens[1],
and Saurabh Arora[2]

[1] Macquarie University, Sydney, Australia
{aarthi,vijay,michaelh}@ics.mq.edu.au
[2] The Royal Institute of Technology, Stockholm, Sweden
arora@kth.se

Abstract. Distributed authorization provides the ability to control access to resources spread over the Internet. Typical authorization systems consider a range of security information like user identities, role identities or even temporal, spatial and contextual information associated with the access requestor. However, the ability to include computing platform related information has been quite limited due to constraints in identification and validation of platforms when distributed. Trusted computing is an exciting technology that can provide new ways to bridge this gap. In this paper, we provide the first steps necessary to achieving distributed authorization using trusted computing platforms. We introduce the notion of a Property Manifest that can be used in the specification of authorization policies. We provide an overview of our authorization architecture, its components and functions. We then illustrate the applicability of our system by implementing it in a Web service oriented architecture.

1 Introduction

Distributed computing can be described generally as a collection of individual computers communicating with one another. Recent advances in networking, end node processing power and software technologies have enabled distributed computing to be widely deployed. Distributed systems can be used to share resources as simple as printers or files to anything as complex as large business functions across an organization. When resources are spread across the Internet, controlling access to their usage becomes an important concern. Different resources have different access restrictions based on how important the resource is, who is requesting access, what actions on the resource have been requested and other environmental factors as time and place of request. This makes access control a challenging area for research.

Traditional access control mechanisms like maintaining access control lists cannot sufficiently express all these requirements. Such mechanisms normally suit systems with a centralized authority that administers access control policies where access requestors are known in advance. When systems are decentralized

V. Atluri (Ed.): DAS 2008, LNCS 5094, pp. 222–237, 2008.

in nature, it is possible that both the access requestor and the authorizer are strangers. The authorizer has to rely on third parties for gathering information about the requestors. When access is obtained, entities can further delegate their rights to other parties that they know. Absence of a central authority, reliance on third parties, rich access control requirements and issues like delegation make traditional access control systems unsuitable for distributed systems.

Trust management systems were introduced to address some of these issues. The term 'Trust Management' was first given by Blaze et al [1] when they introduced the PolicyMaker system. It was described as an unified approach to specifying and interpreting security policies, credentials, and relationships that allows direct authorization of security-critical actions. Since then, there have been many implementations of such systems like KeyNote [2], Binder [3], REFEREE [4] and IBM's trust management framework [5]. A trust management system provides a flexible mechanism usually in the form of a policy language to specify the authorization requirements of a system. The heart of a trust management system is the authorization engine that evaluates whether an access request can be granted or not based on a number of conditions. Authorization credentials are loosely coupled to permissions and are usually created, distributed and managed by the trust management system. Furthermore, the framework can itself be extended to support features like delegation and trust negotiation. Trust management systems, thus move the notion of authorization from a closed-centralized approach to a more open and distributed approach.

In this paper we provide the first steps necessary to build a trust management framework using trusted computing platforms. The structure of the paper is as follows. Section 2 discusses about trusted platforms and attestation. In section 3, we motivate the need for a trust management framework based on trusted platforms. Section 4 introduces the notion of a Property Manifest. In sections 5,6 and 7 we define our authorization system, its components and working. Section 8 looks at an application of the proposed system using Web services. Section 9 discusses about some issues and challenges in using trusted platforms for distributed authorization and we conclude in section 10.

2   Trusted Computing Platforms

In the recent years, computers have become complex with large number of software applications running on them. When these computers get connected to the Internet, they risk data exposure and compromise due to software attacks. Computers have also become mobile and are at constant risk of physical theft or loss. As these risks escalate, it has led to the realization that security mechanisms using software alone are in-sufficient. The use of hardware based security is becoming an important approach to protecting information. Trusted computing technology developed by the Trusted Computing Group (TCG) is an effort that aims to provide techniques for achieving security using hardware in computing platforms.

The core of the trusted computing technology is a Trusted Platform Module (TPM) [6] chip that is embedded in the motherboard at the time of manufacture.

A TPM chip is similar to a secure co-processor. It performs certain crypto-graphic functions and provides secure storage for secrets and data. When hardware and software components are manufactured for a trusted platform, they are supported with information regarding the provenance of the component by its manufacturer. The manufacturer provides a 160-bit binary measurement value that indicates a component's good working state. These values are called the reference values and are represented using the TCG Reference Manifest (RM) [2] structure. A Reference Manifest contains information regarding the identity, version and manufacturer of the component along with the measurement. The TPM also creates a public-private key pair called the Attestation Identity Key or AIK. While the public AIK is used to identify a trusted platform associated with an user, the private AIK is used by the TPM for signing purposes.

Perhaps the most important feature of a trusted platform is its integrity measurement mechanism. When a trusted platform boots, all processes starting from the boot measure the next process to be loaded. All measurements are in the form of a 160 bit hash that are stored inside special registers called the Platform Configuration Registers (PCR) within the TPM. As the number of measurements outnumber the available PCRs (usually 16 for a PC), a hash of the concatenation of the new measurement with the old measurement is stored in the PCR. A log of the measurement history is also stored outside the TPM in local storage.

2.1   Attestation in Trusted Platforms

When a communicating host wishes to learn the state of a trusted platform, it initiates a process known as 'attestation'. During attestation, TPM creates the 'Quote' blob by collating the requested PCR values and by signing them using the private Attestation Identity Key. A Platform Trust Service (PTS) then generates an Integrity Report using the TCG Integrity Report [3] structure. The report includes the Quote information, references that point to the Reference Manifests and the measurement log. When the host receives the report, it validates each individual measurement inside the log against the corresponding Reference Manifest value, recomputes the PCR values using the log and matches them against the Quote values. If all the values match, it believes that the trusted platform is integrity proof.

Attestation mechanism which is strongly founded on binary measurements has certain limitations. Hash measurements change every time there is a 'minor' modification in the implementation. Security updates, version updates and patches applied can continuously change the expected measurement of a component. Measurements are also not human understandable as they are stored as binary inside the TPM. These reasons limit the usability of measurement values as authorization parameters in security policies. Another argument is that measurements relate only to the code or logic of a component. This can move the focus to implementations rather than properties of systems favoring certain vendors and their products. Recent efforts like Property based attestation [7,8,9], an extension of the attestation mechanism try to address these issues by combining binary measurements with security properties of systems. Property based attestation aims to prove that the availability of a certain measurement guarantees the availability of a certain security property thereby abstracting low level binary values to more meaningful attributes.

WS-Attestation [10] proposed by Yoshihama et. al. extends the attestation architecture on the Web services framework. To include the attestation architecture for Web services, it extends the bootstrapping process. The root of trust is a trusted BIOS which begins the measurement process and measures all the components up to and including the middleware layer. The middleware then measures all data it loads or uses in the platform. This way the transitive chain of trust is built from the trusted boot all the way up to a Web service application loaded on the platform.

3 Authorization Using Trusted Platforms

In a distributed system like Web services, there are Service Providers (SP) who provide services and there are Service Requestors (SR) who receive services. When SP receives a service request, it has to answer at least two questions. Is SR the one it claims to be and does it have the necessary privileges for the requested service. These two basic questions relate to the issues of authentication and authorization. The authorization requirements in distributed applications are much richer than the authentication both in terms of the types of privileges required and the nature and degree of interactions between participating entities.

Authorization systems have usually been able to define policies from a user's context and not based on the user's computing environment. Users here we mean human beings who wish to have access to a certain service. Of course, one can think of simple policies like those based on the network address of a requestor or the application (e.g the browser) from which a request has been made. But the ability to include useful information like security properties or behaviour of platforms has been very limited. This is because it is difficult to remotely identify a platform and validate its claims. Software can either be manipulated to produce false claims or the validation technique itself can be manipulated to prove non-existing claims. Therefore, it is common practice to assume that the underlying platform from which a request is made is sufficiently 'secure'.

With the introduction of trusted computing, it is possible to address such limitations. Trusted computing provides mechanisms to both identify platforms and validate claims made about a platform. All users receive Attestation Identity Key credentials that identify them with respect to that platform. AIK keys could be used to identify a platform on the Internet rather than using identities like MAC addresses and IP addresses. Attestation keys which are created and stored inside the TPM may not be as easily spoofed as MAC or IP addresses. Secondly, trusted platforms support attestation which is founded on hardware based trust. Attestation provides a mechanism to validate actual measurements of components against the reference values. When combined with property based attestation, a platform can guarantee the existence of certain security properties.

In this paper we extend the notion of traditional trust management systems from an user-only approach to an user and platform based approach. We provide the necessary first steps towards achieving platform and property based authorization. Firstly, we believe defining suitable credentials for property based attestation is important. We introduce the notion of a Property Manifest that has been discussed in detail in section 4. An overview of the authorization system and its components is available in section 5. Section 6 discusses about the interactions between the entities of the system using the push, pull and delegation models. Section 7 outlines our extensions to XACML to support platform based authorization.

4   Property Manifests

In this section, we introduce the notion of a Property Manifest. Property Manifest (PM) is the representation of a platform's security properties. It is created and issued by a Certification Authority (CA) which can be a trusted third party, e.g manufacturer of a component. The purpose of a Property Manifest is to support the mapping of a component to its security properties. Each Property Manifest may describe a trusted platform as a whole or a component of the platform. However, there may be sub-components each of which may have corresponding Property Manifests. A Property Manifest is represented in an XML based Property Manifest structure. It contains information such as the component identity, manufacturer, model or version number, and others. In order for the Property Manifest to be useful with in a given context, the Reference Manifest data must be made available.

Security properties are closely bound to components that they belong to. Therefore, with a given security property, it might actually be possible to detect some information about the component. This is specially possible when certain properties are unique to components. This defeats the purpose of property based attestation in the first place because property based attestation tries to hide the implementation details of a component. Revealing security properties of components can therefore pose some privacy concerns for a trusted platform. For this reason, we define properties at three different levels of granularity (of course, more levels of granularity are possible). At Step 1 of the pyramid or S1, properties are very coarse. S1 properties are helpful to prove that some security property is available in the component without revealing the implementation details. For example, a Service Provider application guarantees 'confidentiality' and 'privacy' of a Service Requestor's data without revealing how this is actually achieved. At Step 2 or S2, properties reveal more detail. Service provider guarantees 'confidentiality by encryption' and 'privacy by data deletion' pushes the properties to the next level of granularity. At step 3 of the pyramid or S3, properties reveal implementation details of a component. For example, Service Provider guarantees 'confidentiality by encryption using DES' and 'privacy of data by deleting it on the 7th day after transaction' are very fine grained policies.

The Property Manifest schema consists of the following elements. A 'Property' element of complex type that includes property related information PropertyID, Name, Value and Type. 'PropertyID' is the unique identifier of a property and 'Name' is the simple name given to a property. 'Value' is the element that indicates if the value of the property has been evaluated as true or false or undetermined. 'Type' is the element that includes property granularity information like S1, S2 or S3. Property Manifest schema also includes the ManifestID, ComponentID and the Certification Authority elements. 'ManifestID' is the unique identity (e.g. UDDI) of a Property Manifest. 'ComponentID' is a set of attributes accommodating a wide range of change management schemes that when combined uniquely identifies a particular version of a component. It is drawn from the Core Integrity Schema [11] which is also used in the Reference Manifests. The 'Certification Authority' element contains attributes of a CA like name, identity and signature details. More details of the core schema itself can be found at [11].

5   Overview of the System Architecture

In this section, we provide an overview of the system architecture for distributed authorization using Web services. The architecture consists of three main entities, the Service Requestor or SR, the Service Provider or SP and a trusted third party called the Validation Service or VS. The Service Provider hosts and publishes one or more Web services. It has several access control requirements for each of the services it offers. Requirements differ based on the type of service offered and the type of requestor requesting the service. Requirements may also depend on other factors such as time of the day, place of request or other environmental attributes. A Service Requestor is an entity that discovers the services offered by Service Provider and makes a request for one or more of these services. A Validation Service VS is a trusted third party that performs one or more functions on behalf of AP or AR. Its main function includes the verification of the Integrity Report. However, it can also be used for the verification of authorization policies. This is especially useful if many entities have shared policies and trust the VS to do policy verification on their behalf. Reference Manifest repositories and Property Manifest repositories store the Reference Manifests (RM) and the Property Manifests (PM) respectively. There is also a Policy Repository (PR) that stores the authorization policies of the Service Provider. We choose XACML policy language [12] to define authorization policies as it is well suited for Web services. All entities with in the system communicate using Web services.

5.1   System Components

We now define each component and its sub-component that have been implemented in the system.

1) **Service Provider (SP)** is a hardware platform that hosts different Web services. SP can be any type of hardware platform and not necessarily a trusted platform. Its main functions include receiving a request, checking if access can be

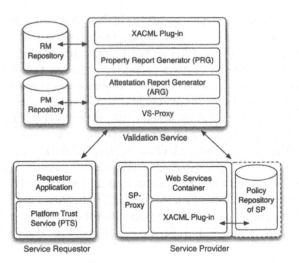

Fig. 1. System Architecture

allowed, and servicing or denying the request. It consists of the sub-components Proxy, WS Container, XACML plugin API.

SP-Proxy is a sub-component of the Service Provider. Proxy is also the first point of communication to an SP hosted Web service. It can be thought of as an abstraction of a Web service application which performs certain functions on its behalf. Its main functions include acting as the central point of communication between the different SP components, and communicating with the Service Requestor and Validation Service.

Web Service Container (WSC) is a collection of Web services offered by the Service Provider each of which can be discovered and invoked by a Service Requestor.

XACML Plugin provides an API for the inclusion of a standard XACML engine inside the provider. An XACML engine is the core component of the XACML access control model and is complex in its functionality. In short, it accepts requests for policy evaluation. It collects the necessary policies from the repositories. It evaluates the policies and resolves conflicts to arrive at a decision. It passes its decision on to the requester for necessary action to be taken. We do not discuss the XACML working model in detail and the specification [12] can be referred for more information.

Policy Repository (PR) is a repository that is used to store all the authorization policies of a Service Provider. This repository can be located anywhere in the Internet especially if the Service Provider is distributed in nature. As the repository is administered by the Service Provider, this association is shown using dashed lines in the diagram.

2) Service Requestor (SR) is the entity that requests access to a service from SP. It is a trusted computing hardware. It is assumed that all the components of the platform have the corresponding Reference Manifests and Property Manifests in some repository. It the Manifests are not available, then it is assumed that they can be obtained on demand. It consists of the Platform Trust Service and Requestor Application.

Platform Trust Service (PTS) on a trusted platform performs the function of generating an Integrity Report (IR) as defined in section 2.1. At the time of attestation, PTS collates the TPM signed PCR values, Reference Manifests or their pointers, Property Manifests or their pointers and the measurement log information into an Integrity Report. This report known as the Integrity Report is used during attestation.

Requestor Application is the component that invokes a request on a Service Provider. It is ideally a Web browser. It can also communicate with the Validation Service.

3) Validation Service (VS) is a third party trusted by both the Service Provider and the Service Requestor. It can be located any where in the Internet, can be any type of platform and should be accessible by the Service Requestor and the Service Provider. It consists of the VS-Proxy, Attestation Report Generator, Property Report Generator, and an XACML plug-in API. In the proposed system, a VS primarily serves three different purposes. It is used for attestation verification, Property Report generation and policy verification.

VS-Proxy is the first point of communication to a VS. SP and SR communicate with the VS-Proxy to start the attestation verification process. It aids communication between the different components of VS like PRG and ARG. It can also invoke other Web services on behalf of VS. For example, it communicates with PTS to request for an Integrity Report.

Attestation Report Generator (ARG) is responsible for the verification of the Integrity Report. ARG is presented with an Integrity Report, the Reference Manifests and the measurement log as inputs. Using these, it verifies the Integrity Report as defined in 2.1. After verification, it generates an Attestation Report that includes the result of the verification process.

Property Report Generator (PRG) performs the functions of a Property Report generation. When VS receives an Integrity Report, it verifies whether the binary values are validated using the Reference Manifests. If the measurements are valid and the component is integrity protected, it looks up the Property Manifest to check if that component satisfies any property (a property satisfied by a component becomes invalid if the component is not in its measured state). It picks up the properties satisfied by that component and collates them into a Property Report. A Property Report is heavily drawn from the Core Integrity Schema [11]. It includes details of components, their properties and property type information along with the signature of the Validation Service. A Property

Report can be thought of as a summary sheet of all the properties satisfied by a trusted platform.

XACML-plugin is available in the Validation Service also. It provides an API for the inclusion of a standard XACML policy engine with in the Validation Service. This enables a Validation Service to not only generate attestation credentials and Property Reports but also to validate policies on request. In such cases, it also has access to SP's policy repository for policy evaluation.

4) Reference Manifest (RM) Repository is responsible for storing the Reference Manifests of different components of a trusted platform. Each component manufacturer can stand-up its own Reference Manifest database for all its products, or such a database can be made available by a third party. RM Repositories can be located anywhere in the Internet and be accessed by SP and VS when required.

5) Property Manifest (PM) Repository. The PM repository is responsible for storing the Property Manifests of different components of the platform. Each manufacturer can stand-up its own Property Manifest database for all its products. A trusted third party can also host a Property Manifest repository for all the components that it has evaluated.

6   Authorization of Web Services

In this section we provide an overview of the authorization mechanism of a Web service. This system supports three different authorization models which are push, pull and delegation. We provide a brief description of each of the models.

The Pull Model. The pull model authorization is initiated when the Requestor Application of SR makes a service request to the provider's Proxy. Like in standard authorization systems, the Integrity Report is appended to the request in order to prove the possession of necessary privileges to access a service. If the Integrity Report is not available during request, then SP-Proxy can initiate a report request and obtain it from the PTS. Once the Integrity Report is received, SP-Proxy invokes the ARG service of VS using the VS-Proxy. The Integrity Report is first validated by ARG using the Reference Manifests from the RM repository. Then the request is passed on to PRG with the Attestation Report. For all the components whose binary measurements have been validated, the property information is looked up in the Property Manifests available in the PM repository. The Property Report is then generated, signed and sent back to the SP-Proxy. The SP-Proxy then sends the request from the requestor and the Property Report from VS to its XACML engine. The XACML engine verifies the request against the access control policies available in the policy repository. It arrives at a decision and sends its decision as allow or deny back to the SP-Proxy. The Proxy then forwards the decision to the Web service in the WSC. Depending on the decision, the service request is either accepted or rejected.

This model has certain design issues to be considered. Firstly, it is assumed that the Validation Service is trusted by SP and more so by SR. This is because, VS is chosen by SP in this model and SR should trust that VS will generate a correct Property Report about its platform. There can be an initial negotiation phase where SP and SR agree on the Validation Service that will be used. Secondly, the provider has to wait until the Integrity Report has been verified and a Property Report is generated. If the provider trusts VS enough, then it can make its policies also available along with the Integrity Report. VS can now not only generate the Property Report, but also validate the policies on behalf of the provider and pass its decision to SP. Thirdly, when the Property Report is being generated, if certain components exists in the platform whose measurements do not validate against the reference values, then the Property Report can include a list of such component identities. This could be useful for the requestor to subsequently take the necessary actions (as re-installation of components) in order to ensure that those properties are made available. Also, when the access control policies are being verified against the Property Report, if certain properties are missing in the report that may be required by the policy, the response from the XACML engine could include a list of missing properties that are required.

The Push Model. In the push model, Property Report generation is initiated by the Requestor Application of SR. The Requestor Application first invokes VS-Proxy by providing its Integrity Report. ARG of VS generates the Attestation Report which is then passed on to the PRG. PRG generates the Property Report using the Property Manifests and sends it to the Requestor Application. The Requestor Application now invokes the Web service of SP with the Property Report. The SP-Proxy receives the Property Report which it forwards to the XACML engine. The engine verifies policies as usual and determines if the properties in the Property Report is sufficient to allow access to the service. The XACML engine sends its decision to the Proxy which is then forwarded to the Web service for action.

The obvious disadvantage of this approach is the time of creation and time of use problem. As the Property Report is created much in advance before the request is initiated, the Service Provider cannot be sure that the report reflects the most recent state of the requestor's platform. The provider can also have policies to define how fresh it expects the property credential to be. In this model also, if SP wishes to use a Validation Service for policy evaluation, it's Proxy can invoke the XACML engine of VS by forwarding the Property Report obtained from the requestor along with its access control policies. When the Proxy receives the policy decision from VS, it can forward it to the SP Web service. Again, there can be an initial negotiation phase on which VS the requestor can use and which VS the provider can use as the VS's can be different entities.

The Delegation Model. In the delegation model, a Service Provider delegates the Validation Service to do all the work on its behalf. When SP's Proxy receives a service request from a requestor, the request is automatically forwarded to the VS-Proxy of the Validation Service. VS-Proxy receives the request and checks if the Integrity Report is available. If the report is not available, it invokes the PTS service of the requestor (it can be assumed that the requestor's URL is available in the request and its PTS service is discoverable). VS-proxy first communicates with ARG to generate the Attestation Report and then with PRG to generate the Property Report. If required, it also evaluates the access control policies and forwards its decision to the SP-Proxy. SP-Proxy then sends the decision to the Web service which acts accordingly.

7   Policy Extensions

Languages for access control aim to support the expression of authorization policies. While a policy language should be simple enough to understand and manage, it should also be expressive enough to accommodate all the authorization requirements of the system. Recently, there has been a lot of work on mark up language based access control policy languages like SAML [13], IBM's XACL [14] and XACML [12] due to their applicability in Web services. XACML has been already accepted by the Web services community and the WS-XACML specification [15] provides ways to use XACML in the context of Web services for authorization, access control, and privacy policies. In this section we briefly explain the extensions to the XACML policy statements necessary to include platform related property information.

7.1   XACML Policy Statement Extensions

The XACML specification, defines a <Subject> element in <Target> as the actor to whom the policy may be applicable to. Here, a subject could refer to the human user that initiated the application from which the request was issued or the application's executable code responsible for creating the request or even possibly the machine on which the application was executing. Although, the specification has some provision for limited platform related information, it is not expressive enough to include the components of a platform and their properties. Extensions to the <Target> element are *Rule/Target/Platforms* to include platform details, *Rule/Target/Platforms/Platform/Components* to include platform component details and *Rule/Target/Platforms/Platform/Components/Component/Properties* to include properties of components and their types.

7.2   Extensions to XACML Context Request and Response

An XACML context is a canonical representation for the inputs and the outputs of the policy evaluation engine. The input context is called the context request and the output context is called the context response. The <Request> element is a top-level element in the XACML context schema which contains the <Subject>, <Resource>, <Action> and <Environment> elements. Similarly, The <Response> element is a top-level element in the XACML context schema. The <Response> element encapsulates the authorization decision produced by the policy evaluation engine after the policy evaluation process has been completed.

The <Result> element includes the <Decision> element with the policy decision, the <Status> element to indicate whether errors have occurred during the evaluation process and the <Obligation> element that need to be sent to the Service Provider. We refer the reader to [12] for more information on the XACML context schema.

The context <Request> is extended to include information about the requesting platform, its components and its properties. For the context <Response> element, the <MissingAttributeDetail> element inside <Status> is extended to include the details of the component and its properties that were missing or unverified at the time of policy validation.

8   Application Scenario

In this section, we provide a sample scenario for the application of property based trust management to protecting medical records in hospitals and clinics. Many people consider their health issues as very private and expect the strongest protection against misuse. Medical records always need to be transferred between different entities who may not all be trusted. Health records need to be shared by different hospitals because the patient might not always visit the same hospital (in case of an emergency, or moving cities etc). Within the same hospital, different doctors and health workers like nurses need to access information based on who is attending the patient. There are also other entities like government agencies, pharmaceutical companies, insurance companies, ambulance services, and others who might require access.

In this section, we provide an example to show the applicability of trust management with trusted platforms in protecting medical records. Let us imagine that a patient Bob who normally visits hospital Hosp-A needs a specialist's consultation at Hospital Hosp-B. All hospitals register to one or more trusted third party brokers who aid in the sharing of information and protecting the interest of a patient. The first time Bob visited Hosp-A, Bob was asked to chose one such broker on his behalf if in the future, information has to be transferred to another hospital. Bob chose Brok-A. Hosp-A has promised Bob that 1) information will be securely transferred such that no illegitimate party can gain access 2) His health records will not be manipulated on transfer 3) Hosp-A will maintain a audit on all transfers and 4) Hosp-B will not store the information for more than one month without Bob's consent.

Hospital A (Hosp-A). Hosp-A is the Service Provider entity. Hosp-A hosts a 'Records Provider' service as a Web service. Any authorized party can invoke this request providing a patient ID as input. The service either rejects the request or provides the ID's corresponding medical history record as output.

Broker A (Brok-A). Broker is the Validation Service entity and performs functions as described in section 5. The broker provides the 'Delegation Proxy' service as a Web service. It is invoked by a delegation request with Patient ID and requestor ID as inputs. The output is either a 'permission granted' or

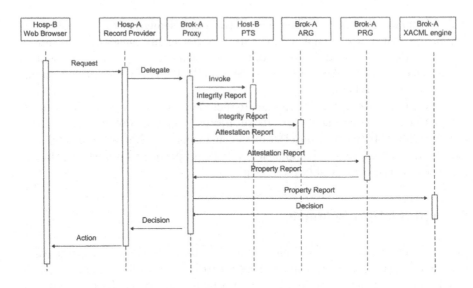

Fig. 2. Sequence Diagram

'permission rejected' response. Its main functions are to invoke the Platform Trust Service (PTS) of the Service Requestor and to communicate internally for generating the Property Report. Brok-A also has access to Hosp-A's XACML policy describing the conditions under which Bob is willing to disclose his data.

Hospital B (Hosp-B). Hosp-B is the Service Requestor. It is identified using an ID that is unique in the Internet (e.g UDDI). It has a Requestor Application that can invokes a request to another hospital providing the patient's ID and its own ID. All requests are sent out from trusted machines in the hospital (with a TPM). Host-B supports attestation mechanism using its PTS service.

The following diagram shows the sequence of events between Hosp-A, Brok-A and Hosp-B. We assume that the scenario follows a delegated model as described in 6. When Bob arrives at Hospital B to consult a specialist, Hospital B's platform launches a request on Hospital A's record provider service by entering Bob's patient ID and its ID. This request on Hosp-A recogizes Bob's ID and checks for his preferred broker. It identifies Brok-A and automatically delegates the request by invoking the Brok-A's Proxy. The Proxy first invokes the PTS service of Host-B (it is assumed that the Proxy can discover PTS of Hosp-B). PTS generates the Integrity Report and presents it to the Proxy. Proxy uses the Integrity Report to invoke the Attestation Report Generator service in VS. ARG now generates the Attestation Report by looking up the Reference Manifests and returns it to the Proxy. Proxy invokes the Property Report Generator service in VS. PRG generates the Property Report looking up the Property Manifests and returns it to the Proxy. Essentially, the Property Report must contain information that will suffice the four conditions of Bob. Hosp-B could achieve this by installing the necessary components that will provide confidentiality of data for condition 1, integrity of data for condition 2, a logging component for condition 3, a policy enforcer that ensures that data will be deleted after one month for condition 4. Hosp-B then proves that all these components are integrity protected and that they have the necessary Property Manifests. When Brok-A Proxy receives the Property Report, it presents the report to the XACML engine. The XACML authorization engine checks if PR has the necessary properties to satisfy the policies of Hosp-A available in the Policy Repository. It arrives at a decision, either to allow or deny the request which it forwards to the Proxy. Proxy forwards this decision to the Record Provider service which enforces the action accordingly. If the decision is to allow, it sends Bob's medical history file over to Hosp-B.

9 Discussion

In this section we discuss some issues that are relevant to property based attestation. One important issue to be considered is how much flexibility should one have when it comes to software updates such as patches, given that state of the platform and configuration will change in these circumstances. One of the main motivations to use properties instead of hashes of configurations is that properties do not necessarily change as often as hashes do. On the one hand, we do want to reflect state changes of the attesting platform to the challenger to decide whether it should interact or not. However if every time a 'minor' change happens, a new Property Manifest needs to be generated, this would limit the usage flexibility. of course, here the issue is to determine what changes are 'minor' and do not affect the 'security and trust' on the platform. Such policy issues also need to be designed and negotiated between the involved parties.

Another concern is related to the area of privacy. On the one hand, a trusted platform can gain confidence (and hence trust) of a challenging host it is communicating with by validating its state. But on the other hand, from the privacy point of view, it may not be appropriate for the challenging host to learn complete information about the components and state of the requestor's platform. At first glance, property based attestation may seem to abstract the low level implementation details to a higher level and thereby provide more privacy. However, deeper inspection will reveal that properties can be 'reverse engineered' to determine the implementation details of a platform. For example, certain components might have unique properties that may not be available in other components or a component can be challenged for different properties to work out what implementations are available and what is not. One recent proposal to enhance privacy in Property Based Attestation is based on the Zero Knowledge Protocol [16]. The protocol assumes that a property certificate is issued as a mapping between a state of a component and its properties. Using the zero knowledge protocol, a trusted platform proves to the challenger that there exists a valid link between the state measured by the Certificate Authority and the property requested without actually revealing the state information in the certificate.

In other words, the protocol allows for a simple equality check between the measured state of the platform and the certified state but hides the state values. If the equality check is successful, the verifier believes that the trusted platform has the certified properties. The problem however is, the certified state cannot be the overall state of the platform. This is because, we cannot guess all the possible platform values to create property certificates that match up. On the other hand, the certified state cannot be a component's state as well. This is because an individual measurement of a component is invalid without the transitive chain of measurements. This in turn will require the log of measurements to be made available in order to verify the chain of trust. Providing the log will defeat the purpose of the zero knowledge protocol. Alternatively, a chain of property certificates can be verified to maintain the trust chain. Another simple approach that we have adopted for privacy in this paper is to slice the properties at different granularities. A trusted platform and a verifier can negotiate in the beginning as to what properties will be revealed and at what granularities. This could enable better privacy for the trusted platform.

Other issues that can be addressed by our architecture are primarily extensions to the current implementation. The example illustrated in section 8 is a sample scenario only. One can imagine that there are many design issues possible here. For example, When Brok-A invokes the PTS service of Hosp-B, both the parties can enter a negotiation phase to determine what properties will be disclosed, at what granularities (S1,S2 or S3) and what actions should be taken if the necessary properties are unavailable. Hosp-B can also have a trust management system of its own to determine what Brok-A should do with Hosp-B's property information e.g delete immediately after use etc. Similarly, Hosp-A can have an agreement with Brok-A on which of Hosp-A's policies will be disclosed to Brok-A, for which patients, under what circumstances and what Brok-A can do with those policies. We can therefore see that each of the entities can themselves have a trust management system on their own. We are considering such extensions to the overall architecture.

10   Conclusion

In this paper, we proposed an authorization architecture for distributed systems leveraging trusted computing platforms. We believe that unlike hash measurements, security properties provide a neat way of defining security policies for systems. We introduced the notion of a Property Manifest, similar to the Reference Manifest to represent security properties. Properties in Manifest were expressed at different steps of granularity S1,S2 etc. We then provided an overview of our system architecture and its components. Like in any distributed system, the authorization mechanism supported different strategies like push, pull and delegation. The system has been implemented using Web services with policy extensions for XACML. We concluded with some interesting thoughts that need to be considered while using property based authorization.

There are many avenues for future work. Presently, we are trying to understand the notion of a property and the issues associated with its evaluation and certification. This will enable us to specify an algebra for trusted platforms, their components and properties. Using this algebra, one might be able to reason out if a certain platform has the necessary 'privileges' to access a certain resource. We will then try to combine user based authorization with platform based authorization to see how it impacts a security decision.

References

1. Blaze, M., Feigenbaum, J., Lacy, J.: Decentralized Trust Management. In: Security and Privacy, pp. 164–173 TY - CONF. (1996)
2. Blaze, M., Feigenbaum, J., Ioannidis, J., Keromytis, A.: The KeyNote Trust-Management System Version 2 (RFC 2704). Internet Engineering Task Force (September 1999)
3. DeTreville, J.: Binder, a Logic-Based Security Language. In: SP 2002: Proceedings of the 2002 IEEE Symposium on Security and Privacy, Washington, DC, USA, p. 105. IEEE Computer Society, Los Alamitos (2002)
4. Chu, Y.-H., Feigenbaum, J., LaMacchia, B., Resnick, P., Strauss, M.: Referee: Trust Management for Web Applications. World Wide Web J. 2(3), 127–139 (1997)
5. Herzberg, A., Mass, Y., Michaeli, J., Ravid, Y., Naor, D.: Access Control Meets Public Key Infrastructure, Or: Assigning Roles to Strangers. In: SP 2000: Proceedings of the 2000 IEEE Symposium on Security and Privacy, Washington, DC, USA, p. 2. IEEE Computer Society, Los Alamitos (2000)
6. Trusted Computing Group: TCG TPM Main Specification Version 1.1b (2005)
7. Poritz, J., Schunter, M., Herreweghen, E.V., Waidner, M.: Property Attestation: Scalable and Privacy-Friendly Security Assessment of Peer Computers. Technical report, IBM Research (May 2004)
8. Sadeghi, A.R., Stueble, C.: Property-Based Attestation for Computing Platforms: Caring about Properties, not Mechanisms. In: NSPW 2004: Proceedings of the New Security Paradigm Workshop (2004)
9. Nagarajan, A., Varadharajan, V., Hitchens, M.: Trust Management for Trusted Computing Platforms in Web Services. In: STC 2007: Proceedings of the 2007 ACM workshop on Scalable Trusted Computing, New York, NY, USA, pp. 58–62 (2007)
10. Yoshihama, S., Ebringer, T., Nakamura, M., Munetoh, S., Maruyama, H.: WS-Attestation: Efficient and Fine-Grained Remote Attestation on Web Services. Technical report, IBM Research (February 2005)
11. TCG Infrastructure Working Group: Core Integrity Schema Specification (November 2006)
12. OASIS XACML Technical Committee: eXtensible Access Control Markup Language 3 (XACML) Version 2.0 (February 2005)
13. Hughes, J., Maler, E.: Technical Overview of the OASIS Security Assertion Markup Language (SAML) V1.1. OASIS (May 2004)
14. Kudo, M., Hada, S.: XML Document Security Based on Provisional Authorization. In: CCS 2000: Proceedings of the 7th ACM conference on Computer and Communications Security, pp. 87–96. ACM, New York (2000)
15. OASIS XACML Technical Committee: Web Services Profile of XACML (WS-XACML) Version 1.0 (December 2006)
16. Chen, L., Landfermann, R., Löhr, H., Rohe, M., Sadeghi, A.R., Stüble, C.: A Protocol for Property-Based Attestation. In: STC 2006: Proceedings of the first ACM workshop on Scalable Trusted Computing, New York, NY, USA, pp. 7–16 (2006)
17. Balacheff, B., Chen, L., Pearson, S., Plaquin, D., Proudler, G.: Trusted Computing Platforms - TCPA Technology in Context. Hewlett-Packard Books (2003)

Sharing but Protecting Content Against Internal Leakage for Organisations

Muntaha Alawneh and Imad M. Abbadi

Information Security Group, Royal Holloway, University of London
Egham, Surrey, TW20 0EX, UK
{M.Alawneh,I.Abbadi}@rhul.ac.uk

Abstract. Dishonest employees, who have privileges to obtain corporate critical information and access internal resources, cause the problem of internal leakage. Employees, who have such privileges and know from where to obtain corporate sensitive information, are far more dangerous than outsiders. This paper proposes a mechanism for protecting information inside organisations against unauthorised disclosure by internal adversaries. It mainly focusses on sharing and simultaneously guarding information assets from one another. This paper proposes a novel solution for binding sensitive content to organisation devices, thereby preventing uncontrolled content leakage to other devices. In the proposed solution we used trusted computing technology to provide a hardware-based root of trust on client side.

1 Introduction

Organizations consist of groups of employees performing business activities in order to achieve a particular goal [7]. There are different structures for organisations based on the type of the organisation [6]. Each has its own specific policy and process workflow. Organisations are generally divided into multiple groups/departments. Each group/department performs a specific function for the organisation. In addition, a department/group is typically structured into different levels specifying the seniority of employees, e.g. senior managers' level, managers' level, supervisors' level...etc. For example a department might has manager(s) who manages team leaders. A team leader supervises a group of employees. A group of employees with the team leader need to share specific organisational information assets. This sharing is required for accomplishing the organisational tasks assigned to this specific group. Such data needs to be shared but protected from getting accessed by other unauthorised employees. Sharing content is categorised as horizontal and vertical sharing.

- Horizontal sharing means providing the ability to share information by users at the same level; e.g. sharing information between all managers, between team leaders, between a group of employees performing a task for a specific project.
- Vertical sharing means providing the ability to share information between higher and lower levels; e.g. between managers and employees, between team

V. Atluri (Ed.): DAS 2008, LNCS 5094, pp. 238–253, 2008.

leaders and managers, and between a department manager and all employees in the department.

Proposing a solution that can directly be applied to different kinds of organisations is not practical. However, organisations have common requirements that would vary in specific details. Thus, for a solution to be practical it must focus on organisational common requirements. Each specific type of organisation then can customise the solution to satisfy its specific requirements. Organisations typically have the following common requirements specific for sharing its informational assets.

- Flexibility as organisations might change process workflow, employees, infrastructure, etc.
- Share but protect. As described above, organisations require sharing pools of content between different employees, and simultaneously protecting the content from getting transferred to others not authorised to access the pools of content. Content sharing could either be horizontal or vertical as defined above.

The main problem, which is the focus of this paper, is how to share content with a group of users, and simultaneously preventing a member user in the group, who is authorised to access the content, from accidentally or deliberately transferring the content to others not authorised to access such content. This is what we referred to as an internal content leakage. *"The quest for secure information sharing has been a central but elusive goal for information security for over three decades. The stumbling block is simple to understand but difficult to solve. Digital information is easy to copy and transport, and read access to any copy is as good as read access to the original"* [13]. Employees, who have privileges and know from where to obtain corporate content, are by far more dangerous than outsiders. Thus, the cost of insiders' threat exceeds outsiders' threat. Also, the greater an individual's authorisation for accessing corporate content, the greater the potential threat from that person. In this case, using password for user authentication is not enough for ensuring sharing and protecting content. This is because, a dishonest user can transfer his authentication credentials to others not authorised to access the content.

Satisfying the requirement of sharing but protecting content needs binding content to devices requiring access to content, and, simultaneously, ensuring that only authorised users having access to such devices using well know user authentication techniques; see, for example, [4,8].

Objectives: The main objectives for this paper are the following:

- Enabling sharing (the horizontal and vertical sharing) of content between a group of users in an organisation, and simultaneously protecting content from getting leaked accidentally or deliberately to unauthorised parties.
- Satisfying other organisation requirements as discussed above.

Internal content leakage has a major impact on organisations, for example, leaked information could be abused by committing an identity fraud or for marketing purposes. According to the 2002 CSI/FBI Annual Computer Crime and

Security Survey, "*insider misuse of authorised privileges or abuse of network access has caused great damage and loss to corporate information*" [10]. There are several real examples of information leakage, for instance, "*Jonathan Pollard, who had high-level security clearance, was arrested for passing tens of thousands of pages of classified U.S. information such as satellite photographs, weapon systems data, etc., to Israelis. A Libyan intelligence agent obtained the U.S. Military's officers' directory through his wife, who worked at the Department of Transportation and had access to the database of the Metropolitan Washington Council*" [9].

2   Dynamic Domain Definition

A dynamic domain consists of one or more devices owned by a specific organisation. We used the word dynamic to refer to its nature of being fleaxiable for adding and removing devices from it, i.e. the dynamic domain can be moved across organisational devices based on the organisation needs. Each dynamic domain has a unique identifier i_D and a unique symmetric key k_D. The dynamic domain-specific symmetric key is used to protect the domain-specific pool of content that can only be accessed by the domain-specific set of devices. This key is only available inside member devices of the domain, thus only domain devices can access the pool of content bound to the domain. The dynamic domain creation process is performed by organisation authorised security administrators, who choose devices that need to be bound to a dynamic domain based on the organisation requirements. This binding is performed using an organisation-specific master control device, as will be explained later in this paper. For example, assume an organisation has a department or a group of users, which require its devices to access a specific pool of content, and it does not want the pool of content to leak to other departments/groups. In this case the organisation needs to create a dynamic domain consisting of all devices that need such an access, and simultaneously the organisation needs to bind the pool of content to the dynamic domain. Authorised users, who use member devices in a specific dynamic domain can access the protected content bound to that domain. On the other hand, users cannot access the protected content from devices not members in the dynamic domain even if they have a copy of the protected content. This is because devices not member in the domain do not possess a copy of the domain-specific key, and hence cannot decrypt the domain-specific content. The dynamic nature of the domain enables adding more devices to the domain, and removing member devices in the domain, which should be based on the organisation needs.

Organisation system administrators create dynamic domains, assign devices to dynamic domains and destroy dynamic domains based on organisation needs. A device can join multiple domains to access all content bound to these domains.

3   Hardware and Software Requirements

In this section we describe the main entities constituting the proposed model.

3.1   Organisation Devices

Software-only techniques cannot provide a high degree of protection for organisation domain credentials; for example, Apple FairPlay[1], which uses software-only techniques, has been hacked multiple times; see, for example, [11] and the Hymn project[2]. In the proposed solution we require that organisation devices to be compliant with the Trusted Computing Group (TCG[3]) specifications [17,18,19]. TCG compliant trusted platforms (TP) are not expensive, and are currently available from a range of PC manufacturers, including Dell, Fujitsu, HP, Intel and Toshiba [12]. In addition, since early 2006, all Intel-based Apple computers are TCG compliant [20].

3.2   TCG Overview

This section provides a very brief overview of the main entities in TCG compliant platforms, which are required in the proposed scheme. TCG is a wide subject and has been discussed by many researchers; we will not address the details of TCG specifications in this paper for space limitations. For further details about this subject see, for example, [12,16,17,18,19].

TPM. The TCG specifications require each TP to include an additional inexpensive hardware chip to establish trust in that platform. This chip is referred to as the Trusted Platform Module (TPM), which has protected storage and protected capabilities. In order to reduce the TPM cost, the TCG specifications only require the TPM to be used for functions requiring protected storage and capabilities. Functions that do not require protected storage and capabilities could run using the platform main processor and memory space. The TPM is typically implemented as a processing engine that is separate from the TP's main processing environment. A TPM incorporates various functional components and features including: I/O; a cryptographic co-processor that supports the following: asymmetric key generation, asymmetric encryption/decryption, hashing and random number generation; generation, storage and protection of symmetric keys; HMAC engine; SHA-1 engine; power detection; non volatile memory; volatile memory; platform configuration registers (PCRs), which are shielded locations inside the TPM used to store integrity measurements; and an opt-in component that provides mechanisms and protections to allow the TPM to be turned on/off, enabled/disabled, activated/deactivated.

Protected Storage. Once a TPM has been assigned an owner, it generates a new Storage Root Key pair (SRK), which is used to protect all TPM keys. The private part of the SRK is stored permanently inside the TPM. Other TPM objects (key objects or data objects) are protected using keys that are ultimately protected by the SRK in a tree hierarchy structure. The entries of a

---

[1] http://www.apple.com/lu/support/itunes/authorization.html
[2] http://hymn-project.org
[3] http://www.trustedcomputinggroup.org

TPM PCRs, where integrity measurements are stored, are used in the protected storage mechanism. This is achieved by comparing the current PCR values with the intended PCR values stored with the data object. If the two values are consistent, access is then granted and data is unsealed[4]. Storage, and retrieval are carried out by the TPM. Therefore, if a software process relies on the use of secrets, it cannot operate unless it and its software environment are correct. The latter ensures that the software process that implements this scheme is trusted to operate as expected.

A TPM can generate two types of keys, known as migratable and non-migratable keys. Migratable keys can be transmitted to other TPs if authorised by both a selected trusted authority and the TPM owner. A non-migratable key is bound to the TP that created it. The TP associates the current platform Software State, which is stored in PCRs, with the non-migratable key, and then protects them using the SRK. Stored secrets are only released after the platform's PCRs have been compared with the values associated with the stored key. Data encrypted using a non-migratable key can leave the TP if and only if the software agent (whose execution status matches the one associated with the non-migratable key, i.e. is authorised to read data encrypted using the non-migratable) authorises the release of the data to other platforms.

Attestation. Establishing trust in a TP is based on the mechanism that is used for measuring, reporting and verifying platform integrity metrics. TP measurements are performed using the RTM (Root of Trust for Measurement), which measures software components running on a TP. The RTS (Root of Trust for Storage) stores these measurements inside TPM shielded locations (i.e. the PCR). Next, the RTR (Root of Trust for Reporting) mechanism allows TP measurements to be reliably communicated to an external entity in the form of an integrity report. The integrity report is signed using an AIK[5] (Attestation Identity Key) private key, and is sent with the appropriate identity credential. This enables a Verifier to be sure that an integrity report is bound to a genuine TPM[6].

3.3 Trusted Software Agent

Trusted software agents act as trusted reference monitors that need to be installed into domain devices and the master control device, and which are required

---

[4] Seal/unseal are TCG terms used for encrypting/decrypting a data object. Seal binds a data object with an integrity measurement that must match the platform PCR value when unsealing the object. Also, a data object must be unsealed on the same TPM that sealed the object.

[5] AIKs are signature key pairs function as aliases for the TP; they are generated by the TPM, and the public part is included in a certificate known as an Identity Credential, signed by a trusted third party called a privacy certification authority (privacy CA). The identity credential asserts that the (public part of the) AIK belongs to a TP with specified properties, without revealing which TP the key belongs to.

[6] One might argue that the device states might change after getting attested. This is solved by using the new generation of Intel/AMD hardware technology that stops DMA or by using Virtualisation technology as has been described in [12].

to implement the proposed scheme; i.e. creating and managing dynamic domains, protecting content and binding it to a specific dynamic domain, permitting the creation and accessing of content on member devices of a specific dynamic domain.

We require that each organisation possesses three different types of trusted software agents[7]. The first is to be used by the master control device for implementing its functionality as discussed in section 3.4; the second is to be used for devices requiring creating and binding content for dynamic domains; and the last is to be used for accessing content. These agents are the only entities authorised to read 'data protection keys' encrypted using a **non-migratable key**[8] specific to each device in a domain. This is because the non-migratable key object is sealed with the integrity metric of the trusted software agent. The trusted software agents need to be implemented so that they will not release the 'data protection keys' to others. Also, they should be designed in such a way they will not release the data protected using these keys 'unprotected' outside the TP boundaries[9].

TCG compliant hardware ensures that the only means to access the protected content is through the trusted software agent. The trusted software agent, in turn, is responsible for ensuring that access to cleartext content is provided only to authorised users.

TCG compliant hardware provides the main functions required by the trusted software agent, e.g. basic cryptographic functions, local and remote platform and application attestation, and sealed storage for 'content protection keys'. The hardware-based root of trust provides the trustworthiness of the software agent. In this a challenger can verify that a platform is trustworthy by validating the platform integrity metrics. The TP measures the integrity of software executed from platform start-up and stores the result in the platform's PCRs; this provides assurance to the challenger that the OS, and of any other measured software, is running as expected on the platform. The trusted software agents are considered to be trusted if their PCR values are as expected. Therefore, if the OS, running applications, and the trusted software agents are as expected, then the execution environment of the TP is trusted. Hence the secrecy of organisation data is subsequently guaranteed.

3.4   Master Control Device

The master control device is a trusted device that has all TP features, as defined in section 3.1. Each organisation has a specific master control device in charge of managing the organisation dynamic domains and all devices membership in

---

[7] The three types of software agents could be integrated in one package or three packages. The way this is designed and implemented is outside the scope of this paper.

[8] See section 3.2.

[9] Such trusted Software agents can easily be designed to cover the assumptions, as DRM techniques has designed their own agents based on similar assumptions; see, for example, [3].

each dynamic domain. The trusted software agent in the master control device is in charge of creating and managing dynamic domains involving the following:

- Securely generating and storing each dynamic domain-specific unique identifier, protection key, and a public key list which includes the public keys for all member devices in each dynamic domain.
- Attesting to the execution environment status of devices added to a dynamic domain, ensuring they are trusted to securely store domain keys and execute as expected.
- Adding devices to a dynamic domain by releasing the domain-specific key (i.e. the content protection key) to member devices in the domain.

4   Process Workflow

The workflow of the proposed system is divided into the following phases (for simplicity we refer to the trusted software agent on a device performing certain action, by just using a device performing certain action i.e. we implicitly assuming that trusted software agents discussed in section 3.3 perform the proposed scheme functionality).

4.1   Master Control Device Initialisation

This section describes the process of initialising the master control device. The first time the master control device is initialised, it instructs the organisation security administrators to provide their authentication credentials. The master control device then stores in its protected storage[10] the authentication credentials of the organisation security administrators associated with its trusted execution environment state (i.e. the integrity measurement, which is stored in the TPM's PCR as described in section 3.2). The authentication credential[11] is used to authenticate security administrators before using the master control device. The master control device is used each time the security administrators want to create, expand, shrink or change a dynamic domain.

4.2   Dynamic Domain Establishment

Whenever an organisation wishes to protect a type of content in such way it only can be accessed by a set of devices, it needs to create a dynamic domain consisting of these devices. The process of creating a dynamic domain is done as follows (figure 1 summarises the protocol for this stage).

1. The organisation decides how many devices need to access a specific type of content, say N. N would be the initial size of a dynamic domain. The organisation also decides which devices will access this type of content. This should

---

[10] We mean by storing data in a protected storage is 'sealing data' in TCG terms, as described in section 3.2

[11] User authentication mechanism is outside the scope of this paper, and it has been discussed in [2].

be based on organisational needs. For example, a dynamic domain could consist of devices used by managers' level, devices used by supervisors' levels. This case covers horizontal sharing. A dynamic domain could be selected to cover vertical sharing. In this case the dynamic domain would consist of devices mixed between different levels. Each group of devices constitutes a specific dynamic domain.

2. The security administrators instruct the master control device to create a new dynamic domain. The master control device then authenticates the organisation security administrators, e.g. using a password.

3. If authentication succeeds, the master control device instructs the security administrators to provide the number N, and the public keys of devices that will be in the dynamic domain.

4. The master control device then securely generates a dynamic domain specific symmetric key k_D, and a dynamic domain specific identifier i. The master control device creates a public key list for this domain consisting of the provided public keys. It then ensures that the size of the public key list equals to N. k_D and i are associated with the public key list and the value of N, and then stored in the master control device protected storage and bound to a trusted execution environment based on TCG specifications; see, for example, section 3.2.

4.3 Adding Devices into a Domain

This section describes the process for adding a device into a dynamic domain, which is performed as follows (figure 2 summarises the protocol for this stage).

1. From each device in the public key list, the organisation security administrators sends a join domain request to the master control device to install the dynamic domain specific key. This request includes the dynamic domain specific identifier i identifying which domain to join.

2. The master control device and the joining device mutually authenticates each other conforming to the three-pass mutual authentication protocol de-

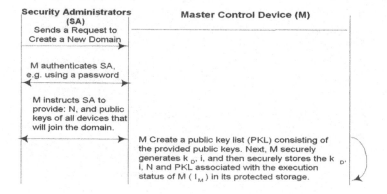

Fig. 1. Dynamic Domain Establishment Protocol

scribed in [5]. The master control device then attests to the execution environment of the joining device and validates its trustworthiness; as described in section 3.2.

3. If the joining device execution environment is trusted, the master control device checks if the device's public key is included in the public key list for the dynamic domain (as specified in step (1) above). If so, it securely releases the dynamic domain specific key to the device.

4. The device stores the domain key in its protected storage, and binds it to a specific execution environment. This device is now part of the domain, as it possesses a copy of the domain key and its public key matches the one stored in the master control device.

5. Now, all member devices of the domain can access the encrypted pool of content related to that domain. All these devices have a copy of the dynamic domain-specific key k_D. Therefore, these devices can access the domain-specific content as protected using the key k_D.

4.4   Binding Content to a Specific Domain

Most organisations create and manage their own content, e.g. creating patient records in clinics, creating bank accounts for customer. As we described in this paper there are different kinds of organisations, each has its own requirements and process workflow. Such requirements and process workflow determine who would create content, and how content should be bound to a domain. Usually departments in organisations create their own content by a group of users in the organisation. These users might be in one department or split across deferent departments. For simplicity, in this paper we consider a single case, which could be easily modified to be suitable for other kinds of organisations. Herein, we assume that an organisation firstly needs to define a group of devices that need

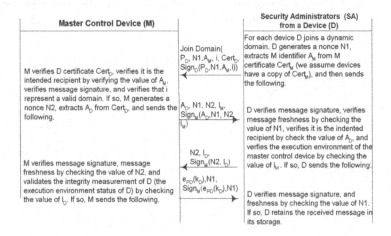

Fig. 2. Adding a Device into a Domain Protocol

to be in a domain to share a specific pool of content. Security administrators then instruct the master controller to create a dynamic domain for this group. Secondly, the third type of the trusted software agent (as described in section 3.3) is used to create content and to specify for which dynamic domain the content belongs. Authorised users (who are allowed to access the trusted software agent) have the ability to create content and assign it to the domain.

We now describe the process for adding content into a domain in a context of a scenario. Assume an organisation needs to work on a new project. This project requires sharing a specific pool of content. Employees working on this project need to share the pool of content, in such a way the content is protected against internal leakage. In this case, the organisation security administrators create a dynamic domain identified by an identifier i. This dynamic domain consists of all devices that need to share the pool of content specific for this project. Authorised employees, which either could be from this group or from a different group create content for this project. Next, the trusted software agent transfers the created content associated with the domain identifier i to the master control device. The master control device identifies the dynamic domain using i, and then encrypts the received content with the dynamic domain-specific key. The encrypted content is typically stored in a dynamic domain-specific location[12] (e.g. a relational database management system, a shared network file system, or others, which should depends on organisational policy.). If someone copied such content he/she will not be able to access it except on devices holding the content-specific dynamic domain key, i.e. member devices in the content-specific dynamic domain.

Next, each member device in a dynamic domain can download the protected content belonging to this domain, typically, from a dynamic domain-specific location or receive it from another device. In this case, only member devices in the same domain i.e. hold a copy of the dynamic domain-specific key k_D, can decrypt and then access the dynamic domain content. As we described earlier, different departments/groups in an organisation, sometimes, require sharing but protecting information. Our solution considers this requirement by allowing devices, which need to share content with other departments or other dynamic domains, to be able to join multiple dynamic domains. Therefore, a single device could join, for example, three domains and so having three dynamic domains-specific keys enabling it to access these dynamic domains content.

5   Domain Management

In order for a solution to be accepted and be widely used, it should adapt with organisations dynamic structure; for example, an organisation might need to change its strategy, layout, business work flow, and/or replace its devices. In this section we discuss how the proposed scheme covers these requirements, i.e.

---

[12] We assumed in this paper that content are stored in a dynamic domain specific location. This is because this way is the most commonly used in practical life. However, our solution does not make this as mandatory assumption, i.e. content could be stored anywhere based on the organisational policy.

removing a device from a dynamic domain, adding a device into a dynamic domain, and key revocation.

5.1   Domain Shrinking

An organisation might need to enable accessing for a pool of content on fewer number of devices than it is currently use, or it might need to replace its devices for several reasons, e.g. a hardware failure and the device cannot be recovered, or replace the device with newer technology. In these cases the organisation should be given the flexibility to do these changes.

The way to remove a device from a dynamic domain is as follows. The master control device needs to attest to the execution status of the device ensuring it is trusted to remove the dynamic domain key from its storage (based on TCG specifications; see, for example, section 3.2). If the device is trusted, the master control device instructs the leaving device to delete all dynamic domain keys for which the device is leaving. The master control device then removes this device public key from the public key list of the dynamic domain, and decrements the value of N. On the other hand, if the execution status of the device is not trusted, the master control device will not remove this device; i.e. it will not decrement the value N, will not remove the device public key from the dynamic domain-specific public key list. Also, security administrators should still know that this device is still have the content.

5.2   Domain Expansion

An organisation can expand a dynamic domain, for example, when adding more employees to perform a new business requirement or to help existing employees if business expands. In this case, the master control device instructs the security administrators to provide the public keys of the new devices. The master control device then adds the number of the new devices to N. The master control device securely stores the new value of N and updates the public key list with the added values, and finally it allows the new devices to join the domain as described in section 4.3.

5.3   Key Revocation

Hacking a dynamic domain specific key only affects the dynamic domain-specific pool of content. As a precautionary measure, security administrators need to revoke the dynamic domain key, and generate a new domain key, which can be done as follows. The security administrators instruct the master control device to change the key for a specific dynamic domain. The master control device then authenticates the organisation security administrators. If authentication succeeds, the master control device generates a new domain-specific key, and then replaces the old copy of the domain key with the new domain key in its protected storage. The master control device then reinstall this key on domain devices; the master control device identifies devices using their public keys, which are securely stored inside the master control device, as described in section 4.2. For each device, the master control device releases the new value of the domain key encrypted using the device public key. The device replaces the domain key with the new value in its protected storage and binds it to the same execution environment used for the old key, as it has already been verified as trusted; see section 4.3.

6 System Analysis

In this section we discuss how the proposed solution meets our objectives defined in section 1.

▷ The proposed solution allows content sharing but protection against internal leakage. Authorised users can freely transfer content amongst each other and share it. Our solution protects content leaks accidentally or deliberately to unauthorised users. We achieve this requirement by using two security levels, the first is device base level and the second is user level. Device based level means binding content to a domain where authorised users can freely access content. Each device in the domain possesses a copy of the domain key, which is used to protect a pool of content that needs to be shared between the dynamic domain devices. In the proposed solution we ensure that the domain key will not be released to unauthorised devices by securely generating it, transferring it and storing it. Content cannot be transferred unprotected to other devices in the organisation, which means devices only receive protected content. In this case the recipient device either could be an authorised device for accessing content or it could be a device that is not authorised to access the content. Authorised devices can decrypt the content and access it because they already possess a copy of the content protection key. However, unauthorised devices are not capable to access the content because they do not have a copy of the key. For achieving user level protection a specific mechanism needs to be integrated with the proposed scheme ensuring only authorised users accessing devices. The details of this important point is outside the scope of this paper and has been discussed elsewhere; see , for example, [4].

▷ Allows horizontal and vertical content sharing across organisation structure. Devices require accessing shared content must join all dynamic domains where shared content is bound. For example, for a chief information officer (CIO) of an organisation to be able to access all organisation shared but protected information, the CIO device needs join all organisation dynamic domains.

▷ Flexibility. This is realised as follows.

• As it is known, organisations have different layers, e.g. managers, seniors. In addition, organisations are organised into different business processes, e.g. a newspaper type of organisation has an editorial work flow, a publishing workflow and page layout. A dynamic domain can contain devices from a single layer, or from different layers, based on organisation requirements. This provides an organisation the flexibility to bind content on devices based on the organisation functionality.

- An organisation can dynamically move devices between dynamic domains based on changes in its needs. For example, if an organisation requires changing its layout, say after one year, this might require content re-binding. When a device is reallocated to be used by a new layer (i.e. different business process) that requires accessing different kind of content, it can join all dynamic domain where the content is bound. The device also needs to remove all dynamic domains specific keys it no longer authorised to access its content (the device will remove the domain keys, as it is trusted to perform as expected).

▷ Reduces the impact if a domain key is revealed. Because we are using trusted computing that provides hardware based root or trust, it is very unlikely for the domain key to be revealed. In the unlikely event of hacking a domain key, only it affects content bound to a single specific domain, i.e. it does not cause a global impact on other domains content.

7   Related Work

In our proposed solution we mainly focused on achieving two main goals:

- Enabling sharing for content by a group of devices, and simultaneously preventing internal information leakage.
- Satisfying organisation requirements such as: vertical and horizontal 'sharing and protection' of content across groups of devices, adapting with changes in organisational business processes, e.g. adding more employees, reducing the number of employees, changing the IT infrastructure.

In the following paragraphs we analyse current solutions based on the above two points. Current access control techniques such as Discretionary Access Control (DAC) and Role Based Access Control (RBAC) are based on the standard assumption that users are trusted and they will not misuse their authorisation. Also, access control is only enforced at content source. Moreover, DAC and RBAC techniques have security flows and usability limitations when talking about information sharing but protection, as has been widely discussed in many literatures (see, for example, [13]).

The second approach is generally called MAC, as has been analysed by Sandhu et al.[13] which attempts to "solve" the secure information sharing problem in a very specific and rigid framework. This makes it to be not very common over the past three and a half decades. In addition, MAC only allows objects to flow in one direction in a lattice of security labels, i.e. MAC does not allow object owner to share and protect an object amongst other users at the same or higher security levels. This means it does not provide flexible vertical information sharing and protection. MAC can be characterised as a coarse-grained one-directional secure information sharing. Therefore, it is clear that MAC does not satisfy organisation dynamic structure.

DRM schemes proposed in [1,2,3] involve creating a domain owned by a single owner, where all devices joining the domain are bound in some way to the domain owner. These schemes allow secure content sharing between devices in a domain, and prevent the illegal copying of content to devices outside the domain. These schemes focus on protecting copyrighted content in personal network. Organisation networks have different requirements than personal networks. These are as follows. (i) A personal network is composed of a single domain, on the other hand, an organisation consists of multiple domains. Consequently, a device in a personal network should be bound to a single domain. However an organisational network requires that each device to join multiple domains managed by the organisation security administrators. (ii) In personal networks each domain is bound to a single user; however, in the organisation multiple employees are members in an organisation domain, and each employee can be member in multiple domains. (iii) Devices in a personal network need to share but protect content between its all devices. On the other hand, an organisational network needs to share but protect pools of content across groups of devices, each (group) forming a dynamic domain. Most importantly, personal network does not have the concept of internal leakage.

There is another technique attempting reducing content leakage once the content in the hands of authorised individuals by proposing a method for monitoring the activities actioned on content. Park et al. [9] *provides scalable and reusable mechanisms to monitor insiders' behavior in organizations, applications, and operating systems based on insiders' current tasks.* This is by monitoring if an authorised user is performing an abnormal activity on content. Although this method attempts to detect information leakage, however it does not provide mechanism for preventing internal and external leakage, which we have addressed in this paper. We believe preventing information leakage should come before detecting a leakage. However, this is not to lower the importance of detection, which should follow the prevention as there is nothing like hundred percent secure system; i.e. any one attempts tampering with the system, he/she will be discovered at an early stage. Such a mechanism could be integrated with our proposed scheme to achieve other objectives.

The work done in [21] proposes a solution for content sharing, where content is accessed from a centralised location in a read only mode. This solution is useful in organisations that constitute one group and where data is located in a centralised location. Our proposed solution is for different kind of organisations, which have multiple groups each of which share a specific data, and also multiple combination of users within these groups might need to share specific data.

The problem of information sharing has also been addressed by other approaches, such as Windows folder sharing[13] (and windows domains), Network File System (NFS) [15], and resource sharing in P2P networks [14]. Although these approaches proposes different mechanisms for sharing content between groups of users; however, these mechanisms do not address internal content leakage (as defined in this paper). For example, a member in a group who is

---

[13] www.microsoft.com

authorised to access content shared using any of these techniques can transfer the shared content to others.

8 Conclusion

In this paper we propose a solution for protecting content against leakage in organisations. The proposed solution uses dynamic domains, consisting of devices owned by an organisation. Devices can be dynamically reallocated between dynamic domains based on the organisation needs. This protects content against leakage, and simultaneously allows content to be shared amongst devices in the same domain.

Acknowledgment

The author would like to thank Jason Crampton and Allan Tomlinson for their useful discussion, which have improved the paper.

References

1. Abbadi, I.: Authorised domain management using location based services. In: Cheak, A.D., Chong, P.J., Seah, W., Ping, S. (eds.) Mobility 2007: proceedings of the 4th International Conference on Mobile Technology, Applications & Systems, September 2007, pp. 288–295. ACM Press, New York (2007)
2. Abbadi, I.: Digital rights management using a master control device. In: Cervesato, I. (ed.) ASIAN 2007. LNCS, vol. 4846, pp. 126–141. Springer, Heidelberg (2007)
3. Abbadi, I., Mitchell, C.: Digital rights management using a mobile phone. In: ICEC 2007: Proceedings of the ninth international conference on Electronic commerce, pp. 185–194. ACM Press, NY (2007)
4. Ferraiolo, D., Chandramouli, R., Kuhn, R.: Role-Based Access Control. Artech House, Norwood (2003)
5. International Organization for Standardization. ISO/IEC 9798-3, Information technology — Security techniques — Entity authentication — Part 3: Mechanisms using digital signature techniques, 2nd edn. (1998)
6. Miles, R.E., Snow, C.C. (eds.): Organizational Strategy, Structure and Process. Stanford University Press (2003)
7. Oh, S., Sandhu, R., Zhang, X.: An effective role administration model using organization structure. ACM Trans. Inf. Syst. Secur. 9(2), 113–137 (2006)
8. Park, J., Sandhu, R.: Towards usage control models: beyond traditional access control. In: SACMAT 2002: Proceedings of the Seventh ACM Symposium on Access Control Models and Technologies, pp. 57–64. ACM, New York (2002)
9. Park, J.S., Ho, S.M.: Composite role-based monitoring (CRBM) for countering insider threats. In: Chen, H., Moore, R., Zeng, D.D., Leavitt, J. (eds.) ISI 2004. LNCS, vol. 3073, pp. 201–213. Springer, Heidelberg (2004)
10. Power, R.: CSI/FBI computer crime and security survey. Computer security issues & trends (2002)
11. Rowell, L.F.: The ballad of DVD JON. NetWorker 10(4), 28–34 (2006)

12. Sadeghi, A.: Trusted computing — special aspects and challenges. In: Geffert, V., et al. (eds.) SOFSEM. LNCS, vol. 4910, pp. 98–117. Springer, Berlin (2008)
13. Sandhu, R., Ranganathan, K., Zhang, X.: Secure information sharing enabled by trusted computing and pei models. In: ASIACCS 2006: Proceedings of the 2006 ACM Symposium on Information, Computer and Communications Security, pp. 2–12. ACM Press, New York (2006)
14. Schoder, D., Fischbach, K.: Core concepts in peer-to-peer (p2p) networking (2005)
15. Inc. Sun Microsystems. NFS: Network File System Protocol specification. RFC 1094, Internet Engineering Task Force (March 1989)
16. Trusted Computing Group. Infrastructure Working Group Architecture, Part II, Integrity Management. Specification version 1.0 Revision 1.0 (2006)
17. Trusted Computing Group. TPM Main, Part 1, Design Principles. Specification version 1.2 Revision 94 (2006)
18. Trusted Computing Group. TPM Main, Part 2, TPM Structures. Specification version 1.2 Revision 94 (2006)
19. Trusted Computing Group. TPM Main, Part 3, Design Principles. Specification version 1.2 Revision 94 (2006)
20. Weiss, A.: Will the open, unrestricted PC soon become a thing of the past? Journal of Trusted Computing 10(3), 18–25 (2006)
21. Yu, Y., Chiueh, T.: Display-only file server: A solution against information theft due to insider attack. In: Feigenbaum, J., Sander, T., Yung, M. (eds.) Proceedings of the 4th ACM workshop on Digital Rights Management, pp. 31–39. ACM Press, New York (2004)

Regulating Exceptions in Healthcare Using Policy Spaces

Claudio Agostino Ardagna[1], Sabrina De Capitani di Vimercati[1],
Tyrone Grandison[2], Sushil Jajodia[3], and Pierangela Samarati[1]

[1] University of Milan, Italy
[2] IBM Almaden Research Center, USA
[3] George Mason University, USA

Abstract. One truth holds for the healthcare industry - nothing should interfere with the delivery of care. Given this fact, the access control mechanisms used in healthcare to regulate and restrict the disclosure of data are often bypassed. This *"break the glass"* phenomenon is an established pattern in healthcare organizations and, though quite useful and mandatory in emergency situations, it represents a serious system weakness.

In this paper, we propose an access control solution aimed at a better management of exceptions that occur in healthcare. Our solution is based on the definition of different policy spaces regulating access to patient data and used to balance the rigorous nature of traditional access control systems with the prioritization of care delivery.

1 Introduction

Healthcare systems support interactions among patients, medical practitioners, insurance companies, and pharmacies. The very sensitive nature of the information managed by these systems requires the balance between two contrasting needs: the need for data, to guarantee a proper delivery of care, and the need for keeping data secure, to properly protect the privacy of patients. Access control is the base mechanism that healthcare systems adopt for protecting medical data. Traditional access control models and policies are based on the assumption that the authorizations regulating access are known in advance. However, since in healthcare systems an important requirement is that "nothing interferes with the delivery of care" [12], access control restrictions may need to be bypassed in case of emergencies and care delivery, especially when there is a risk for the patient's health. For instance, in case of emergency, a nurse may require (and should be granted access to) data that during the "normal" working she cannot access. This phenomenon is usually referred to as "break the glass". While useful and mandatory in the name of care delivery, such a situation may represent a weak point in the system that can easily be the target of abuses, for example, if breaking the glass becomes the norm [19].

The access control system should then be designed to be flexible and extensible, and should not be limited to a particular model or language (depending on

V. Atluri (Ed.): DAS 2008, LNCS 5094, pp. 254–267, 2008.

the context, different solutions might be utilized). Also, the access control system should minimize the uncertainty by limit those cases in which no regulation applies and the break the glass principle is used. Finally, the access control system should protect the privacy of the patients, and should not allow exchange of identity data that violates government legislations, such as, the Health Insurance Portability and Accountability Act (HIPAA) [15] in the United States.

In this paper, we address the need for developing a flexible and powerful access control system for healthcare scenario by proposing an access control model that attempts to balance, on the one hand, the rigorous nature of traditional access control models and, on the other hand, the priority of care delivery in healthcare. We introduce the definition of *policy spaces* regulating access to medical data and we describe how policies are specified and enforced within each space and how their combination works. Our approach regulates the whole set of accesses, which would otherwise fall into a possible "break the glass" policy, and is aimed at a better treatment of "unusual" access requests.

The remainder of this paper is organized as follows. Section 2 introduces policy spaces and describes the properties that an access control system for healthcare should satisfy. Section 3 illustrates the considered scenario and how the policies in the different spaces are defined. Section 4 describes the policy evaluation process and illustrates a possible use case. Section 5 discusses related work. Finally, Section 6 presents our concluding remarks.

2   Exception-Aware Access Control Spaces for Healthcare

Traditional access control models and languages (see Figure 1(a)) are based on the definition of two spaces: *authorized accesses* ($\mathcal{P}^+$), regulating common practice requests; and *unplanned exceptions* ($\mathcal{E}^U$), regulating all requests that are not managed by $\mathcal{P}^+$. Since nothing should interfere with the delivery of care, space $\mathcal{P}^+$ may be bypassed especially when a patient's health is at risk. In such situations, an access request that falls into space $\mathcal{E}^U$ is authorized although the requester was not previously allowed to access what she requests, thus enforcing the break the glass principle. This makes the system vulnerable to malicious users that may exploit the break the glass principle for breaching the patient's privacy also when it is not strictly necessary.

To limit the possible damages caused by the break the glass, we put forward the idea of defining a solution based on the following extended set of *policy spaces* (see Figure 1(b)).

Authorized Accesses ($\mathcal{P}^+$). It corresponds to traditional access control policies. Intuitively, $\mathcal{P}^+$ includes the authorizations regulating *'common practice'*.

Denied Accesses ($\mathcal{P}^-$). It corresponds to access control policies that are used to prevent abuses. Denials are meant to be strictly enforced and do not allow any exception. They can be specified *a priori* to eliminate accesses that should never be authorized (i.e., accesses that cannot be bypassed by the break the glass) or inserted *a posteriori* because of observed abuses.

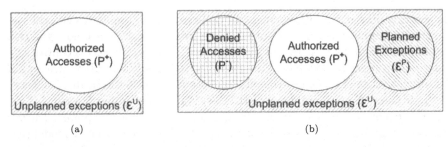

Fig. 1. Traditional access control (a); access control based on policy spaces (b)

Planned Exceptions $(\mathcal{E}^P)$. It corresponds to policies regulating access requests that do not fall into the normal routine as well as activities that should not be normally allowed. Policies in $\mathcal{E}^P$ are evaluated if and only if there are no applicable policies in $\mathcal{P}^+$ and $\mathcal{P}^-$, or applicable policies have no effect. This space regulates access requests that are managed as exceptions and can be foreseen, for example, according to past observations. Traditionally, space $\mathcal{E}^P$ is included in space $\mathcal{E}^U$.

Unplanned Exceptions $(\mathcal{E}^U)$. It corresponds to policies regulating all access requests not covered by the previous policy spaces $(\mathcal{P}^+, \mathcal{P}^-,$ and $\mathcal{E}^P)$. Accesses regulated by $\mathcal{E}^U$ are inserted into an auditing log for subsequent analysis and integration into the other spaces.

An important characteristic of these spaces is their *modularity*, since they are not limited to a particular access control model, language, or implementation. As a consequence, our solution allows the incorporation of policy languages that better suit the requirements of each particular situation. Furthermore, our spaces are fully compatible with traditional approaches and can be incrementally populated by analyzing accesses in $\mathcal{E}^U$ through an auditing process. In particular, the auditing process can show access requests that: *i)* correspond to common practice and should be explicitly permitted by appropriate policies in $\mathcal{P}^+$; *ii)* should be never admitted and should be explicitly denied by defining appropriate policies in $\mathcal{P}^-$; *iii)* are frequent but not common and should be captured by appropriate exceptions in $\mathcal{E}^P$.

As a result, the number of access requests granted by breaking the glass is considerably reduced and the probability of abuses decreases. Also, the modularity of our solution and the independence from the specific adopted language allow *backward compatibility* of the policy spaces definitions, meaning that our solution can immediately take the place of traditional access control models with limited effort.

3   Policy Spaces Language

We consider a scenario where *users* can connect to the system and make access requests of the form $\langle$*user_id, action, object, purposes*$\rangle$, where *user_id* is the unique identifier characterizing the requester, *action* is the action that is being requested, *object* is the object on which the requester wishes to perform the action and may correspond to the personal information of patients, and *purposes* is the purpose or a group thereof for which the object is requested. We assume that the personal information of patients is collected for the *purpose* of providing patient care. Also, in addition to the user id, each user is characterized by other properties (e.g., name, address) that are collected and stored into *profiles* associated with each user. A profile can therefore be seen as a container of pairs of the form ⟨*attribute_name,attribute_value*⟩, where *attribute_name* is the name of the attribute and *attribute_value* is its value. Such a user-related information is both *static* and *dynamic* in nature. Static information includes information that does not change or that does not change frequently (e.g., name, address, date of birth). Dynamic information includes context information that may depend on the specific user session. For instance, in healthcare systems based on the role-based access control model [20], the roles activated during a user session are an example of dynamic information that is stored within the corresponding user's profile.

Medical data to be protected are referred to as *datasets*. Each dataset is characterized by a unique *object identifier* (object id, for short). Datasets can be organized in classes containing groups of datasets that can be collectively referred to with a given name and are associated with *metadata* that provide additional contextual information.

We finally assume that for each of the spaces introduced, the policy evaluation can result in three outcomes: *i) true,* positive evaluation; *ii) false,* negative evaluation; *iii) unknown,* no applicable policy is found. Policy evaluations are then combined to grant or deny the access (we will discuss the policy evaluation process in Section 4).

3.1 Policies for Spaces $\mathcal{P}^+$ and $\mathcal{P}^-$

Policies in $\mathcal{P}^+$ regulate normal accesses and correspond to positive authorizations managed by traditional access control systems. For instance, an authorization can state that a user can access the medical data of her patients when she activates the Doctor or Nurse role.

Policies in space $\mathcal{P}^-$ correspond to access control policies that are used to prevent abuses. These policies represent negative authorizations and identify accesses to be denied. Denials are strictly enforced and do not allow exceptions, meaning that exception policies in $\mathcal{E}^P$ and $\mathcal{E}^U$ are evaluated if and only if negative authorizations in $\mathcal{P}^-$ do not apply or their evaluation is 'false'. The main goal of $\mathcal{P}^-$ policies is to limit the number of access requests evaluated in the exception spaces $\mathcal{E}^P$ and $\mathcal{E}^U$. Negative authorizations are specified *a priori* for those unwanted accesses that can be foreseen at system setup, or inserted *a posteriori* because of abuses observed through the analysis of audit logs produced by accesses in $\mathcal{E}^U$.

Our approach is orthogonal to the specific policy adopted for regulating access and allows for incorporating any policy model and language in spaces $\mathcal{P}^+$ and $\mathcal{P}^-$ [10,16].

3.2   Exception-Based Policies for Space $\mathcal{E}^P$

Space $\mathcal{E}^P$ allows the definition of fine-grained policies used to regulate requests that cannot be considered 'normal routine' and that usually fall in $\mathcal{E}^U$ (e.g., a nurse on duty can access medical data of patients entering the trauma ward). Among them, we consider:

- *emergency requests*, which include all accesses necessary to preserve the health of patients;
- *on demand requests*, which include all accesses requiring an interaction with patients.

By taking a look at these types of access requests, we note that there are situations where the application of the break the glass principle is constrained by the fact that some conditions *must* be satisfied for an access to be granted and that, if at least one condition is not satisfied, the access should not be granted. For instance, suppose that even in case of emergency, access to medical data can be allowed *only* to the medical staff. It is then easy to see that such a restriction cannot be simply represented as a rule stating that the medical staff can be authorized. In fact, while the single rule presents the desired behavior, its combination with other rules specified for the same subject, object, and action may not, since typically an access request is permitted when there is at least a rule that allows the request, thus violating the *only* constraint. From what we said, it is clear that an approach of specifying exceptions as positive permissions for the access is not sufficient. Consequently, even if we do not make any assumption on the language for specifying policies $\mathcal{E}^P$, we propose a language inspired by the work in [4,5] that supports the definition of two sets of rules: a set of *restrictions*, denoted $\mathcal{R}_E$, and a set of *authorizations*, denoted $\mathcal{A}_E$. Intuitively, restrictions are useful to specify requirements of the *only if* form stated above; while authorizations specify requirements in the traditional positive *if* form.

A *restriction* rule specifies requirements that are *necessary* (but not sufficient) to have the request satisfied and is defined as follow.

Definition 1 (Restriction rule). *A restriction rule has the form* ⟨*subject_id*⟩ [*WITH* ⟨*subject_expression*⟩] *CAN* ⟨*actions*⟩ *FOR* ⟨*purposes*⟩ *ON* ⟨*object_id*⟩ [*WITH* ⟨*object_expression*⟩] [*ONLYIF* ⟨*conditions*⟩] [*FOLLOW* ⟨*consequences*⟩], *where:*

- subject_id *and* object_id *are the identifiers of a user and object, respectively;*
- subject_expression *is a boolean formula of terms that allows referring to a set of subjects depending on whether they satisfy given conditions that can be evaluated on the subject's profile;*
- actions *is the action (or class of actions) to which the restriction refers;*
- object expression *is a boolean formula of terms that allows referring to a set of objects depending on whether they satisfy given conditions that can be evaluated on the object's metadata;*
- conditions *is a boolean formula of conditions that every request to which the restriction applies must satisfy;*

- consequences (*or obligations [2,8,9]*) *is a boolean formula of actions that must be either performed after an access has been granted or that need to be performed in the future, based on the occurrence of well defined events (e.g., time-based or context-based events);*
- purposes *denotes the purposes for which the information can be collected and used. In other words, purposes represent the reason for which an access is requested. Abstractions can be defined within the domain of purposes to refer to purposes with common characteristics and to refer to a whole group with a name.*

Lack to satisfy any of the restriction rules that apply to a given request implies the request will be denied. By definition, these rules are equivalent to negative authorizations, where *conditions* are negated, and are ANDed. In this work, we rely on restriction rules for planned exceptions, since they are usually more intuitive and easy to define than negative authorizations. Also, restriction rules give a clear separation between the expressions (i.e., *subject_expression* and *object_expression*) that are evaluated to identify the applicable rules, and the necessary conditions that the request have to satisfy. As an example, notice the difference between rules like "users can read data only if they are Doctors and fill in a form" and "Doctors can read data only if they fill in a form". The first rule prohibits access to non-doctor since the state of being a doctor is defined in the only if part of the rule and then represents a necessary condition to gain the access; the second rule instead uses the condition to be a doctor only as a condition of the applicability of the rule.

An *authorization* rule specifies permission to be satisfied to have the access granted and is defined as follow.

Definition 2 (Authorization rule). *An authorization rule has the form:* ⟨*subject_id*⟩ [*WITH* ⟨*subject_expression*⟩] *CAN* ⟨*actions*⟩ *FOR* ⟨*purposes*⟩ *ON* ⟨*object_id*⟩ [*WITH* ⟨*object_expression*⟩] [*IF* ⟨*conditions*⟩] [*FOLLOW* ⟨*consequences*⟩], *where* subject_id, object_id, subject_expression, actions, object_expression, consequences, *and* purposes *have the same syntax and semantics as in restrictions, and* conditions *is a boolean expression of conditions whose satisfaction authorizes the access.*

Authorization rules are similar to positive authorizations managed by traditional access control systems. In case multiple authorization rules are applicable to a given request (i.e., rules where the conditions before the IF part are satisfied), they are all evaluated and the results are ORed. Unlike for restrictions, lack of satisfaction of a condition in an authorization simply makes the authorization inapplicable but it does not imply that the access will be denied. In particular, access can be authorized if there is at least one authorization that applies to it for which the conditions are satisfied.

Syntactically, subject expressions, object expressions, conditions, and consequences are always represented as boolean formulas of terms of the form predicate_name(*arguments*), where *arguments* is a list, possible empty, of constants or attributes. Single attributes appearing in profiles of the users and

Table 1. An example of authorization and restriction rules in $\mathcal{E}^P$

Rule	Description
A1 *any* WITH equal(user.*role*,'*Nurse*') CAN *read* FOR *emergency* ON MedicalData WITH notequal(meta(object).*nurseId*, user.*id*) IF fill_in_form(*privacyform*)	A Nurse can read the Medical Data of patients not under her responsibility in case of emergencies after filling in a privacy form
A2 *any* WITH equal(user.*role*,'*Doctor*') CAN {*read, write*} FOR *emergency* ON MedicalData WITH notequal(meta(object).*doctorId*, user.*id*)	A Doctor can read or write the Medical Data of patients not under her responsibility in case of emergencies
A3 *any* WITH equal(user.*role*,'*PoliceMan*') CAN *read* FOR *investigation* ON MedicalData IF in(*time*, user.*startDuty*, user.*endDuty*) FOLLOW notify(meta(object).*dataOwner*)	A Police Man on duty can read the Medical Data of each patient in case of criminal investigation, notifying the data owner
R1 *any* WITH equal(user.*role*,'*Nurse*') CAN *read* FOR *emergency* ON MedicalData WITH notequal(meta(object).*nurseId*, user.*id*) ONLYIF in(*time*, user.*startDuty*, user.*endDuty*) FOLLOW {notify(meta(object).*dataOwner*), audit()}	A Nurse can read Medical Data of patients not under her responsibility in case of emergencies *only if* she is on duty, and notifying the data owner. Access must be audited
R2 *any* WITH equal(user.*role*,'*Doctor*') CAN {*read, write*} FOR *emergency* ON MedicalData WITH notequal(meta(object).*doctorId*, user.*id*) ONLYIF in(*time*, user.*startDuty*, user.*endDuty*)	A Doctor can read or write Medical Data of patients not under her responsibility in case of emergencies *only if* she is on duty
R3 *any* WITH equal(user.*affiliated*,'*yes*') CAN *read* FOR *emergency* ON MedicalData WITH notequal(meta(object).*doctorId*, user.*id*) ONLYIF notin(*time*, meta(object).*doctorId.startDuty*, meta(object).*doctorId.endDuty*) FOLLOW notify(meta(object).*doctorId*)	A user affiliated with the hospital can read Medical Data of patients not under her responsibility in case of emergencies *only if* the doctor responsible for the patient is not on duty and then notifying the doctor responsible for the patient

metadata associated with objects are referenced via the usual dot notation. For instance, `Alice.Address` indicates that `Alice` is the user id (and therefore the identifier for the corresponding profile), and `Address` is the property. Also, to refer to the requester (i.e., the subject) and the target (i.e., the object) of the request being evaluated without the need of introducing variables in the language, we use keywords **user** and **object**, respectively, whose appearances in a conditional expression are intended to be substituted with actual request parameters during run-time evaluation of the access control policy. Keyword *any* is used to refer to any subject id and object id, and function `meta(object_id)` is used to refer to the metadata associated with *object_id*.

The conditions specified in the *conditions* element of restriction and authorization rules can be classified into two main categories: *static* conditions, which are similar to subject expressions and evaluate conditions on users' profile; *dynamic* conditions, which can be brought to satisfaction at run-time processing of the request. For instance, `fill_in_form(`*privacyform*`)` is a dynamic condition that is evaluated to true if the privacy form has been filled in by the requester. Table 1 illustrates an example of authorization and restriction rules in $\mathcal{E}^P$.

Evaluation of Planned Exceptions. Restrictions and authorizations are evaluated separately. The set of applicable restriction rules $\mathcal{R}_E$ is first calculated. The applicable restriction rules are those rules for which their *subject_id, actions, object_id,* and *purposes* elements include the *user_id, action, object,* and *purposes* specified in the access request, and the profile associated with the *user_id* and the metadata of *object* satisfy all conditions specified in *subject_expression* and *object_expression*, respectively. If at least one applicable restriction rule in $\mathcal{R}_E$ is such that the *conditions* element evaluates to false, the access is denied. Otherwise, the applicable authorization rules in $\mathcal{A}_E$ are selected. If at least one applicable authorization rule is such that *conditions* element evaluates to true, the access is granted; if $\mathcal{A}_E$ is empty or all the applicable rules evaluate to false, the access request is redirected to $\mathcal{E}^U$.

3.3   Exception-Based Policies for Space $\mathcal{E}^U$

The space of unplanned exceptions $\mathcal{E}^U$ regulates those access requests that do not fall or cannot be evaluated in the spaces just introduced (i.e., $\mathcal{P}^+$, $\mathcal{P}^-$, and $\mathcal{E}^P$). Policies in $\mathcal{E}^U$ should be simple and must always grant access according to the break the glass principle since the promptness in reacting against exceptions is fundamental for preserving patients health. As a consequence, we adopt a solution different from the work in [17] where the concept of access request redirection is introduced to allow denied accesses in case of emergencies. In particular, space $\mathcal{E}^U$ regulates access by providing post-incident capabilities (i.e., auditing) to be used subsequently to better redistribute policies and requests among the spaces. The auditing process provides then logging facilities [3] that can be used a posteriori for overseeing the access requests in a given domain (e.g., a hospital department). To this aim, objects and classes of objects are associated with supervisors that are responsible for their management. Such supervisors monitor all the access requests that fall in $\mathcal{E}^U$ and directed to a set of objects in a given domain. Also, based on log files, they can take countermeasures for misbehaving subjects or formalizes common behavior by defining additional policies in spaces $\mathcal{P}^-$, and $\mathcal{P}^+$ or $\mathcal{E}^P$, respectively. Cross-domain activities will be managed by the collaboration of different supervisors. This allows the mitigation of the risk of malicious supervisors and incorrect policy definitions.

To better clarify the concept, suppose that an employee of the hospital responsible for cleaning the surgical equipment reads the type of patient disease to prepare the suitable cleaning protocol (as each cleaning protocol is different for each infectious diseases). For each request submitted by this employee and allowed in $\mathcal{E}^U$, an auditing process must be performed and the access is logged. Since, the request is perfectly admittable and should be always allowed, a policy should be defined in $\mathcal{E}^P$ by the supervisor to regulate this scenario. By contrast, suppose that a malicious employee, in addition to the type of patient disease, also accesses the personal data of the patient to sell them to an insurance company. In this case, the supervisor is able to apply remedies, for example, initiating termination procedures and defining additional policies in $\mathcal{P}^-$ to avoid other future, similar unauthorized accesses.

4   Policy Evaluation and Enforcement

When an access request is received the policies in the different spaces are evaluated and enforced in sequence. Figure 2 shows the policy evaluation flow, where each policy space is modeled as a box that receives as input an access request and returns as output an evaluation response (i.e., true, false, or unknown). Based on the response the access request is granted, denied or forwarded to another policy space.

Access Denied   **Access Granted**

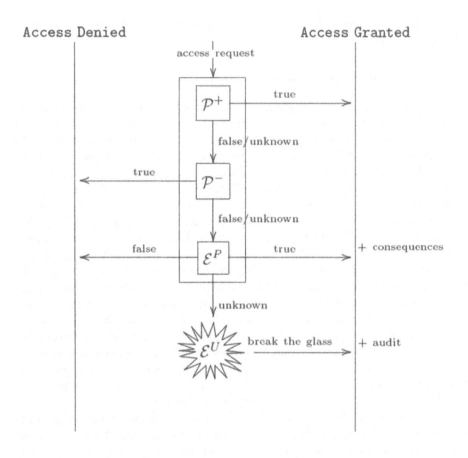

Fig. 2. Policy evaluation flow

First, policies in $\mathcal{P}^+$, which govern *'normal access'* to medical data, are evaluated against the access request. If the evaluation result is 'true', the access is granted. Otherwise, if there are no applicable policies ('unknown' evaluation) or the policies have no effect ('false' evaluation), the request is redirected and evaluated in space $\mathcal{P}^-$. If the result of the evaluation of policies in $\mathcal{P}^-$ is 'true', the access is denied. Otherwise, if there are no applicable policies ('unknown' evaluation) or the policies have no effect ('false' evaluation), the evaluation proceeds by evaluating exceptions in space $\mathcal{E}^P$.

Since policies in $\mathcal{E}^P$ are either authorization rules or restriction rules, the evaluation process in this space is more complex (see Section 3.2 for more details). If at least one applicable restriction in $\mathcal{R}_E$ is not satisfied, the evaluation result is 'false' and the request is denied. Otherwise, if all the applicable restrictions in $\mathcal{R}_E$ are satisfied (or $\mathcal{R}_E$ is empty) and at least one applicable authorization in $\mathcal{A}_E$ is satisfied, the evaluation result is 'true', the access request is granted and the possible involved *consequences* are enforced. If also the applicable authorizations are not satisfied (or $\mathcal{A}_E$ is empty) the request must be forwarded to space $\mathcal{E}^U$.

Here, the access request is inserted into a log file and is granted. The supervisor involved in the access request is then able to perform a subsequent analysis to possibly individuate abuses or access requests that should be regulated by the definition of a proper set of rules in spaces $\mathcal{P}^+$, $\mathcal{P}^-$, or $\mathcal{E}^P$.

4.1 Use Case

We consider the case of Timothy, who is four years old, and currently being examined at Mount Cedar (MC) Hospital. Timothy was brought into MC's first aid clinic by his mother, Eva, late Wednesday evening. The admitting staff observed that Timothy suffered from several contusions all over his body, a fractured rib and a distorted shoulder. There are main stakeholders in this scenario:

- *the child* who might have been abused;
- *the child's mother* who brought the child to the hospital;
- *the child's doctor* who is responsible for providing care to the child;
- *the child's nurse* who is responsible for helping the doctor;
- *the child's social worker* who is responsible for helping the child address the trauma or abuse;
- *the police man* who is responsible for investigating the case and establishing possible criminal charges and responsibilities.

The policies that govern access at MC's computer system are defined in Table 1. Let's walk through the events that would occur in this all too common situation.

Initially, Timothy's doctor in the first aid clinic, Dr Murthy, takes a history, fills in the electronic patient record, assigns the patient to a care team, and orders a series of examinations. When the results return, Dr Murthy suspects child abuse and initiates the protocol defined for cases of *suspected child abuse*.

As a consequence, the police and social services are informed of Timothy's situation. Now, the police officer responsible for the criminal investigation, Lt. Starke, requires access to Timothy's medical information. As this kind of request is neither *normal practice* nor an *access abuse*, the evaluation of policies $\mathcal{P}^+$ and $\mathcal{P}^-$ results in 'false' and the request is redirected to space $\mathcal{E}^P$ where policies in Table 1 are evaluated. No restriction rule is selected (unknown evaluation) and authorization rule A3 is selected and evaluates to true. According to the discussion in Section 3, access is allowed and Lt. Starke informs MC of the access.

At the same time, the social worker responsible for helping abused kids reported by MC's staff, Miss Woodrow, requests access to Timothy's health record. As was the case with Lt. Starke, neither the $\mathcal{P}^+$ nor the $\mathcal{P}^-$ policies evaluate to true and the request gets redirected to space $\mathcal{E}^P$. However, this time the $\mathcal{E}^P$ policy evaluation results in 'unknown', since no authorization and no restriction rules are applicable, which means the request is redirected to space $\mathcal{E}^U$. Here, access is granted to Miss Woodrow and because she has *broken the glass*, the supervisor is awakened and the audit process starts.

Since, Miss Woodrow's access is common in this case, the supervisor may define an additional policy in $\mathcal{E}^P$ to manage such a request in future and avoid further *break the glass* accesses.

Let's suppose that Timothy's health deteriorates and Dr Murthy is not on duty. If the current doctor on duty, Dr Wright, submits an access request to read Timothy's medical data, under emergency circumstances, then the request falls in $\mathcal{E}^P$ and the applicable rules are selected. If Dr Wright satisfies all applicable restriction rules (i.e., rules R2 and R3) and all applicable authorization rules (i.e., rule A2) in Table 1, she is given access to the data and Dr Murthy is informed of the access.

5   Related Work

A number of projects and research works about access control models and languages have been presented in the last few years [1,7,10,16], although they do not address the issues and requirements that characterize the healthcare scenario. Jajodia et al. [16] define the *Flexible Authorization Framework* (FAF), a powerful framework that addresses many traditional access control policies as well as many protection requirements existing in real world applications. FAF allows one to specify accesses to be granted or denied in a declarative manner by defining expressive logic-based rules. The FAF language allows the definition of both positive and negative authorizations. The framework incorporates notions of authorization derivation, conflict resolution, and decision strategies, which rely on the hierarchical organization of objects, users, groups, and roles. Bonatti et al. [6] provide an algebra for combining security policies, which are defined as expressions of the algebra, with its formal semantics. The authors define a policy composition framework allowing the integration of different component policies while retaining their independence. The authors define a translation of algebra expressions into equivalent logic programs, which represent the basis for the implementation of the language.

In this work, we do not aim at providing new access control languages, but rather we are focused on formalizing a language-independent model and infrastructure, which regulate the management of exceptions in healthcare. Below we describe some approaches for regulating exceptions. Gert [11] discusses how emergencies in a healthcare scenario are different from other situations. The author argues that same moral rules apply to all situations, although some actions are permissible in emergencies situations only. Reichert and Dadam [18] study the problem of applying workflow management systems to dynamic business processes. The authors present a formal foundation for the support of dynamic structural changes of running workflow instances and criteria to identify and handling the possible exceptions resulting from a workflow change. Han et al. [14] analyze the problem of managing medical workflow exceptions by giving an overview of past works in such a field and by proposing future research issues and solutions. The paper is focused on three main topics that would improve the quality of the medical procedures: representing, handling, and analyzing exceptions. Rostad and Odsberg [19] claim that exception mechanisms used to ensure access in critical situations increase the threats to patient privacy. Also, they provide an analysis of access log that results in a study of access control requirements for healthcare systems. In particular, using audit trails of access logs of Central Norway Health Region (CNHR), they aim at uncover information about the real user needs to provide a better access control mechanism for healthcare. Gupta et al. [13] provide a criticality-aware access control model for pervasive applications based on the calculation of a criticality level depending on critical events that happen in the system. Based on such a criticality level, they define two access control modes: a normal mode and a criticality-aware access control mode, which exploits a *promoterole* function improving the role privileges of the users to manage such critical cases. With respect to our solution, we do not provide different access control modes. Rather we provide a traditional positive authorization space together with several spaces managing access control exceptions. These spaces manage critical situations through the definition of policies supporting context-based conditions. Also our solution never changes users classifications or privileges for managing emergencies or critical events, but it defines policies to be considered in requests that do not satisfy traditional access control policies. Keppler et al. [17] discuss the problem of managing requests that are denied, by providing a range of other possible actions to use in emergencies situations. The framework extends the Flexible Authorization Framework (FAF) [16] with a sharing policy language for request and data redirection. Finally, Bhatti and Grandison [3] provide PRIMA, a system that improves privacy policies satisfaction in healthcare scenario. The implemented solution is based on the concepts of policy coverage and refinement. In particular, the coverage between the ideal state of the system, that is, the policy defined by system administrator, privacy officer, and the like, and the real state of the system, that is, the policies logically tied to the audit logs, is calculated and then a refinement of policies is provided aimed at maximizing policy coverage itself.

6   Conclusions

We presented an exception-based access control solution whose main goal is to better control the break the glass attempts in healthcare systems to reduce possible breaches in the patients' privacy. We introduced the definition of policy spaces that balance the rigorous nature of traditional access control systems with the prioritization of care delivery. We illustrated how policies are specified and enforced within each space, and how these policy spaces are combined.

Acknowledgments

The research leading to these results has received funding from the European Union within the 6FP project PRIME under contract n° IST-2002-507591, the European Community's Seventh Framework Programme (FP7/2007-2013) under grant agreement n° 216483, and the Italian MIUR within PRIN 2006 under project n° 2006099978.

References

1. Ardagna, C., Cremonini, M., De Capitani di Vimercati, S., Samarati, P.: A privacy-aware access control system. Journal of Computer Security (JCS) (to appear, 2008)
2. Bettini, C., Jajodia, S., Wang, X.S., Wijesekera, D.: Provisions and obligations in policy management and security applications. In: Proc. of the 28th Conference Very Large Data Bases (VLDB 2002), Hong Kong, China, (August 2002)
3. Bhatti, R., Grandison, T.: Towards improved privacy policy coverage in healthcare using policy refinement. In: Proc. of the 4th VLDB Workshop on Secure Data Management 2007, Vienna, Austria (September 2007)
4. Bonatti, P., Damiani, E., De Capitani di Vimercati, S., Samarati, P.: An access control system for data archives. In: Proc. of the 16th International Conference on Information Security, Paris, France (June 2001)
5. Bonatti, P., Damiani, E., De Capitani di Vimercati, S., Samarati, P.: A component-based architecture for secure data publication. In: Proc. of the 17th Annual Computer Security Applications Conference (ACSAC 2001), New Orleans, Louisiana, USA (December 2001)
6. Bonatti, P., De Capitani di Vimercati, S., Samarati, P.: An algebra for composing access control policies. ACM Transactions on Information and System Security 5(1), 1–35 (2002)
7. Bonatti, P., Samarati, P.: A unified framework for regulating access and information release on the web. Journal of Computer Security (JCS) 10(3), 241–272 (2002)
8. Casassa Mont, M.: Dealing with Privacy Obligations: Important Aspects and Technical Approaches. In: Katsikas, S.K., López, J., Pernul, G. (eds.) TrustBus 2004. LNCS, vol. 3184, Springer, Heidelberg (2004)
9. Casassa Mont, M., Beato, F.: On parametric obligation policies: Enabling privacy-aware information lifecycle management in enterprises. In: Proc. of the 8th IEEE Workshop on Policies for Distributed Systems and Networks (Policy 2007), Bologna, Italy (June 2007)
10. eXtensible Access Control Markup Language (XACML) Version 2.0 (February 2005),
    http://docs.oasis-open.org/xacml/2.0/access_control-xacml-2.0-core-spec-os.pdf
11. Gert, H.: How are emergencies different from other medical situations? The Mount Sinai Journal OF Medicine - Issues in Medical Ethics Conference on Special Challenges of Emergency Medicine 72(4), 216–220 (2005)
12. Grandison, T., Davis, J.: The impact of industry constraints on model-driven data disclosure controls. In: Proc. of the 1st International Workshop on Model-Based Trustworthy Health Information Systems (MOTHIS) 2007, Nashville, Tennessee, USA (September 2007)
13. Gupta, S., Mukherjee, T., Venkatasubramanian, K.: Criticality aware access control model for pervasive applications. In: Proc. of the Fourth Annual IEEE International Conference on Pervasive Computing and Communications (PERCOM 2006), Pisa, Italy (March 2006)

14. Han, M., Thiery, T., Song, X.: Managing exceptions in the medical workflow systems. In: Proc. of the 28th international conference on Software engineering (ICSE 2006), Shanghai, China (May 2006)
15. Health Insurance Portability and Accountability Act,
    http://www.dhhs.gov/ocr/hipaa/
16. Jajodia, S., Samarati, P., Sapino, M., Subrahmanian, V.: Flexible support for multiple access control policies. ACM Trans. Database Syst. 26(2), 214–260 (2001)
17. Keppler, D., Swarup, V., Jajodia, S.: Redirection policies for mission-based information sharing. In: Proc. of the ACM Symposium on Access control Models and Technologies (SACMAT 2006), Lake Tahoe, California, USA (June 2006)
18. Reichert, M., Dadam, P.: Adeptflex-supporting dynamic changes of workflows without losing control. Journal of Intelligent Information Systems (JIIS) 10(2), 93–129 (1998)
19. Rostad, L., Edsberg, O.: A study of access control requirements for healthcare systems based on audit trails from access logs. In: Proc. of the 22nd Annual Computer Security Applications Conference on Annual Computer Security Applications Conference (ACSAC 2006) (December 2006)
20. Sandhu, R., Ferraiolo, D., Kuhn, D.: The NIST model for role based access control: Towards a unified standard. In: Proc. of the 5th ACM Workshop on Role Based Access Control, Berlin, Germany (July 2000)

Towards Automation of Testing High-Level Security Properties

Aiman Hanna, Hai Zhou Ling, Jason Furlong, and Mourad Debbabi*

Computer Security Laboratory, CIISE,
Concordia University, Montreal (QC), Canada
{ahanna,ha_ling}@encs.concordia.ca,
furlong.jc@forces.gc.ca, debbabi@ciise.concordia.ca

Abstract. Many security problems only become apparent after software is deployed, and in many cases a failure has occurred prior to the awareness of the problem. Although many would argue that the simpler solution to the problem would be to test the software before deploying it. Although we support this argument, we understand that it is not necessarily applicable in a modern development environment. Software testing is labor intensive and is very expensive from a time and cost perspective. While much research has been undertake to automate software testing, very little has been directed at security testing. Additionally, the majority of these efforts have targeted low-level security (safety) instead of high-level security. In this paper, we present elements of a solution towards automation of testing security properties and for the generation of test data suites for detecting security vulnerabilities in software.

Keywords: Security Testing, Dynamic Analysis, Data Dependency, Test Data Generation, Control Flow Analysis.

1 Introduction

When Von Neumann published his famous architecture in June of 1945, as part of the first draft of EDVAC, he might have anticipated, the potential power of that architecture. The evolution from a strictly single-function piece of hardware to a system that can behave in dramatically different ways through the use of software is is a significant technological advancement that has been exploited by virtually every major industry. However, it is unfortunate that the exponential growth of software in the past few decades has not met with an equivalent, or even relative, growth of concern with respect to software security. Although the problem is much more visible today than few years ago, security problems are still present even in most trusted software, such as operating systems. Many security problems only become apparent after software is deployed, and in many cases a

---

* This research is the result of a fruitful collaboration between CSL (Computer Security Laboratory) of Concordia University, DRDC (Defence Research and Development Canada) Valcartier and Bell Canada under the NSERC DND Research Partnership Program.

V. Atluri (Ed.): DAS 2008, LNCS 5094, pp. 268–282, 2008.

failure has occurred prior to the awareness of the problem. Software testing is the most prominent way to eliminate many of these problems. While considerable research energies have been expended to automate software testing, very little has been directed at security testing. In order to find a security vulnerability in a program, four questions need to be answered:

1. What security property need to be tested?
2. How can security analyst state the property in concern?
3. How vulnerabilities can be located?
4. How test data can be generated to prove that a vulnerability not only exists, but will indeed take effect?

This list emphasizes that the range and nature of possible security vulnerabilities in software is very broad and detecting one of these vulnerabilities or another may require totally different approaches. Many vulnerabilities can be detected through static analysis of the source code. For instance, the password aging vulnerability, which occurs when a system does not enforce the policy that passwords need to be changed over time, has the potential to diminish password integrity. Yet, static analysis is sufficient for detecting vulnerabilities such as these. This can be achieved by checking for the existence of routines that validate the timestamp on passwords and then ensuring that the system utilizes these routines. While static analysis can be very useful in detecting many types of vulnerabilities, others will remain hidden. In such cases, dynamic analysis is needed. The focus of our research is on the detection of security vulnerabilities where dynamic-analysis needs to be conducted.

The answer to the first question falls within the domain of the security analyst. In answering the second and third questions, we have previously introduced extensions to GCC for code instrumentation, as well as Team Edit Automata (TEA) [14]. Used together, these promise to be a powerful tool for the analyst to state security properties, both formally and efficiently for the detection of a wide range of safety and security vulnerabilities.

In this paper, we provide elements of an answer to the fourth question, which concerns the generation of test data for testing security vulnerabilities. Previously published research has focussed on the following approaches: random test data generation [1], directed random test data generation [9], genetic and evolutionary algorithms [5,6], path-oriented test data generation [2,4,7], goal-oriented [10], and the chaining approach [8]. These approaches use different types of information to achieve their goals: Some of them rely on the control flow of the program, while others rely on data dependency to guide their search process. While we highly regard each of these approaches, we need to point that the classification of these approaches as whether or not they are viable depends on the desired outcome. Path-oriented approaches, which rely on control flow analysis, can be viewed as very useful if full path coverage is needed. If the desired goal is to achieve a specific program target, then a path-oriented approach may be very inefficient since a lot of search effort may be wasted exploring parts of the program that have no relation to the target. Goal-oriented approaches, which attempt to lead program execution towards a specific target may also fail for the same reason because they too depend on control flow analysis. Frequently, finding approaches that are both efficient and exacting, require executing parts of the program that are seemingly, from control flow graph perspective, unrelated to the solution [11]. The chaining approach uses both control flow and data dependency analyses that generate test data to reach designated targets in the code.

While none of these approaches targets security testing specifically, we view the chaining approach as as the most likely to facilitate efficient security testing. The nature of many security vulnerabilities is such that they tend to occur at identifiable locations in the code which we will designate *security targets*.

In the next section, we briefly present the chaining approach and its limitations in terms of testing for security properties. Section 3 provides a brief description of some of the most significant low-level and high-level security vulnerabilities. In Section 4, we present the security chaining approach. Section 5 provides an overview of our system and finally, Section 6 provides a conclusion of the work presented in this paper.

2   The Chaining Approach

The main goal of the chaining approach [8] is to find a data set with which a program execution can reach a specific node, referred to as the target node. The target is a node in the Control Flow Graph (CFG), which represents the objective of the test analysis. A simple definition of the approach is as follows: Given node Y in a program, the goal is to find a program input x on which node Y will be executed. The approach is an extension to the goal-oriented approach [12]. The goal-oriented approach classifies the different branches of a program as: *critical, semi-critical, non-essential,* and *required.* A branch is critical if and only if the execution of this branch would permanently drive the execution away from the target node. A semi-critical branch would also drive the execution away from the target node, but not permanently; i.e. through the execution of the back branch of a loop, the program execution may return back to a previous node where alternative branches leading to the target can be taken. A branch is a non-essential if the execution, or non-execution, of this branch does not affect reaching the target. A required branch is a branch that must be executed for the program to reach the target. To illustrate the approach, consider the C++ code fragment given in Figure 1, and its corresponding control flow graph shown in Figure 2.

Since goal-oriented approach relies merely on control flow analysis, both branches to nodes 6 and 8 are considered to be non-essential. That is the case since the execution of either branch will eventually lead back to node 4, and assuming that the loop at that node is not infinite, the execution will either way move towards the target, node 12. The goal-oriented approach will fail since the execution of node 9, which is treated as a part of a non-essential branch, is actually vital to reaching the target.

The chaining approach overcomes this shortcomings by extending the goal-oriented approach to consider data analysis as well. The approach views the

```
void GoOrientedApproach() {
1    int i1 = 0, i2 = 0, i3 = 0, i4 = 0, i5 = 0, i6 = 0;
2    cout << "Enter 4 Integers: ";
3    cin >> i1 >> i2 >> i3 >> i4 >> i5;
4    while (i1 < 10) {
5        if (i5==12) {
6            cout << "Point1" << endl;
7            i6++;
         }
         else {
8            cout << "Point2" << endl;
9            i1 *= 10;
         }
10       i1++;
     }
11   i2++;
12   if (i2 < 10) {
13       i3 = i2 - 1;
14       if (i3 % 2 == 0) {
15           cout << "Point3" << endl;
16           i2++;
17           if(i3 > 5) {
18               if (i6 > 0) {
19                   cout << "Target Point" << endl;
                 }
                 else {
20                   i3 -=5;
21                   cout << "Point 4" << endl;
                 }
22               i3--;
             }
         }
     }
     else {
23       i4 = i3--;
24       i5 = i2 + 4;
25       if (i4 == i5) {
26           cout << "Point9" << endl;
         }
         else {
27           cout << "Point10" << endl;
         }
28       cout << "Point11" << endl;
     }
}
```

Fig. 1. Sample Source Code

problem as the set of one goal and multiple subgoals. Assume that data generation is required for some variable in order to reach the target. The approach starts in an identical fashion to the goal-oriented; it randomly selects a input value x_0 and executes the program with this value, then monitors the execution to detect if a critical path is reached. If the execution leads to the target then the goal has been reached and x_0 is the solution to the test data generation problem. However, if a violation occurs along the execution path; that is, a critical path is executed, the approach terminates the execution and considers the node where execution led to a critical branch to be a *problem node*. The focus of the approach at that point shifts from the goal to the subgoal, which is passing through the problem node towards the target. To solve the subgoal, the chaining approach uses a function minimization technique to find an alternative value that will execute the program at the problem node. If a value is found then the execution continues, with the possibility of hitting another problem node whereupon the

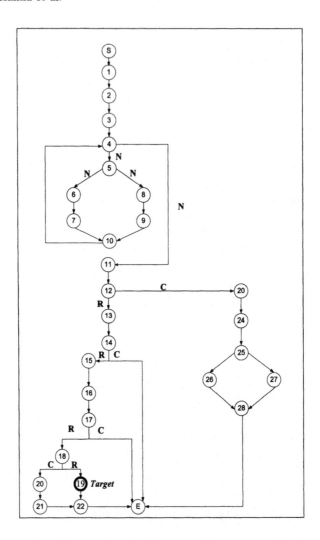

Fig. 2. Corresponding Control Flow of Code in Figure 1

process recursively repeats itself. If, however, function minimization fails to find an alternative value, then the approach switches to a data dependency analysis. To illustrate the idea, we must recall some of the basic concepts considered by the approach as given in [8].

- A flow graph of program Q is a directed graph $C = (N, A, s, e)$ where N is a set of nodes, A is a binary relation on N (a subset of $N \times N$), referred to as a set of edges, and s and e are, respectively, unique entry and unique exit nodes, $s, e \in N$.
- A *node* in N corresponds to the smallest single-entry, single-exit executable part of a statement in Q that cannot be further decomposed.

- An *edge* $(n_i, n_j) \in A$ corresponds to a possible transfer of control from instruction n_i to instruction n_j.
- An *edge* (n_i, n_j) is called a *branch* if (n_i) is a test instruction. Each branch in the control flow graph can be labeled by a predicate, referred to as a branch predicate, describing the conditions under which the branch will be traversed.
- A *use* of variable v is a statement (or predicate) that uses (references) this variable, such as `y=v+1; print(v); if (v!=0){..}`, etc.
- A *definition* of variable v is a statement that assigns a value to this variable, such as `v=15; input (v);` etc.
- Let $U(n)$ be a set of variables whose value are used at node n, and let $D(n)$ be a set of variables whose values are defined at n. There exists a data flow (data dependence) between statement S_1 and S_2 if: (1) S_1 is a definition of variable v, (2) S_2 is a use of variable v, and (3) there exists a path in the program from S_1 to S_2 along which v is not modified.
- A *definition-clear* path from n_{k_1} to n_{k_q} with respect to variable v is a path in the control flow graph, such that: (1) v is defined at n_{k_1}, (2) used at n_{k_q}, and (3) it was not modified along the path between n_{k_1} and n_{k_q}; more formally $1 < i < q, v \notin D(n_{k_i})$.
- *Last definition*: Let p be a node and v be a variable used in p. Last definition of v at node p is defined as follows: A node n, which satisfies the following conditions: (1) v belongs to $D(n)$, (2) v belongs to $U(p)$, and (3) there exists a definition-clear path of v from n to p. Consequently, a *set of last definitions* $LD(p)$ is defined as the set of all last definitions of all variables used in p.

Now, let us revisit Figure 1. The chaining approach starts executing the program with an initial random value x_0. If this input value leads to the target then a solution is found. Assume however, that the execution successfully reaches node 18 but then the critical branch is taken at that node. The approach then attempts to solve that first subgoal, which is to find a value that will still preserve the execution to go all the way to node 18 (this is a constraint), but then changes the execution at that problem node p. Consequently, this is a minimization problem with constraints. If the attempt is successful, then a solution is found; otherwise, the approach attempts to alter the execution at node p by identifying the nodes that have to be executed prior to reaching this node. Effectively, the approach finds a set $LD(p)$ of last definitions of all variables used at problem node p then requires that these nodes be executed prior to the execution of p. By enforcing such a requirement, the chances of altering the execution flow at a problem node may be increased, and hence the desired branch is taken. Such a sequence of nodes to be executed is referred to as an *event sequence* (or *chain*).

An event sequence E is a sequence $\langle e_1, e_2, .., e_k \rangle$ of events, where each event is a tuple $e_i = (n_i, S_i)$ where n_i is a node and S_i a set of variables referred to as a *constraint set*. For every two adjacent events, $e_i = (n_i, S_i)$ and $e_{i+1} = (n_{i+1}, S_{i+1})$ there exists a definition-clear path with respect to S_i from n_i to n_{i+1}.

Generally, event sequences are generated as follows. Initially, for a given target node g, the following event sequence is created: $E_0 = \langle (s, \phi), (g, \phi) \rangle$ If during

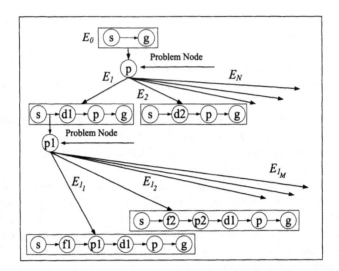

Fig. 3. A Partial Search Tree Generated by the Chaining Approach

program execution, a problem node p is encountered, then: First, find all last definitions at p, $LD(p) = (d_1, d_2, ..., d_N)$, where d_i is a node where last definition of variables at p occurred. Second, Use that set to generate N event sequences. Each newly generated event sequence contains:

- An event associated with problem node p, and
- An event associated with last definition d_i

Consequently, the following event sequences are generated:

$$E_1 = \langle (s, \phi), (d_1, D(d_1)), (p, \phi), (g, \phi) \rangle$$
$$E_2 = \langle (s, \phi), (d_2, D(d_2)), (p, \phi), (g, \phi) \rangle$$
$$\vdots$$
$$E_N = \langle (s, \phi), (d_N, D(d_N)), (p, \phi), (g, \phi) \rangle$$

The approach then selects one of the chains and attempts to find a solution. If another problem node occurred in that chain, a similar list is made as above with this new problem node and its previous LD node included in the chain. For instance, assume E_1 is selected, and that another problem node p_1 is encountered in the execution of E_1. Assume $LD(p_1) = (f_1, f_2, \ldots, f_M)$, then the following event sequences are created:

$$E_{1_1} = \langle (s, \phi), (f_1, D(f_1)), (p_1, \phi), (d_1, D(d_1)), (p, \phi), (g, \phi) \rangle$$
$$E_{1_2} = \langle (s, \phi), (f_2, D(f_2)), (p_1, \phi), (d_1, D(d_1)), (p, \phi), (g, \phi) \rangle$$
$$\vdots$$
$$E_{1_M} = \langle (s, \phi), (f_M, D(f_M)), (p_1, \phi), (d_1, D(d_1)), (p, \phi), (g, \phi) \rangle$$

The process repeats which effectively results in a search tree being created, where E_0 is the root and any other generated event sequence is a child. The chaining approach traverses that search tree in a depth-first fashion, attempting to find an event sequence E for which a program input that executes that selected event sequence is found. A general search tree generated by the approach is partially shown in Figure 3.

3 Low-Level and High-Level Security

The range and nature of security vulnerabilities in software is quite broad. However, at higher abstractions, security vulnerabilities can be classified as either low-level (safety), or high-level (security). For the sake of brevity, we will only indicate some of the most significant.

3.1 Low-Level Vulnerabilities - Safety

Examples of low-level security vulnerabilities include: Buffer Overflow,Heap-based Exploitation, Stack-based Exploitation, Integer Overflow, File Management, and Memory Management.

3.2 High-Level Vulnerabilities - Security

Examples of high-level security vulnerabilities include: Authentication, Privilege Escalation, Inappropriate Authorization, Access Control, Integrity, Confidentiality, Non-Repudiation, Availability, and Cryptographic Vulnerabilities.

4 The Security Chaining Approach

Since the range of security vulnerabilities is quite varied, we must emphasis that a single solution capable of handling all types of vulnerabilities is not feasible. Different solutions for handling specific vulnerabilities, or a group of vulnerabilities, remains within the realm of possibility. In previous work [14], we presented *Team Edit Automata* (TEA) as a powerful model for stating and enforcing safety and security properties. TEA is partially based on *Security Automata* [13] which is proven capable of enforcing all safety properties as well as a limited set of security properties. Building on this research, we will now extend it to facilitate the automatic testing of security vulnerabilities through the security chaining approach.

While we regard the chaining approach well suited for test-data generation, the approach may fail, as it is not intended for security testing. There are many cases where the reachability of a target is insufficient for the detection of security vulnerabilities. To illustrate the idea, let us look at the simple example in Figure 4; the control flow graph corresponding to that code is shown in Figure 5. The program verifies user's role, solicits a PIN from the user, encrypts that PIN, and then sends the encrypted PIN over a network if certain conditions are met. The security analyst is interested in testing the software against a specific security property: All PINs sent over the network must be encrypted.

```
void EncryptAndTransmit() {
1    long int pin, epin;
2    int x1, x2, x3, x4, x5, x6;
3    cin >> x1 >> x2 >> x3 >> x4 >> x5 >> x6;
4    if (x1 > 10) {
5        x4++;
6        if(x2 > x3) {
7            cout << "User Detected as Admin. Enter Admin PIN:";
8            cin >> pin;
9            epin = encrypt(pin);
         }
         else {
10           if(x4 > 12) {
11               cout << "User Detected as Controller. Enter Controller PIN:";
12               cin >> pin;
13               epin = encrypt(pin);
             }else {
14               cout << "User Detected as Supervisor. Enter Supervisor PIN:";
15               cin >> pin;
16               epin = pin;
             }
17           x6 += 25;
         }
18       x6 += 10;
     }
     else {
19       if(x4 > 20) {
20           if(x5 > 15) {
21               x6 += 65;
22               cout << "User Detected as Personal. Enter Personal PIN:";
23               cin >> pin;
24               epin = encrypt(pin);
             }
             else {
25               x6 += 15;
26               cout << "User Detected as Tester. Enter Tester PIN:";
27               cin >> pin;
28               epin = encrypt(pin);
             }
29           x6 -= 4;
         }
         else {
30           cout << "User with Insufficient Permission -Program Will Terminate!.";
31           exit(1);
         }
     }
32   if (x6 > 50) {
33       cout << "User Permission does not Allow Remote Connection.";
     }
     else {
34       cout << "Permissions OK. Encrypted PIN will be Sent Over the Network.";
35       Open_Net_Connection(epin);
     }
36   cout << "Thanks for Using Secure Software! ";
 }
```

Fig. 4. Sample Code for Sending Encrypted Password Over a Network

Clearly, node 35, where the encrypted PIN is sent, is "a" target here. It is also clear that there are multiple paths from start to this node. From the chaining approach point of view, there is only one goal, which is to generate test data to reach this node. However, from security testing point of view, there are multiple goals that must be achieved in parallel to detect any vulnerability. One goal is still to reach node 35. If this node is not reachable, then this code suffers from the availability security vulnerability. Another goal that must be considered is the path taken to reach this target. When the chaining approach attempts to generate test data, it may go through the usual process of hitting problem nodes, attempting to alter executions, generating search trees and

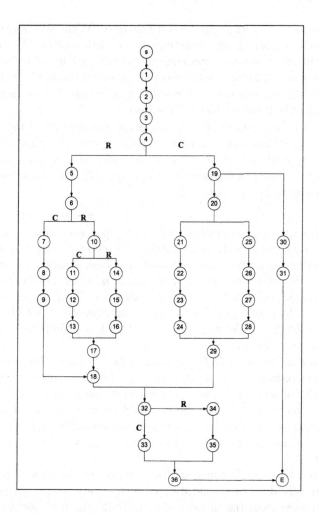

Fig. 5. Corresponding Control Flow Graph of Code in Figure 4

traversing it in depth-first fashion. A successful analysis may generate the following: $x1 = 15, x2 = 1, x3 = 5, x4 = 20, x5 = 10, x6 = 75$, which allows the program to traverse to the target node through the following path: $S \rightarrow 1 \rightarrow 2 \rightarrow 3 \rightarrow 4 \rightarrow 5 \rightarrow 6 \rightarrow 10 \rightarrow 11 \rightarrow 12 \rightarrow 13 \rightarrow 17 \rightarrow 18 \rightarrow 32 \rightarrow 34 \rightarrow 35$. However, such an execution does not suffer any security problems since the PIN would be encrypted at node 13 before being sent at node 35. One possible solution to the problem is to use the chaining approach to generate test data to reach the target, while concurrently executing a finite state machine (FSM) to monitor the status of the encrypted PIN, *ePass*, so that it can only be sent if it is in an encrypted state (that is being assigned a returned value from the *encrypt* function); otherwise the FSM enters an error state. However, this solution will fail for the same reason. If the data generated by the chaining approach is as above then the FSM will not detect any vulnerabilities. Another approach to test the security property in concern, is to use static analysis. While this may work, there is the potential of reporting false negatives. Since static analysis does not require program execution, it has no knowledge of the reachability of a specific point. Consequently, static analysis would report all potential problems, including false positives, which is not scalable to a real-life application. The security chaining approach eliminates these problems altogether.

In addition to the primary goal, which is the reachability of the target, the security chaining approach considers other goals. Specifically, this approach considers another type of event sequence (chains), referred to as the *security chain*, which is directly related to the security property itself. The following basic concepts are introduced by our approach:

- *Security Target*: A security target t is a node that must be: (1) reached, and (2) directly affecting/controlling the security property under test.
- *Last Security Definition*: Let s be a statement related to the security property under scrutiny and v be a variable used in s. Last security definition of v at statement s is defined as follows: A statement n, which satisfies the following conditions:(1) v belongs to $D(n)$, (2) v belongs to $U(s)$, and (3) there exists a definition-clear path of v from n to s. Consequently, a *set of last security definitions* $LSD(s)$ is defined as the set of all last definitions of all security related variables used in s.
- *Undesired Last Security Definition*: Let s be a security target statement - a statement related to the security property under scrutiny. Undesired Last Security Definition is a statment/node n such that if execution goes through that node, no security vulnerability would occur at the security target, s. Consequently, a *set of undesired last security definitions* $ULSD(s)$ is defined as the set of all undesired last definitions of all security related variables used in s.
- A path in a CFG is classified as either *critical* or *required*. A path is critical if and only if: (1) the execution of such a path would permeably drive execution away from the target node, "OR" (2) the path includes a node n that belongs to $ULSD(s)$, where s is the target node. A required path is a branch that: (ι) must be taken in order to reach a target, and ($\iota\iota$) is a part of a path to the target that does not include critical branches.
- *Predomination*: A node n predominates a node k if and only if: (1) There is a path from n to k, and (2) There is no possible way for node k to be reached unless node n is reached.

To illustrate the idea, let us revisit Figure 4 and its CFG shown in Figure 5. The first goal of the approach is to reach node 35, where the security target, the variable *ePIN*, is present. However, reaching that target must be forced through a very specific path for the approach to report a security vulnerability at the given code. The approach starts in an identical fashion to the chaining approach, flagging all critical paths that would permanently lead execution away from the target. The approach then, through code instrumentation and static analysis, detects all the $LSD(\_)$ of the target node (that is $LSD(statement\_at\_node\_35)$ in our example). The approach then flags all undesired last definitions. In our

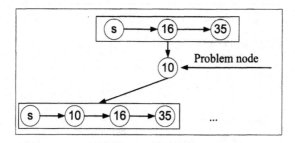

Fig. 6. Search Tree Generated by the Security Chaining Approach

example, there are five $LSD(\_)$ located at nodes 9, 13, 16, 24 and 28. However, nodes 9, 13, 24 and 28 are all flagged as undesired last definitions, since the execution of these nodes would immediately lead to the security property being preserved. At that moment, the approach has one final goal, which is to generate test data to reach node 35 through node 16.

The approach definition of critical paths is significantly different than the one defined by the chaining approach. After the security chaining approach finds an undesired last definition, the approach finds the immediate test node that predominates this node and flags the branch from this test node towards the undesired last definition node as critical. Effectively, all undesired execution paths are eliminated. The approach then attempts to generate test data, in a similar fashion to the one used by the chaining approach. If the generation is successful, then a solution is found; which means a security vulnerability is detected. If all attempts fail to generate the test data, then the path is treated as impossible and no vulnerability is detected by the approach. It should be noted that false negatives are eliminated here since either the approach would report the problem with a set of test data that proves its existence, or nothing is reported if a path is thought of to be impossible after the approach has exhausted all attempts. It should also be noted that the order of flagging paths as critical is important, since it significantly reduces the search overhead. For instance, node 21 in Figure 4 is a chaining approach last definition of variable $x6$ at node 32. However, attempts to alter execution at node 32, should it become a problem node, through the execution of node 21 would never be considered, since this path is already flagged as critical because of the security chaining approach undesired last definition node(node 24).

Effectively, the security chaining approach would result in the generation of only those event sequences that are needed to be executed for security vulnerabilities to be detected. Each one of those event sequences would construct a search tree. In contrast to chaining approach which terminates the search upon one success, the security chaining approach would attempt each one of those trees, since each one represents a potential vulnerability. If the approach cannot find a solution to traverse a tree, then this tree is considered impossible, and hence no vulnerability is detected or reported, eliminating all false positives.

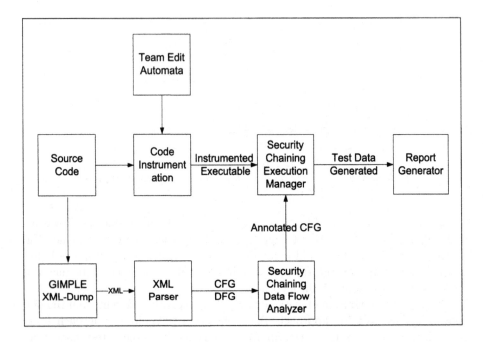

Fig. 7. A High-level View of the System Architecture

For instance, considering the code in figure 4, the approach would initially create a single event sequence, shown in figure 6, which would evolve to a search tree should problem nodes are encountered.

5   Framework Architecture

A high-level view of our system architecture is shown in Figure 7. The System contains 7 main components:

1. GCC Extension for Code Instrumentation: This extension is able to instrument any code at a variety of program points in a source code. This tool injects the additional code which monitors the dynamic behavior of the program.
2. Team Edit Automata: This component describes the security property as selected by the security analyst. The Team Edit Automata model combines the powerful enforcing capabilities of Edit Automata into the component-interactive architectural model defined by Team Automata. The resulting model is a team composed of one or multiple components of edit automata. A team edit automaton connects its component automata through action signatures - definitions that designate the source and destination of actions.
3. GCC Extension for XML-Dump: GCC Extension for GIMPLE XML dumping [3]. The purpose of the tools is to dump the GIMPLE tree into XML format, which is used in the next stage.

4. XML Parser: Parses the XML representation of the GIMPLE tree and generates the CFG for control and data flow analysis.
5. Security Chaining Data Flow Analyzer: This component will perform the data flow analysis, and annotate the CFG by classifying the branch as Critical or Required.
6. Security Chaining Execution Manager: This is the engine of the security chaining approach. It will use the annotated CFG as the guide to run the instrumented executable and to monitor the execution to generate the test data.
7. Report Analyzer: Collects the data generated by the Security Chaining Execution Manager and generates final test reports indicating the presence of any vulnerabilities, their locations and conditions under which these vulnerabilities would be realized.

To sum up, our work is not directly performed on source code, rather on an intermediate representation of it; specifically, a language independent GCC GIMPLE tree. We also utilize some extensions of GCC. First, the GCC extension for XML-Dump is used to generate the XML representation of the GIMPLE tree, then feeds it to the XML Parser to generate the CFG. Given the CFG, the security chaining Data Flow Analyzer is used to perform data flow analysis and to classify the branches of the CFG as *critical*, or *required*. Then, *GCC Extension for Code Instrumentation* we inject the monitoring code and produce the exactable files. Utilizing the annotated GFC, the execution manager runs the produced executable(s) and monitors their execution to generate test data, which is sent to the Report Generator, which produces final reports detailing all the detected vulnerabilities.

6   Conclusion

In this paper, we presented elements of a solution towards automation of software security testing and the generation of test data for the purpose of detecting security vulnerabilities in software. The proposed solution enables the detection of a range of vulnerabilities, both high-level and low-level. The solution utilizes both control flow and data dependency to achieve the needed goals.

While we understand that constructing a single approach that is capable of detecting all possible software security vulnerabilities is not possible, we do believe that multiple components of a single tool may be able to move us forward toward this target. Previously, we introduced TEA [14], which is capable of handling a wide range of safety and security properties. We have incorporated the the Security Chaining Approach into the Security Testing component of our Trusted Free & Open-Source Software suite. This addition not only allows our tool to handle a larger set of security vulnerabilities but to also detect specific set of vulnerabilities that are not, and in most cases could not, be handled by even the best currently available commercial tools for software security testing.

References

1. Bird, D., Munoz, C.: Automatic generation of random self-checking test cases. IBM Systems J. 22(3), 229–245 (1982)
2. Boyer, R., Elspas, B., Levitt, K.: Select - a formal system for testing and debugging programs by symbolic execution. SIGPLAN Notices 10(6), 234–245 (1975)
3. Brandner, F., Ebner, D., Krall, A.: Compiler generation from structural architecture descriptions. In: Proceedings of the 2007 international conference on Compilers, architecture, and synthesis for embedded systems (September 2007)
4. Cadar, C., Engler, D.: Execution generated test cases: How to make systems code crash itself (March 2005)
5. Chakraborty, M., Chakraborty, U.: An analysis of linear ranking and binary tournament selection in genetic algorithms. In: International Conference on Information, Communications and Signal Processing. ICICS (September 1997)
6. Cigital and National Science Foundation. Genetic algorithms for software test data generation
7. Clarke, L.: A system to generate test data and symbolically execute programs. IEEE Transactions on Software Engineering 2(3), 215–222 (1976)
8. Ferguson, R., Korel, B.: The chaining approach for software test data generation. In: ACM Transaction on Software Engineering and Methodology, vol. 5, pp. 63–86. ACM Press, New York (1996)
9. Godefroid, P., Klarlund, N., Sen, K.: Dart: Directed automated random testing (June 2005)
10. Korel, B.: Automated software test data generation. IEEE Transactions on Software Enfineering 16(8) (August 1990)
11. Korel, B., Harman, M., Chung, S., Apirukvorapinit, P., Gupta, R., Zhang, Q.: Data dependence based testability transformation in automated test generation. In: Proceedings of the 16th IEEE International Symposium on Software Reliability Engineering (ISSRE 2005) (2005)
12. Korel, B.: A dynamic approach of test data generation (1990)
13. Schneider, F.B.: Enforceable security policies. ACM Transaction of Information System Security (2000)
14. Yang, Z., Hanna, A., Debbabi, M.: Team edit automata for testing security property. In: Third International Symposium on Information Assurance and Security (2007)

An Attack Graph-Based Probabilistic Security Metric

Lingyu Wang[1], Tania Islam[1], Tao Long[1], Anoop Singhal[2], and Sushil Jajodia[3]

[1] Concordia Institute for Information Systems Engineering
Concordia University, Montreal, QC H3G 1M8, Canada
{wang,t_is,ta_lon}@ciise.concordia.ca
[2] Computer Security Division
National Institute of Standards and Technology
Gaithersburg, MD 20899, USA
anoop.singhal@nist.gov
[3] Center for Secure Information Systems
George Mason University
Fairfax, VA 22030-4444, USA
jajodia@gmu.edu

Abstract. To protect critical resources in today's networked environments, it is desirable to quantify the likelihood of potential multi-step attacks that combine multiple vulnerabilities. This now becomes feasible due to a model of causal relationships between vulnerabilities, namely, attack graph. This paper proposes an attack graph-based probabilistic metric for network security and studies its efficient computation. We first define the basic metric and provide an intuitive and meaningful interpretation to the metric. We then study the definition in more complex attack graphs with cycles and extend the definition accordingly. We show that computing the metric directly from its definition is not efficient in many cases and propose heuristics to improve the efficiency of such computation.

1 Introduction

The traditional binary view of network security (that is, either secure or insecure) is becoming less and less suitable for today's increasingly complex networked environments. In practice, many vulnerabilities may still remain in a network after they are discovered, due to environmental factors (such as latency in releasing software patches or hardware upgrades), cost factors (such as money and administrative efforts required for deploying patches and upgrades), or mission factors (such as organizational preferences for availability and usability over security). To remove such residue vulnerabilities in the most cost-efficient way, we need to evaluate and measure the likelihood that attackers may compromise critical resources through cleverly combining multiple vulnerabilities.

The study of security metrics has recently drawn significant attention (a detailed review of related work is given in Section 5). However, existing network metric standards typically focus on the measurement of individual vulnerabilities. For example, the Common Vulnerability Scoring System (CVSS) measures the potential impact and environmental metrics in terms of each individual vulnerability [13]. This is a major limitation, because the impact, damage, and relevance should be measured against potential compromises of critical resources, which typically require combining more than one vulnerability.

V. Atluri (Ed.): DAS 2008, LNCS 5094, pp. 283–296, 2008.

On the other hand, the causal relationships between vulnerabilities are well understood and usually encoded in the form of *attack graphs* [1,24]. Attack graphs help to understand whether given critical resources can be compromised through multi-step attacks. However, as a qualitative model, attack graph still adopts a binary view towards security, that is, a network is either secure (critical resources are not reachable) or insecure. This is a limitation because it is usually desirable to find a relatively superior option among secure configurations.

Clearly, there is a gap between existing security metrics, which mostly focus on individual vulnerabilities, and qualitative models of vulnerabilities, which are usually limited to binary views of security. To fill this gap, we propose a probabilistic metric for measuring network security. The metric draws strength from both existing security metrics and the attack graph model. More specifically, we combine the measurements of individual vulnerabilities obtained from existing metrics into an overall score of the network. This combination is based on the causal relationships between vulnerabilities encoded in an attack graph. The key challenge lies in handling complex attack graphs with cycles. We first define the basic metric without considering cycles. We provide an intuitive interpretation of the metric. Based on such an interpretation, we extend the definition to attack graphs with cycles. Finally, we study the efficient computation of the metric. We show that computing the metric by using its definition is usually not efficient, and we provide heuristics for optimizing such computations.

The rest of the paper is organized as follows. Section 2 gives a motivating example. Section 3 defines the proposed metric and studies how to handle cycles in attack graphs. Section 4 presents heuristics for efficient computations of the metric. Section 5 reviews related work. Finally, Section 6 concludes the paper.

2   Attack Graph and Motivating Example

Attack graphs model how multiple vulnerabilities may be combined for advancing an intrusion. In an attack graph, security-related *conditions* represent the system state, and an *exploit* of vulnerabilities between connected hosts is modeled as a transition between system states. Figure 1 shows a toy example. The left side is the configuration of a network. Machine 1 is a file server behind the firewall that offers file transfer (ftp), secure shell (ssh), and remote shell (rsh) services. Machine 2 is an internal database server that offers ftp and rsh services. The firewall allows ftp, ssh, and rsh traffic to both servers and blocks all other incoming traffic.

The right-hand side of Figure 1 shows the attack graph (the numerical values are not part of the attack graph and will be explained shortly), which is a directed graph with two kinds of vertices, namely, exploits shown as predicates inside ovals and conditions shown in plaintexts. For example, $rsh(0, 1)$ represents a remote shell login from machine 0 to machine 1, and $trust(0, 1)$ means a trust relationship is established from machine 0 to machine 1. A directed edge from a condition to an exploit means executing the exploit requires the condition to be satisfied, and that from an exploit to a condition means executing the exploit will satisfy the condition. We formalize the attack graph in Definition 1.

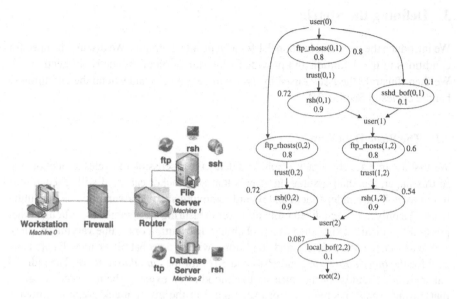

Fig. 1. An Example of Network Configuration and Attack Graph

Definition 1. *An attack graph G is a directed graph $G(E \cup C, R_r \cup R_i)$ where E is a set of exploits, C a set of conditions, and $R_r \subseteq C \times E$ and $R_i \subseteq E \times C$.*

The attack graph in Figure 1 depicts three *attack paths*. On the right, the attack path starts with an ssh buffer overflow exploit from machine 0 to machine 1, which gives the attacker the capability of executing arbitrary codes on machine 1 as a normal user. The attacker then exploits the ftp vulnerability on machine 2 to anonymously upload a list of trusted hosts. Such a trust relationship enables the attacker to remotely execute shell commands on machine 2 without providing a password. Consequently, a local buffer overflow exploit on machine 2 escalates the attacker's privilege to be the root of that machine. Details of the other two attack paths are similar and are omitted.

Informally, the numerical value inside each oval is a probability that indicates the relative likelihood of the corresponding exploit being executed by attackers when all the required conditions are already satisfied. This value thus only depends on each individual vulnerability, which is similar to many existing metrics, such as the CVSS [13]. On the other hand, we can clearly see the limitation of such metrics in assessing the impact, damage, or relevance of vulnerabilities, because such factors are rather determined by the combination of exploits. While we delay its definition and computation to later sections, the numerical value beside each oval represents the likelihood of reaching the corresponding exploit in this particular network. Clearly, a security administrator will be much happier to see the single score beside the last exploit ($local\_bof(2,2)$) than looking at all the eight values inside ovals and wondering how those values may be related to each other.

3   Defining the Metric

We introduce the metric in Section 3.1 for acyclic attack graphs. We discuss the need for conditions in the definition and provide an interpretation of the metric in Section 3.2. We then illustrate the issue raised by cycles in Section 3.3 and extend the definition to handle cycles in Section 3.4.

3.1   The Basic Definition

We first assume acyclic attack graphs and delay the discussion of cycles to Section 3.4. In this paper, we shall assume the events that an attacker can (and will) execute different exploits are independent and regard removing such an assumption as our future work. We only consider a fixed probability for measuring vulnerabilities, although other possibilities clearly exist (such as a probability distribution or a value varying in time).

We associate each exploit e and condition c with two probabilities, namely, $p(e)$ and $p(c)$ for the *individual score*, and $P(e)$ and $P(c)$ for the *cumulative score*. The individual score $p(e)$ stands for the intrinsic likelihood of an exploit e being executed, given that all the conditions required for executing e in the given attack graph are already satisfied. On the other hand, the cumulative score $P(e)$ and $P(c)$ measures the overall likelihood that an attacker can successfully reach and execute the exploit e (or satisfy the condition c) in the given attack graph (the individual score and cumulative score can also be interpreted as probabilities within a Bayesian network [8]).

For exploits, we assume the individual score is assigned based on expert knowledge about the vulnerability being exploited. For conditions, we assume in this paper that the individual score of every condition is always 1. Intuitively, a condition is either initially satisfied (for example, $user(0)$ in Figure 1), or immediately satisfied after a successful exploit (in practice, we can easily remove such assumptions by assigning less-than-1 individual scores to conditions). In Figure 1, we have assigned the individual scores (probabilities shown inside the ovals) based on simple facts, such as a buffer overflow attack requires more skills than executing a remote shell command. In practice, individual scores can be obtained by converting vulnerability scores provided by existing standards, such as the CVSS base score and temporal score [13], to probabilities.

Unlike individual scores, the cumulative score takes into accounts the causal relationships between exploits and conditions. In an attack graph, such causal relationships may appear in two different forms. First, a conjunction exists between multiple conditions required for executing the same exploit. Second, a disjunction exists between multiple exploits that satisfy the same condition. The cumulative scores are defined in the two cases similar to the probability of the *intersection* and *union* of random events. That is, if the execution of e requires two conditions c_1 and c_2, then $P(e) = P(c_1) \cdot P(c_2) \cdot p(e)$; if a condition c can be satisfied by either e_1 or e_2 (or both), then $P(c) = p(c)(P(e_1) + P(e_2) - P(e_1) \cdot P(e_2))$. Definition 2 formalizes cumulative scores.

Definition 2. *Given an acyclic attack graph $G(E \cup C, R_r \cup R_i)$, and any individual score assignment function $p : E \cup C \to [0, 1]$, the cumulative score function $P : E \cup C \to [0, 1]$ is defined as*

- $P(e) = p(e) \cdot \prod_{c \in R_r(e)} P(c)$
- $P(c) = p(c)$, if $R_i(c) = \phi$; otherwise, $P(c) = p(c) \cdot \oplus_{e \in R_i(c)} P(e)$ where the operator $\oplus$ is recursively defined as $\oplus P(e) = P(e)$ for any $e \in E$ and $\oplus (S_1 \cup S_2) = \oplus S_1 + \oplus S_2 - \oplus S_1 \cdot \oplus S_2$ for any disjoint and non-empty sets $S_1 \subseteq E$ and $S_2 \subseteq E$.

In Figure 1, the cumulative scores of two exploits (shown as plaintexts besides corresponding exploits) can be calculated as follows.

1. $P(rsh(0,1)) = P(trust(0,1)) \times p(rsh(0,1)) = 0.8 \times 0.9 = 0.72$
2. $P(user(1)) = P(rsh(0,1)) + P(sshd\_bof(0,1)) - P(rsh(0,1)) \times P(sshd\_bof(0,1)) = 0.72 + 0.1 - 0.72 \times 0.1 = 0.748$

3.2   The Need for Conditions and an Interpretation of the Metric

From the above example, the score of conditions may seem rather unnecessary (as a matter of fact, we do not show the score of conditions in Figure 1). However, the attack graph shown in Figure 1 is a special case where all the causal relationships between exploits happen to be disjunction only. In general, more complicated relationships may arise between exploits, and the cumulative score of conditions will be helpful in such cases. For example, Figure 2 shows the calculation of cumulative scores when a conjunctive, disjunctive, and hybrid relationship exists between exploits, respectively. It would be cumbersome to explicitly deal with such different relationships in defining our metric. However, as long as we include conditions as an intermediate between exploits, we can safely ignore the difference between those cases.

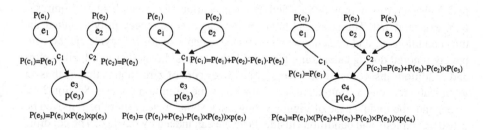

Fig. 2. Examples Showing the Need for Cumulative Scores of Conditions

Using probabilities for a security metric has been criticized as violating a basic design principle, that is, the value assignment should be specific and unambiguous rather than abstract and meaningless [22]. However, there is a simple interpretation for our metric. That is, the individual score $p(e)$ is the probability that any attacker can, and will execute e during an attack, given that all the preconditions are already satisfied. Equivalently, among all attackers that attempt to compromise the given network during any given time period, $p(e)$ is the fraction of attackers that can, and will execute e.

This interpretation of individual scores considers two factors in determining the individual score $p(e)$, namely, whether an attacker has the skills and resources to execute *e* and whether he/she will choose to do so. For example, a vulnerability that cannot be exploited remotely, or the one that requires a valid user account will likely have a lower score due to the first factor (that is, fewer attackers *can* exploit the vulnerability), whereas a vulnerability that can be easily detected, or the one less exposed to the public will likely have a lower score due to the second factor (that is, fewer attackers *will* exploit the vulnerability).

The interpretation of individual scores also provides a natural semantics to the cumulative scores. That is, $P(e)$ or $P(c)$ stands for the likelihood, or the fraction of, attackers who will successfully exploit *e* or satisfy *c* in the given network. The cumulative score of a given goal condition thus indicates the likelihood that a corresponding resource will be compromised during an attack, or equivalently, among all attackers attacking the given network over a given time period, the average fraction of attackers who will successfully compromise the resource. Such a likelihood or fraction is clearly relevant in analyzing the security of a network or in hardening the network for better security.

3.3 Difficulties with Cycles

One complication in defining cumulative scores lies in the effect of cycles in attack graphs. Different types of cycles naturally exist in attack graphs, and they create different difficulties. Namely, some cycles can be completely removed; some cycles can be safely broken, some cycles, however, can neither be removed or broken. Figure 3 shows an example for each type of such cycles.

First, the left-hand side of Figure 3 shows a cycle that can be completely removed because none of the exploits or conditions inside the cycle can ever be reached by attackers. More specifically, executing the exploit e_1 requires both c_1 and c_3 to be satisfied. However, c_3 can only be satisfied by the execution of e_2, which again requires e_1 to be executed first. Therefore, neither e_1 nor e_2 can ever be successfully executed, and thus conditions c_2 and c_3 can never be satisfied. Such a *removable* cycle can be completely ignored during calculating the cumulative scores. In another word, all exploits and conditions inside the cycle have a cumulative score of zero (notice that c_4 thus automatically receives a cumulative score of zero by the definition given in Section 3.1).

Second, the middle case of Figure 3 shows that some cycles cannot be removed because the exploits and conditions inside the cycle can indeed by reached. The condition c_2 can be satisfied by either e_1 or e_2. If c_2 is first satisfied by e_1, then both e_2 and e_3 can

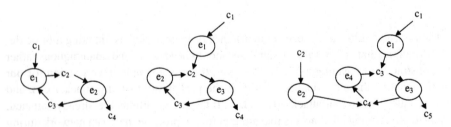

Fig. 3. Cycles in Attack Graphs

be successfully executed. Ignoring such a cycle will thus cause incorrect definition of the metric. Fortunately, this cycle can be easily broken by removing the directed edge from e_2 to c_2. Intuitively, c_2 is only satisfiable by e_1 even though later on it may be satisfied *again* by e_2 (we shall provide a clearer interpretation shortly). After we break the cycle in this way, the cumulative scores can then be easily calculated.

Third, the right-hand side of Figure 3 shows a cycle that can be neither removed nor broken in the aforementioned manner. Both e_1 and e_2 can lead to exploits in the cycle to be executed. There are thus two different ways for breaking the cycle among which we can only choose one. That is, we can either remove the edge from e_4 to c_3 by assuming c_3 is satisfied by e_1, or remove the edge from e_3 to c_4 by considering c_4 to be satisfied by e_2. However, there is no clear reason to prefer any of the two choices over the other. Moreover, removing both edges is clearly not a valid solution (the graph will be separated into two disjoint components). This example shows that removing or breaking a cycle is not a valid solution for all cases.

3.4 Extending the Definition to Handle Cycles

To find a general and meaningful solution, we need to revisit the aforementioned interpretation of the proposed metric. That is, an individual score represents the fraction of attackers who can (and will) execute an exploit or satisfy a condition (in the rest of the paper, we shall refer to both as *reaching*), given that all preconditions are already satisfied; a cumulative score indicates the fraction of attackers who will reach an exploit or a condition. However, when cycles are present in an attack graph, an attacker may reach an exploit or a condition more than once. Clearly, extra caution must be taken in calculating cumulative scores to avoid counting any attacker twice.

Without the loss of generality, we consider the calculation of $P(e_4)$ on the right-hand side of Figure 3. We illustrate those events using Venn diagrams in Figure 4 (the shaded areas can be ignored for now). Notice that the figure depicts cumulative scores for e_1 and e_2 as they are not part of the cycle. Referring to the right-hand side of Figure 3, we shall first calculate $P(e_4)$ by following the cycle clockwise from c_4, through e_4, c_3, e_3, and finally to c_4 again, as follows (each step simply follows the basic definition given in Section 3.1).

1. By abusing notations, denote $P(e_2)$ the set of attackers reaching e_2, represented as an oval in Figure 4.
2. Among the attackers in $P(e_2)$, those who can execute e_4 form the intersection $P(e_2) \cap p(e_4)$.
3. The union of two sets of attackers, $P(e_2) \cap p(e_4) \cup P(e_1)$, will reach c_3.
4. The intersection of the above set with $p(e_3)$, that is, $(P(e_2) \cap p(e_4) \cup P(e_1)) \cap p(e_3)$ will reach e_3.
5. Among those who reach e_3, the attackers originally coming from the set $P(e_2)$ should not be counted again towards satisfying c_4. In another word, only those in $(P(e_2) \cap p(e_4) \cup P(e_1)) \cap p(e_3) \setminus P(e_2) = P(e_1) \cap p(e_3) \setminus P(e_2)$ should be counted.
6. Finally, the set of attackers that can reach e_4 is $(P(e_1) \cap p(e_3) \setminus P(e_2) \cup P(e_2)) \cap p(e_4) = (P(e_1) \cap p(e_3) \cup P(e_2)) \cap p(e_4)$

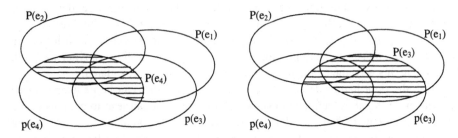

Fig. 4. Calculating Cumulative Scores in the Presence of Cycles

The shaded area in the left-hand side of Figure 4 indicates the final result of $P(e_4)$. The right-hand side of Figure 4 corresponds to $P(e_3)$, which can be calculated similarly. In the above calculation, we essentially break the cycle in the second to the last step, by disregarding those attackers who reach c_4 for the second time. This is reasonable because in measuring the fraction of attackers (or the likelihood of an attacker) reaching c_4, we should only count the fraction of distinct attackers. In another word, although an attacker can repeat an exploit for many times, this should not affect the metric.

There is, however, an alternative interpretation of the final result $P(e_4) = (P(e_1) \cap p(e_3) \cup P(e_2)) \cap P(e_4)$. Intuitively, instead of breaking the cycle when some attackers reach c_4 for the second time, we prevent them from ever leaving e_4. More precisely, when calculating a cumulative score of an exploit (or a condition), we remove all outgoing edges from that exploit (or condition). After removing those edges, some other exploits or conditions may need to be removed if they can no longer be reached. The attack graph will needs to be updated to remove all unreachable vertices. For example, In the left-hand side of Figure 3, to calculate $P(e_1)$, we will remove the edge (e_1, c_2), (c_2, e_2), (e_2, c_3), (c_3, e_1), and finally the exploit e_1 itself (this can be interpreted as $P(e_1) = 0$).

Definition 3 formalizes cumulative scores for general attack graphs. In the definition, the first case corresponds to the exception where e is inside a removable cycle, so its cumulative score is defined (not computed) as zero. In the second case, the cumulative score is defined in $A(G, e)$ instead of G so to ensure that e is not inside any cycle and its cumulative score can thus be calculated based on Definition 2 (however, $A(G, e)$ is not guaranteed to be an acyclic attack graph so Definition 2 does not directly apply).

Definition 3. *Given an attack graph $G(E \cup C, R_r \cup R_i)$, and any individual score assignment function $p : E \cup C \to [0, 1]$, we denote $A(G, e)$ (or $A(G, c)$) an attack graph obtained by removing from G all the outgoing edges at e (or c) and consequently removing all unreachable exploits and conditions from G. The cumulative score function $P : E \cup C \to [0, 1]$ is defined as*

- *If e (or c) does not appear in $A(G, e)$ (or $A(G, c)$), then $P(e) = 0$ (or $P(c) = 0$).*
- *Otherwise, $P(e)$ (or $P(c)$) is equal to its value calculated in $A(G, e)$ (or $A(G, c)$) based on Definition 2.*

Definition 3 satisfies two desirable properties as stated in Proposition 1. The first property guarantees that the cumulative score is defined for all exploits and conditions in the given attack graph G. The second property ensures that the extended definition is still consistent with the aforementioned interpretation of the metric.

Proposition 1. *By Definition 3, for any exploit e (the result applies to a condition c in a similar way),*

- *$P(e)$ can be uniquely determined, and*
- *$P(e)$ represents the likelihood of an attacker (or fraction of attackers) reaching e for the first time in the given attack graph G.*

Proof: We only discuss the case of an exploit e since a condition c is similar. First, e may be unreachable in G because it is inside a breakable cycle, such as the left-hand side of Figure 3. In this case, removing all outgoing edges from e will essentially cause the cycle to be completely removed. We interpret this as $P(e) = 0$, which indicates that no attacker can reach e in G.

Suppose e is reachable. We prove the first claim through induction on the number k of exploits that can be reached before reaching e (we ignore those exploits that are not on any attack path that contains e so any exploit can either be reached before e, or after it). Clearly, for $k = 0$, $P(e) = p(e)$. Suppose the claim holds for any $k - 1$. We consider an exploit e before which k others can be reached. Before any of those k exploits, at most $k - 1$ others can be reached (otherwise, there would be more than k exploits reachable before e), and hence the claim holds for the k exploits that can be reached before e. For exploits that can only be reached after reaching e at least once (notice those exploits could be within a cycle containing e), they will not appear in $A(G, e)$. The claim thus holds for e, because e is no longer in any cycle and the claim already holds for all the k remaining exploits in $A(G, e)$ (except e itself).

For the second claim, it suffices to show that any attacker can reach e for the first time in G iff it can do so in $A(G, e)$. The if part is true because any valid attack path in $A(G, e)$ will also exist in G. The only-if part holds because when we update the attack graph, only those exploits that can only be reached after reaching e are removed, so their removal will not affect any attack path from reaching e in $A(G, e)$, if such a path exists in G. □

4 Computing the Metric

Cumulative scores can certainly be computed directly by Definition 3. That is, for each exploit e (similarly for each condition), we first compute $A(G, e)$ and then compute $P(e)$ on $A(G, e)$. However, this naive approach is inefficient because the removal of outgoing edges (and subsequent updates of attack graphs) is only necessary for vertices inside cycles. More specifically, if a vertex v is not part of a cycle, then on each attack path including v, all vertices can be divided into two sets, namely, the predecessors and successors of v (on the other hand, if v is inside a cycle, then every vertex in the cycle is both a predecessor and a successor of v). Removing outgoing edges from v will cause all successors of v to be removed as well, whereas all the predecessors of v are not affected. Therefore, in Definition 3, if v is not part of a cycle, then calculating the cumulative score of v in $A(G, e)$ will give the same result as calculating it in G.

For vertices not inside a cycle, we use a modified breadth-first search (BFS) to calculate cumulative scores. A normal BFS follows the outgoing edges of a vertex only when it is reached for the first time (cycles are always broken at a vertex with the maximum shortest-path distance from some initially satisfied conditions). However, such a normal BFS is not suitable for calculating our metric. In Definition 3, the cumulative score of any vertex can be calculated only when the cumulative scores of all its predecessors have already been calculated. We thus modify the BFS such that a vertex *receives* a cumulative score from its predecessor, whenever the former is reached from the latter. The outgoing edges of a vertex are followed only when the vertex is reached for the last time (this can be implemented using a counter based on the in-degree of each vertex). At this time, the vertex will have received cumulative scores from all its predecessors, and its own cumulative score can thus be calculated.

The above procedure, however, will terminate upon reaching one or more cycles. Referring to the right-hand side of Figure 3, the search will reach c_3 from e_1 (or, reach c_4 from e_2) and then stop there, because the predecessor e_3 of c_4 (or, the predecessor e_4 of c_3) has not yet been, and will never be, reached. Notice that this is true no matter a cycle is removable (such as in the left-hand side of Figure 3) or not. This termination of the procedure is actually desirable, because it signals that one or more cycles have been reached. It also indicates *entry points* of the cycle, that is, those vertices that have at least one of their predecessors reached, such as c_4 and c_3 in the right-hand side of Figure 3. Upon the termination of the main procedure, a sub-procedure will mark vertices inside the encountered cycle(s), and then calculate their cumulative scores by Definition 3.

One subtlety is that the cumulative score of all entry points of a cycle must be calculated strictly by applying Definition 3. This may not seem to be necessary, since once the calculation is finished for one vertex in the cycle, it is possible to continue without considering the cycle. For example, in the right-hand side of Figure 3, once we calculate $P(c_3)$ by applying Definition 3, $P(e_3)$ can be calculated as $P(e_3) = P(c_3) \cdot p(e_3)$, and $P(c_4) = P(e_3) + P(e_2) - P(e_3) \cdot P(e_2)$. However, while $P(e_3)$ can indeed be calculated this way, the calculation of $P(c_4)$ is incorrect. Figure 5 shows $A(G, c_3)$, $A(G, e_3)$, and $A(G, c_4)$ obtained by Definition 3. Clearly, $P(e_3)$ can be calculated from $P(c_3)$ as $P(e_3) = P(c_3) \cdot p(e_3)$, but the calculation of $P(c_4)$ cannot be based on $P(e_3)$. Actually, it can be observed that $P(c_3)$ and $P(e_3)$ both depend on the individual score $p(e_4)$, whereas $P(c_4)$ has nothing to do with $p(e_4)$.

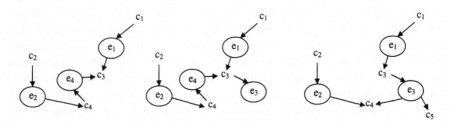

Fig. 5. Computing the Metric for Vertices in Cycles

It is certainly a viable solution to always calculate cumulative scores for all vertices in a cycle by applying Definition 3. However, for those vertices that are not entry points of a cycle, it will be more efficient to calculate their cumulative scores without considering the cycle. In the above example, $P(e_3)$ can be safely calculated from $P(c_3)$. More generally, for any vertex in a cycle that has only one incoming edge, the cumulative score can be safely calculated (after calculation of entry points is finished) as if the vertex is not in the cycle. The reason is as follows. The only incoming edge of such a vertex v must be part of the cycle. Let w be the predecessor of v. When we calculate $P(w)$, we will remove v together with all its successors to obtain $A(G, w)$. When we calculate $P(v)$, we also remove all predecessors to obtain $A(G, v)$. The only difference between the two cases is thus v itself. That is, $P(v) = P(w) \cdot p(v)$ is true. However, if v has more than one incoming edge (and hence multiple predecessors), then to calculate $P(w)$, v may not need to be removed. For example, we do not remove c_4 while calculating $P(e_3)$ in the middle case of Figure 5.

Figure 6 shows an algorithm for calculating the metric in a given attack graph with all individual scores assigned. Lines 1-2 assign the cumulative score of initially satisfied conditions as 1. The main loop between line 3 and line 9 calculates the cumulative score for all other vertices. Each loop is separated into three phases. First, lines 4-5 employs the aforementioned modified BFS to calculate cumulative scores until one or more cycle is encountered and the search terminates. Second, lines 6-7 applies Definition 3 to calculate cumulative scores for vertices in cycles that have more than one incoming edges. Finally, lines 8-9 calculate cumulative scores for other vertices in the cycle in a simpler way (as if they are not in any cycle). After all vertices in the encountered cycles are processed, the main loop will repeat lines 3-9, until all vertices are processed.

Input: An attack graph G with individual scores assigned to all vertices
Output: A set of cumulative scores for all vertices of G
Method:
1. **For** each initially satisfied condition c
2.   **Let** $P(c) = 1$ and mark c as processed
3. **While** there exist unprocessed vertices
4.   **While** there exists an unprocessed vertex v whose predecessors are all processed
5.   **Calculate** $P(v)$ and mark v as processed
6.   **For** each vertex v' in a cycle that has more than one incoming edge
7.   **Calculate** $P(v')$ and mark v' as processed
8.   **For** each unprocessed vertex v'' in the cycles
9.   **Calculate** $P(v'')$ and mark v'' as processed
10. **Return** the set of all calculated cumulative scores

Fig. 6. Algorithm for Calculating the Metric

5   Related Work

General reviews of security metrics are given in [11,2]. The NIST's efforts on standardizing security metrics are in the Technology Assessment: Methods for Measuring the

Level of Computer Security [14] and more recently in the Security Metrics Guide for Information Technology Systems [25]. The latter describe the current state of practice of security metrics, such as that required by the Federal Information Security Management Act (FISMA). Another overview of many aspects of network security metrics is given in [9].

Dacier et al. give intuitive properties that should be satisfied by any security metric [5,6,16]. The difficulty of attacks are measured in terms of time and efforts spent by attackers. Based on an exponential distribution for an attacker's success rate over time, they use a Markov model and the MTTF (Mean Time to Failure) to measure the security of a network. They discuss simple cases of combining individual measures but do not study the general case. Standardization efforts for vulnerability assessment include the Common Vulnerability Scoring System (CVSS) [13], although these generally treat vulnerabilities in isolation, without considering attack interdependencies on target networks. More recently, we propose an attack resistance metric based on attack graph in [31,30]. In this paper, we adopt a probabilistic approach and tackle challenging issues, such as cycles in attack graphs, that are not addressed elsewhere.

The work by Balzarotti et al. [3] focuses on computing the minimum efforts required for executing each exploit. Based the exploitability concept, a qualitative measure of risk is given in [4]. Another approach measures the relative risk of different configurations using the *weakest attacker* model, that is the least conditions under which an attack is possible [20]. Yet another series of work measures how likely a software is vulnerable to attacks using a metrics called *attack surface* [10,12,17,18,19]. These work allow a partial order to be established on different network configurations based on their relative security. However, the treatment of many aspects of security is still qualitative in nature.

Our work on minimum-cost network hardening is one of the first efforts toward the quantitative study of network security [15,29]. This work quantifies the cost of removing vulnerabilities in hardening a network, but it does not consider other hardening options, such as modifying the connectivity. It also has the limitation of adopting a qualitative view of damages (all the given critical resources are equally important) and of attack resistance (attacks on critical resources are either impossible or trivial).

To generate attack graphs, topological vulnerability analysis enumerates potential multi-step intrusions based on prior knowledge about vulnerabilities and their relationships [5,7,16,21,26,33]. Based on whether a search starts from the initial state or the final state, such analyses can be forward [21,26] or backward [23,24]. To avoid the exponential explosion in the number of explicit attack sequences, a compact representation of attack graphs was proposed based on the *monotonicity assumption* saying an attacker never needs to relinquish any obtained capability [1]. On the attack response front, attack graphs have been used for the correlation of attacks, the hypotheses of alerts missed by IDSs, and the prediction of possible future attacks [27,28,32].

6   Conclusion

While removing all vulnerabilities is usually impractical, leaving vulnerabilities unattended may cause significant damages to critical resources in a networked environment.

It is thus critical to understand and measure the likelihood of sophisticated attacks combining multiple vulnerabilities for reaching the attack goal. We have proposed an attack graph-based probabilistic metric for this purpose. We have tackled challenging issues, such as cycles in attack graphs. We showed that the definition of the metric has an intuitive and meaningful interpretation, which will be helpful in real world decision making. Future work will implement a practical tool to measure security risk of enterprise networks.

Acknowledgements. This material is based upon work supported by National Institute of Standards and Technology Computer Security Division; by Homeland Security Advanced Research Projects Agency under the contract FA8750-05-C-0212 administered by the Air Force Research Laboratory/Rome; by Army Research Office under grant W911NF-05-1-0374, by Federal Aviation Administration under the contract DTFAWA-04-P-00278/0001, by the National Science Foundation under grants CT-0627493, IIS-0242237 and IIS-0430402, by Natural Sciences and Engineering Research Council of Canada under Discovery Grant N01035, and by Fonds de recherche sur la nature et les technologies. Any opinions, findings, and conclusions or recommendations expressed in this material are those of the authors and do not necessarily reflect the views of the sponsoring organizations. The authors thank the anonymous reviewers for their valuable comments.

References

1. Ammann, P., Wijesekera, D., Kaushik, S.: Scalable, graph-based network vulnerability analysis. In: Proceedings of the 9th ACM Conference on Computer and Communications Security (CCS 2002) (2002)
2. A.C.S. Associates. Workshop on Information Security System Scoring and Ranking (2001)
3. Balzarotti, D., Monga, M., Sicari, S.: Assessing the risk of using vulnerable components. In: Proceedings of the 1st Workshop on Quality of Protection (2005)
4. Balzarotti, P., Monga, M., Sicari, S.: Assessing the risk of using vulnerable components. In: Proceedings of the 2nd ACM workshop on Quality of protection (2005)
5. Dacier, M.: Towards quantitative evaluation of computer security. Ph.D. Thesis, Institut National Polytechnique de Toulouse (1994)
6. Dacier, M., Deswarte, Y., Kaaniche, M.: Quantitative assessment of operational security: Models and tools. Technical Report 96493 (1996)
7. Farmer, D., Spafford, E.: The COPS security checker system. In: USENIX Summer, pp. 165–170 (1990)
8. Frigault, M., Wang, L.: Measuring network security using bayesian network-based attack graphs. In: Proceedings of The 3rd IEEE International Workshop on Security, Trust, and Privacy for Software Applications (STPSA 2008) (2008)
9. Hoo, K.: Metrics of network security. White Paper (2004)
10. Howard, M., Pincus, J., Wing, J.: Measuring relative attack surfaces. In: Workshop on Advanced Developments in Software and Systems Security (2003)
11. Jaquith, A.: Security Merics: Replacing Fear Uncertainty and Doubt. Addison Wesley, Reading (2007)
12. Manadhata, K., Wing, J., Flynn, M., McQueen, M.: Measuring the attack surfaces of two ftp daemons. In: Quality of Protection Workshop (2006)

13. Mell, P., Scarfone, K., Romanosky, S.: Common vulnerability scoring system. IEEE Security & Privacy Magazine 4(6), 85–89 (2006)
14. National Institute of Standards and Technology. Technology assessment: Methods for measuring the level of computer security. NIST Special Publication 500-133 (1985)
15. Noel, S., Jajodia, S., O'Berry, B., Jacobs, M.: Efficient minimum-cost network hardening via exploit dependency graphs. In: Proceedings of the 19th Annual Computer Security Applications Conference (ACSAC 2003) (2003)
16. Ortalo, R., Deswarte, Y., Kaaniche, M.: Experimenting with quantitative evaluation tools for monitoring operational security. IEEE Trans. Software Eng. 25(5), 633–650 (1999)
17. Manadhata, J.W.P.: Measuring a system's attack surface. Technical Report CMU-CS-04-102 (2004)
18. Manadhata, J.W.P.: An attack surface metric. Technical Report CMU-CS-05-155 (2005)
19. Manadhata, J.W.P.: An attack surface metric. In: First Workshop on Security Metrics (MetriCon) (2006)
20. Pamula, J., Jajodia, S., Ammann, P., Swarup, V.: A weakest-adversary security metric for network configuration security analysis. In: Proceedings of the 2nd ACM workshop on Quality of protection, pp. 31–38. ACM Press, New York (2006)
21. Phillips, C., Swiler, L.: A graph-based system for network-vulnerability analysis. In: Proceedings of the New Security Paradigms Workshop (NSPW 1998) (1998)
22. Reiter, M., Stubblebine, S.: Authentication metric analysis and design. ACM Transactions on Information and System Security 2(2), 138–158 (1999)
23. Ritchey, R., Ammann, P.: Using model checking to analyze network vulnerabilities. In: Proceedings of the 2000 IEEE Symposium on Research on Security and Privacy (S&P 2000), pp. 156–165 (2000)
24. Sheyner, O., Haines, J., Jha, S., Lippmann, R., Wing, J.: Automated generation and analysis of attack graphs. In: Proceedings of the 2002 IEEE Symposium on Security and Privacy (S&P 2002) (2002)
25. Swanson, M., Bartol, N., Sabato, J., Hash, J., Graffo, L.: Security metrics guide for information technology systems. NIST Special Publication 800-55 (2003)
26. Swiler, L., Phillips, C., Ellis, D., Chakerian, S.: Computer attack graph generation tool. In: Proceedings of the DARPA Information Survivability Conference & Exposition II (DISCEX 2001) (2001)
27. Wang, L., Liu, A., Jajodia, S.: An efficient and unified approach to correlating, hypothesizing, and predicting intrusion alerts. In: di Vimercati, S.d.C., Syverson, P.F., Gollmann, D. (eds.) ESORICS 2005. LNCS, vol. 3679, pp. 247–266. Springer, Heidelberg (2005)
28. Wang, L., Liu, A., Jajodia, S.: Using attack graphs for correlating, hypothesizing, and predicting intrusion alerts. Computer Communications 29(15), 2917–2933 (2006)
29. Wang, L., Noel, S., Jajodia, S.: Minimum-cost network hardening using attack graphs. Computer Communications 29(18), 3812–3824 (2006)
30. Wang, L., Singhal, A., Jajodia, S.: Measuring network security using attack graphs. In: Proceedings of the 3rd ACM workshop on Quality of protection (QoP 2007). ACM Press, New York (2007)
31. Wang, L., Singhal, A., Jajodia, S.: Measuring the overall security of network configurations using attack graphs. In: Proceedings of 21th IFIP WG 11.3 Working Conference on Data and Applications Security (DBSec 2007) (2007)
32. Wang, L., Yao, C., Singhal, A., Jajodia, S.: Interactive analysis of attack graphs using relational queries. In: Proceedings of 20th IFIP WG 11.3 Working Conference on Data and Applications Security (DBSec 2006), pp. 119–132 (2006)
33. Zerkle, D., Levitt, K.: Netkuang - a multi-host configuration vulnerability checker. In: Proceedings of the 6th USENIX Unix Security Symposium (USENIX 1996) (1996)

An Opinion Model for Evaluating Malicious Activities in Pervasive Computing Systems

Indrajit Ray, Nayot Poolsappasit, and Rinku Dewri

Department of Computer Science, Colorado State University
{indrajit,nayot,rinku}@cs.colostate.edu

Abstract. Pervasive computing applications typically involve cooperation among a number of entities spanning multiple organizations. Any security breach in any single entity can have very far-reaching consequences. In addition, a number of factors make the task of defending against malicious attacks in pervasive systems even more complex than conventional systems. Foremost among them is that a significant number of the devices deployed in such environments are frequently severely resource constrained. Thus strong security controls cannot be easily deployed on these devices. A second factor is that since a large number of such devices are also involved, attacks can propagate very fast in pervasive environments. These prompt us to propose a model for predicting malicious activities in pervasive systems. Our model is based on a logic of opinion that has been proposed elsewhere. Ours is not an intrusion detection system for pervasive systems but works in tandem with one. The system we propose can be used as a standard interface to analyze pervasive system activities in general and generate an opinion about the possibility of an attack.

1 Introduction

With the growth of mobile and sensor devices, embedded systems, and communication technologies, we are moving towards an era of pervasive computing. Pervasive computing uses numerous, casually accessible, often invisible, computing and sensor devices in addition to conventional computing systems. These devices are frequently mobile and/or embedded in an environment that is mobile. Most of the time these devices are richly inter-connected with each other using wireless or wired technology. Being embedded in the environment and interconnected allow pervasive computing devices to exploit knowledge about the operating environment in a net-centric manner. This enables pervasive computing applications to provide a rich new set of services and functionalities that are not otherwise possible through conventional means and has the potential to impact numerous applications that benefit society. Examples of such applications are emergency response, automated monitoring of health data for assisted living, environmental disaster mitigation and supply chain management.

Pervasive computing applications typically involve many entities that span different organizations interacting in complex and subtle ways. Any attack that causes security breach in a single entity can have very far-reaching consequences. For example, future earthquake monitoring systems are expected to be integrated with electricity grid, gas distribution systems, elevator controls in high rises, traffic monitoring systems etc., that

V. Atluri (Ed.): DAS 2008, LNCS 5094, pp. 297–312, 2008.

are to be switched off when a severe earthquake is detected [3]. Imagine the havoc that can be rendered if such a system is maliciously triggered. However, defending pervasive computing applications against malicious attacks is not easy. Traditional techniques cannot be directly applied. This is because the severe resource constraints inherent to a significant number of the devices [9] – limited energy, processing and memory – complicates the adoption of a vast number of conventional security protocols and renders others completely useless. The widespread use of wireless communication technology further aggravates the problem because attackers can easily intercept, fabricate or jam traffic. Moreover, the rich connectivity among devices enables an attack to spread very rapidly from one device to another across the system. To complicate matters further, security threats in a pervasive computing environment are very application dependent. Thus, it is practically impossible to design a solution that is satisfactory for all applications. It is important, for these reasons, that pervasive computing systems be carefully monitored for malicious activities. This allows one to take just-in-time mitigating actions, if needed by dynamically relocating security controls in the application. In the current work, we propose a model by which we can evaluate the chances of attacks occurring. The model assumes the existence of a activity monitoring system for pervasive applications. and is based on our earlier work on predicting threats from malicious insiders [11].

The rest of the paper is organized as follows. Section 2 discusses how an workflow can be used to model the activities and interactions in a pervasive system. Section 3 presents the attack tree model for this work and discusses how an attack tree can be derived for the pervasive application from its workflow. In section 3.2 we present the opinion model for attack trees. Section 4 presents the quantitative framework for evaluating attacks. Finally section 5 concludes the paper.

2   Modeling Pervasive Applications with Workflows

Security threats in a pervasive environment are application dependent. Consequently, business models incorporating any kind of a pervasive computing paradigm will highly benefit if formalisms are derived to enable a "case-by-case" study of the problem. We, therefore, propose to discuss our approach using an example health care application. We emphasize, however, that our formalization of the model is such that the formulated problems remain independent of any property intrinsic to the healthcare domain only.

The pervasive health care environment consists of devices that measure the vital signs of patients, location sensors that locate mobile resources, location-aware PDAs carried by health-care personnels, and back-end systems storing and processing records of patient data. The devices are connected through wired or wireless medium. We classify these devices into three categories – *adapters, composers* and *back-end*. Adapters are are devices with low capabilities. They collect raw sensor data and forward them to composers for processing. Composers have medium processing capabilities and may have fixed or battery power sources. Back-ends are high processing capability systems whose power may be tapped by composers.

The application consists of different workflows that get triggered by various events. The following example specifies the workflow that handles the situation when an unanticipated change occurs in a patient's vital signs (VS) monitor.

Case 1: The VS monitor tries to detect the presence of the doctor within a wireless communicable distance. If the doctor is present, he can make suggestions which may or may not be based on the patient report stored at the back-end. He may also decide to request the assistance of a nurse, who is located with the help of the network infrastructure. In case of an emergency, the same network infrastructure is used to notify the emergency service.

Case 2: If a doctor cannot be located nearby, there is a search for a nurse. The nurse may have the requisite skills to take care of the situation, perhaps with information obtained from the back-end system. If not, the nurse requests the network infrastructure to locate a remote doctor. The remote doctor can then make his suggestions to the nurse or directly interact with the monitoring devices using the network. Possibilities are also that the doctor feels the need to be immediately with the patient, and informs the emergency service on his way.

Case 3: If a nearby doctor or a nurse cannot be located, the VS monitor communicates with the network infrastructure to locate a remote doctor. The doctor, once located, can remotely interact with the monitoring equipments, or decide to attend to the situation physically, often asking for assistance from a nurse. Emergency services are notified on a need basis. Also, on the event that the network is unable to locate the doctor, it informs the emergency service.

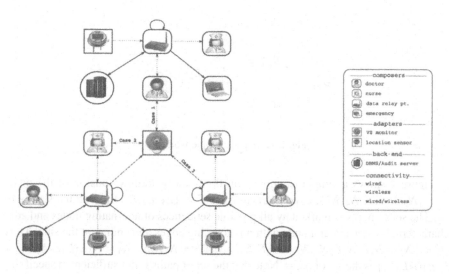

Fig. 1. Constituents of a pervasive healthcare environment

This scenario is represented by the workflow in Fig. 1 and emphasizes the communication links that are used between the nodes in different contexts. The direction of the link indicates the direction of the information flow. The "VS Monitor" node, which is the source node for this workflow can initiate a communication with either a doctor, a nurse or a data relay point. The link between a data relay point and the emergency service is in one direction owing to the specification that the data relay point is only used as an intermediate node to inform the emergency service. How the emergency service handles this notification is outside the scope of the application.

For our purose, a workflow is a tuple $\langle N, E, n, \mathcal{N}, \mathcal{D} \rangle$, where N is a set of *nodes*, E is a set of *edge characteristics*, n is a *sink node*, $\mathcal{N}$ is a set of *paths* and $\mathcal{D}$ is called the *path composition*. A node represents an application executing on a wired or wireless device in the pervasive environment. The application can be broken down into simpler operations. For security analysis we assume that vulnerabilities in these operations are know. An edge characteristic represents a communication channel used between the nodes. Note that we are not identifying an edge by the two nodes it connects, but rather by the characteristics of the communication being performed by the two nodes. Such a definition serves better in the context of attack trees since distinct pairs of nodes may be using a similar communication link (for example an ssh connection), failure or compromise of which can result in faulty (or no) communication between all such pairs. The sink node is representative of the objective that the workflow is designed to achieve. The set of paths represent the interactions between the nodes using edge characteristics. Every member $\mathcal{N}_p = N_{p1}E_{p1}N_{p2}E_{p2}\ldots n$ in this set is a sequence of alternate nodes and edge charateristics, starting with a node in N and ending at the sink node. The path composition specify how different paths interact to accomplish the objective of the workflow.

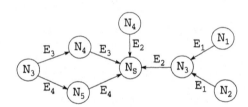

Fig. 2. A simple example workflow

Figure 2 shows a simple example workflow. The workflow consists of the nodes $N = \{N_1, N_2, N_3, N_4, N_5\}$, edge characteristics $E = \{E_1, E_2, E_3, E_4\}$ and the sink node N_s. The set of paths is marked by all possible sequences of alternating nodes and edge characteristics starting at a node with no incoming edges and ending at the sink. Thus, $\mathcal{N} = \{\mathcal{N}_1 = N_1 E_1 N_3 E_2 N_s, \mathcal{N}_2 = N_2 E_1 N_3 E_2 N_s, \mathcal{N}_3 = N_4 E_2 N_s, \mathcal{N}_4 = N_3 E_3 N_4 E_3 N_s, \mathcal{N}_5 = N_3 E_4 N_5 E_4 N_s\}$ is the set of paths. Note that the set of paths is not sufficient in specifying the different ways the objective of the workflow can be achieved. For example, paths $\mathcal{N}_1$ and $\mathcal{N}_2$ cannot individually help realize the objective, but can do so in conjunction. The path composition is thus used to specify any conjunctions, or disjunctions, required among paths to reach the sink. In this particular example we specify this composition as $\mathcal{N}_1 \cdot \mathcal{N}_2 + \mathcal{N}_3 + \mathcal{N}_4 + \mathcal{N}_5$, where we use the "dot" and "plus" notations to denote "AND" and "OR" logic respectively. Besides capturing all possible ways that the objective of the workflow can be achieved, such an expression also lays the ground for the attack tree representation.

3 Modeling Attacks Using Attack Trees

Attack trees have been previously proposed [2, 8, 11, 12] as a systematic method to specify system security based on varying attacks. They help organize intrusion and/or misuse scenarios by

1. utilizing known vulnerabilities and/or weak spots in the system, and
2. analyzing system dependencies and weak links and representing these dependencies in the form of an And-Or tree.

For every system that needs to be defended there is a different attack tree[1]. The nodes of the tree are used to represent the stages towards an attack. The root node of the tree represents the attacker's ultimate goal, namely, cause damage to the system. The interior nodes, including leaf-nodes, represent possible system states (that is subgoals) during the execution of an attack. System state can include level of compromise by the attacker (such as successful access to a web page or successful acquisition of root privileges), configuration or state changes achieved on specific system components (such as implantation of Trojan Horses) and other sub-goals that will ultimately lead to the final goal (such as sequence of vulnerabilities exploited). Branches represent a change of state caused by one or more action taken by the attacker. Change in state is represented by either AND-branches or OR-branches. Nodes may be decomposed as

1. a set of events (attacks) all of which must be achieved for a this sub-goal to succeed; this is represented by the events being combined by AND branches at the node; or
2. a set of events (attacks), any one of which occurring will result in the sub-goal succeeding; this is represented by the events being combined by OR branches at the node.

The notion of attack trees is very similar to the notion of attack graphs that have been proposed by other researchers [1, 4, 5, 10, 13, 14] for network vulnerability analysis. The difference is in the representation of states and actions. Attack graphs describe the sequence of actions that leads to attacks whereas attack trees describe attacks in terms of the sub-goals that need to be reached. Thus attack trees are a more concise representation. A often cited criticism of attack trees (vis-a-vis attack graphs) is that they are not able to model cycles. However, we believe that this criticism is valid only in cases where attack trees are used to represent sequence of operations leading to attacks, not when it is used to represent sequence of states reached. A second criticism of using attack tree to model attack scenarios is that they tend to get unwieldy. Earlier, in one of our works [11], we had shown how we can reduce the size of the attack tree so that it is usable.

We augment an attack tree by associating a label $\langle b, d, u \rangle$ with each branch and node in the attack tree. The augmented attack tree is defined formally as follows:

Definition 1. *An* augmented attack tree *is a rooted tree defined as AAT $= (V, E, \varepsilon, L)$, where*

1. V is the set of nodes in the tree representing the different states of compromise or sub-goals that an attacker need to reach in order to compromise a system. $\mathcal{V} \in V$ is a special node, distinguished from others, that forms the root of the tree. It

---

[1] In real world there can be a forest of trees. However, a forest can be collapsed always to a single tree. So we will assume that there is a single tree.

represents the ultimate goal of the attacker, namely system compromise. The set V can be partitioned into two subsets, $leaf\_nodes$ and $internal\_nodes$, such that
(a) $leaf\_nodes \cup internal\_nodes = V$,
(b) $leaf\_nodes \cap internal\_nodes = \phi$, and
(c) $\mathcal{V} \in internal\_nodes$

2. $E \subseteq V \times V$ constitutes the set of edges in the attack tree. An edge $(v_i, v_j) \in E$ represents the state transition (in terms of actions taken) from a child node $v_i \in V$ to a parent node $v_j \in V$ in the tree. The edge (v_i, v_j) is said to be "emergent from" v_i and "incident to" v_j. Further if edges (v_i, v_j) and (v_i, v_k) exists in the set of edges, then v_j and v_k represent the same node.

3. ε is a set of tuples of the form $\langle v, decomposition \rangle$ such that
(a) $v \in internal\_nodes$ and
(b) $decomposition \in \{AND-decomposition, OR-decomposition\}$

4. L is a set of opinion labels. A label $l \in L$ can be associated with a node or an edge. If $S \in V$ is a node then the opinion label l_S, associated with node S, is given by $l_S = w_S^{Vul}$ and is called the opinion on vulnerability of S. If $e = (v_i, v_j)$ is an edge then the opinion label l_e associated with edge e is given by $l_e = w_{v_i}^{Atk}$, and is called the opinion on attacking activities of e. Each opinion value w, is a tuple of the form $\langle b, d, u \rangle$, where $b, d, u \in [0,1]$ and $b + d + u = 1$, represents respectively, a belief, a disbelief and an uncertainty in the opinion as explained below.

Definition 2. *Given a node v in an attack tree such that $v \in internal\_nodes$, the node is an AND-decomposition if all edges incident to the node are connected by the AND operation.*

Definition 3. *Given a node v of an attack tree such that $v \in internal\_nodes$, the node is an OR-decomposition if all edges incident to the node are connected by the OR operation.*

An AND-decomposition on node v (shown by a single arc among the edges incident to v in figure 3 means that each subgoal of v represented by a child of v needs to be reached in order to reach v. An OR-decomposition (shown by a double arc in figure 3 means that the goal v can be reached only if any one of the subgoals is reached. Note that reaching a child goal is only a necessary condition for reaching the parent goal and not a sufficient condition.

Henceforth we will use the terms attack tree and augmented attack tree interchangeably to mean the latter. Intuitively, the opinion on vulnerability tells us to what degree the current state of the pervasive system is vulnerable. The opinion on attacking activities is a measure of a system monitor's belief that the state transition from one vulnerable state to another will occur.

Definition 4. *Given an attack tree, AAT, an attack scenario, AS of AAT is defined to be a sub-tree of AAT that is rooted at the root of AAT, and follows one or more branches through the tree to end at one or more leaf nodes of AAT such that*

1. *if the subtree has a node that is an AND-decomposition then the subtree must contain all the children of this node, and*
2. *the sub-tree represents one and only one of the many attacks described by AAT.*

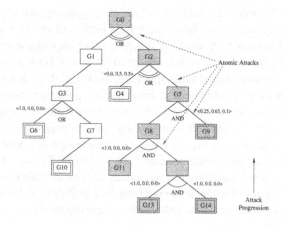

Fig. 3. A possible attack scenario

The following figure shows an augmented attack tree. It helps illustrate the notion of attack scenario. The shaded boxes comprise the nodes in the attack scenario.

Definition 5. *An edge* (v_i, v_j) *in an attack scenario is called an* atomic attack. *The node* v_i *represents the precondition for the atomic attack and* v_j *is the exploitation of the atomic attack.*

Referring to figure 3 some of the atomic attacks have been shown by dashed arrows. Note that to achieve an atomic attack, the attacker must execute some operations that exploit one or more vulnerabilities in the system. Once a vulnerability has been identified the attacker executes a set of "attacking operations" that effectuates an atomic attack. This leads us to the following definition.

Definition 6. *A* suspicious operations set, SO^{attk}, *corresponding to an atomic attack attk, is a set of operations on specific objects that may potentially lead to the culmination of the atomic attack attk.* SO^{attk} *is a set of tuples of the form* $\langle action, object \rangle$.

We can identify two different types of operations in a suspicious operations set SO^{attk}. The first subset of operations is the set *Vul* of vulnerable operations. At least one of the operations in the vulnerable set needs to be executed to exploit a vulnerability. An atomic attack can be launched by exploiting one or more vulnerabilities. Similarly each vulnerability can be exploited by executing one or more vulnerable operations. The second subset of operations is the set *Ao* of attacking operations. All of these need to be executed to accomplish the atomic attack.

3.1 Mapping Workflow to Attack Tree

In order to obtain an attack tree from the workflow corresponding to a pervasive computing application, we assume that the attack trees to compromise a node or an edge characteristic are already known and denoted by $AAT(N_i)$ and $AAT(E_j)$ respectively[2].

---

[2] We have shown earlier in [11] how an attack tree can be build for a system.

We say that $AAT(\cdot)$ is *true* if the root node of the corresponding attack tree (or the goal) has been achieved by an attacker; *false* otherwise. Further, we associate a boolean value $T(\mathcal{N}_p) = \bigvee_i A(x_i)$ to each path, where x_i is a node or an edge characteristic appearing in the path $\mathcal{N}_p$. In other words, a path is disrupted by an attacker if it compromises any of the devices or communication links appearing as part of it. If an attacker is able to disrupt every path, or a subset thereof as necessary, then the application shall have no way of realizing the objective laid down in the workflow. Hence, by replacing the paths by their boolean values in the path composition, we can obtain an expression that is analogous to the attack tree for the workflow. For the example provided in figure 2, the expression for the attack tree would become $T(\mathcal{N}_1) \cdot T(\mathcal{N}_2) + T(\mathcal{N}_3) + T(\mathcal{N}_4) + T(\mathcal{N}_5)$, with the "dot" and "plus" notations now indicating the logical boolean operations. Note that this representation of the attack tree is a boolean expression, and hence standard reduction techniques can be applied to reduce the complexity (node or edge characteristic repetitions) of the attack tree.

3.2 Opinion Model for Attack Trees

The concept of "beliefs, disbeliefs and uncertainty about opinion" is borrowed from the work on subjective logic by Jøsang [6]. In this work, an agent's *opinion* about a proposition x, $w(x)$, is defined in terms of the belief $b(x)$, the disbelief $d(x)$ and the uncertainty $u(x)$, with $b(x) + d(x) + u(x) = 1$. A particular opinion $w(x)$ is represented as a point in the opinion triangle. The triangle itself is defined by the three vertices – [0,0,1], [0,1,0] and [1,0,0] – corresponding to total uncertainty ([0,0,1]), total disbelief ([0,1,0]) and total belief ([1,0,0]) about the proposition.

The following two definitions from [6] help in forming an opinion about the conjunction and disjunction of two propositions x and y. The conjunction of the opinions of two propositions results in a new opinion reflecting the truth of both proposition simultaneously, while the disjunction of the two opinions results in a new opinion reflecting the truth of one or the other or both propositions.

Definition 7. Conjunction of Opinions. *Let x and y be two propositions. Let $w_x = (b_x, d_x, u_x)$ and $w_y = (b_y, d_y, u_y)$ represent an agent's opinion about the propositions. Then the conjunction of the opinion w_x and w_y is $w_x \wedge w_y$ given by*

$$w_x \wedge w_y = (b_{x \wedge y}, d_{x \wedge y}, u_{x \wedge y})$$

and satisfies the following equations.

$$b_{x \wedge y} = b_x \cdot b_y \tag{1}$$
$$d_{x \wedge y} = d_x + d_y - d_x \cdot d_y \tag{2}$$
$$u_{x \wedge y} = b_x \cdot u_y + u_x \cdot b_y + u_x \cdot u_y \tag{3}$$

Definition 8. Disjunction of Opinions. *Let x and y be two propositions. Let $w_x = (b_x, d_x, u_x)$ and $w_y = (b_y, d_y, u_y)$ represent an agent's opinion about the propositions. Then the disjunction of the opinion w_x and w_y is $w_x \vee w_y$ given by*

$$w_x \vee w_y = (b_{x \vee y}, d_{x \vee y}, u_{x \vee y})$$

and satisfies the following equations.

$$b_{x \lor y} = b_x + b_y - b_x \cdot b_y \tag{4}$$

$$d_{x \lor y} = d_x \cdot d_y \tag{5}$$

$$u_{x \lor y} = d_x \cdot u_y + u_x \cdot d_y + u_x \cdot u_y \tag{6}$$

We would like to formalize the notion of an opinion on attack activities based on an opinion on vulnerabilities initially present in the pervasive system. The opinion on vulnerability represents the degree of weakness in the system. For a system to be successfully attacked it must have an initial set of vulnerabilities. As an attack exploits a particular vulnerability it proceeds to the next stage where the system is more vulnerable. This changes our opinion of vulnerability. We represent the vulnerability that results from poor design by the initial subgoal in the attack tree and vulnerabilities that result from the progression of the attack as intermediate subgoals in the attack tree.

The vulnerabilities and the attacking activities are related; the vulnerabilities are the preconditions for an attacker to perform attacking activities. Moreover, a successful attack activity exploits more vulnerabilities. This, in turn, becomes a precondition of a more advanced attack activity. This relationship is formally represented by the following definition.

Definition 9. *Let S be a node in the augmented attack tree AAT* $= (V, E, \varepsilon, L)$*. The opinion on the vulnerability of S, $w_S{}^{Vul}$ is defined as follows:*

1. *if S is an AND-decomposition with m branches then*

$$w_S{}^{Vul} = \left(w_{S_1}{}^{Vul} \land w_{S_1}{}^{Atk} \right) \land \dots \land \left(w_{S_m}{}^{Vul} \land w_{S_m}{}^{Atk} \right)$$

2. *if S is an OR-decomposition with m branches then*

$$w_S{}^{Vul} = \left(w_{S_1}{}^{Vul} \land w_{S_1}{}^{Atk} \right) \lor \dots \lor \left(w_{S_m}{}^{Vul} \land w_{S_m}{}^{Atk} \right)$$

3. *if S is a leaf node then $w_S{}^{Vul} = (1,0,0)$, a constant.*

Definition (9) above represents the relation between two opinions; the opinion on vulnerability in the pervasive system and the opinion on attacking activities. Figure 4 gives the general idea on how we use the augmented attack tree to predict attacks in the pervasive system. When a pervasive computing application is initiated, the intermediate nodes in the augmented attack tree are initiated with total disbelief about any attack. However, the leave nodes are initiated with full belief about an attack. This is because the leaf nodes represent the initial vulnerabilities that exist in the system ready for full and immediate exploitation.

At time t_1 say, the monitoring reports suspicious operation. The system maps the operation to the threats database to identify the corresponding atomic attacks. Assuming Attk$_1$ is the relevant atomic attack, the system computes the opinion on an attacking activity Attk$_1$. The model to compute this is formulated in Section 4. The monitoring system then starts updating the progression of attack against the attack tree. For this purpose, the system evaluates an opinion value for nodes in the attack tree. The edge associated with Attk$_1$ is first updated. Then the opinion value of its immediate parent-level subgoal (subgoal 1 in figure 4) is calculated using the above equations (depending

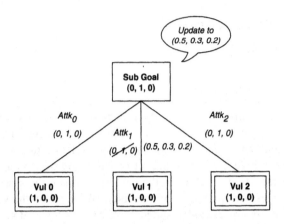

Fig. 4. Attack prediction

on what branch-decomposition this subgoal has). This scenario is shown in figure 4 as the particular node updating the value to (.5, .3, .2). Next comes the next immediate parent-level sub goal. The updating chain continues upwardly to the root of attack tree. Eventually, the updated value at the ultimate goal (the root of the attack tree) announces the current belief in the attack on the system.

4   Quantitative Framework for Evaluating Attacks

Let SO_X be the set of all suspicious operations of an attack in a given attack tree. Let also $SO_X = Vul_X \cup Ao_X$ where Vul_X denotes the set of vulnerable operations and Ao_X is the set of attacking operations. We observe that a monitoring agent that tracks the activities of a given application can reasonably make the following predictions about a malicious attack.

Complete disbelief in an attack. If no operation has been executed by the application that belongs to either Vul_X or Ao_X, then the monitor has complete disbelief in an ensuing attack.

Complete belief in an attack. If all operations in Ao_X and at least one operation in Vul_X has been executed by the application, then the monitor has total belief in an ensuing attack.

Complete uncertainty about an attack. If all operations in Vul_X has been executed and no operation in Ao_X has been executed then the monitor is completely uncertain about an ensuing attack.

We represent these three cases as the three vertices of the opinion triangle representing the monitor's opinion about an attack (see figure 5). We use the symbol D for the total disbelief vertex, B for the total belief vertex and U for the total uncertainty vertex. A point within this triangle, which occurs when some operations in both Vul_X and Ao_X has been executed, will give the monitor's opinion about an ensuing attack. The monitor has to compute this opinion based on the fraction of vulnerable operations that has

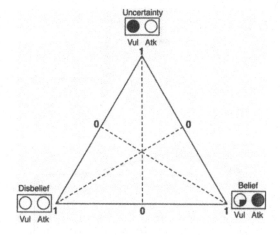

Fig. 5. Opinion thresholds for the model

been executed so far and the fraction of attacking operations. We define the following fractions.

$$m = \frac{\text{Number of vulnerable operations executed so far}}{\text{Total number of operation in } Vul_X} \qquad (7)$$

$$n = \frac{\text{Number of attacking operations executed so far}}{\text{Total number of operations in } Ao_X} \qquad (8)$$

The monitor always starts from the disbelief vertex of the opinion triangle. Since at least one vulnerable operation needs to be executed before any attacking operation can be executed, the opinion of the monitor moves along the $\overline{DU}$ side of the opinion triangle initially. As and when attacking operations gets executed the opinion point begins to move towards the edge $\overline{BU}$. This leads to the following observation.

Observation 1. *The fraction m tends to pull the opinion about an attack towards uncertainty while the fraction n tends to pull the opinion towards belief. The opinion has an initial inertia that tends to keep it at the disbelief end. At any instance the interaction of these three forces keep the opinion in equilibrium.*

This scenario closely resembles the following equilibrium condition arising in mechanics (see figure 6). A ring is attached to a spring which in turn is attached to the vertex D of an equilateral triangle. At the vertices U and B of the triangle are two ideal pulleys that connect two sand buckets to the ring. When the sand buckets are empty the spring keeps the ring at D. As the sand buckets get filled with sand they exert forces on the ring. These forces stretch the spring and move the ring towards U or D. The resulting tension in the string determines the position of the ring within the triangle which can be calculated using the laws of mechanics. In particular, Hook's law gives us that tension in a spring is equal to the product of the stiffness constant of the spring (k) and the elongation of the spring ($\triangle$).

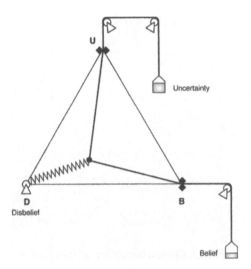

Fig. 6. Analogy of opinion about attacks with equilibrium of forces

We observe that in our model the analogues of the forces exerted by the sand buckets are the fractions m and n from equations 7 and 8. To model our system we need to define the equivalents of the following things: (i) the perimeter of the triangle, (ii) the force exerted by the two sand buckets and (iii) the tension in the spring. The opinion triangle is an equilateral triangle each of whose three sides are 1 unit in length. The resultant of the forces exerted by the two sand buckets can be computed as follows.

Consider the case when all vulnerable operations in the set Vul_X has been executed and no operation in Ao_X has been executed. This corresponds to the case when $m = 1$ and $n = 0$. In this case the opinion point will be at the vertex corresponding to total uncertainty. Thus the spring will be extended along the $\overline{DU}$ edge of the opinion triangle and have a displacement $\triangle = 1.0$ unit. Then the effect of full uncertainty can be expressed by the formula $F_u = k \cdot 1.0$ where k is some constant. Thus, at any instance, the effect of a fraction m of total uncertainty is expressed by the equation:

$$F_u = m \cdot k \tag{9}$$

The effect of total belief needs to be modeled a bit differently. This is because in order for some belief to arise in the opinion, not only some attacking operations need to be executed but some vulnerable operations as well. Moreover at least one vulnerable operation needs to be executed prior to execution of any attacking operation. The effect of execution of any vulnerable operation is to move the opinion point towards uncertainty. Thus, following the same reasoning as for the uncertainty case, if $\lambda \cdot k$ is the extension of the spring along the $\overline{DB}$ side of the opinion triangle, where $0 < \lambda \leq 1$ is a known constant, then the following expression holds for the effect of a fraction n of total belief on the opinion.

$$F_b = n \cdot \lambda \cdot k \tag{10}$$

At some instance the opinion point will be somewhere within the triangle. We use polar coordinate systems to represent the point within the triangle. Let the edge $\overline{DB}$

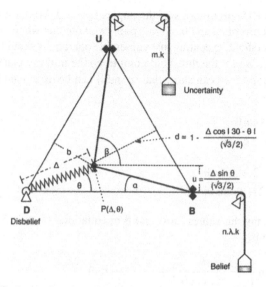

Fig. 7. Computing the values for b, d and u from polar coordinates

represent the X-axis and the point D be the origin. Then any opinion point P in the polar coordinate system can be represented as $P = (\triangle,\theta)$, where $\triangle$ is the point's displacement from the origin and θ is the angle of the displacement with the X-Axis.

Once the polar coordinates $(\triangle,\theta)$ of an opinion point, P, is known we can calculate the corresponding values for disbelief, uncertainty and belief using the laws of trigonometry (see figure 7).

The three values can be expressed in terms of the following equations.

$$u = \frac{\triangle \sin\theta}{\sqrt{3}/2} \tag{11}$$

$$d = 1 - \frac{\triangle \cos|30 - \theta|}{\sqrt{3}/2} \tag{12}$$

$$b = 1 - d - u \tag{13}$$

At any given instance the opinion point, P, is in "equilibrium" within the opinion triangle. In other words, the combined effect of the pull in the uncertainty direction and the pull in the belief direction is balanced by the inertial pull towards the disbelief direction and the resulting effect of the pulls is zero. If we call F_d to be the pull towards the disbelief direction, then the sum of the X-axis components of F_u, F_b and F_d is equal to zero. Similarly the sum of the Y-axis components of F_u, F_b and F_d is zero. We compute these in terms of the angles that the belief, disbelief and uncertainty pulls make with the X-axis, namely α, θ and β respectively (see figure 7).

It can be shown that under equilibrium condition the following equations hold.

$$\lambda n \cos\alpha + m \cos\beta - \triangle \cos\theta = 0 \tag{14}$$

$$\lambda n \sin\alpha + \triangle \sin\theta - m \sin\beta = 0 \tag{15}$$

Equations 14 and 15 are in terms of the angles α and β. We have to find the value of these angles in terms of $\triangle$ and θ. At this point we note that when the opinion values crosses a certain thershold, executing just vulnerable operations should force the system into high alert state. We set the threshold point to be the midway mark between D and B. With this observation we can show that α and β can be expressed by the following equations.

$$\alpha = \arctan \frac{\triangle \sin \theta}{1 - \triangle \cos \theta} \tag{16}$$

$$\beta = \arctan \frac{\sqrt{3}/2 - \triangle \sin \theta}{|1/2 - \triangle \cos \theta|} \tag{17}$$

Finally, substituting the values for α and β in equations 14 and 15 gives us the following two equations.

$$\lambda\, n \cos\left(\arctan \frac{\triangle \sin \theta}{1 - \triangle \cos \theta}\right) + \ - \triangle \cos \theta$$
$$m \cos\left(\arctan \frac{\sqrt{3}/2 - \triangle \sin \theta}{|1/2 - \triangle \cos \theta|}\right) = 0 \tag{18}$$

$$\lambda\, n \sin\left(\arctan \frac{\triangle \sin \theta}{1 - \triangle \cos \theta}\right) + \triangle \sin \theta$$
$$- m \sin\left(\arctan \frac{\sqrt{3}/2 - \triangle \sin \theta}{|1/2 - \triangle \cos \theta|}\right) = 0 \tag{19}$$

From the above modeling we observe that by counting how many of the different types of operations have executed in the pervasive application we can formulate an opinion about the current state of compromise of the system. The complete framework works as follows. When the application starts executing operations, the monitor determines the values of the fractions m and n. This gives rise to the opinion values for branches of the attack tree that are emergent from leaf nodes using equations 18, 19, 11, 12 and 13. These values can be computed all the way up to the root of the attack tree using further the theorems on conjunction and disjunction of opinions. Thus at any point in time, while an application is executing operations, we can estimate what the chances are that this particular application can cause a compromise of the pervasive system.

5   Conclusions and Future Work

In this paper, we have presented a quantitative model for evaluating the chances of an attack occurring in a pervasive computing environment. We make two main contributions. First we develop an augmented attack tree model for representing attacks in a pervasive application. Next we build an opinion model for attacks that is based on monitoring, classifying and counting the different activities that is going on in the application. The opinion model provides three measures, a belief value that an attack is ensuing, a disbelief value that there is an attack and an uncertainty value regarding the other two values. We believe that these three values together gives a good picture of the state of compromise of the pervasive application. Since these values are continuously generated based on signals from the monitoring system, an administrator can use these values to adapt the security controls to the changing scenario.

The challenge is to validate the model in a real world scenario and that is our planned next step for this work. The problem we are facing is the lack of real world data for pervasive applications. As a first step we are using the DARPA Intrusion Detection System Evaluation dataset [7] in a simulated pervasive computing environment. The DARPA dataset will be used to provide a stream of activity records for the application. Results from this evaluation will be presented at a future venue.

Acknowledgment

This work has been supported in part by a grant from the U.S. Air Force Office of Scientific Research (AFOSR) under contract FA9550-07-1-0042. The statements and opinions expressed in this work and the conclusions drawn are those of the authors and do not represent those of the AFOSR or any other federal agencies or their representatives.

References

[1] Ammann, P., Wijesekera, D., Kaushik, S.: Scalable, graph-based network vulnerability analysis. In: Proceedings of the 9th ACM Conference on Computer and Communications Security, Washington DC, pp. 217–224 (November 2002)

[2] Dawkins, J., Campbell, C., Hale, J.: Modeling network attacks: Extending the attack tree paradigm. In: Proceedings of the Workshop on Statistical Machine Learning Techniques in Computer Intrusion Detection, Baltimore, MD. Johns Hopkins University (June 2002)

[3] Elson, J., Estrin, D.: Sensor networks: A bridge to the physical world. In: Raghavendra, C.S., Sivalingam, K.M., Znati, T. (eds.) Wireless Sensor Networks. Kluwer Academic Publishers, Dordrecht (2004)

[4] Jha, S., Sheyner, O., Wing, J.: Minimization and reliability analysis of attack graphs. Technical Report CMU-CS-02-109, School of Computer Science, Carnegie Mellon University (February 2002)

[5] Jha, S., Sheyner, O., Wing, J.: Two formal analyses of attack graphs. In: Proceedings of the 2002 Computer Security Foundations Workshop, Nova Scotia, pp. 45–59 (June 2002)

[6] Jøsang, A.: A logic for uncertain probabilities. International Journal of Uncertainty, Fuzziness and Knowledge-Based Systems 9(3) (June 2001)

[7] Lippmann, R.P., Fried, D.J., Graf, I., Haines, J.W., Kendall, K., McClung, D., Weber, D., Webster, S., Wyschogrod, D., Cunningham, R.K., Zissman, M.: Evaluating Intrusion Detection Systems: The 1998 DARPA Off-line Intrusion Detection Evaluation. In: Proceedings of the DARPA Information Survivability Conference and Exposition, Los Alamitos, CA (January 2000)

[8] Moore, A.P., Ellison, R.J., Linger, R.C.: Attack modeling for information survivability. Technical Note CMU/SEI-2001-TN-001, Carnegie Melon University / Software Engineering Institute (March 2001)

[9] Perrig, A., Stankovic, J., Wagner, D.: Security in wireless sensor networks. Communicaqions of the ACM 47(6), 53–57 (2004)

[10] Phillips, C., Swiler, L.P.: A graph-based system for network-vulnerability analysis. In: Proceedings of the 1998 New Security Paradigms Workshop, Chicago, IL, pp. 71–79 (January 1998)

[11] Ray, I., Poolsappasit, N.: Using Attack Trees to Identify Malicious Attacks from Authorized Insiders. In: Proceedings of the 10th European Symposium on Research in Computer Security, Milan, Italy (September 2005)

[12] Schneier, B.: Attack trees: Modeling security threats. Dr. Dobb's Journal (December 1999)

[13] Sheyner, O., Haines, J., Jha, S., Lippmann, R., Wing, J.: Automated generation and analysis of attack graphs. In: Proceedings of the 2002 IEEE Computer Society Symposium on Security and Privacy, Oakland, CA (May 2002)

[14] Swiler, L., Phillips, C., Ellis, D., Chakerian, S.: Computer-attack graph generation tool. In: Proceedings of DISCEX 2000: DARPA Information Survivability Conference and Exposition II, pp. 307–321 (June 2001)

DIWeDa - Detecting Intrusions in Web Databases

Alex Roichman[1] and Ehud Gudes[2]

[1] Department of Computer Science, The Open University, Raanana, Israel
Alexr@Checkmarx.com
[2] Department of Computer Science, The Open University, Raanana, Israel
and
Department of Computer Science, Ben-Gurion University, Beer-Sheva, Israel
Ehud@cs.bgu.ac.il

Abstract. There are many Intrusion Detection Systems (IDS) for networks and operating systems and there are few for Databases- despite the fact that the most valuable resources of every organization are in its databases. The number of database attacks has grown, especially since most databases are accessible from the web and satisfactory solutions to these kinds of attacks are still lacking.

We present DIWeDa - a practical solution for detecting intrusions to web databases. Contrary to any existing database intrusion detection method, our method works at the session level and not at the SQL statement or transaction level. We use a novel SQL Session Content Anomaly intrusion classifier and this enables us to detect not only most known attacks such as SQL Injections, but also more complex kinds of attacks such as Business Logic Violations. Our experiments implemented the proposed intrusion detection system prototype and showed its feasibility and effectiveness.

Keywords: Intrusion detection, web database security, database vulnerability, SQL content classification.

1 Introduction

Web applications have become very popular in recent years, but their primary focus on functionality and not on security. As a result, there are many security holes in web applications and according to [17], "70% of websites are at immediate risk of being hacked!" Web applications are accessible 24 hours a day, 7 days a week, and have direct access to back-end databases. The attack surface of such databases is very large and the existing technology cannot prevent many attacks.

The best known type of attack is the SQL injection attack and several attempts to deal with it were published (e.g., [3, 5]). However, the above methods cannot defend against another kind of web application attack which is the *Business Logic Violation* attack. For example, in many web forums there may exist a business rule that states that a user must be registered prior to participating in a forum. This logic can be violated at the application level by an intruder who participates in a forum without registering. Such attacks compromise the business logic and can be seen only at the session level. Databases cannot prevent them because the existing database access control can grant or revoke access to resources only according to the user identity or role. It cannot rely on the business logic of an enterprise. Thus the database's access control is inadequate and many web attacks remain unprevented.

V. Atluri (Ed.): DAS 2008, LNCS 5094, pp. 313–329, 2008.

The described situation has some serious impacts. Currently, the only means to prevent attacks on web databases is at the application level. Although many advances have been made in developing secure applications, trusting applications which are developed under time constraints, and by developers who are not security experts, presents a large risk to the database and therefore databases are threatened by these applications. Intrusion detection is therefore an important security measure in these applications.

An enterprise might have several applications, but one database. These applications are changed frequently, thus re-learning the application behavior by IDS requires much effort. On the other hand, business rules which are seen at the database level are stable. Thus, it is preferable to have only one IDS at the database level and to enforce stable business rules, and not to have an IDS for each application which would demand coping with continuous application changes.

Intrusion Detection Systems for operating systems and networks have existed for over 20 years, but IDS for databases is a relatively new field of research that has surfaced in the last few years. Very few practical solutions exist for database IDS (AppRadar, SQLGuard, see [14]) and most of them are signature-based, depend on a specific database provider, and cannot detect many anomalous SQL sessions, especially from web applications. Detection of business logic violations is beyond the scope of these IDS. Thus, despite the existence of academic and industrial research for database IDS, there is no suitable practical solution for web database intrusion detection and many attacks remain unnoticed and unresolved. The absence of an appropriate solution for web databases can be explained by the fact that there are several problems that a web database intrusion detection system must solve:

- In a typical n-tire (web) application, different users can run their SQL statements on the same database connection. This technique is called *Connection Pooling* [18] and contributes to application efficiency. But with this technique, IDS cannot distinguish between legal and intruder sessions. Without finding a way of identifying and partitioning web database sessions, connection pooling makes the web application's access to databases almost untraceable. Since the real user of a web session is unknown at the database level, it is also impossible to apply role base access control to web databases. Sometimes the actual role a user uses is determined dynamically only at run time.

- Web applications have a tendency to use the *Implicit Transaction* where each transaction consists of a single SQL statement. This makes transactional level detection not suitable for web applications. But there exist attacks, such as business logic violations, that cannot be seen at the statement level; they can be seen only at the session level (composed of multiple transactions).

- Many web database attacks are very specific to the enterprise business logic, thus the IDS cannot be signature-based and must be tailored to the enterprise by learning its profiles in a given enterprise. But different roles in an enterprise may have different authorization – what is legal for a one role may be intrusion for another. Thus the best strategy for web database IDS is to build profiles not per an enterprise, but per enterprise roles.

- Building profiles requires a long training period that must be free of attacks. For real web applications it is generally impossible to guarantee a free-of-attack period.

We will present our method for web database intrusion detection that will give a practical solution to the above problems and improve database systems security. Our method works with any existing database and is capable of associating each SQL statement reaching a database with its actual user. We identify database roles from the learnt profiles and look for intrusions from one role to another. We detect intrusions at the session level, thus we are able to detect attacks such as the business logic violation, which cannot be seen at the statement/transaction level. We classify each session by a classifier called the *SQL Content Anomaly* classifier. This approach enables us to detect enterprise roles and analyze an entire session by looking for a deviation from previously learnt roles. Furthermore, our model is able to learn profiles by observing the normal working application with no assumption that the learning period is clear from attacks.

The rest of this article is organized as follows: Section 2 presents related work. Section 3 presents our method and in Section 4 we analyze and evaluate it. The last section concludes the article and discusses future work.

2   Related Work

IDS for databases, and especially web databases, is a relatively new field of research. One such research idea is to learn the structure of each SQL statement possible in the system and to fingerprint that structure. There are a large number of such possible statements, but most of them differ only in constants that represent the user's inputs. If we replace the constants in each statement with variables, we get some high level representation of the SQL sentence called the fingerprint (for more detail, see Section 3.3.1 Fingerprint Set Builder). [3] suggest detecting SQL injections by comparing a fingerprint before inclusion of user input with that resulting after inclusion of input. [5] develop this approach by combining static code analysis and runtime monitoring of possible fingerprints. [7] suggest also imposing order on possible fingerprints. But the disadvantage of these techniques is in its inability to correlate each fingerprint with an appropriate application role

An additional approach is to refer to some interesting properties of each SQL statement such as referenced tables and fields. [2] assign each SQL sentence to some role defined by the SQL's properties. If a new SQL statement arrives, the IDS classifies it to one of the existing roles and compares the predicted role with the role of the user who submitted the SQL query. When the predicted role is different from the user role, the alarm is raised. However, this method is not suitable to the web applications where we do not know the user's role in advance.

Another approach to database IDS is to build profiles for each database user. Users of a database do not usually access all the data, but only a small part of it. [4] identify a working scope of each user and measures the distance of each user's session from the built profiles. When this distance is greater than some predefined threshold, the IDS raises an alert. But for many web applications the number of users is tremendous and it is very difficult to maintain such a great quantity of profiles. Another problem with this approach is erroneously creating a legal working scope for the attacker who accesses the data of different users.

Another approach to the database intrusion detection problem is to search for data dependencies among the data items in a database [see 6, 12]. The data dependencies are the access correlation between the items that are the tables' fields. Transactions not compliant to those dependencies are marked as intrusions. But this method ignores the structure of an SQL sentence and thus may suffer from a high false negative rate.

The proposed methods are capable of detecting several data-centric attacks, but have some weaknesses. When only looking for fingerprints, without associating the fingerprints with roles, many attacks will go undetected. For example, the fingerprint of an SQL run by a professor cannot be used for classification of a student query. Thus it is desired that the IDS will be role-based. But as we already mentioned, for existing web applications roles cannot be known in advance, but must be learned by the IDS. Moreover, when the IDS works only at the SQL statement level, many attacks that can be seen only at the session level remain undetected. Our approach will use new ideas, enabling us to detect previously undetected attacks such as business logic violations. Our model will learn the database access roles (where business rules are wired). With this information, we can look for anomalous sessions which deviate from these roles. In the next section, we will present the architecture of our system and describe how it works.

3   Our Approach

3.1   The Architecture

The software architecture for the proposed IDS design is shown in Figure 1:

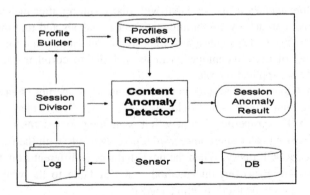

Fig. 1. System architecture

The purpose of the Sensor is to catch every SQL statement that arrives at the database and to write it to the Log. This log is then divided by the Session Divisor to be used by the Profile Builder during the IDS learning phase, and by the Detection

Engine during the detection phase. The profile builder generates sets of application profiles that are stored in the Profiles Repository. The Detection Engine applies the Content Anomaly Detection algorithm to this repository, and outputs the Session Anomaly Result. Next we discuss each of the above components in more detail.

3.2 Session Divisor

All SQL statements submitted by a user from the moment she opens the web application until the application is closed, belong to a user's application session. But because of the connection pooling techniques that are used in web applications, SQL statements of different users from different sessions are mixed. As a result, we cannot distinguish between statements from different sessions without partitioning the SQL log. The first task is therefore, the partitioning of the log by sessions.

Our partitioning algorithm is based on the use of *Parameterized Views* as we proposed in [10]. As has been shown there, parameterized views are used as the means of access control to web databases and each such view retrieves information relevant to the current parameter. This parameter is unique for each session, and is very difficult to fake. For example, in a university system a student can retrieve her marks by selecting a course and submitting the following statement:

```
SELECT * FROM Student_Marks_View(0xA287B5)
WHERE Course_No = 12345
```

Fig. 2. Parameterized view example

The parameter of the view is a random number which the web application uniquely associates with the user and the database has access to it as is depicted in Figure 3.

```
CREATE VIEW Sudent_Marks_View WITH pAS_key
SELECT * FROM Student_Marks_Table WHERE Student_No IN
(SELECT Student_No FROM Users_Table
WHERE Users_Table.AS_key=:pAS_key)
```

Fig. 3. Parameterized view definition

Although the course number 12345 is a user's input and thus the SQL is vulnerable to SQL injection, Student_Marks_View returns only the data of the current student with the parameter of 0xA287B5 and thus SQL injection can affect only the student's data. Namely, the student may access information about her marks for different courses, but not marks of different students (for this she must guess a random parameter belonging to another student- an improbable task). Using the parameterized view technique, we can partition the log by parsing each SQL statement and retrieving its parameter, thus all sentences of the same session will have the same parameter. Furthermore, the actual user of each session is easily identified.

Even without the use of parameterized views, the recent tendency in the development of n-tiered web applications is to transfer the real user identity not only up to the basic application layer, but through all the various layers. Oracle's "lightweight session" [15] allows multiple-user sessions to be maintained within a single database session, so that each user can be authenticated by a database password, without the overhead of a separate database connection. IBM suggested using "trusted context" to connect to DB2 [13]. The last mechanism defines how a trusted application can connect to DB2, and while on the same connection, manage transactions of multiple users simultaneously. Using these techniques, a database continually tracks application users/sessions, and provides the tools ready for partitioning the SQL log.

3.3 Profile Builder

Each profile consists of an SQL Fingerprint Set and a Cluster Set that represents the SQL content of each access role. In the next two sections we will show how DIWeDa builds its profiles. It is important to mention that contrary to previously proposed IDS, our system can learn not only from an attack-free log, but also from any log using a single assumption about the *Session Intrusion Rate*, as is explained in the next section.

3.3.1 Fingerprint Set Builder

The SQL fingerprint is the SQL structure abstraction. Each SQL statement may consist of three types of tokens: reserved words (SELECT, WHERE, AND...), names of database objects (tables, rows, stored procedures...), and constants which only contain user inputs. The SQL fingerprint is generated from each SQL sentence by parsing the SQL and replacing the constants with special place holders. Some attacks, such as SQL injection, work by changing the structure of the SQL. So if we generate all possible fingerprints for a web application, DIWeDa will be able to detect SQL injections as they will not fit into any generated fingerprint [3].

We can create a fingerprint for each SQL sentence submitted by a web application. In this way, we may also fingerprint illegal SQL statements submitted by intruders. To cope with this problem, we define the *Session Intrusion Rate*:

Definition 1: *The Session Intrusion Rate (SIR) is the ratio between the number of attacked sessions and all sessions.*

If we assume that from all user sessions only a few may be under attack, we can define an SIR of 0.01 or less. Notice that for a real web application most of its users are legal ones and not attackers. Our assumption is that the analyzed application is not under DDoS attack during its training phase. But detecting DDoS can be done by other existing DDoS detection tools, see [8].

Definition 2: *The support of an SQL fingerprint is the ratio between the number of application sessions that submit this fingerprint and the number of all sessions in the training set.*

Using the above definition, fingerprints with support that is less than the Session Intrusion Rate can be ignored. In this way, false negatives are avoided when the IDS creates a fingerprint to an SQL sentence under injection attack, and thus erroneously classify an illegal event as a legal one at the detection phase. The Builder uses the log to learn all possible fingerprints with support not less than SIR. The result will be a fingerprint set of size n.

3.3.2 Cluster Set Builder

Each enterprise role accesses different parts of the information in the database and thus the SQL contents of different roles are far apart, while the SQL contents of users from the same role are very close. For example, in the University system both a student and a professor can login to a web application. A student can enroll in a course and a professor can give grades to her students. It is obvious that the SQL content of a student's application session is different from the SQL content of a professor: there are many SQL statements a student can submit that a professor cannot and vise versa. If we are able to differentiate between student and professor session contents, we can detect intrusions from one role to another.

Another example is the Bookstore web application with two different access roles: Searcher and Buyer [16]. One business rule of the bookstore may state that in order to buy a book each Buyer must submit her payment details and receive an invoice. This business logic is implemented in the application, where each Buyer must choose at least one book (select from Books table), submit her credit card details (insert into Credit Card table), order the book (insert into Orders table), and get an invoice (insert into Invoice table). These statements are common only to a Buyer session and do not exist in a Searcher session: when a Searcher suddenly insert into the order table without submitting other statements, her session SQL content is far from the Searcher role (because Searcher never accesses Order table) and from the Buyer role (because Buyer always accesses both Order, Credit Card and Invoice tables). Thus her session violates the business logic and should be classified as an intrusion.

Assume that an application has n different fingerprints. We can associate each application session with its SQL *Session Vector*, which is an abstraction of the SQL content:

Definition 3: *A Session Vector is a binary vector SV with the length equal to the number of fingerprints in the application, where the ith bit is 1 if the application session submits SQL with the ith fingerprint, else bit i is 0.*

The Session Vector enables us to formally define the session's SQL contents. We can think about the web application's SQL content as an n-dimensional space, where n is the number of fingerprints for the application. Then each session's SQL content can

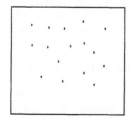

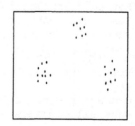

Fig. 4. Abstraction of distribution in the SQL space for an unrealistic application

Fig. 5. Abstraction of distribution in the SQL space for a real application

be seen as a vector in the n-dimensional space. If a session's SQL content was absolutely random then the distribution of vectors in the space should be uniform. But in reality, a session's SQL content is not random and has a very regular structure and the distribution of vectors is not uniform. They are consolidated into several groups (see Figures 4 and 5) where each such group corresponds to an application role.

The distribution is not uniform since two sessions of the same role are likely to produce similar sets of SQL fingerprints. Thus it is reasonable to check the closeness of two sessions by the closeness of their session vectors. If two session vectors are very close, we can assume that they belong to the same role. Each role will be represented by its *Cluster*, and vectors of the same role will be merged to the same cluster.

Definition 4: *A Cluster is a group of highly similar Session Vectors.*

Each Cluster has its mean called the *Cluster Centroid*, which is defined as follows:

Definition 5: *The Cluster Centroid is a vector CC with vector values that are the respective means of the cluster vectors.*

We can define *Support* of a Cluster as follows:

Definition 6: *The Cluster Support is the ratio between the number of Session Vectors belonging to this cluster and the number of all Session Vectors in the training set.*

Definition 7: *The distance D between two clusters presented by their centroids* CC_1 *and* CC_2 *is computed as:*

$$D(CC_1, CC_2) = \sum_{i=1}^{n} \frac{|CC_1[i] - CC_2[i]|}{n}$$

Now a clustering method is applied to produce a set of clusters (roles). If the exact number of distinct roles is known in advance, this is the desired number of clusters. Otherwise the main question is how many clusters should be expected? We propose using the hierarchical clustering algorithm of [1]. The algorithm builds the cluster sets layer by layer; starting with a very large set of clusters and ending with one big cluster (see Algorithm 1 below). The resultant tree is called the cluster Dendrogram tree [11]:

Algorithm 1

```
Build_Dendrogram
{
    1. For each application session build its Session Vector.
    2. Start with each Session Vector as a separate cluster.
    3. Save all clusters received at this stage in a Cluster Set
       CS₁ and initialize i to 1.
    4. Select two closest clusters to merge into a single clus-
       ter.
    5. Compute the new cluster centroid for the merged cluster.
    6. Save all clusters received at this stage in a correspond-
       ing Cluster Set CSᵢ and advance i by 1.
    7. Repeat steps 4-6 until we get a single cluster.
}
```

Figure 6 shows an example of the Dendrogram tree:

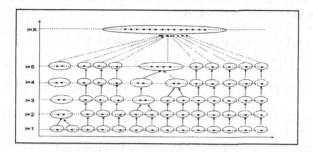

Fig. 6. Dendrogram of clustering algorithm

Our next task is to choose the best Cluster Set (layer of the dendrogram tree) to serve as a profile for DIWeDa. Different strategies exist to make such a choice, and to evaluate cluster set quality [9]. For our purpose, we will use the following criteria:

Definition 8: *Intra-Cluster Distance represents the compactness of clusters in a cluster set and is computed as:*

$$\text{Intra\_Cluster\_Distance}(\text{Cluster - Set}_k) = \sum_{Cluster_j \in Cluster-Set_k} Support_j * \sum_{SV_i \in Cluster_j} D(SV_i, CC_i)$$

where $Support_j$ implies the support of the cluster j (Definition 6). It is zero for the bottom layer of our dendrogram when each cluster contains only one session vector. It increases where the number of clusters decreases and clusters are spread-out. Thus Intra-Cluster Distance is a weighted sum of distances for each cluster in a given cluster set.

Definition 9: *Inter-Cluster Distance represents the isolation of clusters and is computed as:*

$$\text{Inter\_Cluster\_Distance}(\text{Cluster - Set}_k) = \sum_{Cluster_j \in Cluster-Set_k} D(CC_j, Global\_Centroid)$$

where *Global_Centroid* implies the mean of all Cluster Centroids in a given cluster set. It is zero for the top layer of our dendrogram, and it is one at the bottom of the dendrogram when each cluster contains only one session vector.

As can be seen, when Intra-Cluster Distance increases, Inter-Cluster Distance decreases and vice versa. To estimate the quality of each cluster set (layer in dendrogram), we use their intra- and inter-distances with the approach known in the literature as *"Minimum Total Distance"* [9]. This approach finds a cluster set with small specific clusters that are far from the global centroid. By using this approach, DIWeDa will find specific separated roles.

$$\text{Minimum\_Total\_Distance} = MIN\langle \text{Intra\_Cluster\_Distance}(\text{Cluster - Set}_k) + \text{Inter\_Cluster\_Distance}(\text{Cluster - Set}_k)\rangle \mid \textit{for each layer } k \textit{ of Dendrogram}$$

For example, let us assume we found a cluster set which has a minimum cluster distance and this cluster set has 3 clusters which are presented by the following Centroids and have the following Supports:

$$CC_1 = \{0, 0, 0, 1/7, 0, 0, 0\}, \text{Support} = 1/120$$

$$CC_2 = \{1/7, 3/7, 1, 0, 1/7, 3/7, 3/7\}, \text{Support} = 61/120$$

$$CC_3 = \{1, 1, 6/7, 5/7, 1, 6/7, 5/7\}, \text{Support} = 58/120$$

As can be seen, we found 3 roles, but the support of the first role is very small. This can happen in two cases: either this role is not significant at all or this is a role of an intruder. Thus, after finding the best cluster set with the minimum total distance, it is reasonable to delete the clusters (roles) with Support < SIR.

To summarize, the algorithm of building cluster-based profiles is as follows:

Algorithm 2
```
Build_Cluster_Based_Profile
{
    1.  Find all application fingerprints with support > SIR and
        save them in Fingerprint Set
    2.  Run Build_Dendrogram (Algorithm 1)
    3.  Select the appropriate cluster set (layer in Dendrogram)
        with the Minimum Total Distance and save it in Cluster
        Set
    4.  Delete Clusters from the selected Cluster Set with Sup-
        port < SIR
}
```

Note that even when the distinct roles in an application are known precisely, using the above algorithm may be valuable: since some groups of users may behave differently within one application role, applying this algorithm would actually produce two different roles.

3.4 Content Anomaly Detector

At the learning phase, DIWeDa builds its profile that is based on a cluster set. At the detection phase DIWeDa will detect the session content anomalies by first computing the probability of an analyzed session to be abnormal. We assume the following two things influence the anomaly degree of an analyzed session:

- The distance of a session vector to the closest cluster centroid – the farther a session vector is from any existing cluster, the more abnormal a session is.
- The number of unexpected statements (NUS) in a session. An Unexpected Statement is a statement for which DIWeDa finds no corresponding fingerprint. For example, if an attacker changes the SQL structure by an SQL injection attack, DIWeDa will classify such a statement as an unexpected one, since it will not find the corresponding fingerprint in learned profiles. The more unexpected statements a session has, the more abnormal a session is. Notice, sometimes a legal session might have some unexpected statements: these statements are legal ones but simply were not learned during the training phase. But as the number of unexpected statements increases, the probability of a session being legal decreases rapidly.

Definition 10: *the probability of an analyzed session represented by its session vector SV to be abnormal is defined by the formula:*

$$P(SV \text{ is abnormal}) = \frac{MD + NUS^2}{1 + NUS^2}$$

where *MD (Minimum Distance)* is the distance (defined in Definition 7) between SV and the closest *Cluster Centroid* from the cluster set and *NUS* is the *Number of Unexpected Statements* in the analyzed session. Notice, we use NUS^2 since we want to give a high weight to *NUS*.

For example, if we have a set of the two following clusters as the profile, where each cluster represented by its centroid: CC_1 = {0, 0, 0, 1/7, 0, 0, 0}, CC_2 = {1/7, 3/7, 1, 0, 1/7, 3/7, 3/7} and we have a session with no unexpected statements and represented by the following Session Vector: SV = {0, 0, 0, 1, 1, 1, 0}, then the distance to CC_1 is:

$$D(SV, CC_1) = \frac{|0-0|+|0-0|+|0-0|+|1-1/7|+|1-0|+|1-0|+|0-0|}{7} \approx 0.41$$

and the distance to CC_2 is:

$$D(SV, CC_2) = \frac{|0-1/7|+|0-3/7|+|0-1|+|1-0|+|1-1/7|+|1-3/7|+|0-3/7|}{7} \approx 0.76$$

Because $D(SV, CC_1) < D(SV, CC_2)$ we can compute the probability of the session as:

$$P(SV \text{ is abnormal}) = \frac{0.41 + 0^2}{1 + 0^2} \approx 0.41$$

Based on evaluating its SQL content, the last result means that an analyzed session has a probability of 0.41 to be abnormal. Next we show how the result helps to define an analyzed session as legal or intrusive based on the definition of *Session Intrusion Threshold:*

Definition 11: *the Session Intrusion Threshold (SIT) is represented by a number in the range [0, 1], where each session with the probability to be abnormal (Definition 10) is greater than this threshold, will be classified as an intrusion.*

Different choices of the Session Intrusion Threshold will lead to different behaviors of our IDS. A very high threshold will lead to a low false-positive rate, but a high false-negative rate; and low threshold will lead to a high false-positive rate and a low false-negative rate. During the empirical evaluation of our system (Section 4), different thresholds were tried, and for each threshold the ratio between the true positive rate and the false positive rate was computed. This ratio is called the *Receiver Operating Characteristic (ROC)* of the system and is used to estimate the effectiveness of the system for intrusion detection. The interesting thing that was learned from our evaluation was that the best threshold was very close to the *Cluster Set Maximum Distance*.

Definition 12: *the Cluster Set Maximum Distance is the maximum between Cluster Maximum Distances over all clusters in the cluster set.*

where the Cluster Maximum Distance is defined as follows:

Definition 13: *the Cluster Maximum Distance is the maximum distance between a vector in a cluster and its centroid over all vectors in the cluster.*

It seems very rational that sessions with a distance greater than the cluster set maximum will be classified as intrusions, since they are far apart from any existing cluster (role). Thus our proposal to use the Cluster Set Maximum Distance as the Session Intrusion Threshold is very intuitive. In Section 4 we experiment with different thresholds, and show that the system with the best performance results is the one when the threshold is chosen on the basis of the maximum distance.

4 Analysis and Evaluation

4.1 Experimental Setup

We have implemented a prototype of the proposed system and used it to evaluate the system's feasibility, efficiency and correctness. The prototype was developed with C# and SQL Server 2005. The input to the system was a Log file – a text file where each line presents a single SQL statement submitted by an analyzed application. The online bookstore application [16] was used as a web application benchmark. The profiles were built by manually operating this application. The analyzed sessions were created by synthetic data, as will be explained in Section 4.3. We used the following criteria for the quantitative evaluation of our system:

$$\text{True Positive Rate (TPR)} = \frac{\#\,\text{of True Positives}}{\#\,\text{of True Positives} + \#\,\text{of False Negatives}}$$

$$\text{False Positive Rate (FPR)} = \frac{\#\,\text{of False Positives}}{\#\,\text{of False Positives} + \#\,\text{of True Negatives}}$$

$$\text{Receiver Operating Characteristic (ROC)} = \frac{\text{True Positive Rate}}{\text{False Positive Rate}}$$

4.2 Training Set Description

The training set was built by the manual operation of the benchmark application. 200 different sessions were created, from which 198 were legal sessions and 2 with exploiting of application vulnerabilities of SQL injections and business logic violations. Thus, the Session Intrusion Rate (SIR) was 0.01.

All SQL sentences of the 200 sessions were written into the SQL log, which contained 7140 SQL statements. From this log, 165 different fingerprints were deduced by parsing each SQL statement. The 3 fingerprints with support less than SIR were deleted. Notice that of the 3 SQL sentences that have been deleted, two of them were from two different intrusion sessions and the last one was legal, but with a very small support. After this step we had 162 fingerprints in the fingerprint set.

After creating a Session Vector for each session, we used the Dendrogram Building algorithm described in the previous section. From 200 layers of saved cluster sets, using the Minimum Total Distance measure (see Section 3.3.2), we chose the best layer to serve as the DIWeDa profile. The chosen cluster set was a cluster set with 11 clusters, and the maximum distance in this cluster set was 0.07 – this distance was used to define the Session Intrusion Threshold (see Section 3.4).

4.3   Test Set Description

The test-case was built on the following patterns which will be referred to in our Evaluation Discussion Section:

1. Attacks Free Pattern (legal sessions)
2. Where clause modification pattern (sessions built on legal SQLs with where clause modification)
3. Field clause modification pattern (sessions built on legal SQLs with select clause modification)
4. From clause modification pattern (sessions built on legal SQLs with from clause modification)
5. SQL randomization pattern (sessions with randomly created SQLs)
6. Business logic escalation (mix of SQL contents of sessions belong to different roles)
7. Business logic escalation (mix of randomly chosen legal SQLs)
8. Business logic escalation (sessions with random order of SQLs)
9. Business logic escalation (sessions built on SQLs without their original contents)
10. Complex attacks scenario pattern (sessions with mix of previous patterns)

In the following table we summarize our results. The row ROC (Receiver Operating Characteristics) is computed as TPR/FPR and shows the ratio between True Positive Rate (TPR) and False Positive Rate (FPR) for Session Intrusion Thresholds (SIT) from 0.02 to 0.11:

Table 1. Summary of Session Intrusion Thresholds evaluation

	Session Intrusion Threshold								
	0.02	0.04	0.05	0.06	0.07	0.08	0.09	0.1	0.11
TPR	1	1	1	0.925	0.925	0.728	0.728	0.728	0.728
FPR	1	0.3	0.1	0.05	0.05	0.05	0.05	0.05	0.05
ROC	1	3.33	10	18.5	18.5	14.56	14.56	14.56	14.56

The following graph summarizes ROC for thresholds in the range [0.02, 0.11]:

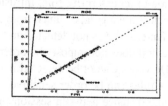

Fig. 7. ROC for different Session Intrusion Thresholds (SIT)

The highest ROC achieved was 0.925/0.05= 18.5 with a Session Intrusion Threshold of 0.07. At this threshold the TPR = 92.5% and the FPR=5%.

4.4 Evaluation Discussion

Table 2 shows the results for each specific pattern.

Table 2. Evaluation summary

Pattern #	# of instances	# of TP	# of TN	# of FP	# of FN
1	200	0	191	9	0
2	5	5	0	0	0
3	5	5	0	0	0
4	5	5	0	0	0
5	10	10	0	0	0
6	5	5	0	0	0
7	5	5	0	0	0
8	5	0	0	0	5
9	15	15	0	0	0
10	5	5	0	0	0

As can be seen in Table 2, all attacks targeting the skeleton of an SQL sentence were detected (Patterns 2–5). This is very important because SQL injection attacks are too common today and many web applications are prone to them.

All cases of business logic escalation (Pattern 6) were classified as intrusion. This pattern merges SQL contents of different roles and shows that, for example, a student who also tries to act as a professor in the University system will have abnormal session SQL contents, and these SQL contents will be detected by DIWeDa.

Very interesting cases are presented in business logic escalation (Pattern 7) and also classified as intrusion by DIWeDa. This pattern shows that the SQL contents of web application sessions are not random, but have a regular structure which can be learned, and deviations from this structure can be detected. We see this by comparing the anomaly degree of the Attack Free Pattern (under 0.05) and the anomaly degree of sessions with random SQL contents (above 0.11). We conclude that the SQL content of a session which is presented by the Session Vector has a regular structure: sessions with the same role are very close one to another and can be consolidated to the same cluster, which is an abstraction of an enterprise role. Intrusion sessions have irregular structure and their session vectors are a great distance from any existing cluster.

Business role escalation (Pattern 8) was not detected and thus, our true positive rate was decreased. Since our method does not impose the order of SQL statements in the session, scrambling of an SQL order cannot be detected in the current system. At this stage, it is clear that business rules can be order sensitive, thus we intend to improve the algorithm by measuring the distance between sessions not only by using common SQL sentences that were issued by both sessions, but also by using the order of these sentences. This will be included in our future work.

All cases of business role escalation (Pattern 9) were classified as intrusion. This pattern shows that a single SQL statement has strong dependencies to other sentences, and if we run some statements without their original SQL contents, DIWeDa can detect the absence of these dependencies and thus is able to detect an intruder, trying to buy books without being authenticated or without paying.

To summarize our true positive rate – we achieved a rate of 0.92, which means that we are able to detect 92% of attacks. Included in the 8% of undetected attacks, there are attacks targeting the order of SQL sentences in a session. This is the main system improvement that can be done in our future work.

Analysis of proposed algorithm's time complexity shows that building profiles is a polynomial task in the number of SQL statements in the log, but analyzing a session is a linear task in the number of session's SQL statements. The following tables summarize the system performance evaluation:

Table 3. Session analyzing performance

# of sessions	Time in sec.
2 Sessions	3
4 Sessions	7
8 Sessions	13
16 Sessions	26
100 Sessions	140
200 Sessions	280

Table 4. Profile building performance

# of sessions	Time in sec.
2 Sessions	2
4 Sessions	3
8 Sessions	5
16 Sessions	32
100 Sessions	215
200 Sessions	480

To summarize our false positive rate – we achieved 0.05 on the test set. This means that 5% of classified sessions are false positives. It should be noted that our system is profile-based and for such systems this rate is low enough (for comparison with other systems, see, for example, Table 2 from [2] or Figure 3 from [6]). Some signature-based systems have achieved false positive rates below our rate, but this is done with a lower true positive rate. The main reason for the level of FPR achieved is that there are legal sessions in which SQL contents are slightly different from learned contents, thus DIWeDa classifies such sessions as intrusion. We assume that our training set, which was created manually, was relatively small and thus DIWeDa was unable to learn all the session's SQL contents. It seems that as real application logs will contain more information, DIWeDa will be able to learn more, thereby possibly making the

FPR less than 5%. We plan to evaluate this on additional web applications in our future work.

5 Conclusions and Future Work

The motivation for this article was to propose a practical solution to the web database intrusion detection problem. DIWeDa profiles the normal behavior of different roles in terms of the set of SQL queries issued in a session, and then compares a session with the profile to identify intrusions. We look for intrusions at the session level and not at the statement/transaction level, as more traditional models do. We learn enterprise roles and look for anomalous sessions far from the learnt roles, enabling us to see anomalies which cannot be seen nor detected using previous models. One possible extension of our algorithm is its ability to deduce enterprise/application roles, which were previously unknown for web applications. RBAC models are widely used for old desktop applications, but most of the web applications do not use roles and the proposed algorithm can be very useful in porting web applications to RBAC models.

As we have demonstrated, our method detects attacks using SQL structures and session's SQL contents based on these structures. This enables us to detect new types of attacks, such as business logic violations. But sometimes data centric attacks can be accomplished without changing the SQL structure, but just by passing unauthorized SQL **parameters.** To detect parameter-based violations, we developed a similar framework and classifiers which are able to learn the distribution of parameters' values and detect deviations from them. We are currently experimenting with detecting such attacks via SQL parameter changes. We are also working on detecting invalid order of SQL statements in a session. We will present our results in a future paper.

References

[1] Berkhin, P.: Survey of Clustering Data Mining Techniques. Tech. rep., In Accrue Software, San Jose, CA (2002)

[2] Bertino, E., Terzi, E., Kamra, A., Vakali, A.: Intrusion Detection in RBAC-administered Databases. In: Proceeding of 21st Computer Security Applications Conference, USA (2005)

[3] Buehrer, T., Weide, B.W., Sivilotti, P.A.G.: Using Parse Tree Validation to Prevent SQL Injection Attacks. In: Proceedings of the 5th international workshop on Software Engineering and Middleware, Portugal (2005)

[4] Chung, C., Gertz, M., Levitt, K.: Demids: A misuse detection system for database systems. In: Proceedings of IFIP TC11 WG11 Third Working Conference (1999)

[5] Halfond, W., Orso, A.: Preventing SQL Injection Attacks Using AMNESIA. In: Proceedings of 28th International Conference on Software Engineering, China (2006)

[6] Hu, Y., Panda, B.: A Data Mining Approach for Database Intrusion Detection. In: Proceedings of the ACM Symposium on Applied computing, Cyprus, pp. 711–716 (2004)

[7] Low, W.L., Lee, S.Y., Teoh, P.: DIDAFIT: Detecting Intrusions in Databases Through Fingerprinting. In: Proceedings of the 4th International Conference on Enterprise Information Systems (2002)

[8] Mirkovic, J., Dietrich, S., Dittrich, D., Reiher, P.: Internet Denial of Service: Attack and Defense Mechanisms. Prentice Hall, Englewood Cliffs (2005)

[9] Raskutti, B., Leckie, C.: An Evaluation of Criteria for Measuring the Quality of Clusters. In: Proceedings of the Sixteenth International Joint Conference on Artificial Intelligence, Sweden (1999)

[10] Roichman, A., Gudes, E.: Fine-grained Access Control to Web Databases. In: Proceeding of 12th SACMAT Symposium, France (2007)

[11] Seo, J., Shneiderman, B.: Understanding Hierarchical Clustering Results by Interactive Exploration of Dendrograms. A Case Study with Genomic Microarray Data, Tech. rep. IEEE Computer Society Press, Los Alamitos (2002)

[12] Srivastava, A., Reddy, S.R.: Intertransaction Data Dependency for Intrusion Detection in Database Systems. Part of Information and System Security course, School of Information Technology. IIT Kharagpur (2005)

[13] Tran, S., Mohan, M.: Use trusted context in DB2 client applications (2006), http://www.ibm.com/developerworks/db2/library/techarticle/dm-0609mohan/index.html

[14] Woo, J., Lee, S., Zoltowski, C.: Database Auditing, http://www.cs.purdue.edu/homes/akamra/cs541/DB_auditing_survey_paper.pdf

[15] Controlling Database Access, Oracle9i Database Concepts Release 2, http://download-west.oracle.com/docs/cd/B10501_01/server.920/a96524/c23acces.htm

[16] Online Book-Store application. The open source from, http://www.gotocode.com/apps.asp?app_id=3&

[17] Acunetix, http://www.acunetix.com/

[18] Connection Pool, http://en.wikipedia.org/wiki/Connection_pool

Securing Workflows with XACML, RDF and BPEL

Vijayant Dhankhar[1], Saket Kaushik[2], and Duminda Wijesekera[3]

[1] Department of Computer Science, George Mason University, Fairfax, VA 22030, USA
dhankhar@gmail.com
[2] Oracle Corporation, Redwood City, CA 94065, USA
saket.kaushik@oracle.com
[3] Department of Computer Science, George Mason University, Fairfax, VA 22030, USA
dwijesek@gmu.edu

Abstract. The XACML is the access controller of the World Wide Web (WWW). The current reference implementation has a single policy decision point and a policy enforcement point. If XACML policies are used to control workflow among cooperating web services, such as those envisioned in more contemporary languages like (BPEL), it requires coordination to be policy compliant. We propose the necessary enhancements required to do so by passing *contextual information* that are needed for the requester to evaluate an access control decision as opposed to the standard four decision values of *permit, deny, indeterminate to make a decision* and *an unforeseeable error occurred during evaluation*. Proposed contextual information is sufficient to coordinate and if necessary synchronize among coordinating policy enforcement points distributed among the WWW. We show how the contextual information can be constructed and verified using the Resource Description Framework (RDF) and the coordination implemented using BPEL.

1 Introduction

In service-oriented architectures, workflows are increasingly being used to provide a single point of access for composite services constructed from multiple sub services. In order to provide a single authority to make yes/no decisions for workflow requests, the individual mechanisms that control the components involved in authorizing the flow should cooperate, requiring distributed evaluation *and* enforcement of the access control decision. Because XACML is the access control language for web services [21], there is a need for distributed accesses controllers using XACML to coordinate in providing secure flow control.

In XACML parlance, a policy based access control decision will be evaluated by (possibly) several so called *policy decision points (PDPs)* [21] collectively; as well as enforced collectively at (possibly) several *policy enforcement points (PEPs)* [21]. This approach has additional advantages, most prominently for the requester, the single service access point provides a service specified by a single access control policy. If implemented, a single access control policy retained at the mother service and be evaluated and enforced distributively by the sub-services. However, current XACML standard and reference implementation [26] lack the desired syntax and enforcement mechanisms for such an access controller. In this paper we supply the necessary extensions to

V. Atluri (Ed.): DAS 2008, LNCS 5094, pp. 330–345, 2008.
© IFIP International Federation for Information Processing 2008

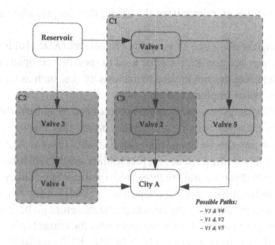

Fig. 1. Use Case

current XACML standard and reference implementation to be able to evaluate and enforce XACML policies in a *fully-distributed* manner. We enhance our previous [11,12] work in achieving this objective in this paper by passing sufficient contextual information between XCAML PDPs and PEPs so that the passed information contain sufficient information to control the distrbuted usage of resources such as flow control ans synhronization. Such techniques can be used in more contemporary workflow languages like BPEL.

For example, consider a hypothesized process of transferring water from a *Reservoir* to a *City A*, enabled through Web Service invocations as shown in Figure 1. In this scenario, for water transfer to take place, the requestor must possess the required authorization *and* the action of opening a valve must be approved by the three companies (*C1, C2* and *C3*) that maintain the grid of water pipelines that connect the reservoir to the city A. In addition, the access controller must check if another request to transfer water is underway or not. This is a necessary environmental constraint because water pipelines have a safety limit as to the amount of pressure they can withstand. As long as there exists a continuous channel from *Reservoir* to *City A*, the water pressure is within safe limits and requestor is authorized, this transfer should be allowed.

Also once the transfer is allowed, it should be run transactionally, i.e. if the downstream valve (*Valve 2* - policy enforcement point) fails to open due to unforseen failure then the upstream valve (*Valve 1* - policy enforcement point) should close, otherwise there is a possibility for an intervening pipeline to burst – another environmental constraint to be met *during* the transfer.

We propose that coordinating access controllers share more than *permit* or *deny* decisions in requesting access to resources controlled by sub-services. Our proposal, described in detail, proposes that they enhance the *permit* or*deny* decision by providing some *context* in which the requester can evaluate the decision. Proposed context information provides the requirements that must be ensured prior to starting the resource usage, the conditions that must be satisfied during the usage and those that must be specified when the requester relinquishes the usage, thereby providing a context for full *usage control* [27].

We propose using the *Resource Description Framework (RDF)* [6] for this purpose of describing the *context*, because RDF can be used to specify a complete *ontology* for the resource usage, including but not limited to exclusivity (i.e. such as writing privileges). We show a snippet of our implementation.

Lastly, the distributed policy enforcement points need to address the control dependencies that exists between policy enforcement points that must exist to ensure the flow. We show how this can be done using the *Business Process Execution Language (BPEL)* [19]. As of this writing we have a preliminary implementation of this.

The significance of this proposal are three fold: Firstly, it can convey synchronization requirements beyond exclusive usage and options. Secondly, it can be customized to the operational interfaces provided by the resource, and therefore go beyond the traditional *read, write, execute* permissions. Lastly, we show how the current collection of semantic web languages and their runtimes (namely, XACML, RDF and BPEL) can be used to implement our proposal. Parts of this proposal have been implemented, and our ongoing work concentrates in making our rudimentary implementation more generic.

The rest of the paper is written as follows. Section 2 describes the current XACML reference implementation. Section 3 provides an overview of RDF. Section 4 describes the enhancements needed to fully distribute the XACML implementation. Section 5 describes some architectural enhancements we are proposing to the existing XACML reference implementation in order to achieve full distribution. Section 6 describes related work and Section 7 has our concluding comments.

2   The XACML Reference Implementation

The current XACML specification has three main entities as shown in Figure 2. As shown, it has the following main components in addition to auxiliary components.

1. **Policy Administration Point (PAP).** Entity that creates policies or policy sets.
2. **Policy Decision Points (PDP).** Entity that evaluates applicable policy and renders an authorization decision. The answer given by the PDP is one of (1) *permit*, (2) *deny*, (3) *insufficient information to decide* or (4) *error*, implying some unforseen error occurred in the execution.
3. **Policy Enforcement Point (PEP).** Entity that performs access control by enforcing authorization decisions.

Figure 2 shows the dataflow of the XACML reference implementation. First, the PAP creates a policy. At request time, an access request arrives at the PEP (flow 1), and is sent to the context handler (flow 2). The context handler determines resources to be accessed and attributes of the requester, resource and the environment, collects all required attributes and forwards them to the PDP (flows 3,4,5,6,7,8). PDP then acquires the policy from PAP (flow 1), evaluates the relevant policy and relays the decision (flows 9, 10) to the PEP through the context handler, which proceeds to enforce the authorization decision.

The policy syntax (XML) includes language constructs to identify the *resource*, the *action* (to be performed on the resource), the *subject*, and *constraints* on the access.

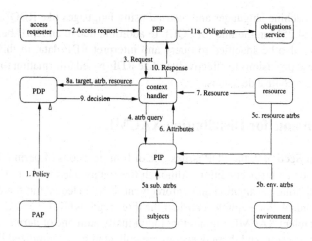

Fig. 2. XACML Architecture

In XACML parlance, this collection of entities is called a *target*. The request syntax (XML) identifies the resource, the action, the subject. The decision engine (PDP) *matches* the incoming request to available policies to discover all applicable policies. If more than one policy is applicable, then the PDP uses a *policy-combination algorithm* [21] to determine the evaluation result. In essence, the combination algorithm states how to combine the result of each applicable policy.

3 RDF Overview

RDF [7,6,15] specify meta-information about *resources*, *i.e.*, entities that can be uniquely identified, and *binary relations* between them so that they can be "machine processed". Such meta information about resources are specified in RDF using binary properties between resources. RDF does so by using the syntax of *triples* where the subject (the first component of the triple) is related by the property (the second component of the triple) to the object (the third component). An RDF schema can be extended further by specifying binary properties between nodes and triples. This process, carried out recursively, is referred to as *reification*. RDF(S) or RDF Schema is RDFs vocabulary description language. It has syntax to describe concepts and resources through meta-classes such as rdfs:Class, rdf:type, *etc.*, and relationships between resources through rdf:property. These meta classes are used to specify properties of user defined schema. Details of RDF/RDF(S) syntax and vocabulary descriptions can be found in [6]. This syntax is readily usable in XACML framework because of the inherent ability of RDF to capture *attribute-value* pairs in its syntax. Attributes are *named-properties* of nodes and their values can be (atomic) data (text, string, integer, etc.) or other nodes.

Multiple RDF triples form a graph (connected or disconnected), *i.e.*, if the object of a triple is the subject of another triple, then the two triples are merged together retaining the common object only once (with one incoming edge and one outgoing edge) [16]. Since RDF expresses binary relationships, RDF triples and graphs can be interpreted by machine languages and *queried* using languages like RDQL, SPARQL, *etc.* [8,9,18,22,24,25] (on the lines of SQL). In addition, due to an XML-based syntax, *XSLT Rules* can also be specified to query and interpret RDF data. In this work, we make use of these provisions to effectively utilize RDF-based information for enforcing distributed access control decisions.

4   Requirements for Distributing XACML

As described in Section 2, the PDP issues one of four decisions of permit, deny, inapplicable policy or an error condition. Although these may adequately reflect the case of a centralized policy evaluation and enforcement, it it inadequate in the case of distributed flow control. For example, consider the three regions C1, C2 and C3 controlled by three independent XACML engines that individually emit one of *permit, deny, inapplicable policy* or *error*, and these decisions are collected by a centralized PDP to give the final decision. The last two decisions from either component should result in denial of permissions for the transfer request of water. For example, if the request to transfer 2000 gallons of water per minute to city A from the reservoir as drawn in Figure 1, and the master PDP request the slave PDP's governing regions C1 and C2 for a subsequent request to transfer water, then they must come back with a reply saying the amount of water they are willing to transfer and what other conditions must be satisfied in order to grant this request. For example, PDP governing region C1 may say that it can grant this request by opening *Valve 1* and *Valve 2*, and closing *Valve 5* provided that *Valve 3* is closed. Simultaneously, the PDP governing region C2 may say that it is willing to grant the request provided that *Valve 3* and *Valve 4* are open and *valve 2* is closed. Consequently, the master PDP must now decide on which path it chooses, provide that all pre-requisite conditions can be met. Otherwise, it has to *Deny* this request. Consequently, there is a need for the secondary PDPs to convey to the master PDP the pre-requisite state information for the former to grant the request, the state that it expects the concerned resources to maintain while the granted resources are being used and the post-requisite state of the resources that it expects the resources to be in when the requestor relinquishes the use of the resource. Because the granted permission or denial are conditional upon these state information, we call it the *decision context*. Consequently, the decision is valid only if the context is satisfied during the enforcement process, consequently providing support for usage control [27]. Furthermore, this *decision context* of how PDP reached a policy decision has to be made available to *PEP's* for the correct enforcement of the *PDP's Decision*. As stated in Section 2, the preferred syntax to state properties of resources on the WEB is RDF, we provide a preliminary definition for the *decision context* using RDF as follows, and refine it in Section 5.

Definition 1 (preliminary definition of decision context). *The decision context consist of a triple of RDF statements, referred to as pre-context, during-context and post-context.*

The *decision context* is different than *obligations* as the latter imposes future requirements on that the PEP must adhere to. The XACML specification specifies an *obligation* as an action performed by the PEP in conjunction with the enforcement of an authorization decision. This definition separates the enforcement action from obligation processing. Such a system where the enforcement is distributed should be able to maintain transactional semantics based on the *decision context*.

Another important aspect of the decision context is that if the decision is not going to be valid during the enforcement of the decision, the actions of the PEP should be rolled back. In the previous example if Valve 1 fails to enforce the policy decision (fails to open), the decision context (both Valve 1 and Valve 2 should open) is invalid and hence Valve 2 must also be closed (rolled back). This transactional semantics based on the decision context should be adhered to by *PEP's* execution.

5   Architecture and Design

In order to enforce distributed access control using XACML, we propose having a separate PDP at every *site* that need to evaluate a local access control policy. Then these local policies communicate their decisions with the encompassing context to the master PDP that collects all such decisions and renders the final access control decision to the external requestor. This arrangement can be repeated recursively, creating a hieararchy of PDPs that are arranged in a tree structure. Consequently, the arrangement applicable to our example scenario is given in the left hand side of Figure 3. For the example given in Figure 1, because the web services are arranged so that the top level service depends upon sub-services C1, and C2, and C1 depends on C2. Consequently, the PDPs given in the left hand side of Figure 3 inherits the same hierarchical structure. Consequently, the corresponding policy enforcement points of these services C1, C2 and C3 should be coordinated in the same hierarchical manner. The right hand side Figure 3 is there to show that the latter coordination can be specified and enforced using the *Business Process execution Language (BPEL)* and will be explained shortly. Accordingly, these PEPs need to agree to enforce the decision within the decision context that all PDPs will pass along with the decision.

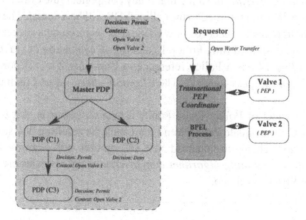

Fig. 3. Architecture and Design

5.1 Context

Because the decision context expresses constraints under which permissions can be granted to acquire resources, we express them as RDF statements. Because the request to the resource has three constraints, these are a triple of RDF constraints, referred to as the pre-context, during-context and the post-context, as defined in Definition 1. (We provide an example, soon after we show how the *decision context* is used).

In order to use this context elements, we alter the access control policies and make the *decision context* conditionals in the access control policies. We do so by using the ⟨*Conditional*⟩ in XACML policies. Furthermore, in order to express and evaluate the enriched policies, we have enriched the XACML runtime. In order to minimize the alteration, we pass the *design context* as a *MetaBoolean* type in XACML, so that it the XACML runtime allows us to use our own evaluator, for which we use and RDF evaluation engine. We formally define the *MetaBoolean* type in XACML as follows.

```
1 <xs:element name="MetaBoolean" type="xacml:MetaBoolean"/>
2 <xs:complexType name="MetaBooleanType">
3     <xs:sequence>
4         <xs:element ref="xacml:Context" minOccurs="0" maxOccurs="unbounded"/>
5     </xs:sequence>
6     <xs:attribute name="eval" type="http://www.w3.org/2001/XMLSchema#boolean" use="required"/>
7 </xs:complexType>
```

Type 1: MetaBoolean Type

In order to give examples of the *decision context* and its embedding as a conditional in the access control policy as a *MetaBoolean* type, consider the case where a request to transfer 3000 gallons of water is received by the master PDP in Figure 1. In response to the request, the PDP retrieves the appropriate policy, given as `Policy 1`.

As shown, the top level policy expressing Company 1's (i.e. the one that governs region c1) in line 1 says that it consists of a policy set. Although the target of this policy is omitted for brevity, it has a set of rules starting in line 8. For brevity we show only one rule, the one starting in line 8 and ends in line 14. Line 1 says that these rules are to be applied in the *denial override*, meaning that if any component rule evaluates to a denial, then the resulting decision returned to the calling PDP will be a denial. The reason being that a synchronous delivery succeeds only if all of its requirements succeed.

In line 8 of the described rule, Policy 1 calls for an evaluation of (*c1:policy-check-valve-1*) and in line 17 has a Policy reference to Company 2's (c2) policy for opening Valve 2 (*c2:policy-check-valve-2*). The *c2:policy-check-valve-2* listing is shown in `Policy 2`.

The intended effect of Policy 1 and Policy 2 taken together is that it will ask the PDP governing C2 to evaluate Policy 2 and send back the resulting decision along with its decision context. Then our enhanced XACML runtime will combine the decisions by using the *policy-combining-algorithm:deny-overrides* algorithm before returning the Decision to the PEP Coordinator.

```
1 <PolicySet PolicySetId="c1:policyset-check-reservoir-city:a" PolicyCombiningAlgId="policy-combining-
    algorithm:deny-overrides">
2   <Target>
3     ....
4   </Target>
5   <Policy PolicyId="c1:policy-check-valve-1" RuleCombiningAlgId="rule-combining-algorithm:deny-overrides">
6     <Target/>
```

```
7    <Rule RuleId="c1:valve-1-scheduling-check" Effect="Permit">
8      ....
9      <Condition>
10       <Apply FunctionId="c1:function:schedeule-valve-1">
11       </Apply>
12     </Condition>
13   </Rule>
14     ....
15   </Policy>
16   <PolicyIdReference>c2:policy-check-valve-2</PolicyIdReference>
17 </PolicySet>
```

Policy 1: Top-Level C1 PolicySet

```
1  <Policy PolicyId="c2:policy-check-valve-2" RuleCombiningAlgId="rule-combining-algorithm:deny-overrides">
2    <Target/>
3    <Rule RuleId="c2:valve-2-scheduling-check" Effect="Permit">
4      ....
5    <Condition>
6      <Apply FunctionId="c2:function:schedule-valve2">
7      </Apply>
8    </Condition>
9    </Rule>
10     ....
11 </Policy>
```

Policy 2: C2's Check for Valve-2

We now provide examples of *decision contexts* returned by the evaluators of these two policies.

```
1 <MetaBoolean eval="true">
2   <Context>
3     <PreContext>
4       <rdf:RDF xmlns:rdfs="http://www.gmu.edu/xacml/owl/ontology/#" xmlns:rdf="http://www.w3.org/1999/02/22-rdf-
          syntax-ns#" xmlns:gmu="http://www.gmu.edu/xacml/rdf#">
5         <rdf:Description rdf:about="http://gmu/valve1">
6           <gmu:state xml:lang="http://www.w3.org/2001/XMLSchema#string">close</gmu:state>
7           <gmu:ID>Valve1</gmu:ID>
8         </rdf:Description>
9       </rdf:RDF>
10    </PreContext>
11    <DuringContext>
12      <rdf:RDF xmlns:rdfs="http://www.gmu.edu/xacml/owl/ontology/#" xmlns:rdf="http://www.w3.org/1999/02/22-rdf-
          syntax-ns#" xmlns:gmu="http://www.gmu.edu/xacml/rdf#">
13        <rdf:Description rdf:about="http://gmu/valve1">
14          <gmu:capacity xml:lang="http://www.w3.org/2001/XMLSchema#int">1000</gmu:capacity>
15          <gmu:state xml:lang="http://www.w3.org/2001/XMLSchema#string">open</gmu:state>
16          <gmu:ID>Valve1</gmu:ID>
17        </rdf:Description>
18      </rdf:RDF>
19    </DuringContext>
20    <PostContext>
21      <rdf:RDF xmlns:rdfs="http://www.gmu.edu/xacml/owl/ontology/#" xmlns:rdf="http://www.w3.org/1999/02/22-rdf-
          syntax-ns#" xmlns:gmu="http://www.gmu.edu/xacml/rdf#">
22        <rdf:Description rdf:about="http://gmu/valve1">
23          <gmu:state xml:lang="http://www.w3.org/2001/XMLSchema#string">close</gmu:state>
24          <gmu:ID>Valve1</gmu:ID>
25        </rdf:Description>
26      </rdf:RDF>
27    </PostContext>
28  </Context>
29 </MetaBoolean>
```

MetaBoolean 1: Generated by valve-1-scheduling-check

The *decision context* returned by the evaluation of Policy 1 is given in *Metaboolean 1*. As the listing shows, the evaluation returned is *true* conditional upon the the pre-context, during-context and post-context given between lines (3-13), (14-25) and

(26-36). As shown, all three of them refer to an RDF descriptions in lines 8, 19 and 31. The three lines immediately following the references to RDF descriptions, namely (9-10), (20-22) and (32-33) describe the three *decision contexts*. The pre-context in lines 9-10 says that the *state* property of *valve 1* must be closed. The during-context in lines (20-21) says that the the *state property* of *valve 1* must be open and further state that the *capacity* property of the valve must be set to 1000 gallons per minute. It is conceivable that the RDF semantics of a valve is such that other properties such as the time duration that it remains open should also be specified. Note that these properties can be specified using RDF polices for the individual resources that are pertinent for the requests to be completely specified so that the PEP can enforce the permission. The post context contained in lines (32-33) say that *close* property of the *valve* must be closed.

Similarly, *Metaboolean 2* given below states the *decision context* returned by the PDP that governs region C2 to the master PDP. As previously explained, if Rule *c2: valve-2-scheduling-check* evaluates to *permit* the function *c2:function-schedule-valve-2* within the conditional returns a *decision context* that requires *valve 2* to be closed prior to granting the requests and it be opened during the usage at the rate of 1000 gallons per minute.

```
1 <MetaBoolean eval="true">
2  <Context>
3    <PreContext>
4      <rdf:RDF xmlns:rdfs="http://www.gmu.edu/xacml/owl/ontology/#" xmlns:rdf="http://www.w3.org/1999/02/22-rdf-
          syntax-ns#" xmlns:gmu="http://www.gmu.edu/xacml/rdf#">
5        <rdf:Description rdf:about="http://gmu/valve2">
6          <gmu:state xml:lang="http://www.w3.org/2001/XMLSchema#string">close</gmu:state>
7          <gmu:ID>Valve2</gmu:ID>
8        </rdf:Description>
9      </rdf:RDF>
10   </PreContext>
11   <DuringContext>
12     <rdf:RDF xmlns:rdfs="http://www.gmu.edu/xacml/owl/ontology/#" xmlns:rdf="http://www.w3.org/1999/02/22-rdf-
          syntax-ns#" xmlns:gmu="http://www.gmu.edu/xacml/rdf#">
13       <rdf:Description rdf:about="http://gmu/valve2">
14         <gmu:capacity xml:lang="http://www.w3.org/2001/XMLSchema#int">1000</gmu:capacity>
15         <gmu:state xml:lang="http://www.w3.org/2001/XMLSchema#string">open</gmu:state>
16         <gmu:ID>Valve2</gmu:ID>
17       </rdf:Description>
18       <rdf:Description rdf:about="http://gmu/valve5">
19         <gmu:state xml:lang="http://www.w3.org/2001/XMLSchema#string">close</gmu:state>
20         <gmu:ID>Valve5</gmu:ID>
21       </rdf:Description>
22     </rdf:RDF>
23   </DuringContext>
24   <PostContext>
25     <rdf:RDF xmlns:rdfs="http://www.gmu.edu/xacml/owl/ontology/#" xmlns:rdf="http://www.w3.org/1999/02/22-rdf-
          syntax-ns#" xmlns:gmu="http://www.gmu.edu/xacml/rdf#">
26       <rdf:Description rdf:about="http://gmu/valve2">
27         <gmu:state xml:lang="http://www.w3.org/2001/XMLSchema#string">close</gmu:state>
28         <gmu:ID>Valve2</gmu:ID>
29       </rdf:Description>
30     </rdf:RDF>
31   </PostContext>
32 </Context>
33 </MetaBoolean>
```

MetaBoolean 2: Generated by Rule valve-2-scheduling-check

There are two pertinent issues here. The first is that either C1 or C2 can consult its own policy and decide how to internally schedule water flow and control their own rates. Secondly they can consult their own scheduling rates so that the resource usage adheres to its own semantics of operations. Our ongoing work addresses these two issues. We now describe the Policy evaluation process used by a master PDP to evaluate an XACML request, upon receipt of *decision contexts*.

5.2   Evaluating the Decision Context

As shown the decision context consists of pre-context, during-context and post-context. Consequently, every child PDP sends its decision context to its parents PDP as a response to a distributed request.

The parent PDP then collects all decision context of its children and combine them to determine if the collected decision context ate consistent. In order to do so, the PDP evaluation collects all *pre contexts*, *during contexts* and *post contexts* separately, and if all of them are determined to be consistent, then evaluate the design context to be consistent. Conversely, if either of them is found to be inconsistent, then the design context is determined to be inconsistent. Conversely, if any of the design context are determined to be Indeterminate, then the design context is said to be indeterminate.

The consistency of the decision context are determined using an RDF rule evaluation engine. The rules supplied to this engine define which contexts are consistent. The RDF rules state which combination of RDF property instances imply falsehood. This process, we refer to as *decision context unification* is performed in a hierarchical manner as shown in Figure 4.

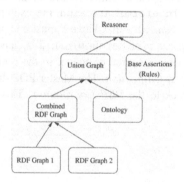

Fig. 4. Context Unification

In order for the process to work, we construct an OWL Ontology and feed it to an RDF reasoner. The Ontology defines the model and specifies the restrictions on the model. A brief snippet of the ontology used to reason about the water system is shown in the listing Valve Ontology.

```
1  <owl:Class rdf:ID="Valve">
2    <owl:Restriction>
3      <owl:onProperty rdf:resource="state"/>
4      <owl:cardinality>1</owl:cardinality>
5    </owl:Restriction>
6  </owl:Class>
7  ....
8  <owl:DatatypeProperty rdf:ID="capacity">
9    <rdfs:range>
10     <rdfs:Datatype>
11       <xsp:base rdf:resource="&xsd;int"/>
12       <xsp:minInclusive rdf:datatype="&xsd;int">0</xsp:minInclusive>
13       <xsp:maxInclusive rdf:datatype="&xsd;int">4000</xsp:maxInclusive>
14     </rdfs:Datatype>
15   </rdfs:range>
16 </owl:DatatypeProperty>
```

Valve Ontology

The important facts stated in the *valve ontology* are as follows:

1. Cardinality of state of a valve is one.
2. for valve 1 the capacity can not be more than 4000 gallons/min.

```
1 [ rule-conflict:
2   ( ?v1 <http://www.gmu.edu/xacml/rdf#MUST_VALVE_CLOSE> ?bag1 )
3   ( ?bag1 ?m ?v2 )
4   ( ?v3 <http://www.gmu.edu/xacml/rdf#MUST_VALVE_OPEN> ?bag2 )
5   ( ?bag2 ?m ?v2 )
6   (?m rdf:type rdfs:ContainerMembershipProperty)
7   ->
8   ( ?v1 <http://www.gmu.edu/xacml/rdf#conflict> ?v3 )
9 ]
```

Valve Conflict Rule

In addition to the ontology, there can be user specified rules that must not be violated. These rules could capture other business/state requirements not captured by the ontology. The listing `Valve Conflict Rule` states that the same valve can not be open and closed at the same time.

If the *Context Unification* leads to a conflict (based on the OWL/RDF Rules) the policy evaluation results in an `Indeterminate` result. For example, if the `MetaBoolean` 1 specified in the < *DuringContext* > that Valve 5 must be open then this would be in conflict with < *DuringContext* > of `MetaBoolean` 2 because the Ontology has cardinality restriction on the *state* resource of Valve. In the running example, there are not conflicts after the *Context Unification*. The Master PDP thus evaluates the request and the decision is sent back to the *PEP Coordinator*. This is shown in the listing `Decision 1`.

```
1  <Response>
2   <Result ResourceId="water:3000">
3    <Decision>Permit</Decision>
4    <Status>
5     <StatusCode Value="urn:oasis:names:tc:xacml:1.0:status:ok"/>
6    </Status>
7    <Context>
8     <PreContext>
9      <rdf:RDF xmlns:rdfs="http://www.gmu.edu/xacml/owl/ontology/#" xmlns:rdf="http://www.w3.org/1999/02/22-rdf-
         syntax-ns#" xmlns:gmu="http://www.gmu.edu/xacml/rdf#">
10      <rdf:Description rdf:about="http://gmu/valve1">
11       <gmu:state xml:lang="http://www.w3.org/2001/XMLSchema#string">close</gmu:state>
12       <gmu:ID>Valve1</gmu:ID>
13      </rdf:Description>
14      <rdf:Description rdf:about="http://gmu/valve2">
15       <gmu:state xml:lang="http://www.w3.org/2001/XMLSchema#string">close</gmu:state>
16       <gmu:ID>Valve2</gmu:ID>
17      </rdf:Description>
18     </rdf:RDF>
19    </PreContext>
20    <DuringContext>
21     <rdf:RDF xmlns:rdfs="http://www.gmu.edu/xacml/owl/ontology/#" xmlns:rdf="http://www.w3.org/1999/02/22-rdf-
         syntax-ns#" xmlns:gmu="http://www.gmu.edu/xacml/rdf#">
22      <rdf:Description rdf:about="http://gmu/valve1">
23       <gmu:capacity xml:lang="http://www.w3.org/2001/XMLSchema#int">1000</gmu:capacity>
24       <gmu:state xml:lang="http://www.w3.org/2001/XMLSchema#string">open</gmu:state>
25       <gmu:ID>Valve1</gmu:ID>
26      </rdf:Description>
27      <rdf:Description rdf:about="http://gmu/valve2">
28       <gmu:capacity xml:lang="http://www.w3.org/2001/XMLSchema#int">1000</gmu:capacity>
29       <gmu:state xml:lang="http://www.w3.org/2001/XMLSchema#string">open</gmu:state>
30       <gmu:ID>Valve2</gmu:ID>
31      </rdf:Description>
32      <rdf:Description rdf:about="http://gmu/valve5">
33       <gmu:state xml:lang="http://www.w3.org/2001/XMLSchema#string">close</gmu:state>
34       <gmu:ID>Valve5</gmu:ID>
35      </rdf:Description>
36     </rdf:RDF>
37    </DuringContext>
38    <PostContext>
```

```
39    <rdf:RDF xmlns:rdfs="http://www.gmu.edu/xacml/owl/ontology/#" xmlns:rdf="http://www.w3.org/1999/02/22-rdf-
        syntax-ns#" xmlns:gmu="http://www.gmu.edu/xacml/rdf#">
40    <rdf:Description rdf:about="http://gmu/valve1">
41      <gmu:state xml:lang="http://www.w3.org/2001/XMLSchema#string">close</gmu:state>
42      <gmu:ID>Valve1</gmu:ID>
43    </rdf:Description>
44    <rdf:Description rdf:about="http://gmu/valve2">
45      <gmu:state xml:lang="http://www.w3.org/2001/XMLSchema#string">close</gmu:state>
46      <gmu:ID>Valve2</gmu:ID>
47    </rdf:Description>
48    </rdf:RDF>
49    </PostContext>
50    </Context>
51  </Result>
52  </Response>
```

Decision 1: Permit under Top-Level PolicySet

5.3   The Decision Enforcement Process

The XACML specification places no restrictions on the policy enforcement point (PEP). Our additions require PEP to be able to execute PDP decisions transactionally. In order to do that we have the PEP associated with master PDP, referred to as the PEP coordinator, that communicates and with slave PEPs (i.e. PEP that correspond to slave PDPs).

Finally, because the decision was permitted only if the *decision context* is valid, it becomes the responsibility of the PEP to ensure that the policy decisions are enforced in the *decision context*. In order to do so, The PEP coordinator also needs to be able to understand the RDF model specified by the PDP Decision and follow the state transition specified in Figure 5. This implies that it should be able to monitor the state of the control system and abort if global state is in conflict with the *decision context*. The

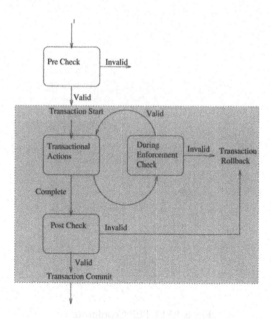

Fig. 5. Context Evaluation within PEP

algorithm used by our PEP coordinator is given in Algorithm **??** in the Appendix Section. As shown in the Figure 5, the

1. **PreContext.** Is checked for consistency before the start of the Transactional actions of PEP. Only when the pre check is valid that the decision holds.
2. **DuringContext.** If the decision holds (pre check passes), the PEP makes sure that during enforcement context of the decision is valid throughout the execution of the transactional actions of PEP. If at any point during enforcement context becomes invalid then PEP needs to roll back the transactional actions.
3. **PostContext.** Finally post check context verifies that post conditions of the decision hold. If it isn't valid then PEP needs to roll back the transactional actions.

The BPEL workflow engine is adequate to provide the above mentioned behavior of coordinated PEPs. Because BPEL natively does not understand RDF, we use a RDF Interpreter Web Service for that domain to synthesize the RDF generated by the PDP.

The construction of BPEL workflow is shown in Figure 6.

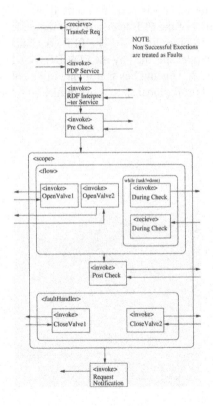

Fig. 6. BPEL PEP Coordinator

6   Related Work

Bertino *et al.* [4] propose an extension to BPEL [19] for expressing RBAC-like [23] authorization requirements (called RBAC_WS_BPEL) for BPEL workflows. The authors propose to encode RBAC requirements in XACML syntax (much like the XACML-RBAC profile [20]) and depend upon the BPEL engine to enforce this specification. However, the authors do not consider a use case for distributive access control requirements as introduced in this paper and consequently they cannot support practical access control requirements, such as those requiring separation duty principle etc, because as far as we know existing XACML runtimes do not support them. We enhance XACML syntax with contextual information and implement a fully-distributed access controller to enforce practical access control use-cases.

FlexFlow [10] is another general purpose modeling language for capturing work-flow representations in tree structure and expressing/enforcing access control requirements on the work-flow. Flex flow is based syntactically on *FAF [14]* (locally stratified Horn-clause programs). However, the work is semantic-web agnostic, and consequently authors ignore real-life scenarios such as those programmable using BPEL. The main disadvantage of using FlexFlow for BPEL security is the simplifying assumptions made in the design that do not take into account the *distributed-ness* of the access decision evaluation and enforcement.

Atluri, Huang *et al.* [2] consider a related security problem of multi-level secure work-flow systems, where work-flows at a higher security label should not be dependent upon work-flows at a lower security label. The authors identify dependencies in the work-flows into different categories, thus identifying security issues (*i.e.*, high to low dependency) and prevent them. This work is orthogonal to our domain, where we aim to secure any workflow based on the security policy – enforcing it throughout the work-flow, including at distributed Web Services that are the part of the secured workflow.

Bertino, Ferrari and Atluri in [5] present a logical language for generic workflows that can be broken down to a sequence of tasks. The main aim of this work is to be able to express RBAC-like authorization constraints and enforce them for workflows. However, this work does not consider the runtime issues like policy enforcement distribution, exclusive usage etc that require more complex control algorithms between enforcement points. In this aspect, our work provides a complete end to end security cover for workflows. Because we use XACML based policies for expressing security requirements, we can utilize earlier extensions like the *lock manager enhancements* by Dhankhar *et al.* [11] to enforce RBAC-like authorization constraints.

Several query languages have been proposed for querying RDF meta-data [8,9,22,24,25], *etc.* These query languages have been used to implement RDF reference implementations like Jena [17], Redland [3], ICSForth Suite [1], *etc.* In this work we use Jena RDF API and reference implementation for integrating XACML with BPEL. The choice is purely due to the free availability of this API and reference implementation.

Dhankhar *et al.* have extended reference XACML implementation [26] with extensions to enforce exclusive use [11] and distributed policy evaluation [12] within a nested transaction tree framework. This paper extends their work to *fully distribute* evaluation and enforcement of XACML policies. In that sense we extend their work to include distributed policy enforcement, including conflict management during policy enforcement.

Fox in [13] provides several examples where contextual information is necessary for decision evaluation. Though we don't consider context at the level of granularity as described by Fox, but, it is a validation of our claim that decisions are arrived in a particular context and valid only within a related context.

7   Conclusion

Following our previous work, we are in the process of fully decentralizing the XACML reference implementation. That is, we would like to have the XACML reference implementation be able to evaluate and enforce policies that refers to resources available anywhere on the world-wide web. That entails the policy decision point (PDP) to be able reach the appropriate policy and access governing authority of the referenced resource and be able to seek and obtain the permissions for the requestor.

During our research and development process, we realized that in such a decentralized system, the resource owners may impose condition that the requestor has to adhere to in order to use the resource as requested. They have been named *decision context* because the PDPs decisions are to be evaluated under these conditions. They are passed on to the request originators PDP and are passed back to the policy enforcement points.

The *decision context* we designed have been specified using RDF and OWL, that specify how the resource can be used. In addition, other rules that constitute consistent use is also passed to a PDP. The PDP then evaluates if the request is permitted, and if so under which amalgamated request and passes that information to a master PEP, that distributes them over to all other PEPs.

We have also realized that our PEP coordination can be specified and enforced using BPEL. Our initial experiments in implementing the stated examples have resulted a reasonable performance. Our ongoing work addresses the process of auto-generating all *decision context* and passing and enforcing them using a BPEL process in a more general context.

References

1. Alexaki, S., Christophides, V., Karvounarakis, G., Plexousakis, D., Tolle, K.: The ICS-FORTH RDFSuite: Managing voluminous rdf description bases. In: Second International Workshop on the Semantic Web (SemWeb 2001) (May 2001)
2. Atluri, V., Huang, W., Bertino, E.: A semantic-based execution model for multilevel secure workflows. Journal of Computer Security 8(1) (2000)
3. Beckett, D.: The design and implementation of the Redland RDF application framework. In: Tenth International World Wide Web Conference (WWW10) (May 2001)
4. Bertino, E., Crampton, J., Paci, F.: Access control and authorization constraints for WS-BPEL. In: IEEE International Conference on Web Services (ICWS 2006), pp. 275–284 (2006)
5. Bertino, E., Ferrari, E., Atluri, V.: A flexible model supporting the specification and enforcement of role-based authorization in workflow management systems. In: ACM Workshop on Role-Based Access Control, pp. 1–12 (1997)
6. Brickley, D., Guha, R.: Resource Description Framework (RDF) Schema Specification 1.0: RDF schema. W3C working Draft (2003)

7. Brickley, D., Guha, R., McBride, B.: RDF vocabulary description language 1.0: RDF schema. W3C Recommendation (February 2004)
8. Broekstra, J., Kampman, A.: SeRQL, a second generation RDF query language. In: SWAD-Europe Workshop on Semantic Web Storage and Retrieval, Amsterdam (November 2004)
9. Chen, L., Gupta, A., Kurul, M.E.: A semantic-aware RDF query algebra. In: 12th International Conference on Management of Data (COMAD), Hyderabad (December 2005)
10. Chen, S., Wijesekera, D., Jajodia, S.: Flexflow: A flexible flow control policy specification framework. In: 17th Annual IFIP WG 11.3 Working Conference on Data and Applications Security (DBSec 2003), pp. 358–371 (2003)
11. Dhankhar, V., Kaushik, S., Wijesekera, D.: XACML policies for exclusive resource usage. In: 21st Annual IFIP WG 11.3 Working Conference on Data and Applications Security (DBSec 2007) (2007)
12. Dhankhar, V., Kaushik, S., Wijesekera, D., Nerode, A.: Evaluating distributed XACML policies. In: 2007 ACM Workshop on Secure Web Services (SWS 2007) (November 2007)
13. Fox, M.S.: Knowledge Representation for Decision Support Systems. Elsevier, Amsterdam (1985)
14. Jajodia, S., Samarati, P., Sapino, M.L., Subrahmanian, V.S.: Flexible support for multiple access control policies. ACM Transactions on Database Systems 26(2), 214–260 (2001)
15. Kaushik, S., Farkas, C., Wijesekera, D., Ammann, P.: An algebra for composing ontologies. In: International Conference on Formal Ontology in Information Systems (FOIS 2006) (November 2006)
16. Klyne, G., Carroll, J.J., McBride, B.: Resource description framework (RDF): Concepts and abstract syntax. W3C Recommendation (2004)
17. McBride, B.: Jena: Implementing the rdf model and syntax specification. In: Second International Workshop on the Semantic Web (SemWeb 2001) (May 2001)
18. Miller, L., Seaborne, A., Reggiori, A.: Three implementations of SquishQL, a simple RDF query language. In: Horrocks, I., Hendler, J. (eds.) ISWC 2002. LNCS, vol. 2342, pp. 399–403. Springer, Heidelberg (2002)
19. OASIS. Business process execution language for web services (May 2003)
20. OASIS. XACML profile for role based access control (rbac) (February 2004), http://docs.oasis-open.org/xacml/cd-xacml-rbac-profile-01.pdf
21. OASIS. Extensible access control markup language (February 2005)
22. Prud'hommeaux, E., Seaborne, A.: SPARQL query language for RDF (April 2005), http://www.w3.org/TR/rdf-sparql-query
23. Sandhu, R., Ferraiolo, D., Kuhn, R.D.: The NIST model for role based access control: Towards a unified standard. In: 5th ACM Workshop on Role Based Access Control (July 2000)
24. Seaborne, A.: A query language for RDF (2004), http://www.w3.org/Submission/2004/SUBM-RDQL-20040109
25. Sintek, M., Decker, S.: Triple, an RDF query, inference and transformation language. In: Deductive databases and knowledge management (DDLP) (2001)
26. Sun Microsystems. Sun's XACML implementation (July 2004), http://sunxacml.sourceforge.net/index.html
27. Zhang, X., Park, J., Parisi-Presicce, F., Sandhu, R.: A logical specification for usage control. In: SACMAT 2004: Proceedings of the ninth ACM symposium on Access control models and technologies, pp. 1–10. ACM Press, New York (2004)

Author Index

Abbadi, Imad M.   238
Adam, Nabil   144
Alawneh, Muntaha   238
Anderson, Ross   64
Ardagna, Claudio Agostino   254
Arora, Saurabh   222

Barker, Ken   65
Barker, Steve   1, 219
Brodsky, Alexander   190

Caballero-Gil, Cándido   175
Caballero-Gil, Pino   175
Carminati, Barbara   81
Chadwick, David   219
Crampton, Jason   219

Debbabi, Mourad   268
De Capitani di Vimercati, Sabrina   254
De Decker, Bart   97
Delgado-Mohatar, Oscar   175
Dewri, Rinku   297
Dhankhar, Vijayant   330
Diepold, Klaus   113
Dong, Changyu   127
Dulay, Naranker   127
Duta, Angela C.   65

El-Fotouh, Mohamed Abo   113

Ferrari, Elena   81
Furlong, Jason   268

Goyal, Vikram   33
Grandison, Tyrone   254
Gudes, Ehud   313
Gupta, Anand   33
Gupta, S.K.   33

Hanna, Aiman   268
He, Xiaoyun   144
Hernández-Goya, Candelaria   175
Hitchens, Michael   222

Islam, Tania   283

Jajodia, Sushil   190, 254, 283

Kaushik, Saket   330

Lapon, Jorn   97
Li, Yingjiu   159
Ling, Hai Zhou   268
Long, Tao   283
Lu, Haibing   144
Lupu, Emil   219

Ma, Di   48
Molina-Gil, Jezabel   175

Naessens, Vincent   97
Nagarajan, Aarthi   222
Nigusse, Girma   97

Poolsappasit, Nayot   297

Ray, Indrajit   297
Ray, Indrakshi   17
Roichman, Alex   313
Russello, Giovanni   127

Samarati, Pierangela   254
Singhal, Anoop   158, 283

Tan, Shaohua   205
Tang, Shiwei   205
Tao, Youdong   205
Thuraisingham, Bhavani   219
Toahchoodee, Manachai   17
Tong, Yunhai   205
Tsudik, Gene   48

Vaidya, Jaideep   144
Varadharajan, Vijay   222
Verhaeghe, Pieter   97
Verslype, Kristof   97

Walleck, Daryl   159
Wang, Lingyu   190, 283
Wijesekera, Duminda   330

Xu, Shouhuai   159

Yang, Dongqing   205

Zhang, Lei   190

Lecture Notes in Computer Science

Sublibrary 3: Information Systems and Application, incl. Internet/Web and HCI

For information about Vols. 1– 4690
please contact your bookseller or Springer

Vol. 5120: S. Helal, S. Mitra, J. Wong, C.K. Chang, M. Mokhtari (Eds.), Smart Homes and Health Telematics. XV, 220 pages. 2008.

Vol. 5094: V. Atluri (Ed.), Data and Applications Security XXII. IX, 347 pages. 2008.

Vol. 5093: Z. Pan, X. Zhang, A. El Rhalibi, W. Woo, Y. Li (Eds.), Technologies for E-Learning and Digital Entertainment. XVII, 791 pages. 2008.

Vol. 5080: Z. Pan, A.D. Cheok, W. Müller, A. El Rhalibi (Eds.), Transactions on Edutainment I. X, 305 pages. 2008.

Vol. 5075: C.C. Yang, H. Chen, M. Chau, K. Chang, S.-D. Lang, P.S. Chen, R. Hsieh, D. Zeng, F.-Y. Wang, K. Carley, W. Mao, J. Zhan (Eds.), Intelligence and Security Informatics. XXII, 522 pages. 2008.

Vol. 5074: Z. Bellahsène, M. Léonard (Eds.), Advanced Information Systems Engineering. XVII, 588 pages. 2008.

Vol. 5069: B. Ludäscher, N. Mamoulis (Eds.), Scientific and Statistical Database Management. XIII, 620 pages. 2008.

Vol. 5066: M. Tscheligi, M. Obrist, A. Lugmayr (Eds.), Changing Television Environments. XV, 324 pages. 2008.

Vol. 5061: F.E. Sandnes, Y. Zhang, C. Rong, L.T. Yang, J. Ma (Eds.), Ubiquitous Intelligence and Computing. XVI, 763 pages. 2008.

Vol. 5053: R. Meier, S. Terzis (Eds.), Distributed Applications and Interoperable Systems. XI, 303 pages. 2008.

Vol. 5039: E. Kapetanios, V. Sugumaran, M. Spiliopoulou (Eds.), Natural Language and Information Systems. XIX, 386 pages. 2008.

Vol. 5034: R. Fleischer, J. Xu (Eds.), Algorithmic Aspects in Information and Management. XI, 350 pages. 2008.

Vol. 5033: H. Oinas-Kukkonen, P. Hasle, M. Harjumaa, K. Segerståhl, P. Øhrstrøm (Eds.), Persuasive Technology. XIV, 287 pages. 2008.

Vol. 5024: M. Ferre (Ed.), Haptics: Perception, Devices and Scenarios. XXIII, 950 pages. 2008.

Vol. 5021: S. Bechhofer, M. Hauswirth, J. Hoffmann, M. Koubarakis (Eds.), The Semantic Web: Research and Applications. XIX, 897 pages. 2008.

Vol. 5017: T. Nanya, F. Maruyama, A. Pataricza, M. Malek (Eds.), Service Availability. XII, 225 pages. 2008.

Vol. 5013: J. Indulska, D.J. Patterson, T. Rodden, M. Ott (Eds.), Pervasive Computing. XIV, 315 pages. 2008.

Vol. 5006: R. Kowalczyk, M. Huhns, M. Klusch, Z. Maamar, Q.B. Vo (Eds.), Service-Oriented Computing: Agents, Semantics, and Engineering. X, 154 pages. 2008.

Vol. 4997: B. Monien, U.-P. Schroeder (Eds.), Algorithmic Game Theory. XI, 363 pages. 2008.

Vol. 4993: H. Li, T. Liu, W.-Y. Ma, T. Sakai, K.-F. Wong, G. Zhou (Eds.), Information Retrieval Technology. XIII, 685 pages. 2008.

Vol. 4976: Y. Zhang, G. Yu, E. Bertino, G. Xu (Eds.), Progress in WWW Research and Development. XVIII, 699 pages. 2008.

Vol. 4956: C. Macdonald, I. Ounis, V. Plachouras, I. Ruthven, R.W. White (Eds.), Advances in Information Retrieval. XXI, 719 pages. 2008.

Vol. 4952: C. Floerkemeier, M. Langheinrich, E. Fleisch, F. Mattern, S.E. Sarma (Eds.), The Internet of Things. XIII, 378 pages. 2008.

Vol. 4947: J.R. Haritsa, R. Kotagiri, V. Pudi (Eds.), Database Systems for Advanced Applications. XXII, 713 pages. 2008.

Vol. 4936: W. Aiello, A. Broder, J. Janssen, E.E. Milios (Eds.), Algorithms and Models for the Web-Graph. X, 167 pages. 2008.

Vol. 4932: S. Hartmann, G. Kern-Isberner (Eds.), Foundations of Information and Knowledge Systems. XII, 397 pages. 2008.

Vol. 4928: A.H.M. ter Hofstede, B. Benatallah, H.-Y. Paik (Eds.), Business Process Management Workshops. XIII, 518 pages. 2008.

Vol. 4918: N. Boujemaa, M. Detyniecki, A. Nürnberger (Eds.), Adaptive Multimedial Retrieval: Retrieval, User, and Semantics. XI, 265 pages. 2008.

Vol. 4903: S. Satoh, F. Nack, M. Etoh (Eds.), Advances in Multimedia Modeling. XIX, 510 pages. 2008.

Vol. 4900: S. Spaccapietra (Ed.), Journal on Data Semantics X. XIII, 265 pages. 2008.

Vol. 4892: A. Popescu-Belis, S. Renals, H. Bourlard (Eds.), Machine Learning for Multimodal Interaction. XI, 308 pages. 2008.

Vol. 4882: T. Janowski, H. Mohanty (Eds.), Distributed Computing and Internet Technology. XIII, 346 pages. 2007.

Vol. 4881: H. Yin, P. Tino, E. Corchado, W. Byrne, X. Yao (Eds.), Intelligent Data Engineering and Automated Learning - IDEAL 2007. XX, 1174 pages. 2007.

Vol. 4877: C. Thanos, F. Borri, L. Candela (Eds.), Digital Libraries: Research and Development. XII, 350 pages. 2007.

Vol. 4872: D. Mery, L. Rueda (Eds.), Advances in Image and Video Technology. XXI, 961 pages. 2007.

Vol. 4871: M. Cavazza, S. Donikian (Eds.), Virtual Storytelling. XIII, 219 pages. 2007.

Vol. 4858: X. Deng, F.C. Graham (Eds.), Internet and Network Economics. XVI, 598 pages. 2007.

Vol. 4857: J.M. Ware, G.E. Taylor (Eds.), Web and Wireless Geographical Information Systems. XI, 293 pages. 2007.

Vol. 4853: F. Fonseca, M.A. Rodríguez, S. Levashkin (Eds.), GeoSpatial Semantics. X, 289 pages. 2007.

Vol. 4836: H. Ichikawa, W.-D. Cho, I. Satoh, H.Y. Youn (Eds.), Ubiquitous Computing Systems. XIII, 307 pages. 2007.

Vol. 4832: M. Weske, M.-S. Hacid, C. Godart (Eds.), Web Information Systems Engineering – WISE 2007 Workshops. XV, 518 pages. 2007.

Vol. 4831: B. Benatallah, F. Casati, D. Georgakopoulos, C. Bartolini, W. Sadiq, C. Godart (Eds.), Web Information Systems Engineering – WISE 2007. XVI, 675 pages. 2007.

Vol. 4825: K. Aberer, K.-S. Choi, N. Noy, D. Allemang, K.-I. Lee, L. Nixon, J. Golbeck, P. Mika, D. Maynard, R. Mizoguchi, G. Schreiber, P. Cudré-Mauroux (Eds.), The Semantic Web. XXVII, 973 pages. 2007.

Vol. 4823: H. Leung, F. Li, R. Lau, Q. Li (Eds.), Advances in Web Based Learning – ICWL 2007. XIV, 654 pages. 2008.

Vol. 4822: D.H.-L. Goh, T.H. Cao, I.T. Sølvberg, E. Rasmussen (Eds.), Asian Digital Libraries. XVII, 519 pages. 2007.

Vol. 4820: T.G. Wyeld, S. Kenderdine, M. Docherty (Eds.), Virtual Systems and Multimedia. XII, 215 pages. 2008.

Vol. 4816: B. Falcidieno, M. Spagnuolo, Y. Avrithis, I. Kompatsiaris, P. Buitelaar (Eds.), Semantic Multimedia. XII, 306 pages. 2007.

Vol. 4813: I. Oakley, S.A. Brewster (Eds.), Haptic and Audio Interaction Design. XIV, 145 pages. 2007.

Vol. 4810: H.H.-S. Ip, O.C. Au, H. Leung, M.-T. Sun, W.-Y. Ma, S.-M. Hu (Eds.), Advances in Multimedia Information Processing – PCM 2007. XXI, 834 pages. 2007.

Vol. 4809: M.K. Denko, C.-s. Shih, K.-C. Li, S.-L. Tsao, Q.-A. Zeng, S.H. Park, Y.-B. Ko, S.-H. Hung, J.-H. Park (Eds.), Emerging Directions in Embedded and Ubiquitous Computing. XXXV, 823 pages. 2007.

Vol. 4808: T.-W. Kuo, E. Sha, M. Guo, L.T. Yang, Z. Shao (Eds.), Embedded and Ubiquitous Computing. XXI, 769 pages. 2007.

Vol. 4806: R. Meersman, Z. Tari, P. Herrero (Eds.), On the Move to Meaningful Internet Systems 2007: OTM 2007 Workshops, Part II. XXXIV, 611 pages. 2007.

Vol. 4805: R. Meersman, Z. Tari, P. Herrero (Eds.), On the Move to Meaningful Internet Systems 2007: OTM 2007 Workshops, Part I. XXXIV, 757 pages. 2007.

Vol. 4804: R. Meersman, Z. Tari (Eds.), On the Move to Meaningful Internet Systems 2007: CoopIS, DOA, ODBASE, GADA, and IS, Part II. XXIX, 683 pages. 2007.

Vol. 4803: R. Meersman, Z. Tari (Eds.), On the Move to Meaningful Internet Systems 2007: CoopIS, DOA, ODBASE, GADA, and IS, Part I. XXIX, 1173 pages. 2007.

Vol. 4802: J.-L. Hainaut, E.A. Rundensteiner, M. Kirchberg, M. Bertolotto, M. Brochhausen, Y.-P.P. Chen, S.S.-S. Cherfi, M. Doerr, H. Han, S. Hartmann, J. Parsons, G. Poels, C. Rolland, J. Trujillo, E. Yu, E. Zimányie (Eds.), Advances in Conceptual Modeling – Foundations and Applications. XIX, 420 pages. 2007.

Vol. 4801: C. Parent, K.-D. Schewe, V.C. Storey, B. Thalheim (Eds.), Conceptual Modeling - ER 2007. XVI, 616 pages. 2007.

Vol. 4797: M. Arenas, M.I. Schwartzbach (Eds.), Database Programming Languages. VIII, 261 pages. 2007.

Vol. 4796: M. Lew, N. Sebe, T.S. Huang, E.M. Bakker (Eds.), Human–Computer Interaction. X, 157 pages. 2007.

Vol. 4794: B. Schiele, A.K. Dey, H. Gellersen, B. de Ruyter, M. Tscheligi, R. Wichert, E. Aarts, A. Buchmann (Eds.), Ambient Intelligence. XV, 375 pages. 2007.

Vol. 4777: S. Bhalla (Ed.), Databases in Networked Information Systems. X, 329 pages. 2007.

Vol. 4761: R. Obermaisser, Y. Nah, P. Puschner, F.J. Rammig (Eds.), Software Technologies for Embedded and Ubiquitous Systems. XIV, 563 pages. 2007.

Vol. 4747: S. Džeroski, J. Struyf (Eds.), Knowledge Discovery in Inductive Databases. X, 301 pages. 2007.

Vol. 4744: Y. de Kort, W. IJsselsteijn, C. Midden, B. Eggen, B.J. Fogg (Eds.), Persuasive Technology. XIV, 316 pages. 2007.

Vol. 4740: L. Ma, M. Rauterberg, R. Nakatsu (Eds.), Entertainment Computing – ICEC 2007. XXX, 480 pages. 2007.

Vol. 4730: C. Peters, P. Clough, F.C. Gey, J. Karlgren, B. Magnini, D.W. Oard, M. de Rijke, M. Stempfhuber (Eds.), Evaluation of Multilingual and Multi-modal Information Retrieval. XXIV, 998 pages. 2007.

Vol. 4723: M. R. Berthold, J. Shawe-Taylor, N. Lavrač (Eds.), Advances in Intelligent Data Analysis VII. XIV, 380 pages. 2007.

Vol. 4721: W. Jonker, M. Petković (Eds.), Secure Data Management. X, 213 pages. 2007.

Vol. 4718: J. Hightower, B. Schiele, T. Strang (Eds.), Location- and Context-Awareness. X, 297 pages. 2007.

Vol. 4717: J. Krumm, G.D. Abowd, A. Seneviratne, T. Strang (Eds.), UbiComp 2007: Ubiquitous Computing. XIX, 520 pages. 2007.

Vol. 4715: J.M. Haake, S.F. Ochoa, A. Cechich (Eds.), Groupware: Design, Implementation, and Use. XIII, 355 pages. 2007.

Vol. 4714: G. Alonso, P. Dadam, M. Rosemann (Eds.), Business Process Management. XIII, 418 pages. 2007.

Vol. 4704: D. Barbosa, A. Bonifati, Z. Bellahsène, E. Hunt, R. Unland (Eds.), Database and XML Technologies. X, 141 pages. 2007.